Regior...
Chang...

Science, Technology and the International Political Economy

Series Editor: John de la Mothe

The upheavals of the international political economy during recent decades have fundamentally altered the relationships between firms and states, citizenship and management, social institutions and economic growth. The changing pace of competition, firm performance and geo-economics is shifting the pressures on public policy and corporate strategy alike. As a result, our conceptual frameworks for analysing key events, emerging trends and driving forces are being challenged. As unclear as the future is, what remains certain is that science, technology and innovation will occupy a central place. By looking at a wide array of issues – ranging from security and foreign affairs, the environment, international institutions, corporate strategy and regional development to research policy, innovation gaps, intellectual property, ethics and law – this series will critically examine how science and technology are shaping the emerging international political economy.

Published titles in the series:

The Complexity Challenge by Robert W. Rycroft and Don E. Kash

Evolutionary Economics and the New International Political Economy edited by John de la Mothe and Gilles Paquet

Global Change and Intellectual Property Agencies by G. Bruce Doern

The Governance of Innovation in Europe by Philip Cooke, Patries Boekholt and Franz Tödtling

Systems of Innovation edited by Charles Edquist

Universities and the Global Knowledge Economy edited by Henry Etzkowitz and Loet Leydesdorff

Forthcoming titles in the series:

Developing Innovation Systems by Mario Cimoli

Innovation and the Service-Based Economy edited by Ian Miles and Mark Boden

Innovation Strategies in Middle Power Countries edited by John de la Mothe and Gilles Paquet

Science and Technology and Governance edited by John de la Mothe

Proposals for books can be sent directly to the series editor:
  John de la Mothe
  Program of Research on International Management and Economy (PRIME)
  Faculty of Administration
  University of Ottawa
  275 Nicholas Street
  Ottawa, Canada K1N 6N5

Regional Innovation, Knowledge and Global Change

Edited by
Zoltan J. Acs

PINTER

London and New York

Science, Technology and the International Political Economy Series
Series Editor: John de la Mothe

Pinter
A Cassell Imprint

Wellington House, 125 Strand, London WC2R 0BB
370 Lexington Avenue, New York, NY 10017–6550

First published 2000

British Library Cataloguing-in-Publication Data
A catalogue record for this book is available from the British Library.

ISBN 1-85567-442-4 (hardback)
1-85567-443-2 (paperback)

Library of Congress Cataloging-in-Publication Data
Regional innovation, knowledge, and global change / Zoltan J. Acs, editor
     p.   cm.—(Science, technology, and the international political economy)
   Includes bibliographical references and indexes.
   ISBN 1–85567–442–4 (hardbound)
   ISBN 1–85567–443–2 (pbk.)
     1. Technological innovations — Economic aspects.   2. Regional economics.
3. Competition.   I. Acs, Zoltan J.   II. Series: Science, technology, and the international political economy series
   HC79.T4 R433 2000
   338'.064—dc21   99–34140
                                                                                                              CIP

Typeset by York House Typographic Ltd, London

Printed and bound in Great Britain by
The Cromwell Press, Trowbridge, Wiltshire

Contents

Contributors

Zoltan J. Acs is McCurdy Professor of Economics, Entrepreneurship and Innovation, University of Baltimore, USA

Allan N. Afuah is Professor of Strategy, University of Michigan, USA

Philip Cooke is Professor of Regional Development, University of Wales, UK

John de la Mothe is Associate Professor of Science and Government, University of Ottawa, Canada

Richard Florida is H. John Heinz Professor of Regional Economic Development, Carnegie-Mellon University, USA

Helen Lawton Smith is Reader in Local Economic Development, Coventry University, UK

Edward Malecki is Professor of Geography, University of Florida, USA

Rebecca Morales is Associate Professor of Management, University of Illinois at Chicago, USA

Richard R. Nelson is Professor of Economics, Columbia University, USA

Gilles Paquet is Professor of Economics and Management, University of Ottawa, Canada

AnnaLee Saxenian is Professor of City and Regional Planning, University of California at Berkeley, USA

Donald F. Smith, Jr, is Co-Director of the Center for Economic Development, Carnegie-Mellon University, USA

Rolf Sternberg is Professor of Regional Development, University of Cologne, Germany

James M. Utterback is Professor of Management and Engineering, Massachusetts Institute of Technology, USA

Attila Varga is Research Fellow, Austrian Academy of Sciences, Austria

CHAPTER ONE

Introduction

Zoltan J. Acs

There is little question that every aspect of economic activity is being affected by the processes of globalization. As we approach the twenty-first century, a worldwide system of production and distribution is evolving, in much the same way as national markets evolved from local and regional networks during the nineteenth century (Chandler 1990). In nearly every economically active country of the world, the importance of international trade and foreign direct investment (FDI) has risen significantly over the past decade. (For a review of the multinational corporation in the 1980s see Kindleberger and Audretsch 1983.) The growth of FDI has been particularly dramatic, increasing more rapidly than either world production or world trade. As a result, both in-bound and out-bound FDI stocks have increased relative to total investment and gross domestic product in nearly every country (Dunning 1995). Cross-border intra-firm activities are now the norm rather than the exception.

'Globalization' refers to the web of linkages and interconnections between states, societies and organizations that make up the world economic system. Globalization creates new structures and new relationships, with the result that business decisions and actions in one part of the world have significant consequences in other places. The growth of global markets stimulates competition and forces governments to adopt market-oriented policies, both domestically and internationally. Modern technologies have greatly reduced the cost of information and the capability to participate in the global economy (Dunning 1993). Countries must join the club. Policies that aim to exclude global participation via trade and investment barriers can be easily circumvented, and they keep no hostages, but they do deprive the countries of global prosperity.

Underlying and reinforcing these globalization trends is the rapidly changing technological environment, particularly in biotechnology, information processing and telecommunications. Changes in telecommunications and data-processing capabilities make it possible to coordinate research, marketing and production operation around the world. Almost instantaneous communication makes it possible to trade financial instruments twenty-four hours a day (de la Mothe and Paquet 1998), making the location of resources within firms, industries and countries more sensitive. Contemporary technical advances are demanding a much closer synthesis and more integrative learning between innovative and production activities.

The pressures of global competition force producers to continually innovate and to upgrade the quality of existing products. Yet, at the same time, many firms can no longer acquire or afford all the technological and human resources that they need. Increasingly, they form interdependent and flexible relationships with other firms –

including suppliers and competing firms – to fully capitalize on their core competencies (Gomes-Casseres 1996). Interdependence calls for a capacity on the part of firms, individuals and governments to interact with speed, flexibility and creativity to the actions of other agents (de la Mothe and Paquet 1996a).

In order to better understand international changes in the late twentieth century we need first to establish an interpretation of globalization.[1] Globalization is a dynamic Schumpeterian evolutionary process on a global scale (Schumpeter 1934). Imagine that the world is segmented by formidable natural and artificial barriers hindering information flow, trade and investment. The world changes; segmented localities are now physically connected by improved means of communication and transportation and, also, artificial barriers to information flow, trade and investment are broken down. The old equilibrium, which is composed of autarky equilibrium in each segment, is not sustainable. The new environment has profitable trade and real investment opportunities which were previously unavailable because of natural (e.g. high transportation costs) and artificial barriers (e.g. trade and investment barriers). As firms and individuals actualize these opportunities, there will be international reallocation of production and factor inputs, changes in output and factor prices, and general changes in income and consumption patterns. The world undergoes structural adjustment.

The shift from the old equilibrium to the new equilibrium relies on the discovery and appropriation of profit opportunities, which Kirzner (1997) refers to as entrepreneurial discovery. An integral component of globalization is therefore international expansion of firms' operations, which is often typified by foreign direct investment. The model below is applicable not just to foreign direct investment, but to other forms of international expansion. For convenience, we start with a theoretically and empirically well-received foreign direct investment theory, which is 'internalization'. In our opinion, the theory implies that international expansion of firms' operations is a process of 'creative destruction'.

The internalization theory starts with the assumption that indigenous firms usually have advantage over outsiders. The reason is that indigenous firms know more about the local environment and already have established relationships with vertically related business, ranging from intermediate suppliers of goods to local government to local consumers. Foreign entrants need to possess unique superior capabilities to overcome indigenous firms' home-court advantage. These are information-based capabilities in technology, production, marketing and management, which are often referred to as intangibles.

Because they are information based, intangible assets behave like public goods: they have intrinsic economies of scale and scope. Firms can leverage the value of their intangible assets by expanding their scale and scope of application. Because of well-known transactions difficulties in arm's-length trade of information-based assets, firms often have to retain direct control in expanding the application of their intangible assets. In other words, firms internalize the markets for their intangible assets. When firms expand the application of their intangibles internationally by retaining direct control of them, these firms become multinational firms. Empirical tests of the internalization theory in an international setting are reported by Morck and Yeung (1997). Internalization implies that multinational firms manage to capture the overseas profit opportunities their intangibles create. The overseas profit opportunities exist because their intangibles allow them, as foreign entrants, to overcome local indigenous firms' home-court advantage and thus to capture local indigenous firms' markets.

In other words, firms are able to internationalize because of the superior competitive advantage of their intangibles. Recall that intangibles are information-based capabilities with respect to marketing, production and management. To the extent that local indigenous firms do not possess these intangibles, they are innovations from the perspective of local indigenous firms. Seen in this light, a firm's cross-border expansion is an internationalized Schumpeterian evolution; and it is an indispensable component of globalization.

In this new environment knowledge and intellectual labour are being mobilized on a more collaborative basis. Firms must develop human resource strategies based on synthesis with educational institutions. They must locate design and production facilities in metropolitan areas that allow partnerships with suppliers and educational institutions, and in places served by governments committed to business-friendly policies. The main form of economic organization in intermediary product markets is increasingly a network of inter-firm cooperative arrangements, rather than the large hierarchical firm (Reich 1992).

Much work has been done in the tradition of neo-Schumpeterian evolutionary economics to advance our understanding of the micro-foundations of innovation. Perhaps the touchstone volume of this tradition is Nelson and Winter's *Evolutionary Theory of Economic Change* (1982). In recent years, efforts have been made to percolate general theoretical and empirical observations from this literature up into a conceptual framework capable of guiding policy and loosely organized around the idea of a 'national system'. 'Systems of innovation' represents a new approach to the study of innovation in the economy that has emerged during the past decade (Lundvall 1988, 1992; Edquist 1997).

Innovation processes occur over time and are influenced by many factors. Because of this complexity, firms almost never innovate in isolation. In the pursuit of innovation they interact with other organizations to gain, develop and exchange various kinds of knowledge, information and other resources. These organizations might be other firms (suppliers, customers, competitors), or universities, research institutes, venture capitalists, government agencies. The behaviour of firms is also shaped by institutions that constitute constraints and/or incentives for innovation, such as laws, health regulation, cultural norms, social rules and technical standards. Interaction between various organizations operating in different institutional contexts is important for processes of innovation. The actors, as well as these contextual factors, are all elements of systems for the creation and use of knowledge for economic purposes. Innovation emerges in such systems.

Readers might ask, 'Why do we focus on regional innovation instead of national innovation?' Krugman (1995) has suggested that as economies become less constrained by national frontiers – as globalization spreads – they become more geographically specialized. Important elements of the process of innovation tend to become regional rather than national. The trends are most important in the science-based and high-technology industries. Some of the largest corporations are weakening their ties to their home country and are spreading their innovation activities to source different regional systems of innovation. And regional networks of firms are creating new forms of learning and production. These changes are important and challenge the traditional role of national systems of innovation.

Although national innovation systems still play an important role in supporting and directing processes of innovation and learning, 'both globalization and region- alization might be interpreted as processes which weaken the coherence and importance of national systems' (Lundvall 1992: 3). Therefore, in this book we choose to focus on regional innovation.

In Part I of the book we develop a conceptual framework for the study of innovation systems. A framework is a useful generalization about hypotheses and gathering empirical generalizations. The systems of innovation approach is certainly not a formal theory. It does not provide convincing propositions as regards estab- lished and stable relations between variables. The most it does provide is a framework for the formulation of conjectures. As a framework it is fairly advanced and has great potential.

In Chapter 2 Richard Nelson sets the stage by reviewing a fifteen-nation study of national innovation systems. It seems useful to review that study here, considering some of the analytical issues it had to address, and some of the key conclusions of that study. The chapter starts out with an analysis of the innovation system concept itself, and asks if it makes much sense in a globalized world. The chapter next examines the country differences and what lies behind them, and then looks at what is required for effective innovative performance. The chapter finishes up by asking, 'What remains "national" about innovation systems?'

In Chapter 3 John de la Mothe and Gilles Paquet critically examine innovation systems. First they examine national innovation systems, suggesting that the con- ceptual framework of national systems suffers in so far as it is itself not so much an explanatory variable as a dependent variable. They explore the complex issues of a meso-analytical framework of social learning that underpins innovation. They examine the different subprocesses that partition the socio-economy and suggest ways in which we can use these new parts to build a meso-analytical perspective that is adequate or robust enough to take into account the full complexity of the innovation process.

In Chapter 4 we begin by sketching the new paradoxical logic that appears to drive the world production system towards both an increasing degree of globalization and an increasing degree of subnational regionalization. We focus on the balkanization of national economies on the one hand and on the devolution of governance systems on the other. The paradoxical consequences of globalization have been not only to generate balkanization but also to create the need for new forms of organization. We suggest that while hierarchies have limited learning abilities and markets have limited capacities to process information effectively, networks combine to overcome both limitations. We next sketch out the elements of regional innovation. This is deliberately done in a somewhat synthetic and sketchy fashion, for no fewer than six of the chapters deal with this issue specifically. These new socio-economic dynamics have dramatically influenced the way in which individuals, organizations and institu- tions have done their own learning in the recent past.

These three opening chapters provide the conceptual background for a systemic approach that is conducted for both Europe and the United States in the next two parts.

Part II presents three broad and contemporary views of regional innovation from Europe. In Chapter 5 Philip Cooke sets the stage for a detailed examination of business processes in regional innovation systems in the European Union. The chapter presents findings from regions of nine European Union member countries from the perspective of firms in key regional industrial sectors or clusters. The study covers (a) the importance of regions in the key function of firms, (b) competitiveness, competitive challenges and responses of firms, (c) the innovative practices of firms, (d) partnership for innovation among firms, and (e) cooperation between firms and the innovation infrastructure.

In Chapter 6 Helen Lawton Smith examines the difficulties of firms in Oxfordshire, England, in acquiring external knowledge and information in their production process. Since both regions and firms benefit from technology transfer and technology sharing, the proximity of these is important and can be augmented by the institutional framework. However, this idea is tempered by a raft of context-dependent factors relating to the historical characteristics of the region. Barriers to technology transfer at the local level might either be manifestations of failures in the system as a whole, or be local difficulties arising out of the characteristics of local firms and institutions. This chapter identifies the sources of local difficulties in the case of Oxfordshire.

In Chapter 7 Rolf Sternberg deals explicitly with university–industry relationships in Germany. The chapter pays particular attention to the state of Baden-Württemberg, considered to be a prime example of a German industrial district because of its tightly woven networks, dominance of small and medium-sized firms, strong influence of regional politics, and high degree of technology transfer between universities and firms. The central hypothesis of the chapter is that the national innovation system in Germany is influenced by several regional innovation systems, all quite different in nature, which subdivide a rather homogeneous country. Three types of regions are analysed, using as examples one representative region for each. The emphasis of the empirical analysis is on innovative linkages between the two most important actors within a regional innovation system, these being firms and universities.

Part III presents three complementary vignettes of the regional innovation system in the United States. In Chapter 8 AnnaLee Saxenian compares California's Silicon Valley and Route 128 in Massachusetts to suggest the limits of the concept of external economies and proposes an alternative, network approach to analysing regional economies. The common notion of external economies is based on an assumption that the firm is an atomistic unit of production with clearly defined boundaries. By drawing a sharp distinction between what occurs inside and what occurs outside the firm, scholars overlooked the complex and historically evolved relations between the internal organization of firms and their connections to one another and the social structures and institutions of a particular locality. The network perspective helps explain the divergent performance of apparently comparable regional clusters, such as Silicon Valley and Route 128, and provides important insights into the local sources of innovation in an increasingly global economy.

Whereas Chapter 8 examines the role of universities in two regions, in Chapter 9 Attila Varga asks the question, 'To what extent can university-based economic development be successfully replicated in any regional innovation system?' Using

data on US commercial innovations and university research expenditures, he investigates the extent to which universities are important actors in any local innovation
system. Applying US county and metropolitan data to 134 metropolitan areas, he
suggests that universities can indeed be important actors in local innovation
systems.

In Chapter 10 Rebecca Morales examines the formation of super-regional pacts
that have been designed to stimulate trade and investment, not necessarily encourage innovation. As the influence of super-regional pacts continues to grow, spurred
by the integration of regional markets, the need to define an explicit innovation
policy is likely to increase. In anticipation of such questions the chapter examines the
concept of a super-regional system of innovation to assess its implications for North
America. Because North America combines nations of vastly different capability,
the thrust is one of identifying the issues within a context of unbalanced multi-state
regional growth.

Part IV shifts the lens from regions to firms and the role of innovation management in regional innovation systems. Why do some regions or nations have a
competitive advantage in some industries? And if some environments are better
sources of competitive advantage than others, how do such environments come
about? In Chapter 11 James M. Utterback and Allan N. Afuah explore both
questions by focusing on the evolution of the technologies that underlie a firm's low
cost and product differentiation. The thesis of this chapter is that the local environment that is the source of national or regional competitive advantage is the result of
the process of technological evolution driven by some initial and prevailing condition. The type of environment that emerges is a function of how these initial
conditions, chance events and the reaction (by firms and regional policy-makers) to
firms' performance influence the process of uncertainty resolution, capabilities
building and survivor selection that are characteristic of technological evolution.

In Chapter 12 Edward J. Malecki examines broad national differences regarding
broad corporate strategies for new technologies. Japanese firms, for example,
routinely enlarge their technology base and product range through an expansion of
technological applications. This is contrasted to European firms, which centre on
networks as a mechanism for learning within firms and regions.

Venture capital plays a critical role in technological innovation and economic
development. In Chapter 13 Donald Smith and Richard Florida examine the role of
venture capital in the new regional political economy over the past fifteen years.

Part V, The City and the World, tries to connect up regions and the global
economy. In Chapter 14 Richard Florida suggests that regions (and not nations) are
becoming the focal points of knowledge creation and learning in the new age of
global, knowledge-intensive capitalism, as they in effect become learning regions.
These learning regions function as collectors and repositories of knowledge and
ideas, and provide the underlying environment or infrastructure which facilitates the
flow of knowledge, ideas and learning.

In the final chapter we suggest a 'cosmology' through which to think of the new
knowledge-intensive capitalism. It will become clear as the reader progresses
through the book that this is not simply a collection of disparate papers. The
chapters together represent important elements for the construction of an alternative way to look at innovation systems.

I am most grateful to the colleagues who have agreed to take part in this dialogue and share some of their results with us in this book. Many of the contributions are themselves part of a larger research project. I would especially like to thank John de la Mothe, series editor and long-time friend, who first suggested the idea to me several years ago as an outcome of several cross-border visits between Ottawa and Baltimore. Richard Florida, Rebecca Morales and Attila Varga have been the source of much inspiration over the years. Finally, I would like to thank Petra Recter for moving from manuscript to final product with a minimum of impediments.

Note

1. This section draws heavily on Acs and Morck (1999).

PART I

The Framework

CHAPTER TWO

National Innovation Systems

Richard R. Nelson

The concept of an 'innovation system', defined globally or at the level of the nation, industrial sector, technology or region, is attracting much attention these days. It is hard to recall that as recently as a decade ago, the concept was a relatively novel one, and many people were sceptical about it. (Some still are.) To the best of my understanding, the concept of a national innovation system was proposed virtually simultaneously by Bengt-Åke Lundvall, Christopher Freeman and myself. This was certainly not a case of independent discovery. All three of us were part of a relatively closely connected group of scholars studying technical advance. Our first discussions of the concept were all published in Dosi *et al.* (1988). We talked a lot to each other. The idea clearly was 'in the air'. And the name for that idea was the obvious one.

Christopher Freeman has proposed that in fact the broad idea, if not the name, had been around for a long time. One can find many of the same thoughts in the work of List in the 1840s. The national reports on R&D put out by the Organisation for Economic Co-operation and Development (OECD) in the 1980s were basically about national systems, although defined more narrowly than Lundvall, Freeman and I defined them. At its broadest level, the national innovation systems idea is a way of describing and analysing the set of institutions that generate and mould economic growth, to the extent that one has a theory of economic growth in which technological innovation is the key driving force. The scholars within our extended group clearly did hold to that theory, and by the late 1980s there was a widely shared view of the key institutional structures involved. Thus the time was ripe for a series of studies on 'national innovation systems'.

I was involved in such a particular study (Nelson 1993). As a background for the new work that makes up most of this volume, it seems useful to review that study here, considering some of the analytic issues it had to address (which many of the contemporary studies share), and some of the key conclusions of that study (which mostly are reinforced by the new studies reported in the rest of this volume).

The basic concepts employed

There is, first of all, the not unproblematic concept of a national innovation system itself. Each of the terms can be interpreted in a variety of ways, and there is the question of whether, in a world where technology and business are increasingly transnational, the concept as a whole makes much sense.

Consider the term 'innovation'. In the study in question we interpreted the term rather broadly, to encompass the processes by which firms master and get into practice product designs and manufacturing processes that are new to them, whether or not they are new to the universe, or even to the nation. We did so for several reasons. First, the activities and investments associated with becoming the leader in the introduction of a new product or process, and those associated with staying near the head of the pack, or catching up, are much less sharply distinguishable than is commonly presumed. Second, much of the interest in innovative capability is tied to concern about economic performance, and here it is certainly the broader concept rather than the narrower one (the determinants of being first) that matters. This means that our orientation was not limited to the behaviour of firms at the world's technology forefront, or to institutions doing the most advanced scientific research (although in some countries that is the focus), but was more broadly on the factors influencing national technological capabilities.

Then there is the term 'system'. While to some the word connotes something that is consciously designed and built, this was far from the orientation here. Rather, the concept employed in our study was that of a set of institutions whose interactions determine the innovative performance, in the sense above, of national firms. There was no presumption that the system was, in some sense, consciously designed, or even that the set of institutions involved works together smoothly and coherently. Rather, the 'systems' concept is that of a set of institutional actors that, together, play the major role in influencing innovative performance. The broad concept of innovation that we adopted forced us to consider much more than simply the actors doing research and development. Indeed, a problem with the broader definition of innovation is that it provides no sharp guide to just what should be included in the innovation system, and what can be left out. (More on this later.)

Finally, there is the concept of 'national' system. On the one hand, the concept may be too broad. The system of institutions supporting technical innovation in one field, say pharmaceuticals, may have very little overlap with the system of institutions supporting innovations in another field, say aircraft. On the other hand, in many fields of technology, including both pharmaceuticals and aircraft, a number of the institutions are, or act, transnationally. Indeed, for many of the participants in this study, one of the key interests was in exploring whether, and if so in what ways, the concept of a 'national' system made any sense nowadays. National governments act as if it did. However, that presumption and the reality may not be aligned.

The studies in this project were unified by at least broad agreement on the definitional and conceptual issues discussed above. They were also guided by certain common understandings of the way technical advance proceeds, and the key processes and institutional actors involved, that are now widely shared among scholars of technical advance. In a way these understandings do provide a common analytic framework – not wide enough to encompass all of the variables and relationships that are likely to be important, not sharp enough to guide empirical work tightly, but broad enough and pointed enough to provide a common structure in which one can have some confidence.

In particular, our inquiry was strongly shaped by our shared understandings about the complex intertwining of science and technology that marks the modern world. In the first place, we took the position that technology at any time needs to be recognized as consisting of both a set of specific designs and practices, and a body of generic knowledge that surrounds these and provides understanding of how things work, key variables affecting performance, the nature of currently binding constraints, and promising approaches to pushing these back. In most fields of technology a considerable portion of generic understanding stems from operating and design experience with products and machines and their components, and generalizations reflecting on these. Thus consider a mechanic's guide, or the general knowledge of potters, or steel makers,

However, over the past century science has played an increasing role in the understandings related to technology. Indeed, most modern fields of technology today have associated with them formal scientific or engineering disciplines like metallurgy, computer science and chemical engineering. These kinds of disciplines are basically about technological understanding, and reflect attempts to make that understanding more scientific. An important consequence has been that, nowadays, formal academic training in the various applied sciences and engineering disciplines has become virtually a prerequisite for understanding a technology.

The intertwining of science and technology which began to occur a century ago led to the rise of the industrial research laboratory as the dominant locus of technological innovation, first in the chemical and electrical industries, and then more broadly. These facilities, dedicated to advancing technology, and staffed by academically trained scientists and engineers, were closely tied to individual business enterprises.

It is important to understand that not all of the activities and investments made by firms in innovating are conducted in R&D laboratories, or get counted as R&D. The extent to which they do varies from industry to industry. Where firms are small, or where firms are engaged in designing products to order for individual customers, much innovative work may not be counted as R&D. Nonetheless, while it is not always counted as R&D, and while it often draws extensively on external sources like universities and government labs, in most industries the lion's share of innovative effort is made by the firms themselves.

There are several reasons. First, after technology has been around for a period of time, in order to orient innovative work fruitfully one needs detailed knowledge of its strengths and weaknesses and areas where improvements would yield high pay-offs, and this knowledge tends to reside with those who use the technology, generally firms and their customers and suppliers. Second, profiting from innovation in many cases requires the coordination of R&D, production and marketing, which tends to proceed much more effectively within an organization that itself does all of these. These arguments hold whether one defines the innovation concept narrowly, as the introduction of a product or process that is truly new, or whether one defines it broadly as we did in the study, as the introduction of something that is new to the firm. Thus all the country studies paid a considerable amount of attention to the activities and investments being undertaken by firms.

The other two types of institutional actors with which all of the country studies were concerned were universities (and scientific and technical educational structures more generally), and governments and their policies as these influence industrial innovation. University and kindred institutions play two different kinds of roles in modern industrial innovation systems. They are the place where scientists and engineers who go into industry get their formal training. And in most (but not all) countries they are the locus of a considerable amount of research in the disciplines that are associated with particular technologies. To a much greater extent than commonly realized, university research programmes are not undifferentiated parts of a national innovation system broadly defined, but rather are keyed into particular technologies and particular industries. University training and research that supports technical innovation in farming and the food processing industries simply is very different from university teaching and research that supports the electronic industries. Thus a major question in this study was how the research and teaching orientation of a nation's universities reflected, or moulded, the industries where technological innovation was important in the nation.

And, of course, the individual country studies looked closely at the range of government programmes and policies bearing on industrial innovation. As is the case with the activities of universities, many government programmes are focused specifically on particular technologies or industries, and these obviously were of central interest. However, as noted in my earlier discussion of the meaning of an 'innovation system', given the broad way we used the term 'innovation', innovative performance cannot be cleanly separated from economic performance and competitiveness more broadly. Thus in many cases the examination of government policies bearing on industrial innovation had to get into things like monetary and trade policies.

In designing the study, the participants faced a quandary. From the discussion above, it is obvious that a very wide range of factors influence the innovative performance of a nation's industries. The desire for comparability across the studies seemed to call for a rather elaborate list of things all country studies would cover. Yet it was apparent that the most interesting features of a country's innovation system varied significantly across countries, and we wanted to illuminate these. Limits on resources and space foreclosed doing both. Our compromise involved two strategic decisions. First, we agreed on the limited list of features all country studies were to cover, e.g. the allocation of R&D activity and the sources of its funding, the characteristics of firms and the important industries, the roles of universities, and the government policies expressly aimed to spur and mould industrial innovation. Beyond these the authors were encouraged to pick out and highlight what they thought were the most important and interesting characteristics of their country. But second, considerable effort was put into identifying the kinds of comparisons – similarities or differences – that seemed most interesting and important to make. In general these did not involve comparisons across all countries, but rather among a small group where for various reasons comparison was apt.

The overall project covered three sets of countries where we thought in-group comparisons would be most interesting. The first group consisted of six large (in terms of population) high-income countries; the United States, Japan, Germany, France, Italy and the United Kingdom. The second group consisted of four small high-income countries, with a strong agricultural or resources base: Denmark, Sweden, Canada and Australia. Finally, included in the set were five lower-income countries: Korea, Taiwan, Argentina, Brazil and Israel. While we were interested in the similarities and differences across groups, a considerable amount of thought and effort went into laying out within-group comparisons.

Country differences and what lies behind them

Certainly the broad view of technical innovation which I laid out above and which guided this study implies certain commonalities. That view applies to economies in which profit-oriented firms are the principal providers of goods and services, and where central planning and control is weak. These conditions hold in all the countries in our set, although in some a certain portion of industry is nationalized, and in some governments do try to mould the shape of industrial development in at least a few economic sections. In all the countries in our set the bulk of education, including university education, is conducted in public institutions. In all, the government is presumed to have major responsibility for the funding of basic research, although there are major differences across countries regarding how much of that they do, and where basic research is mostly carried out. From one point of view, what is most striking about the country comparisons is the amount of basic similarity. Had the old Soviet Union been included in the set, or China or Nigeria, the matter would have been different. But as it is, the differences across our set of countries must be understood as differences of individuals of the same species.

Within our group of countries, it would appear that to a considerable extent the differences in the innovation systems reflect differences in economic and political circumstances and priorities. First of all, size and the degree of affluence matter a lot. Countries with large, affluent populations can provide a market for a wide range of manufacturing industries and may engage in other activities that 'small' countries cannot pursue, at least with any chance of success, and their innovation systems will reflect this. Low-income countries tend to differ from high-income ones in the kinds of economic activities in which they can have comparative advantage, and in internal demand patterns, and these differences profoundly shape the nature of technical innovation that is relevant.

The threefold division of our countries into large high-income industrial nations, small high-income countries and low-income countries thus turned out to be a useful first-cut analytic separation. By and large, the economies in the first group had a significantly larger fraction of their economies in R&D-intensive industry, like aerospace, electronics and chemical products, which require large sales to be economic, than economies in the second and third groups. There are some anomalies, on the surface at least. Thus Sweden in the second group, and Israel and Korea in the third, have higher R&D to GNP ratios than several of the countries in the first group. Some of the mystery disappears when Israel's ambitious military R&D is recognized, and Sweden's and Korea's strong presence in several R&D-intensive industries that live largely through exports. Both of the latter two countries also have strong defence programmes, and this also undoubtedly affects their R&D intensities. There are certain interesting similarities between countries in different groups: Japan and Korea, for example. However, by and large there were strong intra-group similarities and strong inter-group differences. Thus the United States and Japan look much less different than advertised, once one brings Australia and Israel into the comparison set. And much of the United States–Japan difference can be seen to reside in differences in their resource bases and defence policies.

Whether or not a country has rich natural resources or ample farming land clearly is another important variable influencing the shape of its innovation system. It turns out that all our 'small' high-income countries also are well endowed in this respect. Among the large high-income countries the United States was far and away the best endowed in this respect. Countries that possess resources and good farmland face a different set of opportunities and constraints than countries without these assets.

Countries that lack them must import resources and farm products, which forces their economies towards export-oriented manufacturing, and an innovation system that supports this. One sees this strikingly in the cases of Germany, Japan and Korea. On the other hand, countries with a rich resource base can support relatively high living standards with farm products and resources and the affiliated industries providing exports to pay for imported manufactured goods. The countries that have been able to do this – Denmark, Canada and Australia stand out in our set – have developed significant publicly supported R&D programmes to back these industries. So also has the United States. While effective agriculture and resource exploitation do require R&D, compared with 'high-tech' industry the R&D intensity here is low.

The discussion above suggests that, to some extent at least, a nation's innovation system is shaped by factors like size and resource endowments that affect comparative advantage at a basic level. But it also is true that a nation's innovation system tends to reflect conscious decisions to develop and sustain economic strength in certain areas; that is, it builds and shapes comparative advantage.

Some of the project members were surprised to find in how many of our countries national security concerns had been important in shaping innovation systems.

In the first place, among high-income countries defence R&D accounts for the lion's share of the differences among the countries in government funding of industrial R&D, and the presence of large military programmes thus explains why government industrial R&D spending in the United States, and the United Kingdom and France, is so much greater than in Japan and Germany. In the second place, the industries from which the military procures tend to be R&D intensive, whether the firms are selling to the military or to civilians. The study of Japan shows clearly that the present industrial structure was largely put in place during an era when national security concerns were strong. This structure, now oriented to civilian products, is one of the reasons for Japan's high R&D intensity. It is possible that, to some extent, this argument also holds for Germany.

Interestingly, every one of the low-income countries in our study has been influenced by national security concerns, or a military government, or both. Thus much high-tech industry in Israel is largely oriented towards the military. The broad economic policies, industrial structures and innovation systems of Korea and Taiwan were moulded in good part by their felt need to have a capable military establishment. The pockets of 'high tech' atop the basically backward Brazilian and Argentine economies clearly reflect the ambitions of their military elites. As noted, all the countries in our set are, basically, ones in which firms are mostly expected to fend for themselves in markets that are, to a considerable extent, competitive. However, all are marked by significant pockets of government overview, funding and protection. In our countries with big military procurement programmes, the defence industries are the largest such pocket. However, in many of our countries government support and protection extends into space, electric power, telecommunications, and other areas of civilian 'high tech'. While by and large these extensions are most significant in the big high-income countries, Canada has large public programmes in electric power and telecommunications, and so does Sweden.

There clearly are significant differences across the nations regarding beliefs about what kind of a role government should play in shaping industrial development. The role of military concerns clearly is a powerful variable influencing this. But a relatively active government also is associated with 'late' development, along the lines put forward by Alexander Gerschenkron (1962). Aside from the arena of national security and related areas, the United Kingdom and the United States are marked by restrained government. On the other hand, all our low-income late developing countries have quite active governments. However, there certainly are exceptions to this rule. France's *étatisme* goes way back in history, and while Italy is a late developer, except during the Fascist era its government has been weak.

The above discussion suggests that one ought to see considerable continuity in a nation's innovation system, at least to the extent that the basic national objectives and conditions have a continuity. Although this proposition clearly has only limited bearing on the countries in our set that were formed or gained independence only in recent years – Israel, Taiwan, Korea – even here one can see a certain consistency within these nations' short histories. All these countries have experienced dramatic improvements in living standards since the 1950s, and their industrial structure has changed markedly. Their innovation systems have changed as well, but as our authors tell the story, in all these countries today's institutional structures supporting innovation clearly show their origins in those of thirty years ago.

For countries with longer histories, the institutional continuity is striking, at least to the study authors. Thus one can see many of the same things in 1990 in France, Germany and Japan that were there in 1890, and this despite the enormous advances in living standards and shifts in industrial structure all have experienced, and the total defeat of the latter two nations in World War II and the stripping away of their military. Britain of 1990 continues many of the institutional characteristics of Britain in 1890, although they seemed to work better then than now.

Indeed, in this author's eyes, of the countries with long histories the one that has changed most, institutionally, is the United States. The governmental roles in funding university research, and defence R&D, which came into place only after World War II, had little precedent prior to the war and profoundly changed the nature of the innovation system.

What is required for effective innovative performance?

We have defined innovation broadly so that the term basically stands for what is required of firms if they are to stay competitive in industries where technological advance is important. Such industries span a large share of manufacturing, many service sectors such as air transport, telecommunications and medical care, and important areas of agriculture and mining. Staying competitive means different things in different national contexts. For firms located in high-wage countries, being competitive may require having a significantly more attractive product or a better production process than firms in low-wage countries. For the latter, being competitive may not require being at the forefront. Indeed, much innovation in low-income countries involves the learning of foreign technology, its diffusion, and perhaps its adaptation to local circumstances of demand or production. But in either kind of country, if technological advance in the industry is significant, staying competitive requires continuing innovation.

We, the group that has produced the country studies, think we can discern several basic features that are common to effective innovative performance, and which are lacking or attenuated in countries where innovation arguably has been weak. First, the firms in the industry were highly competent in what mattered to be competitive in their lines of business. Generally this involved competence in product design and production, but usually also effective overall management, ability to assess consumer needs, links into upstream and downstream markets, etc. In most cases significant investments lay behind these firm capabilities. All this enabled firms to master the relevant technologies and other practices needed to compete and to stay up with or lead with new developments.

This observation does contain a hint of tautology, but is better regarded as confirmation of a point stressed above that the bulk of the effort in innovation needs to be done by the firms themselves. While they may draw on outside developments, significant internal effort and skill is needed to complement and implement these. One cannot read the studies of Japan, Germany, Italy, Korea or Taiwan (all arguably countries where firms have displayed strong performance in certain industries) without being impressed by the authors' description of the firms. On the other hand, one is impressed the other way by the authors' commentary on the weaknesses of firms in certain industries in Britain, France, Australia, Argentina, Israel.

Being strong did not necessarily mean that firms were large. Economists long have understood that while in some industries a firm has to be large in order to be a capable innovator, in other industries this is not the case. Many of the strong Italian, Taiwanese and Danish firms are relatively small. Nor does it mean that the firms spend heavily on formal R&D. In some fields, like electronics, generally it did, at least for firms in our first two groups of countries; however, in Korea and Taiwan electronics firms often were doing well with technical efforts mostly oriented towards 'reverse engineering'. The Italian textile industry is strong on fashion and design, and is highly innovative in these respects, but little of that work is accounted as R&D. Nor does it imply that the firms were not benefiting from publicly funded R&D programmes, or favoured procurement status. However, as our authors described it, the bulk of the inputs and direction for innovative activity were coming from the firms themselves.

While our concept of strong firm entailed an ability to compete, in all of our cases becoming strong involved actually being exposed to strong competition and being forced to compete. As Michael Porter (1990) has noted, in a number of cases the firms faced strong rivals in their own country. Thus the Japanese auto and electronics companies compete strongly with each other; American pharmaceutical companies compete, and Italian clothing producers. However, it is not at all clear that this generalization holds for small countries, where there may be only one or a few national firms, such as Ericsson in Sweden and Nortel in Canada. For these firms most of their competition is with foreign rivals.

Porter (1990) and Bengt-Åke Lundvall (1988) have proposed that firms in industries where a country is strong tend to have strong interactive linkages with their upstream suppliers, which also are national firms. Our studies show many cases where this proposition is verified. The supplier networks of Japanese automobile firms, and the upstream–downstream connections in Danish agricultural product processing, are good examples. The cooperation of Italian textile producers with each other and with their equipment suppliers is another. However, there are a number of examples where the proposition does not seem to hold. Pharmaceutical companies, strong in Germany and the United States, do not seem generally to have any particularly strong supplier connections, international or national. In aircraft production, the producers of components and subcomponents increasingly are located in countries other than that of the system designer and assembler.

A similar observation pertains to the proposed importance of a demanding set of home-market customers. In many cases this holds. But in small countries, or in industries that from their start have been export oriented, the main customer discipline may well come from foreign customers.

While 'strong firms' are the key, that only pushes the question back a stage. Under what conditions do strong firms arise? As the discussion above suggests, to some extent the answer is, glibly, 'spontaneously'. However, our studies do indicate strongly that aspects of the national background in which firms operate matter greatly.

One important feature distinguishing countries that were sustaining competitive and innovative firms was education and training systems that provide these firms with a flow of people with the requisite knowledge and skills. For industries where university-trained engineers and scientists were needed, this does not simply mean that the universities provide training in these fields, but also that they consciously train their students with an eye to industry needs. The contrast here between the United States and Germany on the one hand, and Britain and France on the other, is quite sharp, at least as the authors of our studies draw the picture. Indeed, these studies suggest strongly that a principal reason why the former two countries surged ahead of the latter two around the turn of the century in what were then the science-based industries is that their university systems were much more responsive to the training needs of industry.

While strength in 'high tech' depends on the availability of university-trained people, industry more generally requires a supply of literate, numerically competent, people in a wide range of functions outside R&D, who are trained to industry demands either by the firms themselves (as in Japan) or in external training systems linked to firms (as in several German and Swedish industries). Countries differed in the extent to which their public education and training systems combined with private training to provide this supply, and the differences mattered. Thus among high-income countries Germany, Japan and Sweden came through much more strongly in this respect than Britain and Australia. Among developing countries the contrast is equally sharp between Korea and Taiwan on the one hand, and Brazil on the other.

The examples of Korea and Taiwan, and the other Asian 'tigers', can be read as remarkably successful cases of education-led growth. As the case authors tell the story, the ability of firms in these countries to move quickly from the relatively simple products they produced in the 1950s and 1960s to the much more complex and technologically sophisticated products they produced successfully in the 1980s was made possible by the availability of a young domestic workforce that had received the schooling necessary for and appropriate to the new jobs. On the other hand, the cases of Argentina and Israel suggest that the availability of an educated workforce is not enough by itself. The economic incentives facing firms must be such as to compel them to mind the market and to take advantage of the presence of a skilled workforce to compete effectively with their rivals.

Another factor that seems to differentiate countries where firms were effectively innovative from those where they were not is the package of fiscal, monetary and trade policies. By and large, where these combined to make exporting attractive for firms, firms have been drawn to innovate and compete. Where they have made exporting difficult or unattractive, firms have hunkered down in their home markets, and – when in trouble – called for protection. As I shall indicate later, in some cases at the same time as firms were competing abroad, they were working within a rather protected home market, so the argument is not a simple one for 'free trade'. Rather, it is that export incentives matter significantly because, for most countries, if firms do not compete on world markets they do not compete strongly. Up until recently the United States possibly was an exception to this rule. The US market was large enough to support considerable competition among domestic firms, which kept them on their toes and innovative. No other country could afford the luxury of not forcing their firms to compete on world markets. Now the United States cannot either.

Of course, much of the current interest in national systems of innovation reflects a belief that the innovative prowess of national firms is determined to a considerable extent by government policies. Above, I have identified two features of the national environment in which firms live that seem to affect their ability and incentives to innovate in a profound way, and which are central responsibilities of government in all of the countries in our sample: the education of the workforce and the macro-economic climate. But what of government policies and programmes more directly targeted at technological advance? This is where much of the contemporary interest is focused. How effective have been these kinds of policies?

In assessing this question in the light of the fifteen country systems studied in this project, one strong impression is the wide range of policies targeted at technological advance. Thus in recent years government policies towards industrial mergers and acquisitions, inter-firm agreements and joint ventures, and allowable industry-wide activities have often been strongly influenced by beliefs about the effects of such policies on innovative performance. Many countries (and the European Union) are now encouraging firms to cooperate in R&D of various sorts. Similarly, in recent years a number of governments have worked to restructure or augment financial institutions with the goal of fostering industrial innovation; thus several have tried to establish their analogue to the 'venture capital' market that exists in the United States. As suggested, these policies are a very diverse lot and differ from country to country. Our case studies do provide scattered evidence on them, but, simply because they are so diverse, I cannot see any strong generalizations that can be drawn.

Of course, our country study authors were primed to look at government programmes directly supporting R&D, and here I think the evidence collected is more systematic. It seems useful to distinguish between government programmes that largely provide funds for university research or for research in government or other laboratories not tied to particular business firms, and government programmes that directly support R&D done in firms. I consider each in turn.

Scholars of innovation now understand that, in many sectors, publicly supported research at universities and in public laboratories is an important part of the sectoral innovation system. A substantial share of the funding of such institutions goes into fields that are directly connected with technological or industrial needs – fields like agronomy, pathology, computer science, materials science, chemical and electrical engineering. Do our country studies support the proposition that strong research at universities or public laboratories aids a country's firms in innovation, defining that term broadly as we have? Not surprisingly, the answer seems both to differ from field to field and to be sensitive to the mechanisms in place to mould and facilitate interactions with industry. All the countries that are strong and innovative in fine chemicals and pharmaceuticals have strong university research in chemistry and the biomedical sciences. A strong agriculture and a strong farm product processing industry are associated in all of our cases with significant research going on relevant to these fields in national universities, or in other types of public research institutions dedicated to these industries. By contrast, Argentine agriculture is surprisingly weak, despite favourable natural endowments. The author of the case study of Argentina lays the blame on Argentina's failure to develop an adequate agricultural research system.

Where countries have strong electronics firms, for the most part there is some strong research in university departments of electrical engineering, and this would appear to include Japan. Government laboratories have been important sources of new electronic product designs later taken over by firms in Taiwan. On the other hand, university research does not seem to be of much importance to technical advance in the automobile or aerospace industries.

Where universities or public laboratories do seem to be helping national firms, one tends to see either direct interactions between particular firms and particular faculty members or research teams (as through consulting arrangements) or mechanisms that tie university or public laboratory programmes to groups of firms. Thus in the United States agricultural experimentation stations do research of relevance to farmers and seed producers, and have close interactions with them. Various German universities have programmes designed to help machinery producers. Taiwan's electronics industry is closely linked to government laboratories. In all these cases, the relationships between the university or government labs and the industry are not appropriately described as the universities or public laboratories simply doing research of relevance to the industry in question. The connections were much broader and closer than that, involving information dissemination and problem-solving. Universities and industry were co-partners in a technological community. While this is not important in all industries, a strong case can be made that such technology- and industry-oriented public programmes have made a big difference in many fields.

These programmes are far less visible than government programmes that directly support industrial R&D, and the latter also tend to involve far more money. Countries differ significantly in the extent to which the government directly funds industrial R&D. And while most of such programmes tend to be concentrated on a narrow range of 'high-tech' industries, programmes of this sort vary significantly and have been put in place for different reasons.

I noted above that, in most of our countries, military R&D accounts for by far the largest portion of government funding of industrial R&D. Analysts have been divided as to whether military R&D and procurement has been a help or a hindrance to the commercial competitiveness of national industry. Of the major industrial nations, the United States spends by far the largest share of industrial R&D on military projects. A strong case can be made that in the 1960s this helped the American electronics and aircraft industries to come to dominate commercial markets, but that since the late 1960s there has been little 'spillover'. The United Kingdom has the second largest of the defence R&D budgets among our set of nations, but most of the companies receiving R&D contracts have shown little capability to break into non-military markets. The same can be said for most of the French companies. While until recently civilian commercial spillover has seldom been a central objective of military R&D, except in the sense that it was recognized that selling on civilian markets could reduce the public costs of sustaining a strong military procurement base, it is interesting to try to understand where military R&D did lend civilian market strength and where it did not.

Analysis of the US experience suggests that civilian strength is lent when military R&D programmes are opening up a broad new generic technology, as contrasted with focusing virtually exclusively on procuring particular new pieces of fancy hardware wanted by the military. Increasingly the US military effort has shifted from the former to the latter. A much smaller share of military R&D now goes into research and exploratory development than during the 1960s, and a larger share into highly specialized systems development. And the efforts of the other countries in our set that have invested significantly in military R&D – the United Kingdom, France and Israel – have from the beginning focused largely on the latter.

Space programmes and nuclear power programmes have much in common with military R&D and procurement. They tend to involve the same kind of government agency leadership in determining what is done. They too tend to be concentrated on large-scale systems developments. Spillovers outside the field have been quite limited.

Government programmes in support of company R&D in telecommunications, other civilian electronics and aircraft may overlap the technical fields supported by military and space programmes, and in some cases the support may go to the same companies. These programmes also tend to involve the same blend of industrial R&D support, and protection from foreign competition. However, there are several important differences. One is that, compared with military R&D, the public funds almost invariably are much smaller. Indeed, programmes like EUREKA, ESPRIT, Jessi, Fifth Generation and Sematech are all small relative to industry funding in the targeted areas. Second, the firms themselves usually have a major say regarding the way in which public monies are spent, and the projects are subject to far less detailed public management and overview than are defence projects. Third, these programmes are targeted to firms and products in civilian markets, and while their home base may be protected through import restriction or preferential procurement, the hope is that the firms ultimately will be able to stand on their own.

Thus while they involve a commitment to high R&D spending, these programmes otherwise have much in common with other 'infant industry' protection programmes, many of which have grown up for reasons with no particular connections with national security, or a belief in the importance of 'high tech', but simply because of the desire of a government to preserve or create a 'national' industry. Infant industry protection, subsidy and government guidance are policies that have been around for a long, long time. They mark French policy since the time of Colbert. During the nineteenth century and up until World War II the United States was protectionist. The Japanese and Korean steel and auto industries, which were highly protected up until the 1980s, are more contemporary examples.

Do the infants ever grow up? Well, some do and some do not. The Japanese auto and electronics companies and the Korean chaebol based enterprises are well known examples of presently strong firms that grew up in a protected market, but it also should be recognized that the American computer and semiconductor industries grew up with their market shielded from foreign competition and with their R&D funded to a considerable extent by the Department of Defense. After a period of such shelter and support, these firms came to dominate the world's commercial markets. Airbus may be another successful example. On the other hand, the country studies in this project give many examples of protected and subsidized industries which never have got to a stage where the firms can compete on their own. France's electronics industry is a striking example, but so also are the import-substituting industries of Argentina and Brazil.

What lies behind the differences? If I were to make a bet, it is that the differences reside in two things: first, the education and training systems, which in some cases did and in others did not provide the protected firms with the strong skills they needed to make it on their own; second, at least in today's world, the extent to which economic conditions, including government policies, provide strong incentives for the firms quickly to start trying to compete on world markets, as contrasted with hunkering down in their protected enclave.

The picture of government policies supporting industrial innovation that I have been presenting highlights the diversity of such policies and programmes, and their generally fragmented nature – some supporting research and other activities aimed to help industry in universities or public labs, others connected with defence or space or nuclear power, still others aimed directly at supporting or protecting certain industries or industry groups. This is the broad picture that I draw from the country studies of this national innovation system project. These studies play down the existence of active coherent industrial policies more broadly. The interpretation they present of the industrial policies of nations widely believed to have them is closer to that of modern-day infant industry protection with some R&D subsidy, than to a well-structured and thought-through general, integrated policy.

What remains national about innovation systems?

I have noted a number of difficulties with the concept of a 'national innovation system'. In the first place, unless one defines innovation very narrowly and cuts the institutional fabric to that narrow definition, and we did neither, it is inevitable that analysis of innovation in a country will sometimes get drawn into discussion of labour markets, financial systems, monetary, fiscal and trade policies, etc. One cannot draw a line neatly around those aspects of a nation's institutional structure that are concerned predominantly with innovation in a narrow sense excluding everything else, and still tell a coherent story about innovation in a broad sense. Nonetheless, most of our authors were able to tell a pretty coherent story about innovation in their country, focusing largely on institutions and mechanisms that fit the narrow definition, with discussion of country institutions more broadly serving largely as a frame.

Second, the term suggests much more uniformity and connectedness within a nation than is the case. Thus, one can discuss Canadian agriculture pretty independently of Canadian telecommunications. R&D and innovation in the American pharmaceutical industry and R&D of aircraft by American companies have little in common. And yet, one cannot read the studies of Japan, Germany, France, Korea, Argentina, Israel, to name just a few, without coming away with the strong feeling that nationhood matters and has a pervasive influence. In all these cases a distinctive national character pervades the firms, the educational system, the law, the politics and the government, all of which have been shaped by a shared historical experience and culture.

I believe that most of us would square these somewhat divergent observations as follows. If one focuses narrowly on what we have defined as 'innovation systems', these tend to be sectorally specific. However, if one broadens the focus to the factors that make for commonality across sections within a country, the wider set of institutions referred to above comes into view, and these largely define the factors that make for commonality across sectors within a country.

From the start of this project we recognized that borders around nations are porous, and increasingly so. Indeed, one of the questions that motivated this study was whether or not the concept of *national* innovation systems made sense any more. I suspect that many of us come out on this as follows.

It is a safe bet that there will be increasing internationalization of those aspects of technology that are reasonably well understood scientifically. Efforts on the part of nations, and firms, to keep new understandings won in R&D privy will increasingly be futile. Among firms with the requisite scientific and technical people, the competitive edge will depend on the details of design, of production process, of firm strategy and organization, upstream–downstream connections, etc. Today, this is quite clearly the case in fields like semiconductors, aircraft, computers and automobiles. In these fields, there are no broad technological secrets possessed by individual countries or particular firms. On the other hand, strong firms have a good deal of firm-specific know-how and capability.

It is also a good bet that differences across firms stamped into them by national policies, histories and cultures will diminish in importance. Partly that will be because the world is becoming much more unified culturally, for better or for worse. Partly it will be because firm managers and scholars of management are increasingly paying attention to how firms in other countries are organized and managed. And cross-country inter-firm connections are likely to grow in importance. Firms in industries where there are large, up-front R&D design and production engineering costs increasingly are forging alliances with firms in other countries, to share some of the costs and to get over government-made market barriers. The establishment of branch plants in protected countries or regions is another mechanism. Thus, increasingly, the attempts of national governments to define and support a national industry will be frustrated because of internationalization.

What will remain of 'national systems'? People and governments will have to get used to dealing with plants whose headquarters are abroad. The countries of Europe have been struggling with this matter for some time, and many of the Latin American countries, too. The United States is now having to try to do so, and Japan and Korea are beginning to. As yet, no large country seems to have made its peace with the problem, however. In most countries, resident firms will remain largely national, but the presence of 'foreign' firms in important industries is something that nations will have to learn to cope with better.

We noted earlier the striking continuity of a nation's basic institutions bearing on industrial innovation. A good example is national education systems, which sometimes seem never to change in their basics. While top-level scientists and engineers may be highly mobile, and some high-level students will continue to take training abroad, below the PhD level, by and large, countries will be stuck with their nationals who are trained at home.

Nations' systems of university research and public laboratories will continue to be largely national, particularly the programmes that are specifically keyed to advancing technology or otherwise facilitating technical progress in industry, and with built-in mechanisms for interacting with industry. These programmes will have to work with foreign branch firms as well as domestic ones in certain fields. But the notion that universities and public laboratories basically provide 'public goods' and that therefore there are no advantages to firms that have close formal links simply does not fit the facts in many industries.

A nation's other public infrastructure, and laws, its financial institutions, its fiscal monetary and trade policies, and its general economic ambience will still be a major influence on economic activity, including innovating, and these are very durable. For large high-income countries at least, the lion's share of private investment will continue to be domestic and constrained by domestic savings, and nations will continue to have their own distinctive views of the appropriate relationships between government and business.

And these will strongly influence a nation's policies bearing explicitly on science and technology. From the evidence in this study, these must be understood as an agglomeration of policies directed towards different national objectives, each with a somewhat special domain in terms of the fields and the institutions most affected, rather than as a coherent package.

All can hope that there will be a significant diminution of defence programmes, but it is a safe bet that military R&D will continue to account for the lion's share of government industrial R&D spending in the United States, France, Britain and Israel. It is likely, however, that there will be little commercial 'spillover'.

Outside the sphere of defence and space, a nation's programmes of R&D support will in all likelihood continue to reflect both the needs of industry and the broad attitudes towards what government should be doing and how. While there will be exceptions, particularly when a defence connection is argued, the United States will continue to resist programmes that directly fund industrial R&D, but will use the universities as the base for a variety of programmes including some directly targeted at certain technologies and industries. European countries are likely to make much more use of programmes that directly support civil industrial R&D, either in individual firms or in industry-wide research organizations. And in Japan, France and various other countries, government agencies and high-tech firms will continue to be quite close.

Postscript

As suggested at the start of this chapter, the scholars who engaged in this early project on national systems of innovation understood when the project began that within nations there were enormous differences among the 'innovation systems' associated with different sectors and technologies. And as our discussions proceeded, a number of us became increasingly cognizant of at least broad similarities of the sectoral and technology-level innovation systems across different countries. As a consequence, a group of us began to define our next collaborative project in terms of sectoral innovation systems, in which we would look at a number of different important industries in different countries.

That follow-on project, which is compared with comparative 'sectoral innovation systems', is now complete (Mowery and Nelson forthcoming). Much of its analysis, and many of its findings, are in the spirit of the chapters which follow in this volume.

CHAPTER THREE

National Innovation Systems and Instituted Processes

John de la Mothe and Gilles Paquet

Material and ideal interests directly govern men's conduct. Yet very frequently the 'world images' that have been created by ideas have, like switchmen, determined the tracks along which action has been pushed. (Max Weber)

Over the past twenty years or so, numerous attempts have been made to develop world images that illuminate the contours of the contemporary political economy. These have been largely unsatisfying and unilluminating. One might point as examples to the images, language and frameworks offered in recent years by Lester Thurow's aggressive 'bloc politics' of *Head to Head* (or 'the coming battle between Europe, Japan and America') (1992) and *The Future of Capitalism* (1996), or the hawkish discourse of 'information power politics' that continues still in respect to smart weapons, systems and human intelligence, Internet terrorism and privacy, and so on (Nye 1993), or the work framed by Paul Krugman (1995) on 'strategic trade theory' and policy, or the 'grand chessboard' of the geo-strategist Zbigniew Brzezinski (1997), or the 'turbo-capitalism' of Edward Luttwak (1993).

Much more fruitful has been the work done in the tradition of neo-Schumpeterian evolutionary economics to advance our understanding of the micro-foundations of innovation. Perhaps the touchstone volume of this tradition is Nelson and Winter's *Evolutionary Theory of Economic Change* (1982). In recent years, efforts have been made to percolate general theoretical and empirical observations from this literature up into a conceptual framework capable of guiding policy and loosely organized around the idea of a 'national system'.

In the first section of this chapter – and following Richard Nelson's admissions in Chapter 2 of extreme heterogeneity across countries, sectors and technologies – we review the ideal of national innovation systems. In the second section we examine how innovation systems are related to techno-economic evolution. In the third section we suggest that the innovation process rarely encompasses the national scene but would appear to be congruent with local, regional and/or sectoral realities that are genuine sources of synergies and social learning.

National innovation systems

As Chapter 2 noted, the idea of a 'national system' as a unit of analysis for competitive performance can be traced back to 1841 when the German economist Friedrich List wrote his highly nation-state-oriented *National Systems of Political*

Economy. But the core idea which he developed has only recently grown into something approaching a conceptual framework through the analytic and empirical efforts of B.-Ä. Lundvall (1992), Richard Nelson (1993), Niosi *et al.* (1993), the OECD (1994a, b) and Charles Edquist (1997).

The rise of a notion of 'national' systems has been, in part, driven by a general interest throughout the OECD member countries in understanding the reasons why firms and nations differ in socio-economic performance over time. Why is it, for example, that firms in the same industries, of the same rough size, which compete in markets with similar products, and which feature similar technologies, plant and equipment, differ significantly in performance? In more general terms, interest in this level of analysis is due, in part, to the strong tendency towards an inter-nationalization of trade, capital, technology and production during the post-1945 period. These general concerns with competition and performance have, of course, motivated economists, managers and policy analysts for many years. But the political impetus that was needed to drive this concept came from the OECD in the mid-1980s.

In an OECD report on science, technology and competitiveness, published in 1983, the Scientific and Technological Policy Committee adopted an approach to analysing competition that was based not on prices, costs, access to raw material and resources, and so on, but rather on the following hypothesis:

> the international competitiveness of a national economy is built on the competitiveness of the firms which operate within, and export from, its boundaries, and is, to a large extent, an expression of the will to compete and the dynamism of firms, their capacity to invest, to innovate both as a consequence of their own R&D and of successful appropriation of external technologies; but the competitiveness of a national economy is also more than the simple outcome of the collective or 'average' competitiveness of its firms; there are many ways in which the features and performance of a domestic economy viewed as an entity with characteristics of its own, will affect, in turn, the competitiveness of firms. (quoted in Chesnais 1991)

As Chesnais (1991) points out, the OECD report recognized that the analysis of these overall macro-economic features or structural features is complex. It embraced a wide variety of economic and institutional phenomena that relate to the ways in which 'real economies' operate and behave. Moreover, it recognized the central importance that technological change, carrying capacities and technological trajectories played in determining the possible growth paths of an industry or nation (Dosi *et al.* 1988).

Chris Freeman has amplified these thoughts, writing specifically about national systems from a policy perspective, saying that

> [the] rate of technical change in any country and the effectiveness of companies in world competition in international trade in goods and services, *does not depend simply on the scale* of their research and development. ... *It depends upon the way in which the available resources are managed and organized*, both at the enterprise and the national level. The national system of innovation may enable a country with limited resources ... to make very rapid progress through appropriate combinations of imported technology and local adaptation and development. (1993: 108; emphasis added)

Indeed, to this end, Lundvall (1992) has distinguished five areas where differences between national systems might occur: in the internal organization of firms; in inter-firm relationships; in the role and expectations of the public sector; in the institutional set-up of the financial sector; and in the intensity and organization of R&D. Lundvall's notion, coupled with the suggestion that national systems might be compared, was sufficiently intriguing to encourage scholars to rush to the national system of innovation (NSI) as the basis for a possible conceptual framework.

In 1993 Richard Nelson edited a collection of case studies under the title *National Innovation Systems: A Comparative Analysis*. This was discussed in Chapter 2. These papers described the 'innovation systems' of countries divided between large high-income countries (the United States, Japan, Germany, the United Kingdom, France and Italy) smaller high-income countries (Denmark, Sweden, Canada and Australia) and lower-income countries (Korea, Taiwan, Brazil, Argentina and Israel). Informing this collection was the hypothesis that 'a new spirit of what might be called "techno-nationalism" ... combining a strong belief that the technological capabilities of national firms are a key source of competitive prowess, with a belief that these capabilities are in a sense national, and can be built by national action' (Nelson 1993: 5). Of course, if right, this hypothesis would powerfully illuminate corridors for policy action in the realms of trade, technology, science and industrial policy. And put in these terms, the notion of a national innovation system is sufficiently alluring to conjure up promises of a 'Ponce de Léon strategy' for governments and lagging economies. In their eyes, achieving techno-economic 'catch-up' and systemic revitalization would be tantamount to achieving and being able to manage sustainable economic growth.

The literature that has emerged around the NSI (Patel and Pavitt 1994; Edquist 1997) does provide for a more articulate understanding of the features that matter in the real economy. In particular, we can here draw attention to the fact that, first, the NSI concept emphasizes that firms cannot be viewed in isolation but must be viewed as part of a *network* of public- and private-sector institutions whose activities and interactions initiate, import, modify and diffuse new technologies. Second, it emphasizes the *linkages* (both formal and informal) between institutions. Third, it emphasizes the *flows of intellectual resources* that exist between institutions. Fourth, it emphasizes *learning* as a key economic resource. And fifth – albeit somewhat counter-intuitively, given our globalized economy – it asserts that geography and *location* still matter.

Essentially, then, the idea of a national system of innovation asserts that a country's economy is more than the simple sum of its firms' activities but is rather the result of synergies that arise from the interactions and dynamics between economic actors in a country. In addition, a system of innovation can be thought of as being important because of its *distributive power*: that is, the system's ability to distribute existing knowledge for recombination. But these important observations aside, we would contend that the idea of a 'national system of innovation' *qua* conceptual framework is very crude indeed from a policy analysis or organization management point of view.

Techno-economic change and smart policy

As we have argued elsewhere (de la Mothe and Paquet 1994a), policy-makers need, but do not have, a satisfactory interpretive scheme of the new real economy. Dominant conceptual frameworks continue to privilege commodities (natural resources, physical plant and equipment, and so on) over knowledge (innovation, technologies, 'smart infrastructure', intellectual property rights, and so on). They continue to approach policies relating to trade, investment and technology as if they were independent of each other. Clearly, what is needed is a more robust framework through which policy analysts and policy-makers can organize thoughts, marshal ideas, and dispatch effective and realistic policy actions.

Such an approach requires that the innovation process be embedded very neatly in the evolutionary techno-economic order. For it is only when the process of innovation is defined as an endogenous variable within the cumulative causation representation of techno-economic change that one may expect to have in hand the necessary tools to analyse existing innovation systems and to engineer policy impacts on them. In turn, this sort of broad conceptual schema has to illuminate the interaction between the macro-evolutionary process and the micro-innovation process. Some interesting work on institutional learning (Johnson in Lundvall 1992) has begun to develop a representation of this interface: the economy is perceived as an instituted process *à la* Karl Polanyi that is continually bombarded by external and internal changes in the techno-economic system and reacts through more or less effective institutional adaptation to the pressures and tensions thereby generated; this adaptation is not only a passive adjustment but a creative conversation with the situation that generates learning of different sorts (by doing, by using, by interacting, etc.), and innovation is indeed nothing more than this continuous and ubiquitous increase in knowledge that results from the highest and best use (in the context of a world where bounded rationality is ever-present) through exploring and exploiting of all the resources at hand in the socio-technical setting and under the control of particular organizations. The 'national system' notion, however, does not provide a very useful template for the study of the interface between the techno-economic evolution and the innovation process. This is so for reasons that are germane to (a) the structure of the notion, (b) the unit of analysis, and (c) the new policy dilemmas that are created by the new real economy.

At the level of the structure of the notion, the conceptual framework of 'national innovation systems' suffers in so far as it is itself not so much an explanatory variable as a dependent variable. As Niosi *et al.* (1993) suggest, the idea of an NSI that is comparable between countries is built upon a number of related concentric rings. At the inner core is what Norman Clark (1985) described as 'the science system'. This 'system' involves those agents (government, private non-profit, private and higher education) that both fund and carry out research and development in the natural sciences and engineering. This 'system' was the focus of much OECD discussion throughout the 1980s as national governments tried to evaluate their comparative economic performances with reference to such macro-indicators as their gross expenditures on R&D as a percentage of gross domestic product (GERD/GDP), the number of highly qualified personnel (HQP) per capita, the number of Nobel prizes awarded to nationally based researchers, the number of citations that published papers received, and so on in the hope that if (for example) GERD/GDP ratios were roughly the same, then net economic gains would follow (de la Mothe 1992). However, this sort of super-functionalist approach ignored key questions that were paradoxical in nature (such as the so-called 'Solow Paradox': why 'computers seem to be everywhere *except* in the national productivity statistics' (Solow 1994)).

The idea of innovation, at least as invoked in the notion of a national system, tends to privilege formal R&D whereas much of the new theoretical and empirical research on innovation (e.g. Gibbons 1995) shows that the critical creative and entrepreneurial aspects of innovation are dependent *not* on frontier research, doctoral graduates, gross expenditures, and so on, but on spillovers, linkages, networks, interdependencies, synergies, etc.

At the next level – i.e. one level *above* that of national innovation systems – is the level of national production systems. This subsumes both the role of research and the role of innovation to the function of production and makes any idea of managing the system – via strategy or policy – moot given that the coordination functions that would be operationally required in order to coherently 'handle' a multi-tiered research–innovation–production system would be dazzlingly difficult. This would be augmented in light of the strategic 'manoeuvres' a nation might wish to make in response to actions of a competing nation. The practical operational problems would be well beyond the intellectual capacity of most nation-states, and well beyond the pull of most available levers. Thus the structural design of the 'national innovation system' idea makes it cumbersome in the extreme from a practical policy or managerial-level perspective.

For analysts of NSI, the unit of analysis is the nation-state. First, one must underline the importance of this misplaced concreteness: it is clear that 'the nation' can provide no guide to understanding or action in questions of economic performance and growth. To say, for example, that Canada's growth rate for 1994 was 4.5 per cent or that the United Kingdom's unemployment rate was 10 per cent reveals little about the sources and causes of that growth and about the levers of policy. Worse still, it can lull one into a false sense that those growth, employment (or wealth) indicators are truly representative of and evenly distributed across geography and a population. Clearly, this is not the case, as economies are more and more frequently being driven by local 'growth poles', a point to which we will return shortly.

Second, in adopting the language of 'national systems', analysts run the risk of both accepting and promoting the standard image of the world economy in which nations are sovereign and hold discrete blocs of population and resources, trading a relatively small portion of their national output on international markets and controlling (to some greater or lesser extent) the levels of employment and income, and the value of their currency. However, as Robert Reich (1991) has intimated and more recently Stanley Hoffmann (1995) has emphatically declared, this Westphalian worldview has ended. In today's reality, nations have seen their sovereignty perforated, and their fate has become dependent on political and economic decisions taken elsewhere in the world. Trade flows have grown exponentially, and yet have been outpaced by capital flows that have become fifty times more important than trade flows. Moreover, the international flow of information, knowledge and technologies that takes place on an hourly basis has served both to vitalize new production systems and to make borders irrelevant. Thus, again in sum, the 'nation-state' no longer seems to be the appropriate operational unit of analysis, given that it no longer holds either control or sway over the knowledge-based factors of production.

This is not to say that governments no longer have an important role to play, as Richard Nelson has already noted. But it is to say, as we have argued elsewhere (de la Mothe and Paquet 1994b), that the power of governance is being drawn, not *up* into a hierarchically organized, centralized mind-set, but *down* to the lowest levels of socio-economic activity, where individuals (managers and consumers) can have direct contact with suppliers, financiers and final clients and can have the power to act in a decisive way.

Third, these trends have been amplified by the real economy policy dilemmas that governments are facing. International economic policies are increasingly affecting domestic policy, as trade disputes and the Asian and Russian financial crises, for example, demonstrate. While explicit innovation, trade and investment policies are, for the most part, governed or administered by the nation-state, the policies, institutions and behaviours that affect the pace and nature of innovation are extremely complex and defy national borders. Moreover, technological changes have sharply reduced the effective economic distances between countries, and government policies – which have traditionally dampened cross-border activity – have been deliberately relaxed and dismantled. The combination of these activities has resulted in the nation-state being characterized by fuzzy boundaries.

Furthermore, as technological distances have shrunk and cross-border fences have been lowered, national governments have faced heightened cross-border spillovers and the need to enter into intra-state negotiation in order to determine the new rules of the game in an arena where transnational economic integration is taking place *à la* NAFTA and the Maastricht Accord. Deeper integration and structural interdependencies require the monitoring of virtually every aspect of socio-politico-economic interaction, and yet the speed accorded by technological systems reduces the effective degrees of freedom or deliberate action dramatically (de la Mothe and Paquet 1994a, b).

These problems have been multiplied by a significant factor as a result of the fact that the number of national entities has grown dramatically in the recent past. For example, in July 1944 only 44 countries participated in the Bretton Woods conference which led to the creation of the International Monetary Fund (Gilpin 1989). By 1993 the number of members within the IMF had grown to 178, and there are now said to be more than 200 capitalist democracies worldwide. But the sheer variety of competing capitalist, democratic models that have been constructed in recent years has clearly defied any anticipation of the shaped coevolution between political stability, economic opportunity and social cohesion. The new political economic mosaic has had the effect of diffusing power and pressure, making the role of multinational firms, not nation-states – as creators of technological investment corridors – all the more important.

It is hardly surprising in this context that the selection of the nation-state level as the pre-eminent unit of analysis and locus of meaningful levers for smart policy has been found wanting. One may readily identify a variety of more or less extensive systems of innovation: from those spanning continents and representing truly world innovation systems to continental ones (especially in Europe and in North America) to national systems but also those at the regional, sectoral and technological levels. Indeed, it is the image of a complex intermingling of these different innovation systems that represents best the evolving innovation system. To insist on a simple transdermal nation-state perspective as the dominant one is unlikely to lead to useful insights in most cases. Indeed, it is likely that it is a much smaller unit of analysis like the 'development bloc' that is likely to be most illuminating (Dahmen 1988; Andersen in Lundvall 1992; de la Mothe and Paquet 1994a).

Indeed, from a comparative point of view or from a real economy point of view, the 'nation-state' perspective would appear to be too macroscopic and to illuminate rather badly the interface between the evolving techno-economic change system and the innovation system. A less aggregative unit – between the macroscope at the national level and the microscope directed at firms – at the 'meso level' might indeed prove to be a much more potent *révélateur* of real-world transactions and literature.

Meso systems of innovation

In an economy that is dynamized by information, knowledge, skills and competence, and which is consequently forced to become decentralized, the new relevant (i.e. operational) units of analysis are those that serve as the basis on which to understand and nurture innovation and growth. Focusing either on the firm or on the national economy is misguided: under the microscope, too much is idiosyncratic and white noise is bound to run high; under the macroscope, much of the innovation and restructuring going on is bound to be missed. One may therefore argue, we think persuasively, that the most useful perspective point is the meso perspective which focuses on development blocs, technology districts, subnational fora, etc. where the learning is really occurring, and where the interfaces between the evolutionary techno-economic system and the process of innovation play themselves out (de la Mothe and Paquet 1994b; Acs, de la Mothe and Paquet 1996).

Casual support for this analytical gambit can be gleaned, for example, from the observation that much of the growth in the Italian economy takes place in growth poles in the north around Milan, or that much of the economic growth, job creation, and so on in Canada is found, not evenly distributed across the country, but concentrated in ten 'smart cities', or that the 'Four Motors of Europe', the Silicon Valley (San Jose) and Silicon Hills (Austin) of the United States, etc. are disproportionately responsible for technology development, investment flows, foreign trade, and so on (de la Mothe and Paquet 1998).

We do not know as much as we should about the innovation process and the process of diffusion of technical and organizational innovations in these areas. But work in the past decade has been much influenced by Nelson and Winter. At the core of their schema is the notion of 'selection environment', which is defined as the context that 'determines how relative use of different technologies changes over time' (1982: 61). This context is shaped by market and non-market components, conventions, socio-cultural factors, and by the broader institutional structure. This selection environment constitutes the relevant milieu, which may be broader or narrower, and may be more or less important in explaining the innovative capacity of a given country, sector or region.

The notion of *milieu* connotes three sets of forces: (a) the contours of a particular spatial set vested with a certain unity and fabric; (b) the organizational logic of a network of interdependent actors engaged in cooperative innovative activity; and (c) organizational learning based on the dialectics between *adapting actors* and the *adopting milieu* (Maillat 1992).

Such a milieu is not a necessary condition for innovation. There are innovations and much learning even in the absence of a dynamic milieu. But such a milieu is likely to bring forth innovation networks; and innovation networks, in turn, are a hybrid form of organization that is adapted so much better to competitive environmental conditions of technological and appropriation uncertainty than are either markets or hierarchies, that they are more likely to kick-start the innovation process (DeBresson and Amesse 1991). At the core of the dynamic milieu and of the innovation network are a number of intermingled dimensions (economic and historical; cognitive and normative), but they all depend to a certain degree on trust and confidence, and therefore rest on a host of cultural and sociological factors that have a tendency to be found mainly in localized networks and to be more likely to emerge on a background of shared experiences, regional or community loyalties, etc. (Sabel and Piore in Foray and Freeman 1993).

The innovation process depends much on the central features of a selection environment or milieu. First, innovation is all about continuous learning, and learning does not occur in a socio-cultural vacuum. The innovation network is more likely to blossom in a restricted localized milieu where all the socio-cultural characteristics of a dynamic milieu are likely to be found. Moreover, it is most unlikely that this sort of milieu will correspond to a national territory. Therefore, if one is to identify dynamic milieux as likely systems on which one might work to stimulate innovation, they are likely to be local or regional systems of innovation. Second, some geotechnical forces would appear to generate meso-level units where learning proceeds faster and better. As Storper (1993: 73) argues,

> in technologically dynamic production complexes ... there is a strong reason for the existence of regional clusters or agglomerations. Agglomeration appears to be a principal geographical form in which the trade-off between lock-in technological flexibility (and the search for quasi-rents), and cost minimization can be most effectively managed, because it facilitates efficient operations of a cooperative production network. Agglomeration in these cases, is not simply the result of standard localization economies (which are based on the notion of allocative efficiency in minimizing costs), but of Schumpeterian efficiencies.

Third, the dispersive revolution in public and private governance and the rise of region-states tend to provide a greater potential for dynamism at the meso level.

The available dossier of case studies (see Nelson 1993; de la Mothe and Paquet 1998) tends to show that local systems do indeed exist. It ranges from writings that are commemorative and suffer from boosterism, to carefully documented cases, to anecdotal evidence quoted on the occasion of a paper covering a broader territory, to tentative syntheses on the basis of all of the above. While it is difficult to derive precise general propositions from this highly variegated material, it provides a very rich file documenting the ways in which local systems of innovation have emerged and evolved. But the vast majority of the extant casework is strongly in support of the existence and importance of local systems of innovation (Acs 1995; Acs, de la Mothe and Paquet 1996), and very much can be learned from these documents about the types of policies that have had determining impacts on the success of these ventures.

One may cite Putnam's work on the civic communities of Italy (1993), Saxenian's work comparing Route 128 and Silicon Valley (1994), the work of economic geographers like Storper (1992, 1993) and the work on regional trajectories by Davis (1991a) and Voyer and Ryan (1994). They all document the importance of proximity and the centrality of community, the linguistic and related dimensions as the fabric of the socio-cultural underground on which subnational economic systems of innovation are built.

Somewhat more empirically, Acs and Audretsch (1990) in particular have developed new sources of data on innovative activity at the local level in the United States. They have critically analysed the data of others in an effort to provide extensive analyses of the important activity of small firms and sectoral, locational and organizational factors that explain different dynamics of innovative activity involving a mix of firm sizes and locations in different industries. Together these studies have suggested that small firms are the recipients of key spillovers from knowledge generated in larger centres, firms and universities. These external factors differ from industry to industry but depend on organizational and locational factors. An important observation from the US work is that spillovers from R&D which are among the sources of externalities are greatly facilitated by the geographic coincidence of the different partners (universities, firms, labs) within the state. Not only do innovative activity, growth and job creation increase as a result of high corporate expenditures on R&D, but they also increase as a result of R&D undertaken in public-sector institutions (universities). This sort of work has allowed Acs and others to usefully examine in some detail such local-level activity as the innovative output of large and small firms by state and county, namely R&D inputs.

From these case studies and the parallel empirical work, one may derive a few general elements:

1. A common thread is the way in which relationships develop between private concerns and both the community and the public actors, and the way in which 'enabling agencies' foster collaboration; whether these agencies have materialized in formal mechanisms of governance like metropolitan technology councils or have simply crystallized in the form of an ethos, the instruments of collective coordination based on appeals to solidaristic local values, vision and culture are of central import (de la Mothe and Paquet 1996a).
2. Another common thread is the importance of leadership; leadership is 'what enables the complex inter-institutional and inter-sectoral partnerships to develop and become operational', and it would appear that the ability of communities to shape their future depends much more on social than on technological processes (Davis 1991a; Saxenian 1994).
3. A third common thread is the great fragility of the local systems of innovations because of the fact that they are 'weakly institutionalized'; this is the sort of weakness that suggests the way in which the senior governments might be of most help in getting the local communities to help themselves, i.e. in providing the enabling support to get the communities to invent new instruments and design new policy approaches (Acs, de la Mothe and Paquet 1996).

Conclusion

We have suggested that the idea of a 'national system of innovation' has generated considerable interest as a potential conceptual framework that might guide policy-makers. As we noted at the outset, choosing one framework over another is a consequential decision, for, like a switchman, such decision may guide the policy process either in the most helpful direction or into something of a cul-de-sac. The OECD and many national policy-makers have been mesmerized by the sirens of the NSI and are in danger of convincing those in power that it can provide the 'hands of the compass' that they need in order to navigate safely in the competitive waters of the twenty-first century.

Our words of caution have insisted that the concept is interesting for what it suggests, not for what it provides in terms of guidance. We have suggested that the innovation system is endogenous to the techno-economic system that it animates. As such, it is at the interface between the innovation system and the broader techno-economic system within which it is nested that one must search for the most useful levers likely to influence the innovation process while taking its contexts fully into account.

Given that so much of the real economy 'lives' at the meso level, and that it is at that level that the international forces and the values and plans of local communities interface to create the new rules of the game and deep integration, betting on the national system of innovation as a cognitive map would appear to be dangerously out of focus. Rather we suggest that focusing on a meso perspective at the development bloc level and searching for levers for policy action at that level would be more promising.

Note

The research support of the Social Sciences and Humanities Research Council (Grants 410–0471 and 809–94–0002) is acknowledged with thanks, as is the assistance of Heather Hudson, Jennifer Khurana and Chris Wilson.

CHAPTER FOUR

Regional Innovation: In Search of an Enabling Strategy

Zoltan J. Acs, John de la Mothe and Gilles Paquet

Introduction

As noted in Chapter 2, in the introductory chapter of Nelson's *National Innovation Systems* a central hypothesis is formulated about 'a new spirit of what might be called "techno-nationalism"', combining a strong belief that the technological capabilities of a nation's firms are a key source of their competitive prowess with a belief that these capabilities are in a sense national, and can be built by national action (Nelson 1993: 3). While Richard Nelson and Nathan Rosenberg were careful in this study to explain that one of their central concerns was to establish 'whether, and if so in what ways, the concept of a "national" system made any sense today', they also added that *de facto* 'national governments act as if it did' (Nelson 1993: 5). The purpose of this chapter is to extend our concerns about this hypothesis and to provide a framework to study 'local' systems of innovation as an alternative analytic level.

In the next section of this chapter, we deal with the process of globalization of economic activities and of its impact on the national production and governance systems. This forces one to confront both what John Naisbitt has called the 'global paradox' and what we have called elsewhere the 'dispersive revolution' (Naisbitt 1994; de la Mothe and Paquet 1994a). Subsequently, we review quickly the main features of network dynamics and the way it is stalled by the phenomenon of centralized mind-set: a strong attachment to a tendency to bet on centralized means of problem-solving that almost inevitably lead to compulsive centralization and misguided approaches. We then provide some evidence in support of our local systems of innovation hypothesis, following which we lay out the elements of innovation systems. A final section summarizes the argument.

The paradoxical consequences of globalization

Real-life economics are 'instituted processes'; that is, sets of rules and conventions that vest the wealth-creation process with relative unity and stability by harmonizing the geo-technical constraints that are imposed by the environment on the values and plans found among decision-makers (Polanyi 1968). Modern economies have evolved considerably over the past century. The wealth-creation process of the late nineteenth century was mainly instituted as a 'social armistice' between fairly rigid constraints imposed by technology, geography and natural resources endowments, on the one hand, and the less than perfectly coordinated plans of private and public decision-makers, on the other hand. As both constraints and preferences evolved, national economies came to be instituted differently. They evolved often quite differently because of the degrees of freedom afforded them by the extent to which they were protected from the rest of the world by relatively high transportation costs, transaction costs and tariff walls.

In the recent past, the wealth-creation process has changed dramatically. It has become increasingly dematerialized as its mainsprings have ceased to be natural resources and material production and become knowledge and information activities. Transportation costs, transaction costs and tariff walls tumbled. And, as a result of important information economies and of growing organizational flexibility, transitional firms have become capable of organizing production globally and thus escaping to a great extent the constraints nation-states might wish to impose on them. Therefore, economic activity has become less constrained by geography, and in many instances has become truly deterritorialized.

Globalization cannot be characterized as a simple process of trade liberalization. To be sure, there has been much liberalization, but firms and nations which have become more exposed internationally have also become increasingly dependent on intangibles like know-how, synergies and untraded interdependencies. This new techno-economic world has required important changes in the managerial, strategic and political rules of the game.

First, 'firms', 'governments' and 'third-sector organizations' have become rather fuzzy concepts. It is often no longer possible to distinguish the inside and the outside in the complex web of networks and alliances they are enmeshed in. Second, the knowledge/information fabric of the new economy has led to the development of a large number of non-market institutions as information and knowledge proved to be poorly handled by the market. Finally, the traditional and narrow economic notion of competition has been replaced by the broader and more sophisticated notion of competitiveness as a benchmark for assessing the process of wealth creation and as a guide in designing the requisite web of explicit and organic cooperative links between all stakeholders (Paquet 1990).

As a result, private and public organizations have become more footloose, and as such they have become more compatible with a variety of locations, technologies and organizational structures (de la Mothe and Paquet 1994b). They have also been potentially affected to a much greater extent by the synergies, interdependencies, socio-cultural bonds or trust relationships that are capable of producing comparative advantages. Indeed, the central challenge of the new economy has been to find ways to create an environment in which knowledge workers do as much learning as possible from their experience, but also from each other, from partners, clients, suppliers, and so on. This entails that, for learning to occur, there must be *conversations* between and among partners. But working conversations that create new knowledge can emerge only where there are trust and proximity. These have proved to be essential inputs (Webber 1993).

Two very significant transformations in our modern political economies in the past decades have been ascribable to a large extent to the challenges posed by the new socio-economy: a balkanization of existing national economies *and* a concurrent massive devolution in the governance system of both private and public organizations.

Balkanization of national economies

There are many reasons for balkanization to proceed as globalization sets in. First, global competitiveness has led advanced industrial nations to specialize in the export of products in which they have 'technological' or 'absolute' advantages. And since those export-oriented absolute advantage industries tend to be found in subnational regions, this has led to the emergence of a mosaic of subnational geographical agglomerations and regional 'worlds of production' characterized by *product-based technological learning systems* resting, in important ways, on conventions rooted in the cultures of local economic actors (Storper 1992, 1993).

Second, the pressures of globalization have put so much strain on the nation-state that subnational regions and communities have strongly felt a need for roots and anchors in local or regional bonds of ethnicity, language and culture. This *tribalism* (to use Naisbitt's term) has been reinforced by the fact that it often proved to be the source of a robust entrepreneurial culture and therefore of competitive advantage in the new context (Stoffaes 1987).

Third, the dysfunctionality of the nation-state has triggered the emergence of genuine shared communities of economic interests at the regional level. The dynamics of collective action has led to the *rise of the region-state* when subnational governments, or loose alliances among local authorities, have become active as partners of foreign investors and providers of the requisite infrastructure to leverage regional policies capable of making the region an active participant in the global economy (Ohmae 1993; *The Economist* 1994).

Fourth, as the region-state emerged, it has been in a position to provide support for the subnational development blocs through the nurturing of complementarities, interdependencies and externalities via infrastructure, networking of economic and business competence, etc., and to dynamize the transformation process at the meso-economic level (Dahmen 1988; de la Mothe and Paquet 1994c). This has in turn reinforced the separate internal dynamics and the resilience of the subnational systems.

Devolution of the governance system

Global competitiveness has also triggered a massive devolution in the governance systems of both public and private organizations. The reasons for this are the following. First, the search for speed of adjustment, variety, flexibility and innovation generated by global competitiveness has forced corporations to adapt ever faster and this has led them to 'deconstruct' themselves into networks of quasi-autonomous units capable of taking action as they see fit in the face of local circumstances. Managers ceased to be 'drivers of people' and became 'drivers of learning' (Wriston 1992). This required a shift from hierarchical structures of governance to networking structures that were conducive to innovative conversations.

Second, the same process has been witnessed in the governance of public organizations. The need to do more with less, and the growing pressure for more subnational states to cooperate actively with private organizations to ensure success on the global scene, have led governments into massive privatization or the devolution of power to lower-order public authorities (Rivlin 1992; Osborne and Gaebler 1992; Paquet 1994).

Third, this has led to general praise for the flexibility and genuine *souplesse* of the federal system as a system of governance for both private and public organizations, and to the general celebration of bottom-up management (O'Toole and Bennis 1992; Handy 1992, 1994).

Fourth, in transforming the governance of economic, social and political organizations, the growing search for flexibility has not stopped at decentralization and privatization strategies. There has been a growing pressure to dissolve permanent organizations so as to allow a maximum open use of all the possibilities of networking. This has led to the proposal that virtual enterprises and governments might provide the ultimate flexibility (Davidow and Malone 1992; de la Mothe and Paquet 1994a). This form of dissolution of governance systems not only has proved to be dynamically efficient but also has led to a reinforcement of community bonds as private and public organizations ceased to be the main source of identification.

Network dynamics and centralized mind-sets

Subnational areas have proved to be better loci for 'conversations' likely to foster fast learning. Indeed, it is argued by the defenders of the notion of local system of innovation that such subnational areas are a more supportive underground for the development of multi-stakeholder networks and new forms of cooperation and relational exchange. But this has not deterred those who have a strong taste for national across-the-board interventions. The techno-nationalists emphasize the importance of the national network of institutions, acting as a system and providing the foundations and the underpinnings of the innovation system. This leads them to bet on policies designed to act on the national institutions to stimulate innovations.

The opposition between local and national systems of innovation is rooted in the contrast between two dynamics: the bottom-up dynamics of networks and the top-down dynamics built on the centralized mind-set.

Bottom-up network dynamics

The paradoxical consequences of globalization have been not only to generate balkanization but also to create the need for new forms of organizations. Hierarchies have limited learning abilities and markets have limited capacities to process information effectively. Networks and alliances are ways to counter these failures, ways to combine the benefit of being large and small at the same time. The network is not, as is usually assumed, a mixed form of organization existing halfway on a continuum ranging from market to hierarchy. Rather, it is a generic name for a third type of arrangement built on very different integrating mechanisms: networks are consensus/inducement-oriented organizations and institutions. This suggests that instead of the market–hierarchy dichotomy, one should bet on a partition of institutions and organizations according to three principles of integration: (a) those associated with threat/coercion; (b) those associated with exchange; and (c) those associated with consensus and inducement-oriented systems. This more useful way of classifying institutions has been used by Karl Polanyi (1968), François Perroux (1960), Kenneth Boulding (1970) and more recently Shumpei Kumon (1992).

Networks have two sets of characteristics: those derived from their dominant logic (consensus and inducement-oriented systems) and those derived from the dominant intelligence that emerges from their structure. The consensus dominant logic does not abolish power but it means that power is distributed. A central and critical feature of networks is the emphasis on *voluntary* adherence to norms. While this voluntary adherence does not necessarily appear to generate constraints *per se* on the size of the organization, it is not always easy for a set of shared values to spread over massive disjointed transitional communities: free riding, high transaction costs, problems of accountability, etc. impose extra work. So the benefits in terms of leanness, agility and flexibility are such that many important multinationals have chosen *not* to manage their affairs as a global production engine, but as a multitude of smaller quasi-independent units coordinated by a loose federal structure, because of the organizational diseconomies of scale in building a clan-type organization (O'Toole and Bennis 1992; Handy 1992).

As for the structural characteristics of the network, as embodied for instance in a company or an organization, it will have the following traits: it will be distributed, decentralized, collaborative and adaptive (Kelly 1994: 189). This network structure based on reciprocity and trust is a self-reinforcing mechanism, for it breeds trust and reciprocity, thereby increasing the social capital and generating increasing returns. In that sense, reciprocity that is based on voluntary adherence generates lower costs of cooperation and therefore stimulates more networking as social capital accumulates with trust. The experiences in Emilia-Romagna described by Putnam (1993), its echo effect in Denmark or parallel developments in Silicon Valley described by Saxenian (this volume) are all pointing in the same direction. The site of a dense concentration of overlapping networks of solidarity generates wealth creation on a surprising scale.

Some have argued that new technologies might well generate 'cyberhoods' that would be as potent as neighbourhoods and that maybe the 'local' setting for such networks of solidarity or for a cultural milieu likely to generate much innovation could become truly deterritorialized and completely 'virtual'. But even network enthusiasts are not quite ready to consider the 'virtual community' as anything more than a poor simulacrum of the real community and consequently see it as being unlikely to generate the degree of passion and commitment that is needed to fuel social capital accumulation on the appropriate scale (Rheingold 1993).

The growth of network markets in a number of sectors where mass customization is important has generated a new form of externalities that has yielded important increasing returns, some snowballing effects and some possibilities of lock-in. This is the logic of network economies. But the network externalities and spillovers are not spreading in a frictionless world. Networking casts much more of a local shadow than is usually presumed: 'space becomes ever more variegated, heterogeneous and finely textured in part because the processes of spatial reorganisation ... have the power to exploit relatively minute spatial differences to good effect' (Harvey 1988). Consequently, a network does not extend boundlessly but tends instead to crystallize around a unifying purpose, mobilizing independent members through voluntary links, around multiple leaders in integrated levels of overlapping and superimposed webs of solidarity. This underscores the enormous importance of 'regional business cultures' and explains the relative importance of the small and medium-sized enterprise networks in generating new ideas (Lipnack and Stamps 1994).

Not only are networks generating social capital and wealth, they have also been closely associated with a greater degree of progressivity of the economy; that is, with a higher degree of innovativeness and of capacity to transform, because networks cross boundaries. Indeed, boundary-crossing networks are likely to ignite much innovativeness because they provide an opportunity for reframing and recasting perspectives and for questioning the assumptions that have been in good currency. One might suggest a parallel between boundary crossing and migration into another world in which one's home experience serves as a useful contrast to the new realities. Much of the buoyant immigrant entrepreneurship is rooted in this dual capacity to see things differently and to network within and across boundaries. In the face of placeless power in a globalized economy, seemingly powerless places with their own communication code on a historically specific territory are fitful terrains for local collaborative networks.

Top-down centralized mind-set

In the face of strong *presumptions* regarding the existence of *regional innovation systems*, it is surprising to find that so little has been done to escape the mind-set of 'national systems of innovation'. The reason for this bias is, however, not very difficult to understand. Since the cost of thinking is not zero, humans adopt paradigms and mind-sets to routinize their thinking. Techno-nationalism's appeal is of this sort.

Mitchel Resnick has analysed the *travers* that explains why, in an era of decentralization in every domain, centralized thinking is remaining prevalent in our theories of knowledge, in our ways of analysing problems, and in our search for policy responses. 'Politicians, managers and scientists are working with blinders on, focussing on centralised solutions even when decentralised approaches might be more appropriate, robust, or reliable' (Resnick 1994: 36). As Resnick explained, 'the centralised mind-set is not just a misconception of the scientifically naive'; one may find ample evidence that in science, in governance, there is a strong resistance to the idea of complexity being formed from a decentralized process. The resistance to evolutionary theory is of that ilk. It is more reassuring to presume that every pattern must have a single cause, and therefore an ultimate controlling factor.

This explains the opposition to a bottom-up explanation when this alternative cosmology has been suggested (Science Council of Canada 1984, 1990), even when documentary evidence had been mounted to show that such an approach was not only promising but, *de facto*, building on already impressive accomplishments in a number of metropolitan areas (Davis 1991a). More than a decade after the suggestion by the Science Council that metropolitan technology councils might be the appropriate lever to energize local systems of innovation, the idea is still in limbo. The centralized 'national system of innovations' continues to dominate the policy scene, and the view of a fragmented and localized *set of systems of innovation* that could only be nurtured from the periphery is still not in good currency (Paquet 1992; de la Mothe and Paquet 1994d; Paquet and Roy 1995).

Corroborative evidence: some comparative vignettes

We draw from three sets of corroborative evidence. First, recent exploratory work on network economies has underlined the importance of local spillovers or externalities, but the extent to which these spillover effects are indeed localized has not been sufficiently emphasized. Second, a whole body of observations and descriptive/ ethnographical and empirical studies using alternative databases on innovative activities would appear to provide collateral evidence. Finally, the existing literature of the historical and case study variety shows that indeed innovation systems have blossomed locally.

Inter-firm relationships

A first element of support has emerged in a somewhat oblique way from some recent work on network economies. The economic literature on networks has generated a rekindling of interest in the role of externalities in supply after decades of neglect. At the core of this renewal is the explosion of the new information and communication technologies. These technologies are at the core of a wave of innovations generated and diffused over recent decades and underpin the new centrality of increasing returns and economies of scale. It is to the increased centrality of communication networks that one may ascribe the new emphasis on the basic characteristics of information: interdependence, inappropriability and externality (Antonelli 1992: 6).

The analysis of telecommunication networks has served as a *révélateur*. They represent a sector with a particularly high degree of heterogeneity of components, of technical interrelatedness, of complexity of technological change, and they are exemplars of a sector with much irreversibility in investment, important scale economies and increasing returns, and a broad array of externalities. Indeed, in the 'paradigmatic network industry the market demand schedule slopes *upwards* (due to demand externalities) and the market supply schedule slopes *downwards* (due to indivisibilities and supply externalities)' (David 1992: 104; Acs, FitzRoy and Smith 1999). But the most crucial aspect of this literature is the component suggesting that 'these features apply not only to the increasing number of sectors affected by the spreading of information and communication technologies, but more generally to all the processes of growth and change' (Antonelli 1992: 15).

If such is the case, some interesting results are emerging in six major areas (Antonelli 1992):

1. The rate of introduction of innovations by a firm would appear to be more and more influenced by its capacity to cooperate with other firms.
2. The success of a new technology depends on adoption externalities.
3. Network externalities are determinant in the selection of a technology.
4. Key sectors are the providers of externalities through an array of untraded interdependencies and linkages.

5. Proximity is a strong necessary condition to take advantage of externalities generated by others.
6. Network firms are the result of attempts by firms to internalize externalities.

A critical examination of this new world reveals that three factors will be central to the new dynamics:

1. Networks represent an intermediate solution between the dynamic efficiency of markets and the static efficiency of hierarchical integrated organizations.
2. Selective cooperation is the new pivotal tool for economic agents to internalize externalities.
3. Any change is likely to have a strong *local character* (Piore 1992: 443; Antonelli 1992: 23).

These factors may vary from sector to sector but are at the source of the various clusterings that lead to social learning and to the dynamic reinforcement of the cluster (Porter 1990).

The knowledge infrastructure

In a series of monographs and papers (Acs 1990; Acs and Audretsch 1990, 1993b; Acs, Audretsch and Feldman 1992, 1994a, b; Acs, FitzRoy and Smith 1999; Anselin, Varga and Acs 1997a, b; Varga 1998 and this volume, Chapter 9), Acs and his associates have developed new sources of data on innovative activity in the United States beyond the traditional measure using patents. They have critically analysed new data developed by others, in an effort to provide extensive evidence of the important innovative activity of small firms, and to throw some light on the important sectoral/locational/organizational factors that explain the different dynamics of innovative activity of large and small firms in different types of industries and locations. These studies have suggested that small firms are the recipients of important spillovers from knowledge generated in larger centres in firms and universities. These external effects differ from industry to industry but depend much on organizational and locational factors. These studies have provided important new evidence to help us understand the texture of local systems of innovation and the potential levers that might be used to design a new generation of public policies based on this new learning.

One of the important results generated by these studies is the detailed documentation that R&D spillovers, which are one of the sources of externalities, are greatly facilitated by the 'geographical coincidence' of the different partners (universities, research labs, firms) within the state. Not only does innovative activity increase as a result of high private corporate expenditures on R&D, but it increases also as a result of research undertaken by universities within the area.

While it is difficult to generalize because of the fact that the patterns of innovative activity vary greatly from industry to industry, and because of the fact that local embedding is often intermingled with global networks, it is clear from the literature that the local milieu can be regarded very often as the collective entrepreneur and innovator, rather than the firm. Obviously the capacity for collective entrepreneurship depends greatly on socio-cultural factors resulting from the history of the region, as Putnam has shown in the case of Italy. But much can be gained from the creation of a robust and decentralized system of institutional support to ensure that technical and commercial knowledge is diffused fast and as widely as possible, thereby catalysing the process of social learning (Best 1990; Tödtling 1994; Cooke and Morgan 1994b; Audretsch 1995).

There has been a bit more systematic work on the landscape of innovative activity in the United States using both traditional R&D expenditures and direct measures of innovative activity like the number of innovations commercially introduced derived from a score of technology, engineering and trade journals listing innovations and new products. It has shown that innovative activity is not evenly spread over the territory. Both R&D expenditures by industry and universities are clustered and they have important spatial spillovers that territorialize innovative activity. While small firms or large firms may dominate the scene, the clustering effect is quite clear in the data presented in Table 4.1 for the US states.

This sort of clustering activity is even more evident at the county level. Table 4.2 shows the number of innovations for the 26 most innovative counties in the United States. One can see clearly that most of the innovations are clustered in a few counties. For instance, five counties in California accounted for 80 per cent of the innovations in the state.

None of this is a robust proof that local systems of innovation exist or that public policy should be mainly directed to the local level. We suggest only that there are undeniably important spatial spillovers and that, in an oblique way, the available data on state and county innovative activity would appear to corroborate the local systems of innovation hypothesis.

Community and the public sector

The dossier of case studies tending to show some evidence that local systems of innovation exist and have a dynamic of their own is very extensive. It ranges from commemorative and boosterism writings, to carefully documented cases in monographs and books, to anecdotal evidence quoted on the occasion of a paper covering a broader territory, to tentative syntheses on the basis of all of the above. While it is difficult to derive precise general propositions from this variegated material, it provides a very rich file documenting the ways in which local systems of innovation have emerged and evolved.

There is no unanimity in this dossier. One finds strident critics and vehement apologists of local systems of innovation. But the vast majority of the casework is strongly in support of the existence and importance of local systems of innovation, and very much can be learned from these documents about the types of policies that have had determining impacts on the success of these ventures. They all document the importance of proximity and the centrality of community, linguistic and related dimensions as the fabric of the socio-cultural underground on which subnational systems of innovation are built. From these case studies, one may derive a few elements of learning:

1.   A common thread is the way in which relationships develop between private concerns and both the community and the public actors, and the way in which

Table 4.1 Innovative output in large and small firms and R&D inputs by state

State	Total innovations	Large-firm innovations	Small-firm innovations	Industry R&D expenditures	University research
CA	974	315	659	3883	710.4
NY	456	180	276	1859	371.0
NJ	426	162	264	1361	70.8
MA	360	148	212	954	245.3
PA	245	104	141	1293	139.2
IL	231	100	131	894	254.9
OH	188	76	112	926	76.2
CT	132	77	55	650	54.7
MI	112	61	51	1815	103.2
MN	110	64	46	399	55.7
WI	86	33	53	224	65.0
FL	66	21	45	375	70.1
GA	53	20	33	78	57.8
IN	49	20	29	398	51.3
CO	42	13	29	167	77.2
AZ	41	23	18	201	37.4
VA	38	19	19	207	45.9
NC	38	16	22	193	64.6
RI	24	4	20	32	14.9
OK	20	12	8	93	19.9
IA	20	12	8	135	46.4
KS	15	3	12	66	26.6
UT	11	2	9	72	32.5
NE	9	1	8	9	20.4
KY	9	6	3	72	17.5
LA	5	0	5	65	33.4
AR	5	5	0	9	12.0
AL	5	0	5	54	28.3
MS	4	1	3	420	61.4

Source: Acs, Audretsch and Feldman (1994a)
Note: Industry R&D and university research expenditures are in millions of 1972 dollars and are taken from Jaffe (1989).

'enabling agencies' foster collaboration; whether these agencies have materialized in formal mechanisms of governance like metropolitan technology councils or have simply crystallized in the form of an ethos, the instruments of collective coordination based on appeals to solidaristic local values, vision and culture are of central import (Hollingsworth 1993).

2. Another common thread is the importance of leadership; leadership is 'what enables the complex inter-institutional and inter-sectoral partnerships to develop and become operational', and it would appear that the ability of communities to shape their future depends much more on social than on technological processes (Davis 1991a: 12).

3. A third common thread is the great fragility of many local systems of innovations because of the fact that they are 'weakly institutionalized'; this is the sort of weakness that suggests the way in which the senior governments might be of most help in getting the local communities to help themselves, i.e. in providing

Table 4.2 Number of innovations by county (top 26 counties) 1982

No.	County	State	Innovation
1	Santa Clara	CA	386
2	Los Angeles	CA	178
3	Cook	IL	155
4	Middlesex	MA	145
5	Norfolk	MA	121
6	Orange	CA	117
7	Bergen	NJ	90
8	New York	NY	82
9	Fairfield	CT	76
10	Nassau	NY	73
11	Dallas	TX	64
12	San Diego	CA	63
13	Suffolk	NY	62
14	Cuyahoga	OH	62
15	Essex	NJ	57
16	Westchester	NY	54
17	Ramsey	MN	49
18	Montgomery	PA	45
19	Philadelphia	PA	44
20	Hennepin	MN	42
21	Morris	NJ	42
22	Alameda	CA	39
23	Middlesex	NJ	36
24	Harris	TX	35
25	Somerset	NJ	34
26	Monroe	NY	34

Source: Anselin, Varga and Acs (1997a)

the enabling support to get the communities to invent new instruments and design new policy approaches. But there is also evidence of very robust local systems of innovations (Cooke and Morgan 1994b; Saxenian 1994).

The elements of the system

In this section we sketch out the institutional infrastructure that supports systems of innovation. Innovation is a cumulative process. It is a ubiquitous phenomenon in modern economies. In all parts of the economy we can find ongoing processes of learning, searching and exploring. The first step in this process is to recognize that innovation is a gradual and cumulative process. This suggests that future innovation depends on past accomplishments. This was pointed out by Schumpeter as new combinations. The second step in this process is to recognize learning as fundamental to continued innovation. If innovation reflects learning, innovation must be rooted in the prevailing economic structure. The areas where innovation will take place will primarily be those where a firm is already engaged in routine activities.

The institutional set-up is the second important dimension of the system of innovation. Institutions provide agents and collectives with guideposts for action. Institutions make it possible for economic systems to survive in an uncertain world.

Table 4.3 Systems of innovation

Elements of the system	National systems of innovation	Regional systems of innovation
Inter-firm relationships	Market and hierarchical Authoritarian relationships Emphasis on competition Arm's-length supplier relationships	Network economics Web systems Supplier chains as source of innovation Cooperation and trust
Knowledge infrastructure The R&D system	Formal R&D laboratories Focus on process R&D Federal R&D laboratories Focus on defence	University research Focus new product R&D External sources of knowledge Local R&D spillovers
Community and the public sector	Emphasis on federal level Paternalistic relationship Regulation	Emphasis on regional level Public–private partnerships Community, cooperation and trust
Internal organization of the firm	Mechanistic and authoritarian Separation of innovation and production Multi-divisional firm	Organic organization Continuous innovation Matrix organizations
Institutions of the financial sector	Formal savings and investment Formal financial sector	Venture capital Informal financial sector
Physical and communication infrastructure	National orientation Physical infrastructure	Global orientation Electronic data exchange
Firm strategy, structure and rivalry	Difficult to start new firms No access to new knowledge Little or no entrepreneurship	Easy to start new firms Inexpensive access to knowledge Entrepreneurship is crucial

This is in part because of the stable characteristics of institutions. In an uncertain world, institutions (laws, customs and norms) make life manageable and more comfortable for agents and organizations.

In the previous section we sketched out three elements of the contemporary political economy that support regional innovation: inter-firm relations, the knowledge infrastructure and the public sector. In addition to the three above we also focus on four others: internal firm organization, the financial sector, physical and communication infrastructure, and firm strategy, structure and rivalry. All these elements will be discussed in some detail in the chapters that follow. Table 4.3 outlines the elements of national and regional systems of innovation.

Conclusion

A presumption put forward very cautiously and tentatively by a few scholars a few years ago was that the most effective way to analyse the innovation system and to intervene strategically in it is to tackle the problem at the 'national' level. Yet much recent work has raised serious questions about this hypothesis. Too many forces at work in the world economy would appear to suggest that, as globalization proceeds, national disintegration occurs, and subnational components gain more importance. Consequently, focusing on subnational units of analysis would, in all likelihood, provide better insights into the workings of the 'real worlds of production' and better levers for policy interventions on the innovation front.

One might have been expected that observers, researchers and policy-makers would have been led to focus more of their work and analyses on local innovation systems. However, this would be to discount unduly the power of the centralized mind-set at work in so many sectors of politics, management and science. This mind-set has maintained the dominion of the centralized machine-model of the socio-economy and has kept the decentralized garden-model at bay. The result is a rather misguided pursuit of 'national systems' where there are only 'regional' or 'sectoral' systems.

The costs of such 'national' strategies are likely to be very high if, as we surmise, what is called for is a bottom-up policy. Consequently, it may not be unimportant to call for a return to the cautious and tentative language used by Richard Nelson and to the realization that the hypothesis of 'national systems of innovation' has not been validated yet.

PART II

European Studies

CHAPTER FIVE

Business Processes in Regional Innovation Systems in the European Union

Philip Cooke

Introduction

Today the regional dimension of innovation policy is receiving much more attention than hitherto. This is for at least five reasons. First, the development of multi-level governance, particularly in the European Union, means that many traditional aspects of national industry and competition policy, as well as aspects of regulation, have moved upwards to supranational level. This means that countries are less able to protect either 'national champions' or uncompetitive industries in the ways they once did (see, for example, Begg and Mayes 1993a, b). Thus regional administrations in which uncompetitive industries are located, such as coal, steel, textiles, shipbuilding and some military industry, have been forced to become more active in assisting restructuring and evolution towards new, more competitive and innovative industries.

Second, 'globalization' has meant that financial markets influence national fiscal, budgetary and monetary policies significantly. These are now constrained in ways which limit the powers of national governments to incur public expenditure for regional policies of the more traditional kind. This has meant that regional governance organizations are being required to do more with less public investment. Among the policy areas particularly affected are capital grants and tax reliefs for new or expanding larger firms. More attention has been paid to small and medium-sized enterprises (SMEs), to improving training infrastructures and to supporting innovation policies which are either less expensive or draw on other budgets that are in the control of national states (e.g. education and training budgets).

Third, global competitiveness (fundamentally intra- and inter-Triad trade; see Ruigrok and Van Tulder 1995; Hirst and Thompson 1996; Lundvall 1997) has caused global firms to re-evaluate the importance of regional 'embeddeness' as part of their global strategies (Granovetter 1985; Grabher 1993; A. Scott 1996; Storper and Scott 1995; Florida 1995). Rather than pursuing a policy, as in the past, where foreign or even domestic, inward-investment firms might move from location to location in pursuit of better subsidies, more are now seeking to integrate with their host economies. They now recognize, more than previously, regional advantages to be derived from localized skill pools, industrial cultures and opportunities for local or regional procurement. Moreover, the role of regional governance organizations in tailoring packages of enterprise support to meet investor requirements should not be underestimated.

Fourth, large and small firms are reaping the benefits of *externalization* as large firms seek to source inputs from regionalized supply chains if small and medium enterprises are capable of meeting the exacting, often world-class quality and delivery standards of large customer-firms. Implicit in this are the messages from 'lean management' models, of the advantages of 'co-makership' and the exchange of tacit knowledge, particularly in the product and process (including organizational) innovation chain (Womack and Jones 1996).

Fifth and finally, strong evidence has emerged to support the thesis advanced by, among others, Krugman (1995) that as economies become less constrained by national frontiers they become more geographically *specialized*. This has been shown to be the case in terms of trade flows in general and technological trade flows in particular (Dalum 1995; Archibugi and Pianta 1992). It is also seen to be occurring *within* countries, often at the most localized, not only regional, levels (see Malmberg and Maskell 1997; Isaksen 1997). They demonstrate that as industry shifted regionally in the 1970s and 1980s, often declining in cities and growing outside them, it also increased its spatial and sectoral concentration as measured by Gini coefficients.

Thus regions have become more important bases for specialized externalized industrial activity than they were during the 'Golden Age' up to 1973 when large firms tended to, collectively, develop spatial divisions of labour (Massey 1984). In the corporate spatial hierarchies of the post-war era until the 1970s, command functions (including R&D) were often concentrated in core regions, usually in the capital cities of the advanced economies; skilled work was focused in relatively modern, industrialized regions (e.g. around Birmingham in the United Kingdom, Turin in Italy or Eindhoven in the Netherlands); while new routine assembly plants went to peripheral regions such as Brittany in France, the Mezzogiorno in Italy and areas of Spain and Portugal, or older industrial regions such as the Ruhr in Germany, Liverpool in the United Kingdom and the Belgian part of Limburg. Externalities were internalized within the corporation to a greater extent than today.

Because of these spatial shifts towards a more embedded, cluster-like tendency, the REGIS proposal funded by the European Union-Targeted Socio-Economic Research Programme of Directorate-General (DG) XII sought to explore and understand the extent to which a wide variety of regions in Europe (including two in Central and Eastern Europe) were developing, at the firm or inter-firm and enterprise support organization levels, *systemic* innovation capabilities to meet these new exigencies. In what follows, an account will be given of the main findings for the nine European Union member regions from the perspective of firms in key regional industrial sectors or clusters.

The areas covered include the following:

- the importance of regions in the key functions of firms;
- competitiveness, competitive challenges and responses of firms;
- the innovative practices of firms;
- partnership for innovation among firms; and
- cooperation between firms and the innovation infrastructure.

In later stages of the research a wide variety of public organizations were interviewed with regard to their own innovativeness and the extent of *systemic* interaction with each other and with firms. The key aim throughout the research was to establish the extent to which systemic interactions between firms and the innovation support infrastructure exist at regional level and to identify the relationship of regional-level interactions by firms with those at higher levels, notably the national and supranational. Eventually, when the regional firm-support infrastructure profile for each region emerged, selected firms were interviewed in depth to establish in more detail their competitiveness, innovation and innovation support policy needs for the future. At this stage some preliminary policy implications of the research will be indicated.

Choice of regions and design of the research

In framing the research, importance was placed upon studying a good mix of regions. But first it was necessary to decide what was to count as a region in the first place. The concept 'region' is somewhat contested both intellectually and in practice. Some EU member states have, in effect, no regional level or only rather weakly institutionalized regions while others have strong regions with considerable powers. Federal systems usually have the strongest subcentral administrative structures despite the fact that, in Germany particularly, some of these have larger populations than many EU member states (e.g. North Rhine-Westphalia has a population of 17 million). Nevertheless, in terms of the research, the administrative powers of the *Länder*, especially in respect of their capacity for innovation support, made them excellent candidates for study. In brief, the criteria used, in general, were as follows. First, the areas to be studied should *not* be limited by their size, whether measured in terms of population or in terms of GDP. Second, they should demonstrate homogeneity in terms of certain criteria; importantly, possession of a homogeneous administrative jurisdiction at subnational and supralocal level was one such criterion. Third, the region should also be distinguishable from bordering regions by some attribute or attributes which could be cultural, administrative, political or economic, or some combination of these. Fourth, it should possess some kind of internal cohesion, whether in terms of a historical, cultural, linguistic or territorial identity. In cases of relatively recent regionalization, where a state had marked out modern regions, these should be at least administratively if not politically or culturally meaningful.

After this process, the analysis of the extent to which such regions were in process of developing systemic innovation linkages and relationships was sharpened by identifying regions in terms of their economic characteristics. These included overall economic performance and economic structure, ranging from high performance, through to those having suffered economic adversity – typically in regions experiencing reconversion from dependence on older, heavy industry – to relatively weak performance owing to peripherality, rurality, dependence on smaller firms in traditional industry, and so on. Thus, four categories of region were developed to reflect these research interests (Table 5.1). The division between reconversion regions was based on pre-existing literature, later confirmed by first-stage REGIS project regional profile research (see, for example, Braczyk *et al.* 1997; Tödtling and

Table 5.1 Regional categorization by economic character

Category	Region
High performance	Brabant (NL), Baden-Württemberg (FRG)
Reconversion (upstream innovation)	Styria (AU), Tampere (FIN)
Reconversion (downstream innovation)	Wales (UK), Basque C. (SP), Wallonia (B)
Peripheral (SME and traditional)	Centro (PGL), Friuli (I)

Sedlacek 1997; Grandinetti and Schenkel 1996; de Castro *et al.* 1996) which suggested distinctiveness in the typical disposition of regional firms towards innovation. The 'upstream' category revealed evidence that regional firms were seeking backward innovation linkages to knowledge centres such as universities or research institutes early in the reconversion process. Indications of this occur in the Tampere region, where Finland's most successful regional cluster of spin-off firms linked both to the Technical University and to local large firms such as Nokia was in evidence. In Styria, similarly, the Technical University of Graz is highly proactive in promoting spin-off firms, many of which have then become involved in the regionally promoted automotive industry cluster. Here, product innovations were rather pronounced outcomes of such upstream linkages. In the 'downstream' category, the linkages tend to be between indigenous SMEs and large customer firms, and innovations tend to be more 'near-market' and perhaps process and organizationally inclined. Subsequently, development of linkages towards knowledge centres is also occurring (on this, see also Cooke and Morgan, 1998).

The design of the research which followed this initial analytical phase was to develop a comparative methodology such that for each region a profile report was produced. On the basis of pre-existing research literature, this established whether or not there were predominant industry sectors or industry clusters and provided accounts of their performance in terms of employment and other standard criteria such as sectoral GDP, R&D expenditure, etc. Thereafter accounts were provided for each region on the nature of the *governance* structure, regional technology policies and the role of innovation intermediaries such as training, finance and technology transfer agencies. Finally, preliminary and very general conclusions were drawn concerning any evidence for regional industry and innovation support infrastructure.

The second stage (which this chapter reports) involved researching the competitiveness, innovation and interaction activities of the key sectors or, where identified, industry clusters in each region. A postal questionnaire was administered to some 300 firms in the selected sectors or clusters (up to a maximum of six) with the agreed aim of achieving at least 75 usable responses (i.e. a 25 per cent response rate). This was achieved for all regions. The third stage of the research involved face-to-face interviews with senior personnel of a representative sample of all innovation support agencies in the public and private sectors in all regions. The fourth stage involved face-to-face interviews with a selection of the sampled, respondent firms to investigate in depth and with a view to gaining illustrative case-material on issues requiring clarification arising from the postal survey. The results of this effort are accounts from each region assessing and documenting the extent to which regional innovation is *systemic* and the nature and intensity of linkages among firms and between firms and innovation support organizations in the region and beyond it (see Cooke, Boekholt and Tödtling 1999).

Firm perspectives on competition, innovation and support

Firms were first asked to provide information about themselves in terms of employment, turnover and so on as a prelude to information concerning the functions performed in the region, the sources and destinations of inputs and outputs, the main location of their most important competitors and the location of the partner firms with which they cooperated most. Both large firms and SMEs (which were of course the majority) were asked for this information.

Table 5.2 is a summary of the sectors or clusters targeted in each region. It is worth noting that where sectors were the focus of research, surveyed firms were reasonably clearly located in that specific sector, whereas when clusters were the focus, firms in industries (including services) known to be linked to the industry cluster but not in the core SIC were included in the sample surveyed. Despite this, there is a total overall focus on manufacturing industry, a choice made by all teams independently, reflecting the fact that the need for innovation is perceived to be most acute there, not least because markets, competition and the pressure for innovation are based on more open, global trading than is the case for most service industry.

The importance of regions in firms' functions

Firms were asked to report their regional and extraregional profiles in respect of location of functions, source and destination of inputs and outputs, location of main competitors and cooperation partners. The reasoning behind these questions was that a picture would emerge of the relative openness or otherwise of regions in terms of the spatial organization of production, externalities, firm rivalry and partnership opportunities.

Table 5.3 summarizes the findings regarding key rankings for six variables in respect of regional/non-regional focus. What this table tells us, in brief, is the following:

- In generic terms these regional firms control mainly *production* and *choice of suppliers*. They, least importantly, have *training*, *assembly*, *R&D* and *distribution* responsibility regionally located. Specifically, high-performance and upstream reconversion regions fit the generic pattern most closely, while downstream reconversion and peripheral regions have least *R&D*, *distribution* and *assembly* but also more *strategic planning* (foreign direct investment and SMEs) functions.
- Regarding *geographical* (regional, national, EU, rest of the world) focus of functions and relationships, generically speaking the *national* level is easily the most important for regional firm *inputs* and *outputs*, though it is less so for first sources of *competition* ('EU' being almost as important and 'regional' being a little more represented). This is more the case for *cooperation*, where *regional* and

Table 5.2 Regional sectors or clusters investigated

Cluster	Region	Sector
Electronics Metal/machinery Food Transport/logistics	Brabant (NL)	
Machinery Automotive Electronics	Baden-Württemberg (FRG)	
Machinery Electronics and electrical Metals/steel Automotive Wood and paper	Styria (AU)	
Automotive Electrical (white goods) Machine tools Telecommunications equipment	Basque Country (SP)	
Automotive Electronics	Wales (UK)	Healthcare/medical equipment
	Centro (PGL)	Footwear Ceramics Cork Metal manufacturing Automotive
	Tampere (FIN)	Metals/machinery Electronics textiles Pulp and paper Chemicals Food
	Wallonia (BE)	Food Chemicals Machinery
Furniture	Friuli (I)	Food Electro-mechanical Metals

then *EU* become substantially more important. In more specific terms, the *regional* and *national input–output* focus is especially important for the higher-performance and upstream regions, except Styria, which is rather open to EU suppliers, customers, competition and cooperation. Downstream and peripheral regions are quite nationally oriented yet also rather open to the EU for *input–output* relations and *competition*, but strongly *regional* or, to a lesser extent, *national* for *cooperation*.

In summary, regional geography is important as a site of production and location for choosing suppliers and cooperation partners, but less so as a final market, where the national level is overwhelmingly important, followed by the EU and the region. The national and EU levels are the most important locations for competitors. EU

Table 5.3 Regional sectors or clusters investigated

Region	Variable					
	Functions (important)	Functions (unimportant)	Inputs	Outputs	Location of competition	Location of cooperation
Brabant	1 Prod. 2 Dist.	1 Training 2 Str.plng	1 National 2 Regional	1 National 2 Regional	1 Regional 2 National	1 Regional 2 National
Tampere	1 Prod. 2 Str.plng	1 Training 2 Assembly	1 National 2 Regional	1 National 2 Regional	1 National 2 EU	1 National 2 Regional
Styria	1 Dist. 2 Ch.supps	1 Assembly 2 Prod.	1 National 2 EU	1 National 2 EU	1 EU 2 National	1 EU 2 National
Ba.-Wü.	1 Prod 2 Ch.supps	1 Assembly 2 Dist.	1 Regional 2 National	1 National 2 Regional	1 National 2 Regional	1 Reg & EU 2 Nat. & RoW
Wallonia	1 Prod. 2 Ch.supps	1 Assembly 2 R&D	1 EU 2 National	1 EU 2 Regional	1 EU 2 National	1 EU & Nat. 2 RoW
Friuli	1 Prod. 2 Ch.supps	1 R&D 2 Training	1 National 2 Regional	1 National 2 EU	1 Regional 2 National	1 Regional 2 National
Wales	1 Assembly 2 Str.plng	1 Dist. 2 R&D	1 National 2 Regional	1 National 2 Regional	1 National 2 RoW	1 National 2 Regional
Basque Country	1 Prod. 2 Assembly	1 Dist. 2 Marketing	1 Regional 2 National	1 EU 2 National	1 EU 2 Regional	1 Regional 2 EU
Centro	1 Prod. 2 Str.plng	1 R&D 2 Dist.	1 National 2 EU	1 National 2 EU	1 National 2 EU	1 Regional 2 National

Note: EU, European Union; RoW, rest of the world; Prod., production; Dist., distribution; Str.plng, strategic planning; Ch.supps, choose suppliers

regional firms are remarkably unaffected by 'globalization' since the rest of the world hardly features for either relationships or functions, markets or competitors.

Competitiveness, challenges and firm responses

Firms in the selected EU regions were asked a series of questions concerning how they perceived their competitive advantage, how they would seek to sustain it, what the challenge from competitors was perceived to be, and how they proposed to respond to that. The results of these inquiries are most interesting, and indeed remarkable, in terms of the degree of consistency of answers across diverse manufacturing clusters and sectors and a widely differing set of regions. Table 5.4 summarizes the results in abbreviated rank order of two most and least important factors for each of four variables.

What is fascinating about these results is the high degree of unanimity across sectors/clusters and type of region. In summary terms the following can be asserted with confidence:

- With reference to the frequency of responses and their high ranking, firms in these European Union regions consistently see themselves as competing on *quality* and only secondarily on technological *innovation*. In general, also, they are not competing on *ecological* or *price-sensitive* foundations. Nor does *user-friendliness*

Table 5.4 Competitive strategies of firms

Region	Variable							
	Competitive advantage (important)	Competitive advantage (unimportant)	Sustaining competitive advantage (important)	Sustaining competitive advantage (unimportant)	Competitive challenge (important)	Competitive challenge (unimportant)	Response to competition (important)	Response to competition (unimportant)
Brabant	1 Quality 2 Price	1 Ecology 2 User-fr.	1 Skills 2 R&D	1 Patents 2 —	1 Quality 2 Dmnd ch.	1 Pers.costs 2 New comp.	1 Cut costs 2 Subcontract	1 Coopn 2 —
Tampere	1 Quality 2 Del.time	1 Ecology 2 Service	1 Skills 2 Marketing	1 Patents 2 Coopn	1 Quality 2 Price	1 Pers.costs 2 New comp.	1 R&D 2 Cut costs	1 Outsource 2 Cooperate
Styria	1 Quality 2 Tech.inno.	1 Price 2 User-fr.	1 Skills 2 R&D	1 Support 2 Patents	1 Price 2 Pers.costs	1 New comp. 2 Tech.ch. & prod. dev.costs	1 Cut costs 2 Speed prod.dev.	1 Outsource 2 Subcontr. & mktng
Ba.-Wü.	1 Tech.inno. 2 Quality	1 Price 2 Ecology	1 R&D 2 Skills	1 Support 2 Coopn	1 Price 2 Quality	1 Dmnd ch. 2 New comp.	1 Cut costs 2 Org.ch.	1 Cooperate 2 Subcontr.
Wallonia	1 Quality 2 Tech.inno.	1 Ecology 2 Price	1 Skills 2 Org.	1 Support 2 Coopn	1 Price 2 Pers.costs	1 Tech.ch. 2 Dmnd ch.	1 Cut costs 2 Org.ch.	1 Cooperate 2 Marketing
Friuli	1 Quality 2 Del.time	1 User-fr. 2 Price	1 Skills 2 Org.	1 Support 2 Patents	1 Price 2 Quality	1 New comp. 2 Tech.ch.	1 Org.ch. 2 R&D	1 Cooperate 2 Marketing
Wales	1 Quality 2 Tech.inno.	1 Ecology 2 User-fr.	1 Skills 2 R&D	1 Patents 2 Support	1 Price 2 Quality	1 Pers.costs 2 New comp.	1 Org.ch. 2 Cut costs	1 Cooperate 2 R&D
Basque Country	1 Del.time 2 Quality	1 User-fr. 2 Ecology	1 R&D 2 Org.	1 Support 2 Patents	1 Price 2 Quality	1 Tech.ch. 2 Dmnd ch.	1 Cut costs 2 Org.ch.	1 Outsource 2 Cooperate
Centro	1 Quality 2 Tech.inno.	1 Price 2 User-fr.	1 Org. 2 R&D	1 Support 2 Patents	1 Quality 2 Price	1 New comp. 2 Pers.costs	1 Cut costs 2 Speed prod.dev.	1 Subcontr. 2 Cooperate

Dmnd ch., demand change; New comp., new competitors; Del.time, delivery time; Pers.costs, personnel costs; Tech.inno., technological innovation; Org., organization; mktng, marketing; prod.dev., product development

score highly as a competitive advantage. There is relatively little difference by category in the perception by specific regions of their important and unimportant competitive advantages.

- A comparable unanimity appears in the response by regional firms to the question of how to sustain this quality-led competitiveness. Nearly all regional firms state that their main strategy is to enhance workforce *skills*. By contrast, *patents*, use of public *innovation support* services and *cooperation* with other firms score low. *R&D* investment is, along with *organizational* change, the next-mentioned course of action to sustain competitiveness. These are more important in the capital equipment engineering regions of Baden-Württemberg and the Basque Country, where public innovation sources rank low as a means of keeping ahead.

- Apart from Brabant, Centro and Tampere, for whose firms *quality* is the main challenge from competitors, all other regional firms rate *price* competition as the most serious challenge. Quality, however, comes second for four regions for which price is the most important competitive threat. The unimportant competitive threats tend to be more mixed; *new competitors* are generally considered to be unimportant, as are *personnel costs*, *technical change* and *demand change*. There is little of significance, perhaps surprisingly, to differentiate more from less developed regional economies in these judgements.

- Finally, firms were asked what would be their business response to the perceived challenge of quality/price competition from competitors. The most common, highly ranking response here is to *cut costs*, mentioned first in six cases and second in two others. However, *organizational change* is mentioned first or second in five

Table 5.5 Percentage of firms reporting organizational innovations

Innovation	Brab.	Tamp.	Styria	Ba.-Wü.	Wallon.	Friuli	Wales	Basque	Centro	% Total
TQM	46	39	36	51	59	59	51	59	65	52
Group work	57	54	59	49	53	62	28	54	47	51
Profit/cost centre	31	29	26	28	36	60	44	19	59	37
Networking[a]	28	28	25	11	15	52	15	9	20	22
Benchmarking	10	20	29	9	53	20	32	25	46	27
Flat hierarchy	51	45	71	73	11	49	33	11	28	41
Design teams[b]	7	43	14	20	17	39	24	13	26	22
JIT	40	28	37	24	68	53	45	43	33	41
Outsourcing	47	14	34	41	13	21	22	14	15	25
System supply	16	14	18	19	10	54	9	7	35	20
ISO 9000	24	52	60	68	54	42	70	69	54	55
IT	24	67	51	25	25	63	60	60	30	45

Notes:
[a] Inter-organizational networking
[b] Interdisciplinary design teams

cases while enhancing *R&D* investment and *speed-up of product development* were mentioned only twice each. The unimportant responses were *cooperation* with other firms, *outsourcing*, *subcontracting*, *marketing* and *R&D*. Again, there is little discernible difference among different regional categories.

Hence, these results point to a *universal* characteristic of European Union manufacturing firms (these results arise from some 800 questionnaire responses overall) in which they see themselves as competing primarily on quality, not price or ecological grounds. They seek to sustain this by investing in skills, not patents. Meanwhile, their competitors compete on price first, quality second, causing the main response of cutting costs and making organizational changes rather than seeking external solutions by cooperation, outsourcing, subcontracting with other firms or working more closely with the public enterprise or innovation support infrastructure. In our sample, European firms are internally focused to a very high degree, appearing to see themselves as self-reliant, quality-oriented competitors, needing to cut costs to keep market share.

The innovative practices of firms

Firms were asked questions about the most recently introduced organizational innovations they had made, as well as the sources of innovation information most frequently consulted, their proportions of R&D as percentage of turnover and staff, their main partners in conducting innovation activities, product and process innovations introduced between 1993 and 1996 and the main constraints on innovation they experienced. Table 5.5 summarizes the results for organizational innovation. This question is relevant in light of the relative importance of organizational change as a response to competitive threats. It shows that, on average, marginally the most frequently mentioned change is the acquisition of *ISO 9000*. The variance in this response is also relatively low, with only Brabant markedly out of line. Nearly equal

Table 5.6 Sources of innovation information (percentage of firms mentioning source)

Source	Brab.	Tamp.	Styria	Ba.-Wü.	Wallon.	Friuli	Wales	Basque	Centro	% Total
Journals	28	19	55	52	22	23	51	20	38	34
Conferences/fairs	23	25	57	71	27	29	42	40	66	42
Customers	48	29	55	71	16	23	46	44	31	40
Suppliers	24	17	50	26	20	23	39	25	35	29
Consultants	5	1	4	1	3	11	9	18	14	7
Associations	13	1	4	13	6	3	22	11	15	10
Tech. transfer	3	—	2	6	1	1	4	23	16	6
Universities	8	2	15	8	7	1	20	5	7	8
Higher education	1	—	—	4	1	4	8	3	3	3

Notes:
[a] Industry associations
[b] Technology transfer agencies

as the second most frequently mentioned organizational innovations overall are *total quality management* (TQM) (echoing the emphasis on quality as a competitive advantage, as, to some extent, does ISO 9000) and *group work*. Slightly more than half of the 833 firms surveyed had introduced both. Information technology, flattened hierarchies and just-in-time (JIT) delivery had been introduced by some 40–45 per cent of firms. The less important changes to have been made are *inter-organizational networking* and *interdisciplinary design teams* (22 per cent each). Becoming a system or modular supplier (as distinct from a parts or components supplier) scored lowest overall at 20 per cent, and outsourcing and benchmarking are also rather low at 25 per cent and 27 per cent respectively. These results again suggest relatively introverted rather than strongly associational or cooperative strategies as the main organizational focus.

Interesting differences between the high-performance and upstream reconversion regions and the rest occur with respect to the introduction of *flat hierarchy* (60 per cent compared to 26 per cent) and *benchmarking*, where the higher-performance regions scored less, at 17 per cent, than the others with 35 per cent. This points to recognition by the latter group of a greater need to *learn* improved organizational practices. Outsourcing is also more pronounced in the first group (34 per cent) than the second (19 per cent), suggesting that the former are more conscious of the benefits of externalization than the latter.

Firms were then asked to indicate which, from a range of possibilities, were the main sources of information they used to engage in innovative activities of relevance to product, process or organizational innovation. These results are shown in Table 5.6. Firms were asked to rank sources on a six-point scale. The table contains information on firm rankings of particular sources grouped into the 'important' and 'very important' categories, the two highest. In overall terms, there is a cluster of four sources of innovation information which clearly outweigh the others by a large margin. *Conferences* and *fairs* are the first source, closely followed by *customer* firms, then *journals* (including technical literature) and, a little way behind, *supplier* firms. Added together, 'other firms' (i.e. customers and suppliers) are the main source. Of low but equal importance are *industry associations* and *universities*, ahead of

Table 5.7 Regional R&D activity

R&D	Brab.	Tamp.	Styria	Ba.-Wü.	Wallon.	Friuli	Wales	Basque	Centro	% Total
% of turnover	0.1	8.1	8.4	4.7	5.0	2.9	6.3	10.1	2.1	5.3
% of staff	1.9	9.0	14.9	9.8	11.0	5.9	9.5	6.4	2.2	7.8

consultants, technology transfer agencies and, finally, *higher education (non-university) institutes.*

There is little significant variation between the regional categories, though the peripheral regions (47 per cent) rely on conferences and fairs more than the reconversion regions (38 per cent), but so does high-performance Baden-Württemberg. This suggests that the reconversion economics have a lesser perception of the need to learn from such external sources. Interestingly, the Spanish and Portuguese regions are more reliant than the others on learning opportunities from *technology transfer* centres. Finally, *universities* are relatively important sources in two reconversion regions, Styria and Wales.

Questions were asked about firms' expenditure on R&D both in budgetary terms (per cent of turnover) and direct R&D staff as a percentage of labour force in the region. These results are presented in Table 5.7. They reveal that in 1995, there was wide variation in regional proportions of expenditure and, even more strikingly, staff engaged in R&D. Predictably, perhaps, the peripheral regions scored low, but so, on average, did the high-performance regions, notably Brabant. The higher proportions of *turnover* (8.3 per cent) were in the upstream reconversion regions while even the downstream reconversion regions scored higher than average at 7.1 per cent. Interpreting these higher than average expenditure scores is difficult but may reflect, on the one hand, the effect of older, established, albeit declining, sectors or clusters in combination with a certain dynamism from newer small-firm industries. The pattern for proportion of total *staff* engaged in R&D echoes that for expenditure, with the downstream reconversion regions scoring 9.0 per cent compared to the average of 7.8 per cent and the upstream reconversion regions scoring 12 per cent. Baden-Württemberg's relatively low expenditure but higher than average staff may suggest that innovativeness need not be highly correlated with larger R&D budgets. The higher than average R&D activity of reconversion regions is, to a considerable extent, correlated with higher interaction by their firms with universities, as shown in Table 5.6.

Further investigation of more systemic linkage in the innovation process revealed very convergent results. In most regions the main innovation partner is usually the *customer* firm, with *supplier* firms second. This ranking fails to hold only for Wallonia, Friuli and Centro. In third place are *universities* and *consultants* equally. There is no evident pattern, in terms of regional economic character, in these third-choice partners. What is slightly surprising is the appearance of consultants, given their low average visibility as sources of innovation information (Table 5.6). This may be interpreted to mean that firms use consultants for expertise in problem-solving rather than as sources of innovation ideas.

The geographical location of customer and supplier partners in innovation is predominantly national, followed by European Union-based and regionally based. The use of universities tends to be national and that of consultants regional. Thus a

Table 5.8 Percentage of firms reporting innovations 1993–6

Innovation	Brab.	Tamp.	Styria	Ba.-Wü.	Wallon.	Friuli	Wales	Basque	Centro	% Total
Product	36	76	67	79	74	80	64	66	83	70
New to market	17	44	48	63	43	51	45	26	52	43
Process	28	51	44	39	41	76	52	52	74	50
New to market	8	43	21	13	17	26	20	12	26	21

picture is reinforced of regional firms operating primarily on a national scale with respect to inter-firm relations in rather the same way that they do with respect to inputs and outputs (Table 5.3). The lesser use of innovation partners regionally contrasts with the higher levels of interaction with regional partners for non-innovation activities, again as shown in Table 5.3.

In an attempt to ascertain how innovative firms were, questions were asked of them concerning product and process innovations they had introduced during the period 1993–6 and whether such innovations were new to the market as distinct from being 'reinventions' of products or processes known to be available in other markets (e.g. the United States or Japan) or product or process markets other than those in which the firm principally operated. The results of this investigation are presented in Table 5.8. They reveal remarkably high levels of both *product* and *process* innovation, though lower levels of innovation 'new to the market'. This prompts the obvious question as to the nature of these innovations.

Of interest and, perhaps, concern from these results is the large amount of effort and, presumably, expense being invested in both product and process innovation which is not new to the market. There seems to be identified here, perhaps for the first time, a widespread European business phenomenon of 'reinnovation', perhaps copying or mimicking products or processes that are known to be already available on the market. However, it has to be remembered that much of this could be transferring and adapting innovations from market sectors other than the ones in which the respondent firms are active.

A further question concerns precisely what firms mean when they report 'innovations'. Are these marginal adjustments – changes of colour, design or fabric in, for example, textiles? Or are they true, incremental or even, occasionally, radical innovations? These questions can be seriously addressed only in stage four of the research when firms are interviewed in depth and asked for illustrative case examples of their product and process innovations. It is particularly noteworthy that the two more peripheral regions of Friuli and Centro register well above average levels of both product and process innovations, though those new to the market are closer to the average. Baden-Württemberg scores high on product innovations new to the market, but low on equivalent process innovation, while Brabant scores lowest in all categories, maybe reflecting its very low R&D activity, but perhaps also a commonly used and rigorous definition of what constitutes 'innovation'. The reconversion regions are comparable in their rate of innovation in products and processes, though less so regarding those new to the market, with Tampere scoring twice the average for process innovations new to the market, possibly echoing its

Table 5.9 Constraints on innovation

Constraint	Brab.	Tamp.	Styria	Ba.-Wü.	Wallon.	Friuli	Wales	Basque	Centro	% Total
Funding	27	21	40	25	40	18	18	29	26	27
Know-how	10	18	26	9	11	7	18	15	16	14
Mgt time	39	30	38	17	26	14	35	21	9	25
Skills	12	13	19	20	25	16	31	15	21	19
Pers. costs (research)	20	19	40	40	17	20	17	18	26	24
Finding specialists	—	15	20	6	6	7	6	6	15	9
Customer needs info.	10	12	20	10	11	6	10	6	5	10
Market info	14	9	33	12	12	4	12	4	6	12
Sources of know-how	8	5	22	14	11	4	8	5	9	11
Lack of autonomy	—	4	22	7	15	5	17	4	5	9
Standardized products	10	1	37	5	8	—	13	5	1	9

strong position in process machinery, especially for the pulp and paper industry, and, with Nokia, in electronics.

Finally, firms were asked about the constraints they experienced with respect to innovation. These relativities, measured in terms of firms responding that given variables were either important or very important constraints, are presented in Table 5.9. Predictably, *funding* was the most cited, followed by *management time* and *costs of research personnel*. Relatively unimportant were finding specialist know-how, lack of autonomy and being in standardized product markets. Stronger regions faced a rather higher than average premium on personnel costs of research staff while downstream reconversion regions had more difficulty recruiting appropriately skilled workers. Lack of autonomy was also more of a problem in such regions.

Cooperation in innovation

The final set of questions put to firms concerned cooperation in innovation – the aim being to establish the extent to which network linkages existed among firms, and between them and public or private innovation support agencies. This is a way of beginning to explore whether or not or to what extent system-like relationships exist. The first question concerned partnership with others in innovation and the location of partners, as shown in Table 5.10.

It is apparent, with a few exceptions, that the strong customer–supplier link with respect to innovation information flow is even more pronounced with respect to cooperation in product and process innovation. 'Customers' receive four priority and two secondary rankings at regional level, 'suppliers' less, but innovation support infrastructure such as *technology transfer* centres, grant or *subsidy*-providers and non-grant-giving *government* agencies and *universities* receive some mention as

Table 5.10 Geographical cooperation for product and process innovation

Location and function	Brab.	Tamp.	Styria	Ba.-Wü.	Wallon.	Friuli	Wales	Basque	Centro
	% of firms mentioning								
Region, 1	Tech. trans. 40	Customers 37	Customers 54	Customers 80	Grants 80	Suppliers 16	Govt. agency 28	Tech. trans 28	Customers 30
Region, 2	Uni./HEI 36	Uni./HEI 23	Suppliers 14	Suppliers 71	Uni./HEI 20	Assocs 15	Customers 27	Customers 28	Suppliers 28
Nation, 1	CRO 13	Customers 66	Customers 72	Customers 84	Suppliers 46	Suppliers 31	Customers 53	Customers 27	Suppliers 58
Nation, 2	VC 10	Suppliers 35	Suppliers 18	Suppliers 67	Uni./HEI 24	Customers 25	Suppliers 50	Suppliers 26	Customers 53
EU, 1	Uni./HEI 7	Customers 39	Customers 20	Customers 65	Customers 46	Customers 17	Suppliers 25	Customers 32	Suppliers 63
RoW, 1	—	Customers 22	Customers 11	Customers 39	Customers 9	Suppliers 3	Customers 21	Customers 27	Customers 23

Notes: HEI, higher education institution; CRO, contract research organization; VC, venture capital

Table 5.11 Reasons for not cooperating in innovation

Reason	Brab.	Tamp.	Styria	Ba.-Wü.	Wallon.	Friuli	Wales	Basque	Centro	% Total
Risk of losing know-how	54	11	47	49	30	14	15	15	16	28
Risk of revealing cost structure	37	27	22	27	8	7	11	3	12	17
No suitable partner available	58	40	40	14	17	21	41	29	23	38
External solutions too expensive	46	24	13	26	28	6	17	20	14	27
Problems can be solved internally	71	22	61	58	48	31	37	31	22	43

regional services accessed with moderate intensity. Baden-Württemberg is remarkable for the high intensity of its regional customer–supplier interaction concerning innovation.

Interactions at all other levels are overwhelmingly dominated by firms' innovation cooperation with *customers*, with only very occasional mentions for venture capital, universities, research organizations or even suppliers. Innovation partnership is clearly user-driven in Europe, with little variation between types of region. Generally speaking these interactions are national first, regional and EU second.

When firms do not cooperate with other firms in the innovation process, the reasons are as given in Table 5.11. Clearly, in some cases, cooperation problems elicited a large range and depth of responses among the population of firms surveyed. Interestingly, as we move away from the higher-performance regions, the reluctance to cooperate in general declines, since the percentages measure responses which rated the reasons for non-cooperation important or very important. It appears that as one moves towards the more peripheral or downstream reconversion regions, reluctance to cooperate diminishes in intensity. In general terms, the key reason for non-cooperation is that 'problems can be solved internally' followed by 'no suitable partner available'. Risk of too much openness on costs and know-how is generally perceived to be low, as is the prospect of investing in external solutions. From these statistics, which ask only why firms do not cooperate, in a context where (from Table 5.10) we know there is a significant amount of user-led cooperation in innovation, it appears that firms, once again, tend to internalize their problem-solving once a deal with a user has been struck.

Innovating with public and contract research organizations

To round off the investigation into the extent of systemic interaction by firms in regions, questions were posed about the use they made of the innovation support infrastructure inside and outside the region. Results are presented in Table 5.12. For most regions, *technology transfer* services are mainly accessed within the region or, second, the nation. This is less the case with *innovation finance*, for which the national level is first port of call more often. This relationship reverses, though, regarding interaction with *universities* or *higher education institutions* (HEIs),

Table 5.12 Geographical location of innovation cooperation by service

Service	Brab.	Tamp.	Styria	Ba.-Wü.	Wallon.	Friuli	Wales	Basque	Centro
Technology transfer services									
Region	40	4	18	15	3	5	10	75	11
Nation	7	7	20	5	3	7	6	13	21
EU	3	5	14	1	3	1	6	8	16
RoW	3	4	10	—	—	—	1	—	5
Innovation finance									
Region	13	10	31	7	41	8	18	37	5
Nation	10	12	33	9	16	16	6	21	53
EU	3	1	22	1	8	8	4	14	5
RoW	3	1	8	—	—	—	—	—	—
Interaction with universities or higher education institutions									
Region	30	52	32	17	51	9	42	29	21
Nation	7	25	30	15	41	9	22	11	42
EU	7	1	19	3	19	1	9	—	—
RoW	3	2	12	3	3	—	5	—	—
Contract research organizations									
Region	17	33	23	11	8	18	3	30	5
Nation	17	49	25	8	3	5	2	10	37
EU	3	6	18	—	3	3	—	—	5
RoW	7	2	8	—	3	—	1	—	—

Note: RoW = Rest of World

though not infrequently the national level comes a close second. Finally, contract research organizations tend to be accessed marginally more regionally than nationally. The more peripheral regions tend to be more dependent upon national innovation support organizations, while the high-performance regions are more likely to interact with regional organizations. The upstream reconversion regions interact more intensively with national organizations while the downstream reconversion regions are more able to cooperate with regional service providers. These findings suggest quite strongly that innovation services connected with accessing research results and technology transfer are systematically used in all regions, in overall terms in preference to use of national organizations. Even innovation finance is quite widely tapped at regional level, though less overall than from national organizations.

When firms were further asked about the impact of using such services on their capability, the most common response from firms in all regions is that it 'speeds up the *product* development' process and 'enlarges the firm's *technological* base'. Less important impacts were those on *skills*, and *collaboration* with other firms or encouragement of wider collaboration with R&D centres. Once again, firms use such services for internalized solutions to problems arising in the course of conducting their own business activities. If firms were not participating in publicly funded research projects or, more generally, interacting with the innovation infrastructure, it is typically because 'there is no need to', 'internal solutions are adequate', 'there is a lack of information about services' or because of 'bureaucratic application processes'. Cost was not usually a major consideration, nor was 'risk of losing know-how', though 'quality of services on offer' was a relatively important reason for not using the services of innovation organizations. These findings were broadly common for all types of region, though the ability to access *information* of a technical nature was a key reason for using services in the less accomplished regional economies.

Conclusions and policy implications

A stylized account of these findings on nine EU regions at different stages of development or regeneration of their manufacturing economies gives the following generic characteristics of the extent to which innovation occurs in a regionally systemic way or not. First, regional firms are in control of *production* and *choice of suppliers* but less so *strategic planning* and *R&D*. Stronger regions have more control of planning and R&D as well as the other factors. Firm *inputs* and *outputs* are linked overwhelmingly to the national level, followed at a distance by the EU (outputs especially) and the regional level (inputs especially). Competitor firms are perceived to be national, EU and regional in that order while the reverse is the case where firms engage in cooperation. There is circumstantial evidence of systemic *regional* interaction between firms around the notion 'cooperative supply of inputs'; this is more the case, the stronger the regional economy.

Concerning competitiveness, firms in all regions sell primarily on a perceived *quality* advantage rather than on price (or ecological attributes). They propose, generically, to sustain this by raising *skills* in the workforce, not especially by means of *patents* or wide use of technical or innovation support. Most see *price competition* as the main market threat, not *personnel costs*, or *technical* and *demand changes*. Most plan to meet the price threat by *cutting costs* and engaging in *organizational* innovation, not *cooperation* with other firms, *marketing* or *R&D*. European manufacturing firms are generally strongly introverted in terms of business strategy.

When it comes to innovation, the main organizational innovations undertaken are acquiring *ISO 9000*, introducing *total quality management* and developing *group* or *team work*. More accomplished regional economies have introduced *flat hierarchies*, less accomplished ones *benchmarking*. Outsourcing is already more common in the higher-performance and upstream reconversion regions, a sign of their early engagement in externalization processes. Less accomplished regions are favourably disposed to learning good practices. This is underlined by the results on sources of innovation ideas and information. While *conferences*, *fairs*, *customers*, *suppliers* and *journals* are the main universally used innovation sources, the less accomplished regions rely on *conferences* and *fairs* more than the higher-performance ones. *Universities* are quite notable as innovation sources in some reconversion regions.

R&D expenditure and staff within firms are more pronounced in reconversion than in higher-performance regional firms, but innovativeness is not necessarily closely linked to R&D, as signified by the position of Baden-Württemberg. Most innovation is carried out with *customer* and *supplier* firms, pointing to strong interaction in this as in more general business activities. Consultants seem to be brought in for specific expertise in problem-solving rather than systemic expertise. Innovative interaction is less regionally, more nationally focused than other business interactions. *Product* and *process* innovation are commonly high in all regions but innovations 'new to the market' are only about half of total innovation. This suggests a high level of 'reinnovation' by European firms in all sectors and regions. It also begs questions about firms' definition of 'innovation', which needs further investigation. Constraints on innovation experienced by firms are primarily *funding*, followed by *management time* and *cost of researchers*. Everywhere, cooperation on product and process innovation is overwhelmingly with *customers* and *suppliers* in the main, not infrequently at regional level, supporting a general notion of systemic inter-firm regional innovation. Regional *technology transfer centres* are also noticeable partners, with firms, in innovation. When firms do not cooperate on innovation it is mainly because there is 'no suitable partner' available or because they think that their 'problems can be solved internally'. Costs and know-how erosion are not important reasons for non-cooperation.

Finally, in respect of cooperation between firms and the innovation support infrastructure, this is strongly regional, except for *innovation finance*, which tends to be accessed at the national level. On many of these innovation and cooperation indicators there seems to be more convergence than divergence in the practices of manufacturing firms within the EU's various regions. Universities are important elements in regional provision of services relating to innovation, as are, to a lesser extent, those at national level. Firms gain mainly by speeding up *product* development and enlarging their technological base from such interactions. When such services are not used it is because of lack of information, because solutions can be found internally within the firm or, for innovation projects, because of problems associated with bureaucratic application processes.

The policy impacts are clear and call for recognition that when firms speak of innovation they include quality, organizational change, management priorities, skills and finance as the key means for achieving it. They are open to using public support of the right quality and see universities and technology transfer agencies as useful sources of support. But mainly they are working on an *internalized* problem-solving basis and, maybe, wasting a lot of effort by 'reinnovating' because information on what is available on the market is inadequately diffused. Policy steps which encourage 'information society' diffusion techniques to enable more rapid learning, both electronically and by better inter-firm knowledge diffusion, could assist the problem of excessive dependence on an internalized focus within the firm, missing innovation solutions already in existence. Innovation policy should build on the evidence of regionally based systemic innovation, but it should be defined in ways which enable firms to improve their own perceived competitive advantages by stressing also quality, skills and organizational innovation in a more integrated way. The success of ISO 9000 is interesting in this respect, though in itself it is scarcely a standard that significantly helps firms enhance their innovation potential.

Note

This chapter summarizes the findings of research conducted in the 'Regional Innovation Systems: Designing for the Future' (REGIS) Project. This research was funded by European Commission DG XII under the Fourth Framework: Targeted Socio-Economic Research Programme. All teams contributed equally to the process of generating empirical information. These data were then analysed by the REGIS Editorial Group, P. Cooke (Project Coordinator), P. Boekholt (Netherlands) and G. Schienstock (Finland), and the draft was written by the Coordinator. Teams were then invited to add comments and corrections and those received were incorporated into the present draft. The author wishes to thank the

European Commission on behalf of the nine teams here involved for funding the project. Thanks are also expressed to all teams through project leaders not already mentioned: G. Bechtle (Germany), E. de Castro (Portugal), G. Etxebarria (Spain), M. Quevit (Belgium), M. Schenkel (Italy) and F. Tödtling (Austria). The usual disclaimer applies.

CHAPTER SIX

Innovation Systems and 'Local Difficulties': The Oxfordshire Experience

Helen Lawton Smith

Introduction

The relationship between firms' success, innovation and the use of external techno-logical resources, and localization of economic development are themes currently being explored in the academic literature. The connection between them is clear. It is that as technological knowledge and information are key factors of production, their acquisition from external sources enhances firms' profitability, and that pro-cesses by which they are transferred are more effective when localized. Therefore, the economic performance of regions can be improved when firms are encouraged to become better innovators by interacting both with institutions such as universities and government laboratories and with other firms within their region. Thus the organizing power of proximity can be augmented by technology transfer support from the local institutional framework.

However, this ideal is tempered by a raft of context-dependent factors relating to the geo-historical characteristics of regions, the knowledge infrastructure and knowledge transfer systems, as well as strategies adopted by individual institutions. Indeed, David and Foray's (1994) key organizing concept of 'the distribution power of an innovation system' is designed to identify differences in nations' capacity to ensure timely access by innovators to stocks of knowledge held in institutions and firms. Barriers to technology transfer at the local level might either be manifesta-tions of failures in the system as a whole, or be 'local difficulties' arising out of the characteristics of local firms and institutions. This chapter identifies the sources of local difficulties in the case of Oxfordshire in the United Kingdom. The key theme is that of how variations in 'information conditions' affect how local systems operate.

'Information conditions' refers to the kinds of information which are available in different regions and how their access is determined. This is dependent on the mix of organizations and the forms of ownership of information. Formal ownership of scientific and technological information (codified knowledge) takes several forms. In the public sector, the state owns that held in national laboratories; it can also give agency to institutions such as universities to exploit state-owned assets through patent and licensing arrangements. Private-sector ownership takes the form of intellectual property held by firms. This also includes ownership of intellectual property on industry-funded research projects undertaken in universities, and that held by individuals. Information as a 'free good' (tacit knowledge) is available through informal networks which may coexist with formal channels. Not only can technical information be transferred during informal interaction, but important information about what kind of research is being done, who is doing it and what kind of approach is necessary to gain access to it can be acquired. Both formal and informal conditions are changed by new strategies being adopted by firms and research institutions and by intervention by third parties to encourage flows of information and its utilization.

Innovation systems

The construction of regions

The character of regions is constructed through the 'fundamental processes of mutual interaction and moulding' and the combination of layers of investment and through human agency (Massey 1994: 321). Regions in which highly innovative firms are clustered (innovative milieux, new industrial districts, etc.) have particular characteristics and information conditions, both in the supply of and in the demand for technology and information. Steed and De Genova (1983) broadly classified areas as different kinds of technology-oriented complexes: (a) products of locally initiated firms and spin-offs; (b) science park sites; (c) manufacturing facilities of large companies, for example in south-east England; and (d) areas that receive very large expenditures of government funds – for example the defence and aerospace companies concentrated in the Bristol region (Boddy and Lovering 1991) and near Grenoble in France (Hilpert and Ruffieux 1991: 77–8). More recently Markusen (1996) has produced a new typology of five types of district: Marshallian industrial districts; the Italianate variant of Marshallian industrial districts; hub-and-spoke districts; satellite platforms; and state-anchored districts. This typology also provides indications of the types of information conditions and of barriers to technology transfer. For example, in the Italianate variant of the Marshallian industrial district model, there is a high degree of cooperation among competitor firms to share innovation. In this model, information flows through interaction. In contrast, in the state-anchored model there is a low degree of cooperation among local private-sector firms to share innovation (Markusen 1996: 298–9), and information flows are restricted. At the regional level, therefore, an important variable affecting the type of information conditions prevailing is whether decisions about investment in R&D are made internally or externally to the region. This can have an important bearing on the extent and nature of information flows into and out of firms and research institutions.

The construction of regions is also affected by the representation of particular sectors, the tendency of firms to interact with other firms and local research institutions, and the research intensity of sectors in particular countries. Sectors, even high-tech ones, differ in their general propensity to collaborate with other firms or universities and national laboratories (Pavitt 1984; Nelson and Rosenberg 1993). Faulkner and Senker (1995) found considerable variations in levels of interaction with universities in R&D-intensive biotechnology, engineering ceramics and parallel computing firms in the United Kingdom. Indeed, only in pharmaceuticals, where Glaxo Wellcome is the world's largest R&D spender, is Britain matching international spending rates (*Guardian*, 27 June 1997). Thus regions with concentrations of sectors which are more likely to be seeking external technological resources contain different information demand conditions as compared with those dominated by less innovative or less interactive sectors. Moreover, disparities in research activities and interests between firms and their local institutions will inhibit the formation of effective information and technology transfer systems.

The knowledge infrastructure

A distinction between knowledge infrastructure and knowledge transfer systems is important particularly when discussing the localization of innovation systems. Both formal and informal network conditions operate in any system of innovation. Institutions such as universities and national laboratories constitute the knowledge or 'technological infrastructure' of places (Feldman and Florida in Malmberg 1996: 396). The cumulative impact of relationships between these institutions and industry on local economic development depends on a number of context-dependent factors. These include their position within the national innovation system and their autonomy to develop their own strategies.

In the case of universities, on the one hand the new institutional stance (Feller 1990) can stimulate or induce regional economic development in an indirect way by increasing the region's capacity for technological development (Luger and Goldstein 1991: 8). On the other, nationally determined factors such as funding and accountability and their place within the national innovation system affect the relationship with the local economy. In the United Kingdom, universities are nationally funded, but other countries, such as the United States, operate dual systems of both state and private universities.

A general tendency in advanced industrialized countries since the 1980s has been to cast universities as an instrument of national R&D policy, assigning them a central role in generating knowledge and transferring it successfully to the domestic sphere of industrial application (David, Mowery and Steinmeuller 1994). This process has accelerated as a result of the cutbacks in funding imposed since the mid-1970s in the United Kingdom and elsewhere, and of accountability in the form of 'user relevance'. The United Kingdom has one of the lowest levels of public funding for university research of OECD countries. Since the 1980s there has been a considerable growth in the funds from industry, charities and overseas sources, while government funding has decreased. The government share stood at 81 per cent in 1981 and 73 per cent in 1990 (Save British Science 1994). As a consequence of general cuts in funding, and particularly cuts in research funding, it was recognized that universities would be expected to diversify their resources and reduce their dependence on the state (Committee of Vice-Chancellors and Principals 1986). A further change in the university system came about in 1992 when most of the polytechnics became universities. With that change of status came a greater emphasis on research as the new compete with older universities. As polytechnics have traditionally been more embedded in their local regions, the upgrading of their research means that there are potentially more resources for industry in the region.

The contribution of universities to local development is assumed. The assumption is based on evidence that agglomeration of high-tech industry often takes place near universities. This suggests that knowledge is not so easily transferable and that there are specific services (such as libraries, databases, consultants, etc.) which enjoy locational advantages even though geographical proximity is not a *sine qua non* condition (Varoldo 1991 in Bonaccorsi and Piccaluga 1994: 241). However, the ways in which their influence on flows of technology and information operate are both institution and context dependent. In the United Kingdom there is a marked difference between Warwick University and Cambridge University. Whereas Warwick University has made a deliberate commitment to make links with industry a key element in the university's long-term development strategy, Cambridge University has operated a 'benign supportive and non-interventionist policy' (Segal Quince Wicksteed 1988: 17/22). In Germany each university and technical college in Munich has an agency responsible for technology transfer within the high-tech region of Munich as well as to all other areas (Sternberg 1996b: 12). In Göteborg in Sweden, spin-offs from academia are the most important means of technology transfer. Up to 1995 the universities in the Göteborg region had given birth to approximately 350 university spin-offs (Lindholm 1997).

National laboratories are also affected by a restructuring process by which publicly funded research institutions have become more geared to the needs of industry (Branscomb 1993; Charles and Howells 1992). Variation in roles introduces different sets of accountability and results in particular kinds of information conditions and flows. For example, the French Atomic Energy (CEA) laboratory Laboratoire d'Électronique, de Technologie et d'Instrumentation (LETI) has very different kinds of relationships with industry nationally and within the Grenoble region as compared with those of the UK atomic energy laboratory at Harwell in Oxfordshire with its regional hinterland and national economy (Lawton Smith 1995). The former is much more integrated into its regional economy.

In sum, the types of activities within regions, combined with the kinds of institutions within regions, produce region-specific information supply and demand conditions. A third factor which affects how local innovation systems operate is the quality of the regional 'milieu', or the extent to which a region provides external economies that support technology-based entrepreneurial activity and technology transfer (Luger and Goldstein 1991: 7–8).

Knowledge transfer systems

The relationship between national and regional systems of innovation, and the effectiveness of local knowledge transfer systems, depends on the relative distribution and power of intervention. The national innovation system comprises the set of institutional actors that together play the major role in influencing innovative performance (Nelson and Rosenberg 1993: 4). It includes the allocation of resources to science and engineering activities, both in the public sector (universities and government research establishments, etc.) and in the private sector, as well as the mechanisms available to encourage the generation and transfer of technology. Although the nation-state provides the overall organizing framework, local institutional actors, operating in conjunction with nationally determined strategies, comprise the framework of innovation systems operating at local levels.

The term 'institutional thickness' has been used by Amin and Thrift (1995: 106) to refer to the combining of state and other agencies to produce the capacity of places to act to develop, consolidate and transmit structures of representation, interaction and innovation. Peck (1994: 166) argues that even in the centrally designed and nationally imposed policy programmes of the UK's previous Conservative government, very different effects can be seen in different places and thus play a part in the formation of distinctive regional 'regulatory milieux'. However, there are limits to the organizing power of regulation at the regional level compared to both national policies (Hilpert 1991: 21) and international forces (Lipietz 1992), and because of the limits to resources. In England there are no elected and accountable regional governments equivalent to the German *Länder* or the states of America. County councils are the closest equivalent, and for many of them the resources that are allocated for economic development are small.

The Oxfordshire case

The Oxfordshire region

Oxfordshire's economy has undergone a considerable transformation since the 1960s. From being both a rural county and a centre of car manufacturing it is now one of the United Kingdom's and Europe's most important centres of R&D. It has a high concentration of national laboratories and high-tech firms, and a historic university dating back to the thirteenth century. Oxford City also has the locational attractiveness associated with the picturesque landscape of the nearby Cotswolds. Oxford's favourable locational position based on its technical and cultural assets has been enhanced with the construction of the M25 motorway and the M40 extension. The county is now on major transport routes north and south, and has easy access to Heathrow Airport.

Oxfordshire comprises one of the areas within the 'Western Crescent' (Breheny and McQuaid 1987), a band of high-tech industry running from East Anglia to Hampshire. It specializes in instrumentation, biosciences and motor racing. The number of high-tech firms has grown rapidly in recent years, although the number of firms and of employees depends on the definition used. In October 1995 there were 512 firms employing over 25,500 in Oxfordshire County Council's database, using the 1987 Butchart definition of high-tech. However, this included establishments such as British Telecom offices and dental laboratories, which would not generally be classified as high-tech. An earlier study (Jordan 1995) using NOMIS data selected on Butchart's criteria found employment of 16,000 in 1981 and 16,700 in 1991. As the NOMIS figure for total UK employment in high technology for 1991 was 1,159,200, Oxfordshire's overall contribution accounts for only 1.4 per cent of the UK employment total. On a more restricted definition from an earlier study (Lawton Smith 1990) using a firm-by-firm criterion that establishments undertake R&D, there were some 192 firms and national laboratories employing 15,000. A recent study, described below, using the same definition found 190 firms employing around 17,000. Most are small manufacturing firms, reflecting the county's generally high level of manufacturing employment. However, the county does not have major manufacturing operations of high-tech multinationals in receipt of large amounts of government contracts, which are a key element in the success of Silicon Valley (Saxenian 1991).

The Oxford Instruments Group, which makes a range of medical and industrial instruments, has been the major success story and has been an important contributor to the development of the UK cryogenics industry. In 1994 Oxford Instruments, plus its diagnostic imaging joint venture with Siemens Oxford Magnet Technology, which makes whole-body scanners, employed a total of 1800 (1350 in the UK and 450 overseas). The biotech sector consists of 40 firms employing 2189 people (Mihell 1996); and the motor-racing industry consists of six companies collectively employing 1300 directly and about a further 3000 jobs in smaller firms and indirectly (Willis, Kingham and Stafford 1996).

The trajectory of the county's high-tech sector has been associated with the impact of land-use planning, the lack of engagement of Oxford University and the national laboratories with the local economy, and the unique contribution played by local voluntary organizations. Key dates are listed in Table 6.1.

The knowledge base

In some respects Oxfordshire conforms to Steed and De Genova's fourth category of large government expenditures and Markusen's fifth (state-anchored industrial districts). The county's science and technology knowledge base comprises public investment in the form of four universities, nine hospitals of which seven have university research departments, some ten national/privatizing laboratories, including the Rutherford Appleton Laboratory, and two atomic energy establishments. The county's workforce accounts for a quarter of all R&D workers in the South East. This represents the largest number of people employed in R&D outside London (Jordan 1995). This disproportionate share of workers in innovation is a feature of Markusen's Italianate variant of industrial districts.

Oxford University is comparable only to Cambridge in stature in basic research. It is the second largest university in the United Kingdom after London, with a combined undergraduate and graduate population in October 1995 of nearly 15,000. It receives considerable research income from industry and research councils. Overseas industry funding is dominated by US companies. Income from industry, from both the United Kingdom and overseas, totalled £11.2 million in 1994–5. This was biased towards medical research. The university has 53 units undertaking medical research.

Oxford Brookes University has a much smaller research base than Oxford University. It lacks a strong research culture, except in departments such as Architecture and Town Planning, and in areas of expertise such as joining technology. The national laboratories' 'big science' specializations include nuclear fusion (the Joint European Torus (JET) at Culham) and fission (Harwell), and space (Rutherford Appleton Laboratory).

Table 6.1 Summary of developments in Oxfordshire

At Oxford University	In national laboratories	In the county
	Harwell Laboratory (Atomic Energy: fission) 1946	
	MRC Radiobiology Unit 1947	
	Hydraulics Research Station 1947 (privatized 1982)	
First recorded firm formed by Oxford University academic, Littlemore Instruments, Dr Edward Hall Archaeology Laboratory 1954	Rutherford Appleton Laboratory (research and university research support) 1957	
Oxford Instruments 1959		
University and Industry Committee formed 1968	Culham Laboratory (nuclear fusion) 1961	First structure plan for Oxfordshire 1976
Solid State Logic 1969	Institute of Hydrology 1962	
Research Machines 1973	National Radiological Protection Board 1970	
Oxford Lasers 1977	Institute of Virology 1970	
	Joint European Torus 1978	
Committee on Patents 1980		The Oxford Trust founded 1985
University and Industry Committee disbanded 1986		Modifications to the structure plan to allow science park and location of science-based industries in central Oxfordshire 1987
ISIS Innovation formed 1988		
Oxford GlycoSystems, 1988		
First full-time university industrial liaison officer appointed 1989		
Oxford Molecular 1989		
Oxford Science Park established by Magdalen College 1991	Ending of AEA apprenticeship scheme 1994	M40 extension opened 16 January 1991
Oxford Polytechnic became Oxford Brookes University 1992	AEAT privatized 1996	Oxford Innovation Forum founded 1992
Oxford Molecular floated on stock market 1994		Oxfordshire Investment Opportunity Network 1994
Review of Technology Transfer Arrangements Report 1995		Oxfordshire County Council became member of Thames Valley Economic Partnership 1995
Appointment of biotech specialist to ISIS Innovation 1995		Oxfordshire Business Link March 1996
University statute 'asserts' rights to intellectual property 1996		Oxfordshire BiotechNet established 1997

Knowledge transfer

A prime example of a 'local difficulty' is that Oxford University has not had a strategy for participating in the development of high-tech industry in Oxfordshire. It has not encouraged local access to its research from outside nor its academics to form their own firms. The three major reasons why this has been the case lie in the organizational structure, decisions made within the university on the terms of trade under which its academics engage in technology transfer, and in the position the university has within the national science base.

The first major factor is that Oxford University has not had efficient formal structures to liaise with industry and has never had a single entry point for firms. Until the late 1980s the Research Support Office (RSO) was headed by a part-time rather than a full-time industrial liaison officer. The office has functioned as a research contracts office rather than an industrial liaison service (Lawton Smith 1991: 408).

The second is the position of the university on academic entrepreneurship. Freedom of exploitation of research was given by the recommendations of the Committee on Patents under chairmanship of the Warden of All Souls in 1980. This led the university to waive its intellectual property rights to patentable work by academics that was funded by the university, but not that funded by industry. This allowed academics to form companies. However, academics in some departments, particularly in the medical school and in the engineering sciences department, were discouraged from establishing firms as a means of capitalizing on their research. In spite of this, by the mid-1980s some 35 companies had their origins in its departments, with some 20 others founded by former students. More than half of the founders of the former (19) retained their academic posts (Lawton Smith 1990).

In the late 1980s the university itself became somewhat more entrepreneurial but the emphasis remained on trading of intellectual property (IP) rather than on the active encouragement of academic entrepreneurship. ISIS Innovation was established in 1988 as a wholly owned company of the University of Oxford in order to manage the exploitation of downstream IP dealings with patents and licences, and later to run the Oxford Innovation Society. This was formed so that members (mainly multinational companies) could have a window on Oxford technology. By 1996 ISIS had managed three spin-out firms. The most successful was the Oxford Molecular Group, formed in 1989 and floated on the stock market in 1994. In April 1997 the value of Oxford University's share was estimated to be nearly £16 million. The university also owns a 10 per cent share of Oxford Asymmetry, founded in 1991, which makes chemical compounds that pharmaceutical companies need in order to develop new drugs. The university's stake was expected to be worth at least £5 million when the firm floated on the stock market in 1998. It owns an 8 per cent share in Oxford Biosciences and a 16 per cent share in Oxford Biomedica (*Observer*, 27 April 1997). The importance of exploiting medical research is indicated by the appointment of a biotechnology specialist to ISIS Innovation in 1995.

In the mid-1990s the university's position was that it was losing out on the gains from scientific expertise enjoyed by its academics who founded their own firms. The university therefore set up the 'Review of Technology Transfer Arrangements' in

1994. The report was published in 1995. Rather late in the day, the university had recognized that it was not providing the right kind of support for entrepreneurial academics. The review acknowledged that some academics had formed their own companies privately, independently of the university system. The response of the committee was that the best way to discourage private individuals from doing that would be to show that such individuals would have fared better by using the university's assistance. The report was critical of university practice, and argued that coordination and communication were needed to improve efficient exploitation of research. In July 1995 the university enacted a policy of owning intellectual property generated by its staff and students. The university now has the obligation and responsibility to ensure that arrangements for exploitation of the IPR are efficient and easy to use.

The third major factor is that Oxford's charter is different from that of other universities, except Cambridge. It is expected by the Department of Trade and Industry (DTI) to be both a national and an international resource for industry and not to be involved in local economic development (Director, RSO, personal communication, June 1996). Hence interaction has tended to be with larger, multinational firms.

Oxford Brookes's traditional role as a teaching rather than a research institution meant that in the mid-1980s there was limited interaction with high-tech industry in Oxfordshire and a much smaller number of high-tech entrepreneurs (ten) than Oxford University. In the 1990s the university does not have a well-developed infrastructure for transferring technology. The main liaison unit is a contracts office. Individual academics arrange their own links. However, in the motor racing sector there is the clearest, and perhaps only, evidence of 'institutional thickness': Oxford Brookes has set up an engineering degree sponsored by Reynard and TWR, and others.

The institutional framework within which Oxfordshire's 'big science' national laboratories operate has been a determining factor in the low level of engagement in the development of high-tech industry in the county. The combination of the nature of the research, of the rules governing conditions of employment which inhibited entrepreneurship, and of the 'risk-averse' culture has meant that very few firms have been formed by research scientists. By the mid-1980s only eight advanced-technology firms had been formed by staff from any of the laboratories (Lawton Smith 1990), and only two others formed by ex-employees were mentioned during the recent data-gathering exercise. The most important contribution to advanced-technology industry has been the supply of skilled craftsmen. In the 1960s through to the 1980s, the apprenticeship schemes run by the atomic energy laboratories were an important source of engineering skills for the advanced-technology firms, especially Oxford Instruments. The change in the function and type of research in the United Kingdom Atomic Energy Authority (UKAEA) brought this to an end, and the apprenticeship scheme closed in 1994.

However, in the past decade the national laboratories have become much more commercially oriented, and some have been privatized. For example, on 31 March 1996 AEA Technology PLC was legally separated from the Atomic Energy Authority, whose shares are all owned by the government. Its activities are now fully commercial and include consultancy, contract R&D and technical services. Its constituent businesses compete with both industry and universities. Commercialization has also included more extensive use of the site. In December 1996 the UKAEA created a science park on the Harwell site (*Oxford Times*, 20 December 1996).

Regional development strategies and the local infrastructure

The Structure Plan for the South East (which determines land use) and county, city and district council policies restrict the kinds of industrial activity in Oxfordshire. Planning strategy was and is to protect the environment, character and agricultural resources of the county by restraining the overall level of development, and to promote the 'country towns of Banbury, Bicester, Didcot and Witney' as preferred locations for new development, while limiting development in the rest of the county (Structure Plan for Oxfordshire, Written Statement, May 1987). Although the overall strategy is to contribute to the diversity of the local economy, high-tech industry is central to Oxfordshire's economic development. County council policy is 'To encourage the development of a high wage, high skill, high value added economy which enhances and protects the quality of life of the residents of Oxfordshire and enable them to fulfil their potential' (Oxfordshire County Council 1997: 2). The tendency is to support inward investment of R&D-intensive firms, such as research laboratories, rather than manufacturing firms and warehousing. The exception is Cherwell District Council, which, as partner in the Cherwell–M40 Investment partnership, encourages manufacturing firms to locate in towns such as Bicester and Banbury.

However, Oxfordshire's economic development strategy is arguably under-resourced. The county has one of the smallest innovation support teams in the country. The lack of resources for the economic development team arises from two historical factors:

1. In the recent past, the council was controlled by the Conservative Party, whose philosophy was to spend as little as possible. Therefore resources allocated to all parts of the county's budget were low. Oxfordshire is almost the lowest spender of any local authority in the United Kingdom. This is because of the previous government's policy of capping local government expenditure. Grant allocations are historically based and Oxfordshire has been a low spender.
2. The county has been traditionally rural. There is a tradition among political classes in the broadest sense that Oxfordshire does not need the sort of resources which might be required in other parts of the country (Oxfordshire Economic Policy Adviser, personal communication 1996).

As part of the strategy to increase economies of scale in delivery of support, on 1 April 1996 Oxfordshire County Council became a member of the Thames Valley Economic Partnership, which covers Berkshire, Buckinghamshire and Oxfordshire. This includes the Training and Enterprise Councils (TECs) and chambers of commerce.

Planning policy concerning the green belt delayed the establishment of that symbol of high-tech industry, a science park. It was not until 1991 that Magdalen College, one of the colleges of Oxford University, in a joint venture with the Prudential Assurance Company, created the Oxford Science Park on a 75-acre (30-ha) site at the south-east edge of the city in 1991. This was two decades later than the formation of the Cambridge Science Park.

In May 1987 modifications to the Structure Plan for Oxfordshire proposed and subsequently agreed by the Secretary of State included a statement which could be read as an indication that there was scope for the positive identification of one or more sites as science parks. Policy E4 stated that:

> In Central Oxfordshire, provision will be made and proposals will normally be per-mitted for science based industries concerned primarily with research and development which can show a special need to be located close to Oxford University or to other research facilities in central Oxfordshire.

The first tenant was the European Research Laboratory of the Japanese electronics firm Sharp. By August 1995 there were 35 tenants on the site.

In the vacuum created by weak local and central government coordinating structures, a business elite stepped in to provide innovation support activities. This group includes Sir Martin Wood; the Director of the Oxford Trust, Paul Bradstock; the Director of Sharp European Laboratory, Dr Clive Bradley; and the County Economic Development Adviser, Martin Stott. The leading member of the elite is Sir Martin Wood. His is a unique contribution to the institutional framework of a local area. In 1985 he established the Oxford Trust, a charitable trust whose aim is to encourage science and technology enterprise in Oxfordshire. The Trust has adopted an active role in generating links between firms and institutions within the county. Local innovation support mechanisms are predicated on the belief that there are barriers to interaction between local firms and between firms and research institu-tions, and that these can be overcome by measures targeted to meet particular needs. The Oxford Trust is involved in most local initiatives.

The Trust manages the Oxford Centre for Innovation, which has units for new high-tech firms. It has played a key role in providing help and advice to firms applying for SMART awards, and has also established the Oxford Investment Opportunity Network. This works by companies outlining their plans to an audience of private investors. Six successful matches have been made (*Scintilla*, May 1996: 5). It coordinates the Oxfordshire Innovation Forum and Oxfordshire BiotechNet. The Innovation Forum was set up in 1992 to integrate the powerful interests in the county (universities, business, TECs, etc.) involved in high-tech industry and improve the support infrastructure for innovation. However, it was generally not seen to be effective. It did not represent all high-tech sectors (for example, the hospitals or the biotech/pharmaceuticals sector), and did not have proper representation from some of the other higher education institutes, such as the Royal Military College of Science (RMCS) at Shrivenham. It has now ceased to exist.

The aim of Oxfordshire BiotechNet, which is a DTI initiative, is to double the rate of growth in the biotechnology sector by making it easier for scientists to exploit their ideas (*Scintilla*, February 1997). The objective is to understand the key challenges in the development process of the local biotechnology firms and uncover the means by which these challenges have been met.

The study

The aim in this section is to analyse the relationship between the information conditions identified above and local difficulties. It uses evidence from a recently completed comparative study of Oxford and Cambridge in which a sample of 51 innovating firms in the Oxford and 50 in the Cambridge regions were interviewed between October 1995 and May 1996. (This was the ESRC Centre for Business Research study 'Territorial Development and Innovative Milieux' carried out by David Keeble, Barry Moore, Frank Wilkinson, Clive Lawson and Helen Lawton Smith.) The samples were stratified to reflect the composition of the population. The greater number of high-tech manufacturing firms than service firms in the country is reflected in the split being 28 : 23. Topics covered by the questionnaire included the locational advantages and disadvantages of the two places, and the extent and scope of local and non-local innovation and production linkages.

Technical linkages

The survey showed that there is a strong local clustering of linkages and that the level of interactions with all local institutions has increased over the past decade. Three-quarters of the sample had links with universities and/or government laboratories in general, and half had links with local universities or government laboratories. The majority of firms in the sample are also linked into geographically extensive innovation and production systems (Keeble *et al.* 1996). The level of local interaction is the same as that in Cambridge but surprisingly similar to that found by Foley and Watts (1996) in the mature industrial region of Sheffield. However, there were marked differences in the level of links with different institutions. Table 6.2 shows that 43 per cent had some form of technical linkage with Oxford University, 27 per cent with the national laboratories but only 12 per cent with Oxford Brookes.

The research also showed sectoral differences in interaction. Most of the R&D-based firms had links, but motor racing, plastics, coatings, electrical and electronics firms had no links with any local institutions. The highest percentages of links with Oxford University were the bioscience firms (80 per cent) and R&D-based firms (67 per cent) such as industrial research laboratories. The results should be treated with some caution. The table understates the extent of the medical cluster as some twelve firms' products and services were related to medicine (bioscience firms, medical products manufacturers). The R&D-based firms had the highest level of links with national laboratories.

Links with Oxford University have increased significantly over the past ten years from a time when only 43 firms (26 per cent) from a sample of 164 firms had such links. The founder's academic background was the most important factor in the incidence of links: 57 per cent of establishments formed by graduates of Oxford University used universities as a source of technical links, most of which were with Oxford University (Lawton Smith 1990). Since then, more firms have spun out of the university, particularly in the biosciences sector, but generally not through ISIS innovation. Several firms indicated that they would like to make contact with academics but either had tried and failed, or did not know how to make contact. One such firm was a Formula One racing team.

Table 6.2 Link with local firm or public-sector institution

	No. of firms	Oxford University link	National labs	Oxford Brookes
Software	8	3	2	0
Racing cars	2	0	0	0
Instruments	18	9	7	3
Audio equipment	1	0	0	1
R&D	6	4	4	1
Coatings	1	0	0	0
Electrical	1	0	0	0
Plastics	1	0	0	0
Electronics	2	0	0	0
Biosciences	5	4	0	0
Microscope	1	1	0	0
Medical products	4	1	0	1
Nuclear waste	1	0	1	0
Totals	51	22 (43%)	14 (27%)	6 (12%)

Source: CBR Survey

Linkages with Oxford Brookes University have risen over the ten years to 12 per cent but from a low base of only 3 per cent with technical links with Oxford Polytechnic, the university's previous incarnation. Of the ones in the recent study with links, over half were instrument manufacturers. However, events can move quite quickly and research links, as has already been highlighted, are not the only measure of the impact of universities on local economic development. For example, two of the motor racing firms in the sample subsequently became involved in setting up the degree course at Oxford Brookes, and two recruited graduates from that university.

Linkages between firms and national laboratories were in evidence in the 1980s. Then some 27 firms (16 per cent) of survey firms had research interactions, the majority of them, as in the 1990s, being R&D-based firms (Lawton Smith 1990). In 1996 14 firms (27 per cent) had links with the county's national laboratories. R&D-based firms had the highest percentage (4 firms, 66 per cent), followed by instrumentation firms (7 firms, 39 per cent) and software firms (2 firms, 25 per cent).

Table 6.3 indicates the diverse nature of the range of formal links both with the local universities and government laboratories and with 'others', i.e. such bodies elsewhere in the United Kingdom and overseas. These include academics on boards of companies, technology transfer through patents and licensing, and training programmes. All forms were used by at least a tenth of the sample, except for local research consortia or clubs, including participation in European Commission programmes. The most frequent interaction was in the form of collaborative projects. This was the highest for both local and 'other', but with 'other' outscoring local linkages (about a half compared to a third of firms). This was closely followed by university staff acting as consultants, and there was no difference in percentage for local and 'other' (about a third of firms).

Table 6.3 Forms of interaction between Oxfordshire firms and local universities, and with other universities

	Oxford number (% of sample)	'Other' number (% of sample)
Academics on board	11	5
	(22)	(10)
Collaborative projects with	16	24
universities	(32)	(48)
Collaborative projects with	12	13
government research laboratories	(24)	(26)
Part-time secondment by	9	11
academics	(18)	(22)
Research consortia or clubs	4	12
	(8)	(24)
University staff acting as	15	15
consultants	(30)	(30)
Licensing or patenting university	10	9
inventions	(20)	(18)
Training programmes run by the	6	6
university	(12)	(12)
Other	6	7
	(12)	(14)
Total	29	29
	(58)	(58)

Similar proportions (about a quarter) had collaborative projects with local and non-local government laboratories. Over a fifth of firms had academics in local universities on the boards of companies, compared to a tenth with academics from outside the county.

The evidence shows that links are highly valued by the Oxford firms. Nearly half said that the benefits were either important or very important to their success (Table 6.4). Two-thirds reported that links were at least of significant importance. This might mean that there is a perceptual difference in the value of interaction if it involves formal procedures rather than occurring as a result of personal relationships based on trust and reciprocity.

As an attempt to gauge the organizing power of proximity in overcoming barriers to interaction by familiarity and ease of communication, firms were asked about the kinds of difficulties faced with working with Oxford University. Table 6.5 shows that over a third reported some problems. Closer questioning revealed that these reflected a general tendency consisting of differences in time scales and priorities which have been found in other studies (e.g. Charles and Howells 1992; Lawton Smith 1993) and which are not confined to this institution. Only five firms had problems associated with IPR arrangements.

Inter-firm links

There is some evidence of local inter-firm interaction. Just under half (23, 46 per cent) had close links with other firms in the Oxford region. More manufacturing firms (14, 28 per cent) than high-technology services (9, 39 per cent of service firms)

Table 6.4 Importance of benefits to firms' success of links between Oxfordshire firms and Oxfordshire universities

Importance of links	Number (%)[a]
Not at all important	1 (2)
Of slight importance	2 (4)
Of significant importance	10 (20)
Very important	11 (22)
Extremely important	11 (22)
Total	35 (70)

Source: CBR Survey

[a] As a percentage of all firms with university links

Table 6.5 Problems with interaction with Oxford University in the Oxfordshire sample

	Number (%)
General problems in dealing with Oxford University	14[a] (37)
Intellectual property rights problems	5 (13)

Source: CBR Survey

[a] As a percentage of all firms with university links

had close inter-firm links. The majority of these were instrumentation manufacturers, which comprised 35 per cent of the sample. Inter-firm links based on subcontracting were the most frequent and most important. Firms were also asked to assess the importance of their links with other firms on a scale ranging from 1 to 5, where 1 equals completely unimportant and 5 equals important. Table 6.6 shows the frequency of firms ranking their links with a score of 4 or 5 for each type of link (Lawson *et al.* 1997).

The overwhelming majority of high-technology firms (87 per cent) with close links with other local firms regarded such links as important or very important. Links with local suppliers and subcontractors were cited most frequently as important. Firms providing services, research collaborators and customers were equally second most important.

Conclusions

The chapter set out to investigate the relationships between the information conditions and 'local difficulties in Oxfordshire'. The evidence suggests that Oxfordshire has some features of Markusen's Marshallian industrial districts. It has a high-tech business structure dominated by small firms, with some of the more interactive features of the Italianate variant. It also has a disproportionate share of workers engaged in innovation. It also, like Ottawa, is a composite of all four types of Steed and De Genova's model. It has characteristics of a research-oriented complex, and

Table 6.6 Importance of inter-firm linkages in Oxfordshire

Type of link	Number (%)[a]
Customers	9 (39)
Suppliers/contractors	13 (57)
Firms providing services	9 (39)
Research collaborators	9 (39)
Firms in line of business	3 (13)
Others	0 (0)
Total	20 (87)

[a] Ranking 4 or 5 of all firms with links in Oxfordshire

the third stage involving the addition of private research labs, and to a lesser extent manufacturing facilities. The level of local interaction was of a similar level between firms and with universities and national laboratories (50 per cent compared to 43 per cent). Firms which had links with other firms tended to be manufacturing firms. The long-established instrumentation sector, much of which can be traced back to Oxford University through Martin Wood as the prime agent, has well-established links. Bioscience and R&D-based firms had higher proportions of links than other sectors. The recently established and rapidly growing biosciences sector, which largely comprises small firms, is primarily linked into Oxford University. Firms providing services, including software houses, and some sectors such as motor racing, were far less embedded into a local innovation system. The first conclusion is that a local difficulty is created by the nature of the demand for information, owing to the type of region, as indicated by low levels of interaction and information flows in some sectors.

In Oxfordshire the regimes imposed directly by institutions and by the national government limit information flows. However, more firms had links with Oxford University than with the national laboratories or with Oxford Brookes University. The extent of interaction of Oxford University with local industry is a function of the particular institutional strategy and of its role as a national resource. Local difficulties in technology transfer are shown to exist by Oxford University's own internal review, which identified failure to respond to the signals from its own academics who wished to ensure that their intellectual property became available through commercial channels. Its position within the national innovation system 'crowds out' a local role as its interests are generally not those of economic development. However, this is not the whole story. The information conditions are that access is high in technological specialisms such as bioscience where the state (in universities, medical research council), industry and medical charities have all invested heavily in research. Information flows too have been encouraged through the exploitation of Oxford University's own research, for example through entrepreneurship and firm formation, and the location of firms such as Yamanouchi and British Biotech in the city of Oxford attracted by access made easier by proximity.

The historic lack of embeddedness of the government laboratories in the local industrial structure and associated lack of engagement in local technology transfer is related to regulation at the national level. For the UKAEA laboratories, for example, for universities and other parts of the nuclear industry, and for the Rutherford Appleton Laboratory, contact is primarily with UK universities in general and with the international research community. Informal access by local small business was limited in the days of 'big science', and now links are determined by commercial criteria. There is an indication of increasing interaction, and with different types of firms associated with refocusing of activity, including cooperation at the local level. However, it remains to be seen whether commercialization is the most effective route to encouraging informal interaction.

Markusen assumes strong local government in her Italianate variant of industrial districts. In the UK context that is not appropriate because of the centralized state, and is particularly not the case in Oxfordshire, which historically has a low level of local government resources. Instead, where difficulties have been identified, an elite has sought to encourage local economic development by the use of collective power. The members of the elite have done so by identifying their own interests with those of other organizations. While institutional mechanisms described have been designed to facilitate innovators' access to relevant stocks of knowledge in Oxford- shire – that is, to overcome local difficulties identified as a lack of interaction – the elite have adopted strategies which encourage sector-specific interaction. There is clearly scope for examining the possibility of looking at other sectors, such as software, and at intra-sector interaction. More work needs to be undertaken on evaluating the impact of these and equivalent organizations in other areas. Import- ant questions relate to the degree to which the activities of elites as described here work at the margin or form more significant representational and organizing functions, and whether more resources would improve the quality of the service provided.

Regional innovation systems, or even more local, industrial districts, are shown to have specific information conditions of inclusion, where tacit knowledge is ex- changed through informal interaction, and exclusion, where much of the informa- tion is codified and access is restricted to formal interaction. Demand and supply conditions necessarily vary by region. Moreover, information conditions change over time, and not necessarily because of evolutionary factors. The Oxfordshire case illustrates how local empowerment can create possibilities of invention to over- come local difficulties, and enhance the likelihood of increased localization of the geographic scope of spillovers between knowledge creation and production (see Anselin, Varga and Acs 1997b).

CHAPTER SEVEN

University–Industry Relationships in Germany and Their Regional Consequences

Rolf Sternberg

Introduction

Since the days of the 'economic miracle' in the 1960s, Germany has enjoyed high international acclaim for its economic as well as its technological achievements. This has only changed in recent history in connection with debates about the competitive position of Germany. For more than three decades the technological competitiveness of Germany was based on the outstanding research and educational infrastructure (for example, leading scientific and technical universities or Max Planck institutes), and, in addition, on world-renowned innovative firms (like Siemens and many automobile and chemical companies) and their educational programmes (career-oriented and continuing education). In particular, the company-run educational system in Germany was competitively untouchable for a long time. In the end the medium-sized businesses played a special role in the rise of Germany to the rank of a leading economic and export power – solely and in cooperation with large concerns.

Many non-German scholars of geography have been especially interested in the last aspect – the innovative networks between large and small firms – in connection with the regional implications of technological advance during the past several years. The State of Baden-Württemberg (or parts thereof) is considered abroad to be a prime example of a German industrial district in accordance with Marshall's concept and the typical features of this regional type (importance of intra-regional networks between similar businesses or tightly woven branches, dominance of small and medium-sized enterprises (SMEs), and strong influence of local or regional politics on business innovation behaviour, intensive knowledge transfer between universities or technical colleges and firms; Sabel *et al.* 1987). In spite of numerous studies, few empirically based findings exist verifying a typical industrial district in Baden-Württemberg. Additionally, there are very few analyses checking whether characteristics of an industrial district exist in other German regions and have led to similar economic success.

The central hypothesis of this chapter is that the national innovation system in Germany is in fact influenced by several regional innovation systems which are quite different in nature, and which subdivide a supposedly homogeneous country into many subsystems of innovation – each having specific impacts on regional economic development, but, at the same time, each being influenced by the national innovation system itself. It is not possible to completely describe and explain the whole spectrum of regional innovation systems in Germany. Therefore, three types of regions are analysed with the help of one representative region for each. The emphasis of the empirical analysis is on innovative linkages between the two most important actors within a regional innovation system; that is, firms and universities.

The general relationship between industry and universities in the German innovation system

The German innovation system in the 1990s is characterized by both relative strengths and weaknesses when compared to its competitors in the United States, Japan and Western Europe (see BMBF 1997, 1998; Keck 1993; Boschma 1997; Tylecote 1996). Comparative advantages can be found:

- in strong engineering and natural science departments at universities, as well in some technical colleges and some semi-public research institutes like the Max Planck institutes or Fraunhofer institutes (however, this advantage has been reduced in the recent past);
- in very good career-oriented and continuing education systems (which also have lost importance quantitatively in recent years); and
- in the high educational level of the workforce.

Technology, innovation and education policies are the responsibility of various political departments and are carried out at different political levels (federal, state and sometimes municipal or local); for a long time this was viewed as advantageous as compared with the centrally administered policies of other nations (for a debate over mission-oriented technology policies versus diffusion-oriented technology policies, see Ergas 1987).

Comparative disadvantages cannot be overlooked in the following fields:

- weaknesses in the speedy conversion of technological inventions into new and innovative products – the process of technology transfer;
- a deficit of technology-intensive business start-ups, which can be traced back to particular weaknesses in entrepreneurship (the appropriate incubator facilities, such as large firms and universities, fail to promote start-ups).

It is rather controversial whether the relatively balanced regional structure of the German research and innovation landscape represents an advantage or disadvantage, when compared internationally. In particular, France, with its spatially concentrated research and innovation capacities, as well as Japan, and to a lesser extent the United States (especially the East and West Coasts) and Great Britain (the South East), differ significantly from Germany in this respect (for an international comparison of the leading industrial countries, see Sternberg 1995b, 1996a).

Compared with those of other countries, German firms are characterized by (Tylecote 1996: 47):

- high sector orientation (publicly protected unions, for example);
- limited filière tradition with strong local or regional collaboration in technological matters, but beyond that, strong bonds do not tend to extend beyond broad sectors; and
- innovative linkages with neighbouring universities, which are favoured as useful complements rather than substitutes for in house research; however, international technological collaboration is treated with great reservation.

Main actors governing the innovation process

Private firms and public research institutions are the main actors in the German innovation system. In 1993 there were about 11,500 private firms which performed research; 9200 of them were located in western Germany. The business sector is the dominant actor within the German innovation system. It is responsible for 61 per cent of national R&D financing (DM 50 billion in 1994) and for 66 per cent of R&D performance. Similar results can be found in the other G7 countries. So far as employment is concerned, private companies were responsible for almost 294,000 people (full-time equivalents) in 1993 (the estimate for 1994 is almost 321,000), which means that 62 per cent of national R&D employment arose from private firms. This is a relatively high rate compared to most of the other G7 countries with the exception of Japan. Approximately 90 per cent of the research-active private firms belong to the SME sector with less than 500 employees. However, with respect to R&D expenditure the relevance of large firms is obvious: almost 86 per cent of R&D expenditure from private firms came from large firms with more than 500 employees in 1994. However, the SME share has increased during recent years, in terms both of R&D employment and of R&D expenditure. The simple reason is that the internal R&D expenditures of SME grew by 7 per cent between 1991 and 1994, whereas large firms decreased their R&D expenditures, at least in relative terms. A similar trend can be observed in employment: whereas R&D employment in all private firms decreased by 8.7 per cent between 1991 and 1993, and by 3.2 per cent between 1993 and 1994, the corresponding figures for SMEs are 4.6 per cent and 0.5 per cent respectively (BMBF 1998).

In order to get an adequate impression of Germany's public research potential, it is helpful to distinguish between five types of institutional groups. In 1996 there were 335 public universities (*Hochschulen*), including 222 technical colleges (*Fachhochschulen*), whose main task is to educate and to research. In general, research, as well as education, is more oriented towards theory and basic research at universities, whereas technical colleges focus on practical education and applied research. Figure 7.1 shows the location of Germany's universities and technical colleges.

The Helmholtz Association is the new name (since 1995) for the Arbeitsgemeinschaft deutscher Großforschungseinrichtungen, which links sixteen large research institutes with the equivalent of 21,600 full-time employees (1997). They are co-financed by the federal government (90 per cent) and the respective state (10

Figure 7.1 Regional distribution of universities and technical colleges, 1998
Source: BMBF (1998). Cartography: Stephan Pohl, 1999

per cent) (see Figure 7.6, p. 99). Their tasks include basic research with sophisticated apparatus, collaboration in long-term national research programmes, precautionary research dealing with the treatment of central and long-term problems in environmental and health sciences, and in technology development, especially the fields of

Figure 7.2 Regional distribution of non-university, (semi)public research institutions in Germany, 1996
Source: BMBF (1998: 263, 276, 290, 299). Cartography: Stephan Pohl, 1999

environmental protection, energy supply and future high-technology sectors including space travel (Figure 7.2).

The Max Planck Society serves as a funding organization for approximately 100 research institutes with the equivalent of 11,628 full-time employees in 1998 (up from 9334 in 1993). The institutes are very different in task and size. They are co-financed by the federal government (50 per cent) and the respective state (50 per cent) (see Figure 7.6, p. 99). They carry out basic research in science and social sciences, support new research fields and cooperate with universities, for example in the provision of apparatus for academic use (Figure 7.2).

The Fraunhofer Society serves as a funding organization for 47 research institutes with the equivalent of 6720 full-time employees in 1998 (5965 in 1993). These too are quite different in task and size. The institutionally financed portion of their costs is co-financed by the federal government (90 per cent) and the respective state (10 per cent) (Figure 7.6). Their tasks include contract research for private firms and for the federal and state governments, military research and services (patent office, information centre) (see also Figure 7.2).

Finally, the so-called 'Blue List' (*Blaue Liste*) institutes should be considered. In this list, 82 institutes (1998) are included with the equivalent of approximately 10,000 full-time employees in 1998 (9334 in 1993). Once again, their tasks and sizes vary. Generally, these institutes are co-financed by the federal government (50 per cent) and the respective state (50 per cent) (Figure 7.6). The research institutes or service institutes should be of national importance and scientific interest.

Germany's technological performance and the specific role of industry and universities

In order to maintain a strong position in international competition as a location of production, Germany, like any other country, has to focus on its comparative advantages in technology and know-how. This is especially important because Germany has trailed somewhat in other areas such as finances, growth rates and administration structures. The following remarks emphasize Germany's techno-logical performance by comparing its research and development capabilities, first in the private sector and later in the public sector, with the situation in the most important competing countries. The central findings of this chapter, and most of the figures, are based on a report submitted to the Federal Ministry of Education, Science, Research and Technology, or BMBF (Bundesminister für Bildung, Wis-senschaft, Forschung und Technologie; now called the Federal Ministry of Education and Research), by four leading economic research institutes[1] (BMBF 1997) and on the federal research report by the same ministry (BMBF 1998).

R&D-intensive industries not only are the heart of production of new technolo-gies, products and processes, but also use knowledge from other industries and from public research most intensively. R&D-intensive industries have continually increased their shares in overall industrial output and employment (46 per cent and 43 per cent, respectively, in 1995). However, if one considers recent developments in employment and investment figures, the impact of globalization and international division of labour in R&D-intensive sectors cannot be ignored. The pressure to increase productivity has forced employment levels down continually since 1990, particularly during the ongoing period of weak demand. Even during the most recent phase of slight economic revival in Germany, the R&D-intensive industries have not been able to resume the role they played in the 1980s, when they were a driving force behind the economy. Instead, jobs are being shed at a rapid, previously unknown rate – for example, in mechanical engineering and the aviation industry. As far as gross capital investment in R&D-intensive industries is concerned, the figures show dramatic decreases between 1991 and 1994. This sector is clearly not achieving the growth it recorded during previous phases. However, investment activity expanded in 1995 and 1996 and even exceeded investment activity in non-R&D-intensive industries.

A generally accepted measure for a country's technological competitiveness is its position on international technology goods markets. Using the concept of revealed comparative advantage (RCA) as a measure for the degree of specialization, Germany is particularly specialized in advanced technologies, where it is the only major industrialized country to produce above-average market results even *vis-à-vis* the United States and Japan (Figure 7.3). However, it displays less strength in the area of cutting-edge technologies. In trading of R&D-intensive goods, Germany follows Japan and the United States as the third largest exporter on global markets; the three countries respectively accounted for 16.5 per cent, 20.5 per cent and 18.8 per cent of world trade in R&D-intensive goods in 1994 (Figure 7.4). In terms of trade between industrialized countries only, Germany is the second largest net exporter of advanced technologies (following Japan), with obvious strength in chemical products, machines, motor vehicles and electrical engineering. As regards cutting-edge technologies, however, the United States and Japan are, on balance, the leading technology providers in the world.

We would find very similar results if we used patent indicators like the RPA[2] (relative patent activity). There has been little change in the basic patterns in respective competition over the years. Only Japan could be considered highly specialized in the high-tech sector, more so than the United States and Germany. However, the United States enjoys substantial advantages over Japan in the cutting-edge technologies segment. Germany's domain continues to be advanced technologies with strengths in automotive engineering, mechanical engineering and chemicals – and usually on an across-the-board basis. On the other hand, Germany is not specialized in cutting-edge technologies, except in testing instruments and primary organic products. This statement is clearly confirmed if we examine the technological specialization of Germany by field of technology (Figure 7.5). Germany has comparative technological advantages (i.e. an above-average share of patents) in power engineering, inorganic and organic chemistry and, especially, in mechanical engineering and environmental engineering.

An increasingly important factor determining Germany's technological performance is the decline in industrial research. Innovation intensity – innovation expenditure relative to turnover – totalled 4.1 per cent in 1994 (compared to 5.2 per cent in 1992), while R&D intensity was approximately 2.9 per cent. Thus, budgets for innovation activities have been cut generally, particularly for investment in fixed assets connected with innovation. Measured in terms of added value, West German industry has not increased its R&D input since 1987. There have, however, been areas (e.g. office machines, automobiles, pharmaceuticals) in which 'specific' R&D intensity has increased. On the other hand, R&D intensity has fallen sharply in mechanical engineering, the aviation industry, electrical engineering and the chemical industry. The longer-term decline is related to several factors. Sectoral structural change contributed enormously towards increasing R&D during the 1980s, but has not been favourable to R&D-intensive branches since the late 1980s. The share of investment in fixed R&D assets has been shrinking for years, which is a critical sign

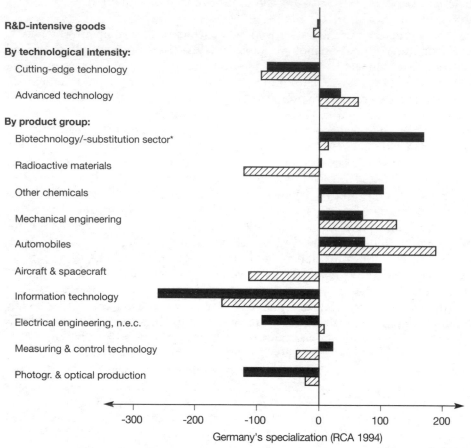

R&D-intensive goods

By technological intensity:

Cutting-edge technology

Advanced technology

By product group:

Biotechnology/-substitution sector*

Radioactive materials

Other chemicals

Mechanical engineering

Automobiles

Aircraft & spacecraft

Information technology

Electrical engineering, n.e.c.

Measuring & control technology

Photogr. & optical production

Germany's specialization (RCA 1994)

* => Includes bioengineered chemical products and traditional chemical products for which the biotechnology field could provide substitutes.
A positive value indicates that the export-import ratio is higher for this product group than for total manufactured goods.

vis-à-vis Japan   vis-à-vis USA

Figure 7.3 Germany's specialization in R&D-intensive goods *vis-à-vis* the United States and Japan (revealed comparative advantage (RCA), 1994)
Source: BMBF (1997: 66), based on OECD: *Foreign Trade by Commodities* and NIW calculations

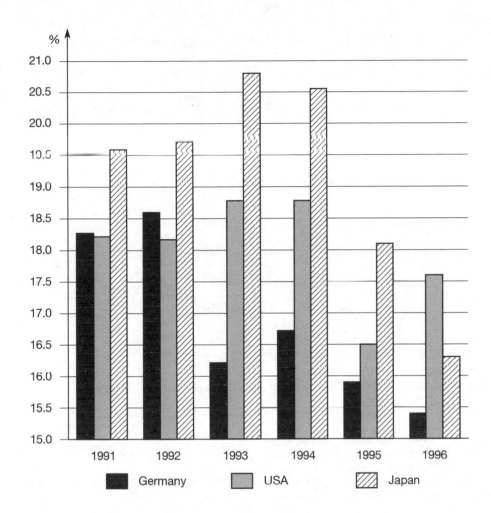

Figure 7.4 World trade shares in R&D-intensive goods held by Germany, the United States and Japan, 1990–4 (per cent)
Source: Modified from BMBF (1997: 9), based on OECD: *Foreign Trade by Commodities*; Federal Statistical Office: *1996 Statistical Yearbook of Foreign Countries*; and NIW calculations

and also a reflection of weakening locational ties in the R&D field. Many very small industrial firms have withdrawn completely from R&D over the years. This trend appears to have been stopped; obviously small firms are becoming increasingly aware of the importance of conducting in-house R&D again. In fact, since the mid-1990s German SMEs have been more likely to maintain their R&D capacity or even expand it, while large corporations have tended to take a more cautious stance. The other three frequently cited reasons for reducing R&D intensity are not, or only

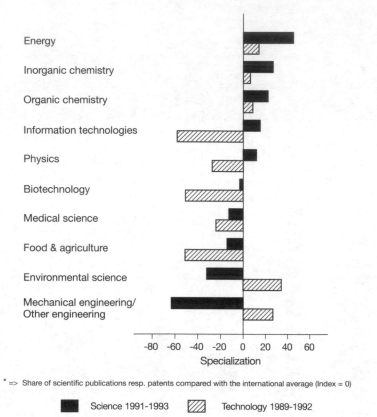

Figure 7.5 Comparison of scientific and technological specialization of Germany by field of technology, 1989–93
Source: BMBF (1996: 17), based on SCI-ISSRN databank and EPA, ISI calculations

partly, valid in Germany. Increasing efficiency of R&D inputs explains only part of the decline, whereas neither outsourcing (i.e. the reduction of the vertical range of manufacturing steps) nor the growing amount of research being conducted abroad serves as an adequate explanation for the declining R&D effort in Germany.

Public research in Germany is conducted and financed by several different types of institutions including universities and technical colleges, and the Helmholtz Association, the Fraunhofer Society and the Max Planck Society each have a specific function within the public research system. The research-related task is to encourage basic research and, in certain cases – more in technical colleges than in universities – applied research. The universities' share in R&D expenditure from Germany's gross domestic R&D expenditure was 19 per cent in 1996 (1991: 16 per cent). The emphasis within the universities' R&D expenditure was in science (28 per cent) and medicine (26 per cent). Engineering and social sciences reached 19 per cent each. The German Research Association (Deutsche Forschungsgemeinschaft) is the most

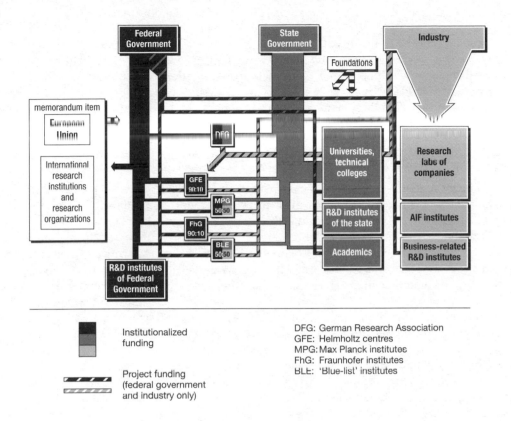

Figure 7.6 System of research funding in Germany
Source: Modified from BMBF (1996: 23)

important funding organization for research at universities. The complex financing mechanism of the German research system is described, in a simplified form, in Figure 7.6. It is obvious that research at universities is mainly financed by the respective federal states, whereas firms predominantly finance their own research.

Of course, universities have to fulfil another task, which at least indirectly has to do with Germany's future research capabilities. The 'human capital' represented by highly qualified workers who receive regular extended vocational training is by far the most important factor for successful R&D activities at universities as well as in private companies. Technical colleges and universities in Germany in particular are key factors in innovation-oriented structural change of the economy. In 1995 Germany expended some DM 283.5 billion, or 8.2 per cent of its gross domestic product, to build up its human capital. Of this amount, about 27.8 per cent was for R&D (5.3 per cent of this was carried out at universities, 4.2 per cent at non-profit organizations and 18.3 per cent in private firms), 58.1 per cent for education and training (8.4 per cent was for universities and 10.5 per cent for private firms), and

14.1 per cent for extended vocational training in firms. Although R&D spending nearly tripled in the years between 1975 and 1989, spending on education and training rose by only 60 per cent, even more slowly than GDP. The 1990s have witnessed a break in this trend: expenditure on education has begun growing at a disproportionate rate again, while R&D spending has increased only slightly. As regards universities, quantitative figures alone do not tell the whole truth. Despite a perpetually increasing number of students at universities (1.9 million in 1995, three-quarters of them studying at universities and the rest at technical colleges), it is likely that a shortage of persons with qualifications essential to the technological innovation process – scientists and engineers – could develop within the next few years, because the number of first-year students in these fields has fallen by 50 per cent since 1990.

In order to assess the quality of university research in Germany relative to other countries one could use the RLA measure, which counts the number of scientific publications by country and technological field. The results clearly show that Germany's scientists are – relatively speaking – strongly present on the international science market in fields where Germany has been traditionally strong, like physics and chemistry, as well as in material sciences. By global standards electrical engineering, telecommunications research and information technology are considerably less pronounced. Measured in terms of demand for published research findings (i.e. the number of times findings are cited), German research findings continue to attract growing international attention in virtually all scientific fields – in Germany's traditional core areas of physics and chemistry in particular and, to an increasing degree, in medicine and pharmaceutical science.

One of the responsibilities of government research institutes, like universities, is to produce marketable findings and to convey them directly from the science system to the industrial system. Patent applications could be used as an indicator of the marketability of government research, because the only way for government R&D facilities to transfer their research findings and inventions to industry is by codifying them in patents. In Germany approximately 4 per cent of all domestic patents came from universities in 1994, and the trend points sharply upward. The respective figures for the other institutional elements of the public research system in Germany are about 1 per cent, 0.9 per cent and 0.2 per cent (Helmholtz centres, Fraunhofer institutes and Max Planck institutes, respectively). In order to compare patent performance of universities and private firms by technological fields, a look at Figure 7.7 may be helpful. The strengths of technology-related research at universities are in the fields of organic chemistry and measuring and control technology, whereas research by private firms is especially patent-intensive in the fields of electrical engineering, machinery and parts, printing and transportation.

If we look again at German scientific publications compared with the international average (Figure 7.5), relative specialization in the public science sector can be seen in chemistry, power engineering, information technologies and physics. Compared with the specialization in technologies (originating from private research), there are significant differences in performance regarding information technologies and physics (strengths in science, but weaknesses in the private sector) as well as in environmental engineering and mechanical engineering (strengths in the private sector).

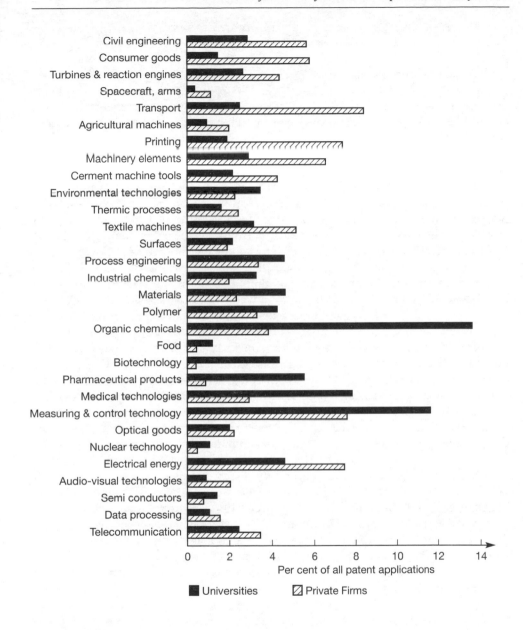

Figure 7.7 Technological profile of universities and private firms in Germany on the basis of 30 technology fields
Source: Adapted and modified from Fraunhofer-Institut für Systemtechnik und Innovationsforschung (ISI) (1997: 19)

Policy strategies and instruments implemented at different spatial levels in favour of innovation and technology transfer

As described earlier, industrial research as a whole has decreased in Germany in recent years. Large German corporations, especially, are following a worldwide trend by reducing domestic research efforts. Basic research departments are being cut back everywhere, and it appears that research is being concentrated on activities with a short-term pay-off, and on areas of core expertise. This core competence strategy could develop into a risk for the economy as a whole, should the focus of research become restricted not only to familiar methods and processes, but in the area of product development as well. In such an event, longer-term innovation potential would dissipate and economic sustainability would be at risk. Additionally, public expenditure for education and training has stagnated in recent years. A question arising from these developments is how the public innovation systems react to this classical kind of market failure. Careful consideration must be given to the direction strategic research should take, the consequences any specific direction would have for the country's national innovation system, and ways to create interfaces with industry. Do cut-backs in industry's basic research activities lead to gaps in know-how? Is the pipeline between science and industry in order? Are we making full use of existing potential? Is the mechanism for transferring know-how via patents functioning correctly? When we examine these questions, it is not immediately obvious that Germany has shifted the focus of its innovation activities to areas whose development depends comparatively little on advances made in the national scientific field. This could mean that Germany's science and research system is not woven tightly enough to allow various parts and potentials to interact on a cross-sectoral basis, which poses challenges for the institutional assistance provided by Germany's state governments and federal government (BMBF 1997).

R&D and innovation policy in Germany is diffusion oriented, i.e. characterized by decentralized forms of organization and by policy instruments with decentralized effects (Ergas 1987; Sternberg 1996a). The measures target SMEs and, thus, the broad effects of the promoted allegedly internationally competitive high technologies. With respect to the organization of the instruments of technology policy, a differentiation in direct, indirect and institutional support has gained acceptance (see Brösse 1996). Direct project support is the most significant form of industrial policy, and occurs when the object seeking support is concretely laid out with respect to content and topic; that is, the support is technologically specific. Large firms are favoured by this type of support. Indirect research support, however, does not favour technologically specific projects. In this case research, development, innovation, diffusion and technological transfers in general, like grants to businesses for the strengthening and maintenance of R&D personnel, are provided with support. A special form is indirect specific aid, which targets a rapid dissemination of certain key technologies such as information technology, but within this group nothing specific is picked out. Finally, institutional support includes the support of facilities that themselves aid or carry out research (e.g. the German Research Association, the Max Planck Society, the Fraunhofer Society and even universities).

It is characteristic of a federally organized country like Germany that the sixteen federal states, the cities and communities pursue their own independent technology policies. In none of the other industrialized countries does the regional level have a comparable quantitative significance in terms of innovation policy. The latest chapter in German innovation policy started in the early 1990s with Germany's reunification and the subsequent special boosting of eastern Germany. For these reasons the following discussion is separated into instruments typical of the techno-logy and innovation policy implemented by the federal government and those implemented by the federal states and cities/communities. In order to consider adequately the theme of this book, the chapter examines the spatial goals and spatial distribution of public R&D funds.

Let us now focus on the spatial consequences and spatial goals of innovation policies in Germany. Until reunification, regional effects were not among the goals of national technology policy. For a long time the BMBF (Bundesministerium für Bildung, Wissenschaft, Forschung und Technologie, called the BMFT – Bundes-ministerium für Forschung und Technologie – until 1994), quantitatively the most important ministry in terms of technology policy, as well as the other ministries, geared their R&D spending exclusively at the available capacities. In the late 1970s two factors led to a debate about innovation-oriented regional policy: the awareness of the spatially non-neutral effects and the failure of the policy of mobility-oriented industrial settlements. There was and still is a call for an increased orientation towards endogenous potential, which, it was claimed, could be activated with the help of external federal promotional R&D funds. The idea of reducing regional innovation disparities marked the discussion about innovation-oriented regional policy. The underprivileged regions (the Saarland and the Ruhr District and, now, eastern Germany) were to receive support from national technology policy through 'a regionalization of existing national R&D incentives in terms of a spatial differ-entiation of rates for clearly delineated problem regions' (Ewers and Wettmann 1980: 173).

The advocates of innovation-oriented regional policies mainly criticized national R&D policies for their concentration on measures of direct project assistance and the resulting promotion of large enterprises and technologies. The federal govern-ment reacted to this criticism by increasing indirect R&D-promotional measures without explicitly considering spatial goals. As a source of regional statistics cover-ing all ministries, this study falls back on project promotion by the former Federal Ministry of Research and Technology between 1985 and 1991 in order to analyse the regional distribution of federal R&D spending.[3] Traditionally this ministry is the major financier of direct project promotion (target for 1997: 47.3 per cent or DM 3.153 billion (BMBF 1998)). The objects of this analysis are the 328 cities and districts in Western Germany. The BMBF's R&D project promotion is heavily concentrated in agglomerations. By absolute criteria, the city of Munich clearly prevails. Indeed, it receives more funds than the cities holding second and third place put together! The region of Munich profits mostly from project promotion by the BMBF. This did not change with reunification, although the total expenditure of the BMBF on direct project promotion has fallen and the number of competing cities has drastically increased.[4] In absolute terms, metropolises like Berlin, Cologne and Hamburg rank high on the list. Differences related to city size are more character-istic of the promotion pattern than large-scale spatial disparities. An analysis of the location quotients of the promotion funds per employee in manufacturing yields a somewhat different picture. With the exception of Munich, undoubtedly Germany's top high-technology region (Sternberg and Tamásy 1999), no large city ranks in the top twelve. Medium-sized towns in North Rhine-Westphalia and Baden-Württemberg dominate here.

The conclusion to be drawn is that in the Federal Republic of Germany before reunification there never was a technology policy pursuing explicitly spatial goals. Nevertheless, the flow of national R&D funds into the regions was very uneven. Agglomerations in general, and large cities in North Rhine-Westphalia, Baden-Württemberg and Bavaria (in essence the region of Munich) in particular, profited. Because of significant changes in the environment of regional technological development, new policy approaches were designed by the federal government. Among them are new promotion measures like 'lead projects' to support regional bio-technology initiatives (see Licht 1997).

Federalism in Germany suggests that, in addition to the federal level, technology policy can be practised on other levels. Indeed, significant amounts of funding from the national R&D budget of all public bodies are allotted to the states and municipalities. In 1993 the federal government spent roughly DM 14.9 billion on R&D, and the states managed to allot DM 13.6 billion on their own (see BMBF 1996). No other large industrial nation places so much importance, in quantitative terms, on the regional level with respect to technology and innovation policy. The relation between federal and state funding as described differs significantly from the national average, depending on the state (see Figure 7.8). Whereas Bavaria's portion of federal funds clearly dominates with 21 per cent (DM 3.1 billion), it ranks only second, behind North Rhine-Westphalia, for R&D expenditures at the state level with DM 1.88 billion (13.9 per cent of R&D expenditures for the states). Immediately behind Bavaria is Baden-Württemberg. In most economically and technologically prosperous states (like North Rhine-Westphalia, Lower Saxony, as well as Hesse, Saarland and Rhineland-Palatinate), state R&D spending is of relatively high importance, since the R&D share of the state is higher than that of the federal government. This also applies to three of the five 'new' (former East German) states (Mecklenburg-Pomerania, Saxony-Anhalt and Thuringia).

The more or less independent technology policy of the states is relatively new. It stems from the concept of an innovation-oriented regional policy – the product of the technology and regional policy discussion. Its supporters plead for a shift in competence and funding of technology policy from the federal to the regional level, especially with regard to questions of innovation support for SMEs. In response, the states and municipalities have established a practically incomprehensible number of technology policy support programmes, since the 1980s. This has been vehemently criticized for reasons of constitutional policy (*Ordnungspolitik*) and on account of non-existent legal safeguards (Staudt 1987/88). With respect to the instruments, numerous parallels can be drawn between the federal government and the states. On both levels, the financial support of R&D projects, the intensification and activation of technology transfers (in particular through a consulting infrastructure), the promotion of technology-oriented business start-ups and the construction of technology and innovation centres are especially favoured (for individual measures, see Brösse 1996). In comparison, at the municipal level the establishment of technology and innovation centres (TICs) is the most popular, although not undisputed,

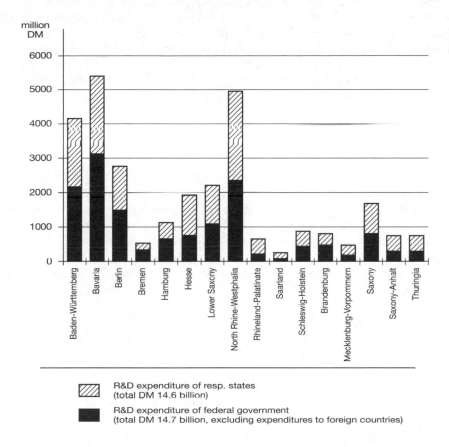

Figure 7.8 Federal government and state government R&D expenditure in each federal state, 1993
Source: Data from BMBF (1998: 448, 449)

measure, and has produced a very dense network of 120 to 200 TICs – depending upon the definition. An empirical check of the success rate shows, indeed, that the regional-economic goals of TICs (promotion of technology transfers, creation of skilled jobs) were less fully achieved than the business management goals (promotion of business start-ups; see Sternberg *et al.* 1996). During the past decade it has become clear that the all-encompassing decentralization of technology policy, which is the aim of the innovation-oriented regional policy, is not practical for the municipalities and communities, since the local conditions differ too strongly. As a compromise between technology support from the federal government and all-encompassing decentralization, the main policy of decentralized stabilization and development (Voelzkow 1990: 242) oriented to the needs of the region has become equally important. These state programmes bear a completely ambivalent relation to the influence of the federal government's technology policy. In some respects they appear to be complementary, in other cases contradictory. The states differ particularly with respect to the regional goals and the acceptance of technology policy guidelines from the federal government. Most of the 'old states' (of West Germany) attempt to supplement the disparity-fostering effects of federal technology policy with their own equalization-oriented R&D policy. In particular, measures taken in Baden-Württemberg, as well as Bavaria and North Rhine-Westphalia to a lesser extent, are addressed first and foremost to the international competitive situation in the state. For this reason, the reduction of intraregional disparities is not an explicit goal of technology policy (see Sternberg 1998).

To summarize, the German innovation system on the national and state level involves an extensive set of instruments and attempts to decrease the transformation gap, which has been complained about for years, between (strong) basic research and knowledge-intensive production (innovation) through appropriate technology and innovation policy measures. In states like Bavaria and Baden-Württemberg positive effects for the regions' economies were undoubtedly triggered by the interaction between state and federal policy. Fundamentally, the problem remains that the national level does not consider the regional effects of its measures sufficiently, and coordination between federal, state and community programmes is minimal.

Germany possesses a very diverse research landscape with different institutional types which often have very different goals. Universities, for example, should never be lumped together with technical colleges, and neither type of institution should be grouped together with non-university research institutes like the Max Planck institutes or the Fraunhofer institutes. This comment also applies to the relationship between private-sector enterprises and the public research or educational institutions.

From a regional perspective, one can observe that the regional aggregation and the local embeddedness of the research institutions is very diverse. In general, universities are most strongly anchored in each region, while the Helmholtz institutes and most Max Planck and Fraunhofer institutes follow a federal orientation with respect to possible clients and partners in scientific and economic cooperation. From the viewpoint of politics, only the universities played a role in the framework of regional policy from the 1960s to the 1980s. At that time, the choice of location for the founding of many universities and technical colleges was based in part on the regional-political effects in the sense of equalization for economic disparities between favoured and disadvantaged areas (e.g. in north-west Lower Saxony and parts of Bavaria). In addition, one must carefully consider the fact that Germany even then possessed – and today this is even more the case – a spatially balanced research and education landscape, when compared to France or the United States. This concentration of a network of research and educational facilities between 1960 and 1980 was followed by the establishment of numerous technology transfer facilities which were affiliated with universities but also involved in commercial enterprises. But these developments could not disguise the fact that a discrepancy exists between the relatively balanced spatial educational infrastructure, the more advanced network of research facilities, and, on the other hand, the spatially concentrated innovative firms. The enduring north–south gap in West Germany with respect to R&D-intensive enterprises (see Sternberg 1998) still persists today, though since reunification it has been overshadowed by the larger east–west gap between the old and new federal states.

This has at least two consequences. First, many regions in both western and eastern Germany which maintain good-quality R&D equipment at public research institutions do not have adequate partners for cooperation from the private side to initiate technology transfers and regional-economic effects. Second, the federal government is following, for the first time in its history, regional goals with its technology policy, namely the support of the five new states with regard to technology and education policy. Since the development of the research infrastructure and their favoured treatment as competitive locations are not only dependent upon federal policy, but also, and perhaps more strongly, influenced by the corresponding sectoral policies of the states and municipalities, the outlook as regards economic and technological prosperity in the various regions is mixed. Comparatively prosperous states (like Baden-Württemberg and Bavaria) and many regions therein (e.g. Baden, Munich) have an easier time maintaining their standard with the help of local politics and backing from the federal government than less-developed regions have of improving theirs significantly and permanently. The technology policy of the federal government is hardly suitable for reducing regional inequalities. The implicit non-intentional regional effects of the federal technology policy favour, furthermore, regions that are relatively well equipped with innovative enterprises and public research facilities (see Sternberg 1998).

Regional case studies: Lower Saxony's research triangle, Baden, Saxony

A sketch of the national innovation system and its effects on the regional development would be incomplete, as it only views the economy as a whole. The regional and local framework conditions are of importance for the concrete relations between industry and universities in certain cities, for more reasons than the federal system of the nation. In this regard not only do the sixteen states differ from one another, but often regions within each state vary too. This great heterogeneity of the national economic and scientific landscape will be taken into account in the following through the analysis of three case-study regions based on extensive surveys. Nevertheless, the results represent only a small part of the total from an extensive and continuing interregional and international comparative research project covering innovation potentials in ten European regions.[5]

The following sections are based upon empirical research in Baden, which is part of the *Land* of Baden-Württemberg;[6] in the so-called 'research triangle' of Hanover–Brunswick–Göttingen in Lower Saxony; and in Saxony.[7] Three slightly different questionnaires, adapted to the three groups of addressees and oriented to the new *Oslo Manual* (OECD and EUROSTAT 1997), were mailed to the three case-study areas: one to manufacturing firms, one to service firms and one to research institutions (universities, technical colleges, Fraunhofer institutes, Max Planck institutes and other public or semi-public research institutions). For populations and sample sizes in each case-study area see Figure 7.9.

A total of 1806 questionnaires were returned by manufacturing firms, 884 by service firms and 1078 by research institutions (see Table 7.1). Table 7.1 shows fairly high response rates of 15 per cent to 44 per cent, with rather high absolute figures. A

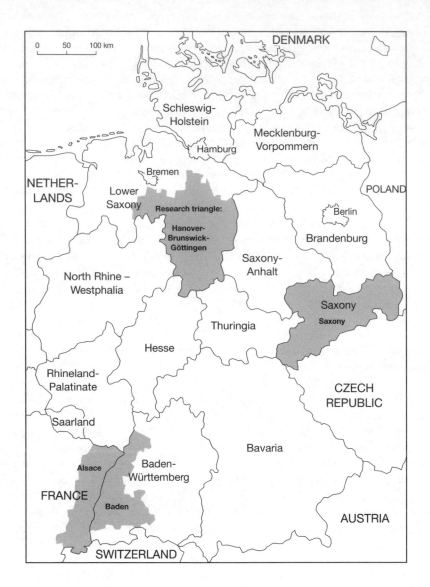

Figure 7.9 Case-study areas
Source: German Innovation Survey, University of Hanover, University of Cologne, Technical University Bergakademie Freiberg, Fraunhofer Institute for Systems and Innovation Research, Karlsruhe, 1997. Cartography by Stephan Pohl, 1997

result like this is a necessary prerequisite for assessing both single-actor groups and intraregional versus interregional linkages between selected groups of actors.

Table 7.1 The innovation surveys: samples and response rates (no. and %) in the case-study areas

Target group	Research triangle Hanover–Brunswick– Göttingen	Saxony	Baden[b]	Total
Manufacturing	1807[a]	3767	2715	8289
	372	1004	430	1806
	20.6	26.7	15.8	21.8
Services	1351	1477	1198	4051
	240	365	279	884
	17.8	24.8	23.3	22.0
Research institutions	610	1405	615	2630
	252	618	208	1078
	41.3	44.0	33.8	41.0

Source: German Innovation Survey, University of Hanover, University of Cologne, Technical University Bergakademie Freiberg, Fraunhofer Institute for Systems and Innovation Research, Karlsruhe, 1997 (surveys of manufacturing firms, surveys of service firms, surveys of research institutions)
Notes:
[a] First line in each cell: no. of questionnaires distributed; second line: usable questionnaires (sample); third line: response rate (%)
[b] A related survey took place in Alsace, the French region bordering on Baden, with the following numbers of usable questionnaires: 263 manufacturing firms (15.0 per cent response rate), 147 service firms (15.4 per cent) and 65 research institutions (43.6 per cent). However, this contribution is restricted to the results in German regions

Regional economic structure of the case-study areas and policies with respect to innovation and technology transfer

The three case-study regions – under the aspects of economics and innovativeness – represent three different types. Until recently, Baden, which is part of the state of Baden-Württemberg, was one of the most innovative and prosperous German regions. Several mainly non-German scholars have characterized it as typical of an industrial district with intensive intraregional linkages between suppliers and customers and between small and large firms with a dominant engineering base and a wide variety of different policy measures especially favouring SMEs in the innovation process (e.g. Cooke and Morgan 1993; see Grotz and Braun 1997 for a more sceptical view from within the region).

Saxony, representing one of the new German states, still suffers from the consequences of the economic (and political) transition following German reunification. Increasing innovation pressure on all German firms resulted from emerging internationalization and globalization processes. However, this pressure is significantly higher in eastern Germany, because there the increasing costs per unit require considerable productivity growth. If Saxony and the other eastern states do not succeed in generating an adequate surge of innovation, that part of Germany may remain underdeveloped for many years to come (see Brezinski and Fritsch 1995).

The Hanover–Brunswick–Göttingen research triangle has comparative weaknesses relative to R&D enterprises, which are especially evident in large companies. In addition, the region's economic structure suffers from its strong dependence on vehicle construction. With regard to new (technology-oriented) establishments, however, the general proposition that years producing substantially more new establishments – even if the rate of bankruptcy among them may be high – contribute to the creation of long-term jobs, does apply to the Hanover region (Gerlach and Wagner 1994). No studies have yet examined whether the risk of insolvency could be reduced if innovative networks were utilized more, or new networks were created.

In terms of the public R&D infrastructure, there is general consensus that its extraordinary innovation potential has not yet been fully utilized (there are nine universities and institutes of higher learning, eight technical colleges, eight institutes of the Max Planck Society, four institutes of the Fraunhofer Society, four large research institutions, the 'Blue List' in seven locations, and eleven locations of federal R&D institutions; both headquarters and branches are included in these figures (see BMBF 1998)). This hypothesis – which holds true for automotive-related research capacities as well (see Gehrke and Schasse 1993) – relates, in particular, to the assumption that interregional interactions between the staff of public research institutions in the study region and enterprises exist, but not intraregional ones. There is little empirical proof of this, though. This assumption would mean that R&D institutions in Hanover, though linked with networks, are not part of the innovative milieu. Transferred to the current regional economic debate on research 'spillovers' (see Anselin, Varga and Acs 1997b), these observations would have to be interpreted to indicate that institutions such as universities and research laboratories located in the study region and generating knowledge have not, so far, effected 'spillovers' of new knowledge in favour of other establishments, particularly small enterprises.

In Hanover, technology policy instruments for the initiation and intensification of intraregional technology transfer, especially in favour of SMEs and new technology-based firms, have been implemented (e.g. innovation centres in Hanover and Brunswick, the Medical Park in Hanover, technology transfer offices at universities and technical colleges; see Sternberg 1992). Although these institutions have been success-ful up to a point, they have not yet been able to improve the 'climate' or milieu.

In an age of global markets and increasingly knowledge-intensive production, most German enterprises are forced to cooperate in the innovation process when they operate in the corresponding markets. In accordance with the theory of flexible production (also for innovations) the firm restricts itself to its core competencies and attempts to compensate for deficits through cooperation. Dealing with the most convincing theoretical explanations for inter-firm technological linkages, Dodgson (1996) distinguishes four broad categories: changing systems of production; the impact of technological change; a focus on firms and their economic and competitive relations; and a final group which addresses organizational learning. However, external technological linkages of firms are not restricted to those with other firms, but should also include research institutions. Concerning innovative firms, the current literature offers several plausible arguments as to why innovative firms, especially small ones, should cooperate with external partners more intensely than non-innovative firms. Some of the reasons include reducing uncertainty; costs and competitive pressure; achieving synergy effects; sharing personnel; and entering new technological fields.

An investigation of the relationship between firms' innovativeness and the existence of external linkages was attempted by asking all manufacturing enterprises in our case-study regions whether or not they had introduced product or process innovations during the past three years, and whether they had established external cooperation in this regard (beyond regular business relations) with external partners, such as customers, suppliers, competitors or public or semi-public research institutions. Our result is a clear and statistically significant proof of the hypothesis mentioned above: that among firms maintaining cooperation, innovative firms are over represented and vice versa. This result holds for each of the three case study regions.

There is clear empirical evidence that the relevance of external cooperation as described above increases with firm size. Four-fifths of all innovative firms with less than 20 employees have external linkages relative to product or process innovations. This share rises to 95.8 per cent with firms of over 500 employees. Similar results were obtained for each of the case-study areas.

In order to assess the importance of firm linkages with universities and other research institutions, it is helpful to compare the frequency of these linkages with those of other types of cooperation partners. Figure 7.10 shows very uniform results for the three case-study regions. Firms cooperate in the innovation process[8] particularly with clients and suppliers (in that order), then come the research institutions and competitors.

How regional is the innovation system? The relationship between intra- and interregional linkages between industry and universities

The survey of research institutions in the three regions clearly reveals how important intraregional linkages are and which firms cooperate (Figure 7.11). Measured by the number of firms cooperating with the research institutions of the three sample regions, 43 per cent of the businesses are allotted to the respective study regions themselves. Thus the regional level is, at least quantitatively, more important than the national level, which includes business cooperation outside the study area, but inside Germany. On the other hand, cooperation with foreign enterprises is on average quite rare for all three regions. German research institutions are less internationally oriented with regard to their contacts to businesses than the German businesses themselves.

Such general remarks about all research institutions hide significant differences between the three regions and between different types of research institutions. The universities and other research institutions (the Max Planck, Fraunhofer and Helmholtz institutions) cooperate primarily with businesses outside the study regions. One can recognize a noticeably strong regional orientation by the technical colleges (on the average between 50 and 67 per cent of the firms cooperating with technical colleges are in the same region; for universities the figure is 37 per cent and for other research institutions it is only between 14 and 31 per cent; see Backhaus and Seidel 1997). The number of foreign firms cooperating with technical colleges (relative to all firms) is correspondingly low. The non-university public research institutions

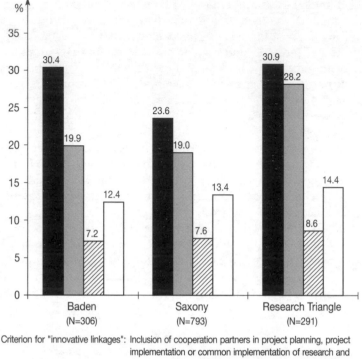

Figure 7.10 Relevance of external innovative linkages of manufacturing firms by type of cooperation partner
Source: Data from German Innovation Survey, University of Hanover, University of Cologne, Technical University Bergakademie Freiberg, Fraunhofer Institute for Systems and Innovation Research, Karlsruhe, 1997 (survey of manufacturing firms)

maintain substantially fewer business contacts than universities – in total and also with each region. The three regions are, thus, representative of Germany as a whole, as the national study by the Zentrum für Europäische Wirtschaftsforschung shows (see Beise and Spielkamp 1996).

In an interregional comparison, the research institutions of Saxony show stronger ties to their own region with respect to cooperation partners from the commercial sector than the institutions in Hanover–Brunswick–Göttingen. In both these regions

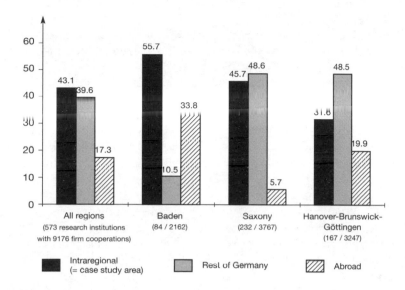

Figure 7.11 Research institutions and their innovative linkages to innovating manufacturing firms in the case study regions (as percentages of all innovative manufacturing firms cooperating with the respective research institutions)
Source: Data from German Innovation Survey, University of Hanover, University of Cologne, Technical University Bergakademie Freiberg, Fraunhofer Institute for Systems and Innovation Research, Karlsruhe, 1997 (survey of manufacturing firms)

the firms from the rest of the country represent the quantitatively most important factor. In Baden the situation is entirely different: the regional connection and the endogenous potential are apparently so strong here that more than half of all businesses cooperating with research institutions are located in the survey regions themselves. Also, the foreign share of a solid one-third is significantly higher than in the other two regions, whereas hardly any cooperation partners from the rest of the nation cooperate with the research institutes of Baden-Württemberg (Backhaus and Seidel 1997). The situation in Baden involves two processes that occur in many national and regional economies: regionalization and globalization. Regionalization means, in this case, the strong intraregional networking of actors in innovation (research institutions and manufacturing firms) in the framework of cooperative research. At the same time, basic and applied research of the highest technological level are carried out in this region, which is linked to worldwide research networks. Thus, both Baden, with its above-average proportion of foreign and regional cooperation in innovation, and Saxony, with its high regional and very low foreign share, deviate from the average values in Germany's national innovation system.

How important are the local innovation climate and regional knowledge and technology transfer agencies for the development of linkages?

In each of the three case-study regions there are different facilities which are supposed to initiate or intensify the transfer of knowledge and technology between the economy and the research institutions. On the business side, the SMEs are the centre of all activities. Appropriate facilities are either financed from the economy (e.g. innovation consulting services of the Chambers of Industry and Commerce or the Chambers of Handicraft) or carried by research institutes (e.g. technology transfer systems at the universities). Before we discuss the importance of such facilities for the actual cooperation between university and business in the regions, it is essential to sketch the regional framework conditions under which the participants in innovation, as well as the local transfer facilities, operate. First of all, it can be seen that there are surprisingly few differences between the three regions with respect to the frequency of business innovation. Of the supposedly innovatively weak Saxon firms, 79.2 per cent implemented a product or process innovation in the three years immediately prior to the survey (1992–5); the corresponding proportions for the research triangle and Baden are only slightly lower (78.2 per cent and 71.8 per cent respectively).

More obvious interregional differences are observable in the impediments which have hindered the firms in their innovation projects (Figure 7.12). Independent of regional differences, one should stress that the level of personnel costs, the difficult prediction of demand development and the absence of personal capital (this, however, only in Saxony) are the three most important hindrances. In contrast – and this observation also applies to each of the three regions – the businesses do not view a lack of cooperation possibilities with other firms or with research institutes as a hindrance to innovation. Obviously, in the eyes of businesses enough potential cooperation partners exist in both innovation participant groups. If innovation projects still encounter difficulties, then these usually have another source. In this respect, significant differences can be determined. The Saxon businesses complain most heavily (with respect to other impediments, as well as other regions) about the deficit of personal capital. In addition, the lack of outside capital is more frequently cited here as a hindrance to innovation than in Lower Saxony and Baden-Württemberg. In that respect, the Saxon firms are typical of many industrial businesses in the new German states, which lack a personal capital base. The industrial enterprises in Baden, on the other hand, are most highly burdened by the high personnel costs and the difficulty of predicting the demand development. Both indicators can be pointers to above-average R&D-intensive products and processes in this region. The firms in the research triangle, compared with the other two regions, view bureaucratic hindrances as a major disadvantage, and high personnel costs, which are typical for West German firms, are also frequently considered to impede innovation.

A further, valuable reference to the framework for innovation projects is provided by the question of the firm's assessment of relevant factors impacting business innovation processes. Political framework conditions can play a special role here. For the assessment of such political measures it is not unimportant to know that in

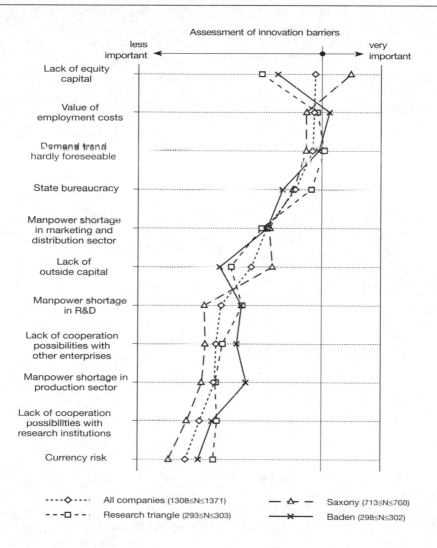

Figure 7.12 Barriers to firms' innovation by case study area
Source: German Innovation Survey, University of Hanover, University of Cologne,
Technical University Bergakademie Freiberg, Fraunhofer Institute for Systems and
Innovation Research, Karlsruhe, 1997 (survey of manufacturing firms)

Saxony more than half the businesses had received funds from public promotion
programmes for innovation projects during the previous three years (see the earlier
comments about the favourable technology policy of the federal government for
East Germany). In the research triangle, on the other hand, the corresponding
proportion is only 23 per cent and in Baden only 19 per cent. Figure 7.13 shows that,
in total, most factors of influence are valued similarly; only the supply of partici-
patory capital is particularly poorly valued, and that is the case in all regions. Several
(partially politically relevant) differences exist between the regions which clearly

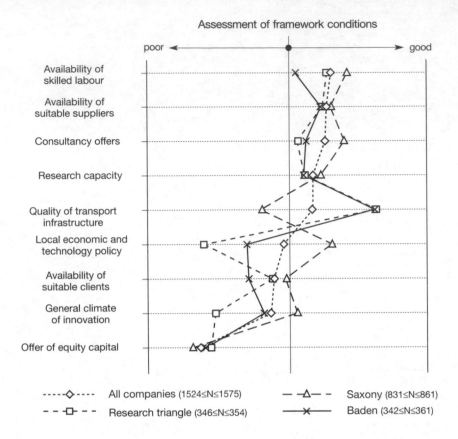

Figure 7.13 Firms' assessment of the regional framework conditions for executing innovations by case study area
Source: German Innovation Survey, University of Hanover, University of Cologne, Technical University Bergakademie Freiberg, Fraunhofer Institute for Systems and Innovation Research, Karlsruhe, 1997 (survey of manufacturing firms)

show anew the East–West differences. The Saxon businesses regard the – mostly locally determined – economic and technological support, consulting, as well as the general innovation climate as being significantly better than do their West German counterparts. From the latter, Baden once again rates better than Lower Saxony. With the exception of the transportation infrastructure, whose shortcomings are complained about by eastern German businesses, the east German firms rank all factors of influence more highly than the firms in western Germany.

The role of intermediate facilities in the innovative integration of industry and research institutions is very different in the three regions. About four-fifths of the surveyed research institutes collaborated within businesses in the three years immediately before the survey. In this respect the three regions differ only marginally, while larger differences arise between the types of research institutes. University institutes cooperate less frequently with businesses than the practice-oriented tech-

Table 7.2 Primary means by which research institutes made business contacts

Contact made via:	Frequency (%)
Congresses, fairs	31.8
Specialist periodicals, publications	17.1
Databanks	0.6
Associations (*Verbände*)	13.4
Knowledge and technology transfer agencies	8.6
Activities of the cooperating company	66.0
Personal contacts of research institution's staff	80.7

Source: German Innovation Survey University of Hanover, University of Cologne, Technical University Bergakademie Freiberg, Fraunhofer Institute for Systems and Innovation Research, Karlsruhe, 1997 (surveys of research institutions)

Note: Up to three nominations per research institution

nical colleges. The highest share goes to the non-university research institutes. From a technology policy perspective the effects of knowledge and technology transfer arrangements on the relationship between research institutes and businesses are of interest. It should be mentioned here that, in total, only 20 per cent of the research institutes utilized such arrangements in recent years; differences between the regions are insignificant. Their value appears to be rather poorly regarded considering the major hopes that are connected to this instrument. Even so, this level of utilization is considerably higher than by businesses. The data suggest a statistically significant connection between both dichotomous variables: 'cooperation with businesses' (yes/no) and 'use of technology transfer arrangements during the past three years' (yes/no). Of the research institutes working together with businesses, a quarter used services from transfer arrangements. Of the non-cooperating research institutes, only 8 per cent used the transfer arrangements. If it was asked how the cooperation between research and businesses came about, the role of transfer arrangements again appeared minimal, although it is their role to mediate such contacts. The mean of 8.6 per cent of the businesses varied only insignificantly in the three regions. As Table 7.2 shows, workers at the research institutes frequently used existing personal contacts during their search for partners in the economy. In two-thirds of the cases the initiative came from businesses. Additionally, conventions played a relatively important role.

In summary, it is important from a regional perspective that the technology transfer arrangements achieve a significance out of proportion to their number when the contacts, especially to firms in the same region, are very intensive. Indeed, there are percentage differences in the influence of such transfer arrangements which are dependent upon the regional connection of such contacts. They are, however, statistically insignificant. In conclusion, it can be emphasized that no matter how widely employed the technology transfer arrangements are, they still play a subordinate role in the achievement and the regional importance of cooperation between research institutes and businesses.

Conclusions for regional innovation theory and policies from German experiences

This chapter was an attempt to sketch the German research and business landscape with particular attention to the connections between the commercial sector and public research facilities. Selected aspects of cooperation between both participants in innovation were empirically shown on the basis of primary statistical data from the three regions.

Conclusions regarding regional innovation theories refer mainly to the following aspects:

- The regional level plays a role in the explanation of innovation processes (stemming from cooperation between public research and business in the economy) that should not be neglected in a nation with a relatively balanced spatial structure like Germany. Thus, spillover effects from research in Germany should also exist, even if no survey has yet been made. For research institutes, as well as businesses, the most important spatial level of measure for external cooperation in innovation is their own region (of more importance than the rest of Germany and abroad). This 'local embeddedness' is most significant in Baden, but even in Saxony and Lower Saxony a majority of businesses and research institutes cooperate on an intraregional basis. The main statement of the industrial district approaches and the knowledge spillover theory thus receive empirical confirmation from those surveyed in this regional study.
- Here one can see several empirical pieces of evidence for the existence of different regional innovation systems, even though the three regions in the study are similar in many aspects related to innovation, such as the negligible importance of technology transfer arrangements, and in terms of intraregional cooperation between industrial enterprises, particularly with universities and technical colleges though seldom with non-university research institutes.

The following discoveries relate to the innovation policy conclusions:

- Technology policy at the federal as well as the regional and local level should develop differentiated measures for technology transfer between small and large businesses, which consider regional peculiarities of technology suppliers (SMEs and, thus, most frequently businesses) and technology demand (especially universities and non-university research institutes).
- Explicit instruments like the widespread knowledge and technology transfer agencies, as well as the increasingly popular innovation centres (similar to British science parks), have rarely led to an intensification of cooperation between business and research in the relevant regions. More important than these examples of explicit technology policy is an implicit technology policy without regional goals, but with regional results. This includes, first and foremost, the research project support from the BMBF with long-standing preferential treatment for southern German states, and especially the region around Munich, which for this reason became the top German high-tech region.
- The days in which an equalization-oriented regional policy by means of R&D facilities (especially universities) was pursued, are gone. In the 1990s Germany's

national innovation system is pursuing consolidation and saving due to tight budgets, and not expansion in the form of new institutions. Thus, regional cooperation between research and business is becoming concentrated in existing locations, rarely in new ones. At present, an explicit technology and educational policy with regional goals exists only in eastern Germany, but even there most of the important points have already been met.

- Regarding the transferability of the results discussed above, it must be remembered that Germany is not representative of other nations because of its special circumstances. For example, there are few private universities; higher education is open to everyone with the appropriate high school diploma (*Abiturzeugnis*), but at a location tightly controlled by a central organization, the ZVS; and little competition occurs among the universities as a whole. Other nations can still recognize that a diffusion-oriented technology policy alone cannot meet the needs of research institutes and businesses with respect to knowledge transfer (particularly intraregionally).

- In the future, a major restructuring of the public research system in Germany is to be expected. Budget restrictions, the new generation of university professors, the shift in academic study preferences of the students, and the growing competition between universities to attract students and funding sources are all examples of a changing landscape. In the business world at the moment, a trend towards relocation of R&D capacities abroad and/or in cooperating firms is indisputable, at least for large concerns. Many small enterprises, on the other hand, appear to have rediscovered the strategic importance of in-house research. These developments influence the knowledge transfer between businesses and public research institutes, as well as the relationships between the regions. It seems reasonable to assume that the spatially relatively balanced research landscape in Germany will experience more disparity in the future than it has in the past.

Notes

1. The German Institute for Economic Research in Berlin (Deutsches Institut für Wirtschaftsforschung, DIW), the Fraunhofer Institute for Systems and Innovation Research in Karlsruhe (Fraunhofer-Institut für Systemtechnik und Innovationsforschung, ISI), the Institute for Economic Research of Lower Saxony in Hanover (Niedersächsisches Institut für Wirtschaftsforschung, NIW) and Centre for European Economic Research in Mannheim (Zentrum für Europäische Wirtschaftsforschung, ZEW).

2. Relative patent activity (RPA) is used to measure the degree of specialization. A country has a positive value when its patent share in a specific technological area is larger than the average for all other countries. The RTP value is negative when the country reports a below-average level of activity in the area under consideration.

3. By now, figures for the regional distribution of BMBF's direct project promotion for all German cities and counties (i.e including the East German ones) are available for 1992 and 1993 only. Because of the danger of statistical distortions (only two years) and the atypical transformation situation of East Germany's economy at the beginning of the 1990s, this part of the empirical analysis is restricted to West German cities and communities. The east German share of BMBF's R&D project promotion in favour of domestic recipients was 12.5 per cent and 21 per cent in 1992 and 1993 respectively (BMBF 'Regionalkatalog 1992 resp. 1993 Direkte Projektförderung'). However, several special measures in favour of eastern Germany are included in this figure.

4. The city and communal district of Munich received 12.4 per cent (DM 414.8 million) of the corresponding BMBF budget in 1993; in 1985 its grant amounted only to 11.9 per cent.

5. In the next phase of this comprehensive research project, seven non-German European regions (Stockholm, Barcelona, Vienna, south Wales, North Holland, Slovenia and Gironde) will be investigated using the same questionnaires in order to enable a comparison of innovative intraregional linkages in different European countries. Empirical work started in 1997.

6. The surveys conducted by the Fraunhofer Institute for Systems and Innovation Research include firms and research institutions in Alsace – the French region bordering on Baden – which are disregarded in this chapter.

7. This research is being funded by the German Research Association (Deutsche Forschungsgemeinschaft, DFG, Award No. Scha 198/32-1) and was designed as a joint research project of the following research teams: the Department of Economic Geography at the University of Hanover (Ludwig Schätzl and Rolf Sternberg – the latter now with the Department of Economic and Social Geography at the University of Cologne – as project leaders and responsible for the research triangle); the Fraunhofer Institute of Systems and Innovation Research in Karlsruhe (Frieder Meyer-Krahmer and Knut Koschatzky, responsible for Baden), and the Faculty of Economics and Business Administration of the Technical University Bergakademie Freiberg (Michael Fritsch, responsible for Saxony). Most of the empirical work was done in 1995 and 1996.

8. The criterion for the existence of innovative linkages is here the valuation (as a very important form of cooperation) of the inclusion of partners in project planning and implementation or the joint implementation of R&D.

PART III

North American Studies

CHAPTER EIGHT

Regional Networks and Innovation in Silicon Valley and Route 128

AnnaLee Saxenian

Introduction

The competitive advantages of regional clusters have become the focus of scholarly and policy attention. Once they were only the province of economic geographers and regional scientists, but the work of Paul Krugman (1991) and Michael Porter (1990) has spurred widespread interest in regions at the same time that economic activity is becoming increasingly global. These newcomers have ignored an already extensive and sophisticated literature on the dynamics of industrial localization (see, for example, Storper 1989; Scott 1988a, b; Vernon 1960). Yet, like their predecessors, they share a reliance on external economies to explain the advantages that are derived from the spatial of clustering of economic activity.

In this chapter I compare California's Silicon Valley and Route 128 in Massachusetts to suggest the limits of the concept of external economies and propose an alternative, network approach to analysing regional economies. The common notion of external economies is based on an assumption that the firm is an atomistic unit of production with clearly defined boundaries. By drawing a sharp distinction between what occurs inside and what occurs outside the firm, scholars overlook the complex and historically evolved relations between the internal organization of firms and their connections to one another and the social structures and institutions of a particular locality. The network perspective helps explain the divergent performance of apparently comparable regional clusters, such as Silicon Valley and Route 128, and provides important insights into the local sources of innovation in an increasingly global economy.

The limits of external economies

Alfred Marshall (1920) developed the notion of 'external economies of scale' to refer to the sources of productivity increase that lie outside individual firms. In the classic view, producers derive external benefits by sharing the fixed costs of common resources, such as infrastructure and services, skilled labour pools and specialized suppliers, and a common knowledge base. In addition, some theorists distinguish external economies that depend on the size of the market, including such factors as a labour pool and specialized supplier base (pecuniary external economies) from those that involve spillovers of knowledge between firms (technological external economies). When these factors of production are geographically concentrated, firms gain the additional benefits of spatial proximity, or 'agglomeration economies'. Once established in a locality, such an advantage becomes self-reinforcing through a dynamic process of increasing returns (B. Arthur 1990; Krugman 1991; Scott 1988b; Storper 1989).

Students of regional development typically treat Silicon Valley and Route 128 as classic examples of the external economies that are derived from industrial localization. They are seen as cumulatively self-reinforcing agglomerations of technical skill, venture capital, specialized input suppliers and services, infrastructure, and spillovers of knowledge associated with proximity to universities and informal information flows (see, for example, Castells 1989; Hall and Markusen 1985; Krugman 1991; Porter 1990; Scott 1988b). Some researchers have compared them to the nineteenth-century industrial districts described by Alfred Marshall (Piore and Sabel 1984).

Yet this approach cannot account for the divergent performance of the two regional economies. In spite of their common origins in post-war military spending and university-based research, Silicon Valley and Route 128 have responded differently to intensified international competition. Both regions faced downturns in the 1980s. Although Silicon Valley recovered quickly from the crisis of its leading semiconductor producers, Route 128 shows few signs of reversing a decline that began in the early 1980s. The rapid growth of a new wave of start-ups and the renewed dynamism of established companies such as Intel and Hewlett-Packard were evidence that Silicon Valley had regained its former vitality. Along Route 128, by contrast, start-ups failed to compensate for continuing layoffs at the Digital Equipment Corporation and other minicomputer companies. By the end of the 1980s, Route 128 producers had ceded their long-standing dominance in computer production to Silicon Valley.

In 1990 Silicon Valley-based producers exported more than $11 billion in electronics products, almost one-third of the nation's total, compared to Route 128's $4.6 billion (*Electronic Business* 1992). Finally, Silicon Valley was the home of 39 of the nation's 100 fastest-growing electronics companies, whereas Route 128 claimed only 4. By 1990 both southern California and Texas had surpassed Route 128 as locations of fast-growing electronics firms.

The concepts of agglomeration and external economies alone cannot explain why clusters of specialized technical skills, suppliers and information produced a virtuous and self-reinforcing dynamic of increasing industrial advances in Silicon Valley, while producing relative decline in Route 128. These theories account for regional stagnation or decline through imprecise references to 'diseconomies' of agglomeration or the accumulation of negative externalities. Yet if such diseconomies are related to the overall size of a regional cluster, the degree of congestion or the costs of production, growth should have slowed in the more densely populated Silicon Valley long before it did in Route 128. The simple fact of spatial proximity evidently reveals little about the ability of firms to respond to the fast-changing markets and technologies that now characterize international competition.

The distinction between internal and external economies is based on the assumption that the firm is an atomistic unit of production with clearly defined boundaries.

Treating regions as collections of autonomous firms has even led some observers to conclude that Silicon Valley suffers from excessive, even pathological, fragmentation (Florida and Kenney 1990). Proponents of this argument overlook the complex of institutional and social relationships that connect the producers in its fragmented industrial structure. Researchers who adopt the broadest interpretations of technological external economies recognize that firms learn from each other through flows of information, ideas and know-how (Storper 1989), but they do so only by denying the theoretical distinction between internal and external economies, between what is inside and outside the firm.

A network approach to regions

Far from being isolated from what lies outside them, firms are embedded in networks of social and institutional relationships that shape, and are shaped by, their strategies and structures (Granovetter 1985). The network perspective helps illuminate the historically evolved relationships between the internal organization of firms and their connections to one another and to the social structures and institutions of their particular localities (Nohria and Eccles 1992b; Powell 1987).

A network approach can be used to argue that, despite similar origins and technologies, Silicon Valley and Route 128 evolved distinct industrial systems in the post-war period. The differences in productive organization have been overlooked by economic analysts or treated simply as superficial differences between 'laid-back' California and the more 'buttoned-down' East Coast. Far from superficial, these variations demonstrate the importance of the local social and institutional determinants of industrial adaptation. In particular, they help explain why these two regions have responded so differently to the same external forces, from the lowering of global trade barriers and the intensification of international competition to cuts in the domestic military budget.

Silicon Valley has a regional network-based industrial system that promotes learning and mutual adjustment among specialist producers of a complex of related technologies. The region's dense social networks and open labour markets encourage entrepreneurship and experimentation. Companies compete intensely while at the same time learning from each other about changing markets and technologies through informal communications and collaborative practices. Loosely linked team structures encourage horizontal communication among firm divisions and with outside suppliers and customers. The functional boundaries within firms are porous in the network-based system, as are the boundaries between firms, and between firms and local institutions such as trade associations and universities.

The Route 128 region, in contrast, is dominated by autarkic (self-sufficient) corporations that internalize a wide range of productive activities. Practices of secrecy and corporate loyalty govern relations between firms and their customers, suppliers and competitors, reinforcing a regional culture that encourages stability and self-reliance. Corporate hierarchies ensure that authority remains centralized and information tends to flow vertically. Social and technical networks are largely internal to the firm, and the boundaries between firms, and between firms and local institutions, remain far more distinct in this independent firm-based system.

Regional networks and industrial adaptation

Understanding regional economies as networks of relationships rather than as clusters of atomistic producers, and thinking of the regions as examples of two models of industrial systems – the regional network-based system and the independent firm-based system – help illuminate the divergent trajectories of the Silicon Valley and Route 128 economies during the 1980s. For example, Silicon Valley's superior performance cannot be attributed to differentials in real-estate costs, wages or tax levels. Land and office space were significantly more costly in most of Silicon Valley than in the Route 128 region during the 1980s; the wages and salaries of production workers, engineers and managers were higher (Sherwood-Call, 1992), and there were no significant differences in tax rates between California and Massachusetts (Tannenwald 1987).

Nor can the differences in regional performance be traced to patterns of defence spending. Route 128 has historically relied more heavily on military spending than has Silicon Valley, and hence is more vulnerable to defence cutbacks; however, the downturn in the Massachusetts electronics industry began in 1984, when the value of prime contracts to the region was still increasing. Although defence spending cannot account for the timing of the downturn in the region's technology industry, the military spending cutbacks that began in the late 1980s exacerbated the difficulties of an already troubled regional economy.

Finally, while it may be tempting to attribute Silicon Valley's prosperity to the ability of local firms to shift low-wage jobs elsewhere, this cannot account for the differential performance of the two regions. Technology firms from both Silicon Valley and Route 128 have, since the 1960s, moved their routine manufacturing operations to lower-wage regions of the United States and the Third World (Scott 1988b; Saxenian 1985).

Route 128's difficulties lie in the rigidities of its local industrial system. The independent firm-based system flourished in an environment of market stability and slowly changing technologies because extensive integration offered the advantages of scale economies and market control (Chandler 1977). It has been overwhelmed, however, by changing competitive conditions. Corporations that invest in dedicated equipment and specialized worker skills find themselves locked in to obsolete technologies and markets, and their self-sufficient structures limit their ability to adapt in a timely fashion. The surrounding regional economy in turn is deprived of resources for self-regeneration because large firms tend to internalize most local supplies of skill and technology.

Regional network-based industrial systems like that of Silicon Valley, in contrast, are well suited to conditions of technical and market uncertainty. Producers in these systems deepen their capabilities by specializing while engaging in close, but not exclusive, relations with other specialists. Network relations promote a process of reciprocal innovation that reduces the distinctions between large and small firms and between industries and sectors (DeBresson and Walker, 1991). Evidence from the industrial districts of Europe suggests that the localization of know-how and information encourages the pursuit of diverse technical and market opportunities through spontaneous regroupings of skill, technology and capital. The region, if not all the firms in the region, is organized to innovate continuously (Best 1990; Sabel 1988).

The competitive advantages of network organizational forms are reflected in the experience of Japanese industry as well. Japanese producers of electronics and automobiles, for example, rely on extensive networks of small and medium-sized suppliers, to which they are linked through ties of trust and partial ownership. Although Japan's large firms may have often exploited suppliers in the past, many firms increasingly collaborate with them, encouraging them to expand their technological capabilities and organizational autonomy (Nishiguchi 1989). Like their Silicon Valley counterparts, these producers tend to be geographically clustered and depend heavily on informal information exchange as well as more formal forms of cooperation (Friedman 1988, Imai 1989).

As the case of Japan suggests, there are large-firm as well as small-firm variants of network-based systems (Dyer 1993; Fruin 1992, 1993; Herrigel 1993). Large corporations can integrate into regional networks through a process of internal decentralization. As independent business units are forced by competition to achieve the technical and productive standards of outsiders, they often rely on external institutions that facilitate knowledge sharing and collaboration with suppliers and customers.

Of course, all economic activity does not cluster within a single regional economy. Firms in network systems serve global markets and collaborate extensively with distant customers, suppliers and competitors. Technology firms, in particular, are highly international. However, the most strategic relationships are often local because of the importance of timeliness and face-to-face communications in complex, uncertain and fast-changing industries (Nohria and Eccles 1992a).

Regional network versus firm-based systems

In the rest of this chapter I use a set of paired comparisons to illustrate the differences in the organization and adaptive capacities of Silicon Valley's regional network and Route 128's independent firm-based industrial systems. The comparison of Apollo Computers and Sun Microsystems – both 1980s-generation start-ups competing in the emerging workstation market – demonstrates how small firms benefit from the open flows of information, technology and know-how in a network system. The comparison of the Digital Equipment Corporation (DEC) and Hewlett-Packard Co. (HP) – the leading computer systems producers in the two regions – in turn shows how regional networks can facilitate the reorganization of large firms.

Clearly, these cases alone cannot encompass the experience of two complex regional economies. For an extended treatment of the origins and evolution of the two regional economies, see Saxenian (1994). Nor can the focus on individual firms fully portray the myriad decentralized relationships in a regional network-based system. Indeed, the resilience of Silicon Valley's network system lies precisely in the fact that it does not depend upon the success of any individual firm. However, these comparisons illustrate the social and institutional dimensions of productive organization that are overlooked in the concept of external economies and the competitive advantages of regional networks in the current economic conditions.

Start-ups: Apollo Computer and Sun Microsystems

The largest wave of start-ups in Silicon Valley's history began in the late 1970s and accelerated during the 1980s. The region was the home to scores of new ventures that specialized in everything from workstations and semi-custom semiconductors to disk drives, networking hardware and software, and computer-aided engineering and design. These start-ups contributed to the diversification of the regional economy away from its original concentration in semiconductors and into a complex of computer-related specialists.

In contrast with the upsurge of entrepreneurial activity in Silicon Valley, the pace of start-ups along Route 128 slowed during the 1980s. Massachusetts experienced lower rates of new high-tech firm formation between 1976 and 1986 than either New England or the United States as a whole (Kirchoff and McAuliffe 1988). Also, the performance of companies founded during the 1980s was disappointing. Nothing in the Route 128 experience matched the spectacular successes of the 1980s generation of Silicon Valley start-ups such as Sun Microsystems, Conner Peripherals and Silicon Graphics. By the end of the decade, public companies that were started in Silicon Valley during the 1980s collectively accounted for more than $22 billion in sales, whereas their Route 128 counterparts had generated only $2 billion (Standard & Poor's 1992).

Investment decisions reflected this divergence. Annual venture capital investments in northern California during the 1980s were double or triple those in Massachusetts. Over the course of the decade, Massachusetts-based companies received some $3 billion in venture capital, or 75 per cent of the total raised in the region, whereas firms in northern California received $9 billion, or 130 per cent of the total capital raised locally. Silicon Valley companies were consistently awarded at least one-third of the nation's total venture capital pool.

By 1992, 113 technology enterprises located in Silicon Valley reported revenues exceeding $100 million, compared to 74 companies in Route 128. Moreover, the great majority of Silicon Valley's $100 million enterprises were started during the 1970s and 1980s, whereas those in Route 128 were overwhelmingly started prior to 1970 (CorpTech 1993).

The comparison of Apollo Computer and Sun Microsystems demonstrates how the autarkic structures and practices of Route 128's independent firm-based system created disadvantages for start-ups in a technologically fast-paced industry. Apollo pioneered the engineering workstation in 1980 and initially was enormously successful. By most accounts the firm had a product that was superior to that of its Silicon Valley counterpart, Sun Microsystems (which was started two years after Apollo, in 1982). The two firms competed neck and neck during the mid-1980s, but in 1987 Apollo fell behind the faster-moving, more responsive Sun, and never regained its lead. By the time Apollo was purchased by Hewlett-Packard in 1989, it had fallen to fourth place in the industry, whereas Sun led the industry with more than $3 billion in sales (Bell and Corliss 1989).

Apollo's founder, 46-year-old William Poduska, one of Route 128's few repeat entrepreneurs, had worked for Honeywell and helped to found Prime Computer before starting Apollo. Not only was Poduska himself well steeped in the culture and organizational practices of the region's established minicomputer firms, but the entire Apollo management team moved with him from Prime. This history contrasts with that of the typical Silicon Valley start-up, in which talent was typically drawn from a variety of different firms, and even industries, representing a mix of corporate and technical experience.

Not surprisingly, Apollo's initial strategy and structure reflected the model of corporate self-sufficiency of the region's large minicomputer companies. In spite of its pioneering workstation design, for example, the firm adopted proprietary standards and chose to design and fabricate its own central processor and specialized integrated circuits. Although it sourced components such as disk drives, monitors and power supplies, Apollo began with a proprietary operating system and architecture that made its products incompatible with other machines. Sun, in contrast, pioneered open systems. The firm's founders, all in their twenties, adopted the UNIX operating system because they felt that the market would never accept a workstation custom-designed by four graduate students. By making the specifications for its systems widely available to suppliers and competitors, Sun challenged the proprietary and highly profitable approach of industry leaders IBM, DEC and HP, which locked customers in to a single vendor of hardware and software.

This strategy allowed Sun to focus on designing the hardware and software for its workstations and to limit manufacturing to prototypes, final assembly and testing. Unlike the traditional vertically integrated computer manufacturers, Sun purchased virtually all its components off the shelf from external vendors and subcontracted the manufacture and assembly of its printed circuit boards. (In the late 1980s Sun began assembling some of its most advanced printed circuit boards internally.) The firm even relied on outside partners for the design and manufacture of the reduced instruction set computing (RISC)-based microprocessor at the heart of its workstations and encouraged its vendors to market the chip to its competitors.

Although specialization is often an economic necessity for start-ups, Sun did not abandon this strategy even as the firm grew into a multi-billion dollar company. Why, asked Sun's vice president of manufacturing Jim Bean in the late 1980s, should Sun vertically integrate when hundreds of Silicon Valley companies invest heavily in staying at the leading edge in the design and manufacture of integrated circuits, disk drives, and most other computer components and subsystems? Relying on outside suppliers greatly reduced Sun's overheads and ensured that the firm's workstations contained state-of-the art hardware.

This focus also allowed Sun rapidly to introduce complex new products and continuously alter its product mix. According to Bean, 'If we were making a stable set of products, I could make a solid case for vertical integration' (Whiting 1987). Relying on external suppliers allowed Sun to introduce an unprecedented four major new product generations during its first five years of operations and to double the price : performance ratio each successive year. Sun eluded clone-makers through its sheer pace of new product introduction. By the time a competitor could reverse-engineer a Sun workstation and develop the manufacturing capability to imitate it, Sun had introduced a successive generation.

As a result, the Sun workstations, although vulnerable to imitation by competitors, were also significantly cheaper to produce and sold for half the price of the proprietary Apollo systems (Bulkeley 1987). Sun founder and chief executive officer Scott McNealy described the advantage for customers:

> We were totally open with them and said, 'We won't lock you into anything. You can build it yourself if we fail', whereas our competition was too locked up in this very East Coast minicomputer world, which has always been proprietary, so that encouraging cloning or giving someone access to your source code was considered like letting the corporate jewels out or something. But customers want it. (Sheff 1989).

It quickly became apparent that customers preferred the cheaper, non-proprietary Sun workstations. However, Apollo, like the Route 128 minicomputer producers, was slow to abandon its proprietary operating system and hardware. As late as 1985 the firm's management refused to acknowledge the growing demand for open standards and even turned down the offer of a state-of-the-art RISC microprocessor from Silicon Valley-based MIPS Computers. Apollo finally committed 30 per cent of its R&D budget to RISC development in 1986, but the effort became an economic burden, and the chip it ultimately developed internally was no faster than the chip it could have bought two years earlier from MIPS.

Sun's innovative computing strategy was inseparable from the firm's location in the sophisticated and diversified technical infrastructure of Silicon Valley. Apollo, in contrast, responded sluggishly to industry changes, in part because of a more limited regional infrastructure. According to Jeffrey Kalb, an engineer who worked for DEC in Route 128 for many years before moving to Silicon Valley to start the MasPar Computer Corporation,

> It's hard for a small company to start in Route 128 because you can't get stuff like IC's and disk drives fast. Route 128 is dominated by large, vertically integrated firms that do everything themselves. In Silicon Valley, you can get anything you want on the market.
> You can get all those things in Route 128 sooner or later, but the decisions are much faster if you're in Silicon Valley. From the East Coast, interacting with the West Coast is only possible for 3–4 hours a day because of the time difference, and you spend lots of time on the phone. It's no one thing, but if you get a 20–30 per cent time to market advantage by being in Silicon Valley, that's really significant. (personal communication 1991)

Apollo's other major misstep was in its 1984 choice of a president and chief executive officer to replace Poduska. Following the tradition of the large Route 128 companies, it hired a long-time East Coast corporate executive who had worked his way up the ranks at General Electric and then become the president of GTE Corporation. The 53-year-old Thomas Vanderslice was asked to bring 'big-company organizational skills' to fast-growing Apollo and help the firm to 'grow up'. He couldn't have had a more different background than the twenty-something graduate students and computer whizzes who had founded Sun Microsystems two years earlier (Beam and Frons 1985).

The media played up the superficial differences between Apollo and Sun: the buttoned-down, conservative Apollo executives alongside the casually attired, laid-back founders of Sun. It made for great journalism: Vanderslice enforced a dress code and discouraged beards and moustaches at Apollo, and Sun threw monthly beer bashes and employees showed up on Halloween in gorilla suits. Whereas Vanderslice was chauffeured to work daily in a limousine, an April Fool's Day prank at Sun involved placing founder Bill Joy's Ferrari in the middle of the company's decorative pond.

However, the important differences between the two firms lay in their management styles and organization: Vanderslice brought in a traditional, risk-averse management team who focused on imposing financial and quality controls, cutting costs and diversifying the firm's customer base. Former Apollo employees describe him as an archetypal 'bean counter' who established formal decision-making procedures and systems in the firm at a time when flexibility and innovation were most needed.

This commitment to formality, hierarchy and long-term stability – which typified most large Route 128 companies – could not have offered a greater contrast with the 'controlled chaos' that characterized Sun (Weiss and Delbecq 1987). Like many Silicon Valley companies, Sun developed decentralized organizational forms in its efforts to preserve the flexibility and enthusiasm of a start-up even as it grew. Corporate strategy was generated by discussions among representatives of autonomous divisions rather than dictated by a central committee, and Sun's culture encouraged informal communications, participation and individual initiative (Levine 1988).

In the late 1980s, when Sun surpassed Apollo in both sales and profitability, more than a dozen Apollo managers defected to their West Coast rival. They joined other experienced and ambitious engineers at ailing Route 128 companies who recognized that opportunities to join or start technologically exciting new ventures lay not in New England, but along the increasingly crowded freeways of northern California. As skilled engineers moved west, the advantages of Silicon Valley's network-based industrial system multiplied.

Large firms: Digital Equipment and Hewlett-Packard

The successes of the 1980s-generation start-ups were the most visible sign that Silicon Valley was adapting faster than Route 128, but changes within the regions' largest firms were equally important. Established producers in Silicon Valley began to decentralize their operations, creating inter-firm production networks that built on the region's social and technical interdependencies and strengthened its industrial system. By institutionalizing long-standing practices of informal cooperation and exchange, they formalized the process of collective learning in the region. Local firms redefined themselves by participating in local production networks, and the region as a whole organized to create new markets and sectors.

Adaptation in the Route 128 economy, by contrast, was constrained by the autarkic organization and practices of its leading producers. Focused inward and lacking dynamic start-ups from which to draw innovative technologies or organizational models, the region's large minicomputer firms adjusted very slowly to the new market conditions. By the end of the decade they were struggling to survive in a computer industry that they had once dominated.

Although it is very difficult to develop accurate and useful measures of vertical integration, one indication of the greater reliance of Route 128 firms on internal production is the lower sales per employee figure shown in Table 8.1 for the leading Route 128 firms and their Silicon Valley counterparts.

The comparison of DEC and HP during the 1980s highlights the differing relationship of large firms to the region in network and firm-based industrial systems. By 1990 both were $13 billion companies and the largest and oldest civilian

Table 8.1 1990 sales per employees: Silicon Valley and Route 128 ($ thousands)

Silicon Valley		Route 128	
Apple	382.6	Prime	128.7
Sun	214.6	Wang	123.7
Silicon Graphics	200.0	Data General	114.8
HP	143.8	DEC	104.4

Source: 'The Electronic Business 200', *Electronic Business*, 22 July 1991, 43–9; Annual 10K Company Reports

employers in their respective regions. (Lockheed Missile and Space and Raytheon Corporation were the largest private employers in Silicon Valley and Route 128, respectively. But both were military contractors with limited commercial business.) Both DEC and HP were vertically integrated producers of proprietary mini-computers with shared origins in an earlier era of computing. Yet the companies responded differently to comparable competitive challenges. HP gradually opened up by building a network of local alliances and subcontracting relationships while strengthening its global reach. DEC, in spite of its formal commitment to decentralization, retained a substantially more autarkic organizational structure and corporate mind-set.

The transformations in the computer industry during the 1980s placed a premium on speed and focus. Computer makers were forced to develop and bring new products to market faster than ever before, often in a matter of months. HP vice president of corporate manufacturing Harold Edmondson claimed in 1988 that half of the firm's orders in any year came from products introduced in the preceding three years (personal communication 1988). At the same time, the cost of developing new products increased as they became more technologically complex. Innovation in all segments of the industry – from microprocessors and logic chips to system and applications software to disk drives, screens, input–output devices and networking devices – meant that it was more and more difficult for a single firm to produce all of these components, let alone remain at the forefront of the underlying technologies. This increasingly competitive environment posed a challenge for established computer makers like DEC and HP. By 1990, however, HP had successfully managed the transition from minicomputers to workstations with open systems, whereas DEC remained dependent on its proprietary VAX line of minicomputers. As a result, even though both enjoyed 1990 revenues from electronics products of $13 billion, HP earned $771 million and DEC lost $95 million.

Variations in corporate performance always have multiple causes, but the firms' organizational structures and their relationships to their respective regions help explain these differences. DEC maintained clear boundaries between itself and other companies or institutions in the region. This was, in part, a result of extensive vertical integration: the firm designed and manufactured internally virtually all software and hardware components for its computers. Moreover, DEC's corporate culture rewarded secrecy and corporate loyalty; departed employees were typically treated like pariahs and cut off from the corporate 'family' (Rifkin and Harrar 1990). As a result, the technical and social networks that mattered were all internal, and there were few opportunities for collaboration, learning and exchange with other local firms.

HP was both less dominant in Silicon Valley and more open to the surrounding economy. DEC dominated the Route 128 region in a way that no firm did in Silicon Valley. With more than 30,000 Massachusetts employees in 1990, DEC accounted for almost 20 per cent of regional high-technology employment, whereas HP's 20,000 Silicon Valley employees made up only 8 per cent of the regional total. HP benefited from a long history of participation in the region's rich associational life and fluid labour markets. Continuous and open exchange about everything from the latest start-ups to technical breakthroughs allowed local engineers to stay at the leading edge of new computing technologies and market trends (C. Vedoe, manager, workstation marketing, Sun Microsystems, personal communication 1990).

HP's decentralized divisional structure also offered an ideal training ground for general managers. Former HP executives were responsible for starting more than eighteen firms in Silicon Valley between 1974 and 1984, including such notable successes such as Rolm, Tandem and Pyramid Technology (Mitchell 1989). A sixteen-year veteran of DEC who now works for HP described how the firm's autonomous divisions preserve opportunities for entrepreneurship:

> Running a business at the division level, you get a chance to be a general manager. You get a chance to learn ... to be creative. ... There are a lot of new divisions springing up [within HP], new ideas springing up, brand new businesses, and old divisions that couldn't make it anymore transform themselves into new businesses. (P. Porter 1993)

In contrast, DEC's matrix organization – which represented only a partial break from traditional functional corporate hierarchies – stifled the development of managerial skill and initiative in the Route 128 region. The matrix demanded continuous negotiations to reach consensus, and despite the addition of cross-functional relations among product groups, final authority remained highly centralized (Schein 1985). As a result, aside from Data General, it is difficult to identify successful spin-offs from DEC.

Both DEC and HP began the 1980s with the bureaucracy and internal conflicts typical of large firms. Both missed opportunities and made false starts in workstation and RISC markets, and both had difficulty keeping up with newer, more agile competitors. Yet HP quickly became the leading producer in the fastest-growing segments of the market. By 1990 HP controlled 31 per cent of the $8 billion RISC computer systems market – a market in which DEC still had no presence. HP also boasted a 21 per cent share of the $7.2 billion workstation market and 13 per cent of the $33 million UNIX computer systems market, compared to DEC's 16 per cent and 8 per cent respectively. In addition, HP controlled 66 per cent of the market for desktop laser printers and 70 per cent of the market for ink-jet printers (Nee 1991).

Hewlett-Packard reinvented itself by investing heavily in RISC microprocessor technology and the UNIX operating system well before most established computer companies recognized the importance of open standards. By betting the future of the computer division (which accounted for 53 per cent of HP revenues) on RISC systems in 1985 and by undertaking internal reorganizations that unified and rationalized the firm's disparate computer divisions and component technologies, HP positioned itself advantageously for emerging markets (Yoder 1991). In 1990, for example, the firm created an independent team to develop a RISC workstation. The ultimate product, the Series 700 workstations, was far ahead of the rest of the industry and allowed HP quickly to become one of the world's biggest sellers of UNIX systems. A financial analyst for Salomon Brothers assessed the situation:

> they [HP] have done an excellent job of identifying trends in the computer market such as Unix, RISC, and PCs. No other major computer company has done a better job of positioning.... They are the one company I can count on surviving. HP has a better base today than IBM or DEC. (Greene 1990)

HP's ability to identify market trends early reflected the firm's openness to external changes and a Silicon Valley location that gave it easy access to state-of-the-art information markets and technologies. This flexibility contrasts sharply with DEC's prolonged denial of the growing demand for personal computers and UNIX-based systems. In the words of a former DEC marketing manager, 'DEC had its head in the sand. They didn't believe that the world would really change. ... They got focused on the internal evolution of the company rather than on the customer or markets' (C. Vedoe, manager, workstation marketing, Sun Microsystems, personal communication 1990). As late as 1985, DEC chief executive officer Olsen referred to personal computers as 'snake oil' (Rifkin and Harrar 1990).

DEC was plagued by ongoing internal conflicts and a series of costly course reversals in its efforts to enter the workstation and open systems markets. The firm's strategy remained confused and inconsistent even after the defection of large customers such as GE and AT&T forced Olsen to authorize a shift to open systems and away from the vision of a single proprietary VMS operating system and VAX architecture for all DEC systems (J. DeNucci, vice president, Entry Systems Group, MIPS Computer Systems, personal communication 1990).

DEC's research lab in Silicon Valley developed state-of-the-art RISC and UNIX technologies in the early 1980s, but its discoveries were virtually ignored by head-quarters, which continued to favour the highly profitable VAX–VMS system (Comerford 1992). Insiders claim that DEC's Palo Alto lab contributed more to other Silicon Valley firms such as Sun and MIPS than it did to DEC because its findings quickly diffused to other Silicon Valley firms through technical papers and local industry forums (T. Basche, vice president, Sparcstation Group, Sun Microsystems, personal communication 1991; T. Furlong, RISC workstation manager, DEC Palo Alto, personal communication 1991).

DEC finally decided to build its own RISC-based workstation in 1986, following conventional wisdom within the firm that the RISC microprocessor should be designed and built in-house. It was not until 1992, however, after a series of costly reversals, that the firm finally introduced its own RISC processor, Alpha (Comerford 1992). By this time, DEC controlled only 13 per cent of the workstation market (McWilliams 1992).

The contrast between DEC's Palo Alto Lab and its East Coast operations is instructive. Engineers who worked at both emphasize how different the two were: DEC East was internally focused, whereas DEC Palo Alto was well integrated into Silicon Valley's social and technical networks. According to Joe DeNucci, a former employee,

> DEC definitely relates differently to the regional economy in Silicon Valley than in Route 128. DEC is the largest employer in Route 128 and you come to think that the

centre of the universe is north of the Mass Pike and east of Route 128. The thinking is totally DEC-centric: all the adversaries are within the company. Even the non-DEC guys compete only with DEC.

DEC Palo Alto is a completely different world. DEC is just another face in the crowd in Silicon Valley; the adversaries are external, firms like Intel and Sun. It forces a far more aggressive and 'prove-it' mind-set. (personal communication 1991)

He described his years with the DEC engineering and development group in Palo Alto:

We had an immense amount of autonomy, and we cherished the distance from home base, from the 'puzzle palace' and from the 'corridor warriors' and all the endless meetings. It was an idyllic situation, a group of exceptionally talented people who were well connected to Stanford and to the Silicon Valley networks. People would come out from Maynard and say, 'This feels like a different company.' The longer they stayed, the more astounded they were. (personal communication 1991)

Tom Furlong, who headed a DEC workstation division in Maynard before moving west in 1985, described the newly formed Workstation Group in Palo Alto as a typical Silicon Valley start-up. The group's autonomy from headquarters allowed members to take full advantage of the local knowledge available within the regional economy. At the same time, the group benefited from the financial backing and reputation of a large, well-established corporation. By 1990 Furlong was the manager of a 275-person group. He compared his experience working in the two locations:

It would be very difficult for me to do what I'm doing here within DEC on the East Coast. I'm a fairly autonomous business manager out here, with all the functions necessary to success reporting to me and the freedom to use outside suppliers. Back East, I would have to rely on DEC's internal suppliers and functional groups for everything.

We're like a start-up organization here. We're not really significant to DEC, we're only contributing $.5 billion to them, but we have the advantages of their resources and name. (personal communication 1991)

He explained the consequences of these organizational differences for new product development:

The same job of bringing a new workstation to market takes two times as long in the East Coast and many more people than it does here. In Maynard, I had to do everything inside the company. Here I can rely on the other companies in Silicon Valley. It's easier and cheaper for me to rely on the little companies in Silicon Valley to take care of the things I need, and it forces them to compete and be more efficient. At DEC, the commitment to internal supply and the familial environment means that bad people don't get cut off. I had to depend on all sorts of inefficient people back at DEC East. (personal communication 1991)

The Workstation Group did not achieve this independent position without resistance: 'It was a huge embarrassment to them that we had to rely on external suppliers such as MIPS. DEC takes great pride in being vertically integrated, in having control over its entire system' (personal communication 1991).

DEC was ultimately unable to assimilate the lessons of its geographically distant Palo Alto group, in spite of its technical advances, and in 1992 transferred it back to Maynard headquarters. Furlong and other members of the workstation team left DEC to work for Silicon Valley companies.

HP began the decade with a comparable level of vertical integration to DEC, but soon recognized that it could not continue to produce everything in-house. In the late 1980s HP began outsourcing most of the sheet metal fabrication, plastics and machining for its computer systems. The firm also consolidated the management of some 50 disparate circuit technology units into two autonomous divisions, Integrated Circuit Fabrication and Printed Circuit Board Fabrication. These divisions were organized as internal subcontractors for the company's computer systems and instrument divisions. They were forced to compete with external vendors for HP's business and expected to remain competitive in technology, service and cost to sell successfully to outside customers.

HP also built alliances with local companies that offered complementary technologies. During the 1980s the firm created partnerships with Octel Communications for voice-data integration, 3Com for local area network-manager servers, and Weitek for semiconductor design. An HP manager explained the acquisition of a 10 per cent stake in Octel: 'In the business and office processing environment, no one company can develop everything on its own, so we're increasingly looking at forming alliances to meet our customers' needs' (Tuller 1988).

The partnership between HP and semiconductor design specialist Weitek illustrates how a large firm benefited from Silicon Valley's networks. Tiny Weitek, which lacked manufacturing capacity of its own, was the leading designer of ultra-high-speed 'number-crunching' chips for complex engineering problems. In 1987 HP opened its state-of-the-art fabrication facility to Weitek for use as a foundry, hoping to improve the performance of the Weitek chips in its workstations. Realizing that the manufacturing process at the foundry Weitek used slowed down the chips, the HP engineers suggested fully optimizing the Weitek designs by manufacturing them with HP's more advanced fabrication process. This culminated in a three-year agreement that allowed the firms to benefit directly from each other's technical expertise.

The arrangement assured HP of a steady supply of Weitek's chips and allowed HP to introduce its new workstation faster than if it had designed the chip in-house. It provided Weitek with a market, the legitimacy of a close association with HP, as well as access to a state-of-the-art foundry. Moreover, the final product represented a significant advance over what either firm could have produced independently. This partnership allowed each to draw on the other's distinctive and complementary expertise to devise novel solutions to shared problems.

HP opened itself to outside influences during the 1980s, creating a model of a large firm that is internally decentralized and horizontally linked to networks of other specialists. DEC's dominant and isolated position in Route 128, by contrast, hindered its efforts to shift to new technologies or a new corporate form. Saddled with an autarkic organizational structure and located in a region that offered little social or technical support for a more flexible business model, DEC's difficulties worsened.

In 1992 DEC chief executive officer and founder Ken Olsen was forced to resign after the company reported a $2.8 billion quarterly loss – the biggest in computer industry history. One year later, HP surpassed DEC in sales to claim the position as the nation's second largest computer company, after IBM. As a final irony, in 1993 DEC moved a design team for its new Alpha microprocessor from the East Coast to Palo Alto to immerse Alpha engineers in the Silicon Valley semiconductor community. According to industry analyst Ronald Bowen of Dataquest, 'Digital is finding the support network of other companies is very, very limited back East. In effect, what's been happening is the people who work on the East coast spend a lot of time flying to San Jose anyway' (Nash and Hayes 1993).

Conclusion: regional networks in a global economy

This comparison of Silicon Valley and Route 128 highlights the analytical leverage gained by treating regions as networks of relationships rather than as collections of atomistic firms. By transcending the theoretical distinction between what lies inside and outside the firm, this approach offers important insights into the structure and dynamics of regional economies. It directs attention to the complex networks of social relationships within and between firms, and between firms and local institutions.

The Silicon Valley experience also suggests that network forms of organization flourish in regional agglomerations. Proximity facilitates the repeated face-to-face interaction that fosters the mix of competition and collaboration required in today's fast-paced technology industries. Yet the case of Route 128 demonstrates that geographic clustering alone does not ensure the emergence of regional networks. Competitive advantage derives as much from the way that skill and technology are organized as from their presence in a regional environment.

These network relationships are not simply local. Regions like Silicon Valley have extensive and important ties to the global economy. The most obvious is their role in international trade. Silicon Valley today is the third largest exporting region in the United States, after the New York and Detroit areas, with $28 billion worth of exports in 1995 (Dorgan 1997). Silicon Valley has also attracted substantial foreign investment, as foreign multinationals seek access to the technological know-how, sophisticated infrastructure and skill base that distinguishes the region. Virtually every industrialized nation in the world today has sought to create a presence in the Silicon Valley networks, whether by establishing a listening post or a research lab, or by creating a partnership or even a full-blown subsidiary in the region (Teece 1992).

The elaboration of the region's supplier networks has reinforced the advantages of locating in Silicon Valley, even as production becomes increasingly globally footloose. Firms locate or expand in the region – in spite of its relatively high costs – in order to become part of its social and technical networks. Geographic proximity enables all firms to monitor emerging technologies closely and avoid being caught off guard by unanticipated breakthroughs. It provides the advantage of speed, as local firms learn about market changes before others do. And it facilitates the frequent face-to-face communications needed for successful collaboration, while also intensifying competitive rivalries.

Obviously not all suppliers are located within the region. Some products and services are not available locally; others are available, but at higher cost. Most Silicon Valley computer firms purchase components such as memory chips and flat panel displays from Asian vendors. Many also rely on offshore fabrication facilities or contract manufacturers to reduce costs when they shift into high-volume production.

As large Silicon Valley producers expand their operations to other parts of the world, they replicate this pattern of geographic localization. Firms such as HP increasingly reject the traditional model of internationalization, which calls for products to be developed at home and low-cost inputs to be purchased from cheap-labour sites, in favour of a strategy that involves building, and even designing, products in the markets in which they are sold. These firms invest in local ties that allow them to accumulate the local knowledge needed to respond more rapidly to the subtle differences between countries and even regions in the ways a product is used and what customers expect of it. Even locations that had once been attractive simply for low-cost labour, such as Singapore and Malaysia, began to upgrade their technology infrastructures during the 1980s, and increasingly offer skilled labour and sophisticated suppliers and customers.

Expanding in distant locations, Silicon Valley firms have thus simultaneously enhanced the capabilities of independent, but linked, regional economies. The lessons of Silicon Valley's network system have thus begun to diffuse to other regions, reinforcing the importance of geographic proximity even in an era of market globalization. The greatest challenge will be to transfer these lessons back to places like Route 128 which have industrial systems that favour stability, self-sufficiency and market control rather than flexibility, openness and continuous innovation.

CHAPTER NINE

Universities in Local Innovation Systems

Attila Varga

Introduction

Subnational regions have increasingly become focal points of contemporary economic activities. Paradoxically, market globalization is a major factor explaining the increasing importance of localities in the spatial organization of economic processes (Acs, de la Mothe and Paquet 1996; A. Scott 1996; Stopford 1996). In the global economy, modern regions are far less subject to changing national policies. Instead, they are increasingly dependent upon the direct effects of world market conditions: the major linkages of regions tend to be not with their host nations, but with the global economy (Ohmae 1993, 1995). Globalization results in expanded markets and increasing competition, strengthening the economic growth potential and the degree of specialization of individual regions (A. Scott 1996).

Besides globalization of economic activities, the recent fact that knowledge has gained a key function in advanced production has a particular relevance for understanding the emerging role of subnational regions in modern economies. Exhibiting exceptional employment and production growth, high-technology industries have moved into a leading-edge position in the past decade (Acs 1996). Unlike traditional production processes, the main economic activities of high-technology industries are related to the production and distribution of knowledge and information, rather than the production and distribution of physical objects (Drucker 1993).

High-technology activities have a predominant tendency to cluster spatially (Audretsch and Feldman 1996; Varga 1998; Varga and Stough 1997). High-technology firms' inherent reliance on external scientific, technological and business knowledge sources is a major explanatory factor behind their spatial concentration. The sensitivity of the transmission of new knowledge to distance provides a principal reason for the development of regional high-technology complexes: the most recent knowledge is usually in such a complex, uncertain and uncodified form that it cannot be transferred over long distances (Storper and Scott 1995). In order to acquire this type of knowledge, firms need to be located in close proximity to each other. It is widely suggested in the literature that local knowledge transmission is facilitated through networks of high-technology firms (Feldman 1994a; Saxenian 1994; Florida 1995).

The emerging importance of knowledge in advanced production challenges the

prevailing notion about the social role of universities. In addition to their traditionally accepted functions as institutions of higher education and basic scientific
research, universities can potentially become major agents of regional economic
growth. The history of the most recognized high-technology centres demonstrates
that the presence of a significant stock of scientific and technical knowledge at
universities can be a critical source of the origin and rapid growth of advanced
technology regions. As illustrated below, technology transfers from university
research to regional high-technology production link academic institutions to the
regional system of innovations.

The oldest and perhaps the best-known high-technology concentrations have
arisen around Boston, Massachusetts, and in San Jose, California. Top research
universities played an active role in the development of both Route 128 (Boston)
and Silicon Valley (San Jose). The economic growth of Route 128 was generated by
the exceptional technological activity of the Massachusetts Institute of Technology
(MIT) (Malecki 1986). MIT not only supported purely academic research, but also
promoted faculty efforts in the areas of application and development. More than
that, university laboratories rewarded researchers who were involved in entrepreneurial activities (Lynn and Long 1982; Teich 1982; Roberts 1981; Saxenian 1994).
As a consequence of this unique, application-oriented research policy, a considerable part of local economic growth has come from a succession of spin-offs from MIT
laboratories (Rogers and Larsen 1984). By the 1960s, 175 firms were identified as
being founded by MIT personnel (Dorfman 1983). Between 1988 and 1993, 40
biotechnology firms were spun off from MIT laboratories, and the university raised
over $70 million in venture capital funds to help create these start-up companies
(Parker and Zilberman 1993). Direct investments of Stanford University in university spin-off companies and Stanford Industrial Park significantly contributed to
economic growth in Silicon Valley (Saxenian 1983, 1985). Compared to MIT,
Stanford was a source of relatively few faculty spin-offs (Malecki 1986); most of the
spin-off companies were established by former university students (Rogers and
Larsen 1984).

In the development of the Cambridge Phenomenon, the role of Cambridge
University in England is comparable to that of Stanford and MIT in the United
States (Wicksteed 1985). Liberal policies towards faculty entrepreneurship encouraged technology transfer and close university–industry research connections. As in
the case of Boston and San Jose, university spin-offs generated much of Cambridge's
high-technology-based economic growth.

The classical examples of Silicon Valley, Route 128 and the Cambridge Phenomenon stimulate regional economic policy-makers to build their own high-technology
centres around research universities. For instance, states in the United States
arrange funding for promising university research projects, help create incentives for
professors to concentrate on commercially applicable inventions, and encourage
faculty spin-offs by making venture capital available for new start-ups (Malecki
1980a, 1986; Osborne 1990; Kelly *et al.* 1992; Isserman 1994).

What is the extent to which university-based local economic development can be
successfully replicated in any regional innovation systems? Can the university be
considered as the centre of modern regional economic growth (as advocated in
Rogers 1986), or is local economic development supported by academic institutions

the privilege of only the most advanced high-technology regions (as argued in Malecki 1991)? Applying data on US commercial innovations and university research expenditures, the rest of this chapter investigates the extent to which universities are important actors of any (and not only the most successful) local innovation systems. In the second section, university technology transfer mechanisms are introduced and classified. This is followed by an exploratory analysis that compares the spatial distribution of academic research and high-technology innovations. In the fourth section, the relative importance of universities in local systems of innovation and the spatial extent of university knowledge transfers are investigated. In the fifth section, the effect of the maturity of a local innovation system on local academic knowledge transfers are demonstrated. A summary closes the chapter.

Local university knowledge transfer mechanisms

Universities are integrated into regional innovation systems via the different mechanisms of local academic knowledge transfers. According to Parker and Zilberman (1993), technology transfer from academic institutions is any process by which basic understanding, information and innovations move from a university to firms in the private sector.

Not every form of university knowledge transfers require spatial proximity. For instance, scholarly journal publications or faculty consulting in industry can convey knowledge from academic institutions to industrial firms over large distances (Brodsky, Kaufman and Tooker 1980). Similarly, different forms of cooperation in research and development between industry and academia, such as industry-sponsored contract research, long-term university–industry research agreements and industry-financed university research centres, channel university expertise between distant locations (National Science Foundation 1982). However, in many cases, especially when academic knowledge is in its evolving, non-codified stage, successful knowledge transfers between university and high-technology firms require spatial proximity. In this chapter local academic knowledge transfer mechanisms are classified into three categories: information transmission via local personal networks of university and industry professionals, technology transfers through formal business relations, and knowledge spillovers generated by industrial applications of university physical facilities.

The *local network of university and industry scientists* is a principal mechanism in the transmission of technological information from academia to high-technology industry. Access to graduate students and a supply of scientists and engineers represent important university–industry linkages (National Science Board 1982; National Governors Association 1983; Johnson 1984). As a consequence, regional labour markets of scientists and engineers are responsible for much of the local academic knowledge flow. Faculty scientists and engineers are more likely to move to nearby firms when changing jobs (Bania, Calkins and Dalenberg 1992; Almeida and Kogut 1995), and trained graduates may look for their first jobs close to the university (Malecki 1986; Kelly *et al.* 1992).

In addition to a local labour market of professionals, several different forms of personal connections strengthen the local network between academia and high-technology industry. Technological knowledge can be disseminated from universities in seminars attended by scientists from industry. Moreover, knowledge transfers can be facilitated in a less formal manner via local professional associations (Bania, Calkins and Dalenberg 1992) or close personal connections (Saxenian 1994; Almeida and Kogut 1995).

Among the *formal mechanisms* of local knowledge transfers, university spin-off firms and technology licensing have gained particular importance. University spin-off firms commercialize economically useful new technical ideas developed by research at the university (Brett, Gibson and Smilor 1991). A large portion of economic growth in major high-technology centres is generated by university spin-off companies (Wicksteed 1985; Osborne 1990; Kelly *et al.* 1992). Licensing technologies originated in university research laboratories can also have significant impact on the local economy. In addition to a positive regional economic effect, royalty incomes generated by licences may form a considerable part of the university budget (Parker and Zilberman 1993; Association of University Technology Managers 1995).

Economically useful knowledge at academic institutions is transmitted to local high-technology industry not only via the network of university and industry professionals and formal business relations between academia and industry, but also via the commercial application of *university facilities* by local high-technology firms. Such facilities are industrial incubators, industrial parks, libraries or computer services (Johnson 1984).

Spatial distribution of innovation and university research

Although the classical cases of university-supported regional growth (i.e. Silicon Valley, Route 128, the Cambridge Phenomenon) are of great importance to an understanding of how universities are embedded in some of the major local innovation systems, these examples have only limited general validity. In order to collect information on local university knowledge transfers that reflects not only the experience of the best-regarded high-technology centres, a different methodology is required. In this section, a large US data set is applied to compare the spatial tendencies of university research with the geographic distribution of commercial innovations. A common spatial pattern of academic research and innovative activity is considered as an indicator of potential university knowledge transfers.

In empirical studies, the most widely used measures of innovative activities are either patents or literature-based innovation output indicators. Because many patents have never been developed into innovations and many innovations have never been patented, the common critique against the patent measure is that it does not cover the whole universe of commercial innovative activities (Griliches 1990). Literature-based innovation output indicators are generated by sampling the 'new product' sections of trade and technical journals. The advantage of these indicators over patents is that they document the ultimate end of every innovation process: the commercialization of technical ideas.

The only available US literature-based innovation output indicator, i.e. the United States Small Business Administration (SBA) innovation citation database, is used in this chapter. To date, this is the best available measure of innovative activity in the United States. It covers the country for one year, 1982. As a result of the review of 46 trade journals, 4476 product innovations were recorded. Of these

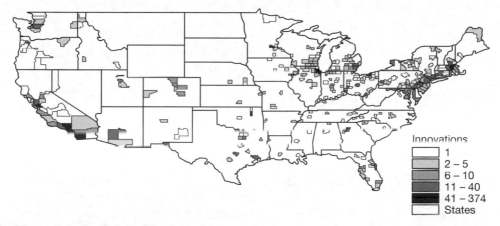

Figure 9.1 Spatial distribution of innovations

innovations, 4200 included information on the location of innovating establishments (i.e. the site responsible for the major aggregations. On the basis of the industrial classification of innovating establishments, each innovation was categorized by a matching entry in the Standard Industrial Classification (SIC) system. (For a detailed description of the data set, see Acs and Audretsch 1990, 1993a.)

National aggregates of the SBA data were previously used for analysis by Acs and Audretsch (1988, 1990). In state-level studies, Acs, Audretsch and Feldman (1991, 1994b), Audretsch and Feldman (1996) and Feldman (1994a) utilized the data. Anselin, Varga and Acs (1997a, b) and Acs, FitzRoy and Smith (1999) used MSA-level aggregates (MSA means US metropolitan area), while Varga (1998) analysed county-level patterns of the innovation data.

Research activities at universities are measured by university research expenditures. The data are collected from the National Science Foundation Survey of Scientific and Engineering Expenditures at Universities and Colleges for the year 1982 (National Science Foundation 1982). Research activities at university departments are matched to the respective high-technology manufacturing sectors on the basis of the scheme of Audretsch and Feldman (1996). In the following analyses, data on 'high-technology industry' consist of the aggregated values of the following sectors: chemicals, industrial machinery, electronics, transportation equipment, and instruments. Applying county-level aggregates of the innovation and the university research data, the rest of this section provides a comparative analysis of the spatial distribution of innovative activities and academic research.

It has been previously recognized by Feldman (1994a) and Audretsch and Feldman (1996) that, even at the level of US states, innovations exhibit a remarkably strong tendency to cluster spatially. According to these studies, the most active states in commercial innovations are California, New York, New Jersey, Massachusetts, Pennsylvania, Illinois, Ohio, Texas, Connecticut, Michigan and Minnesota.

Figure 9.1 maps US high-technology innovations at the level of US counties for the year 1982. As a counterpart to the figure, Table 9.1 presents the number of US counties and counts of innovations by the value ranges used for mapping the data. Three hundred and sixty of the total 3107 continental US counties observed at least

Table 9.1 The distribution of innovations and US counties by innovation value ranges

Innovation value ranges	Innovation counts	Counties in range
0	0	2747
1	127	127
2–5	388	133
6–10	284	38
11–40	967	45
41–374	1659	17

one innovation. Innovation activities are highly concentrated in a relatively small number of counties. (The seventeen top-range counties produced almost half of the total number of innovations.) It is not clear from Table 9.1 whether the concentration in value exhibits concentration of innovations in space as well. However, visual inspection of Figure 9.1 suggests that value concentration is paralleled by the tendency for strong spatial clustering. In Figure 9.1, the two major innovation concentrations are the California and the North Atlantic clusters. The San Diego–San Francisco region constitutes the California cluster, while the North Atlantic cluster consists of the Philadelphia–New York–Boston regions. The California cluster exhibits a centre in the north (around San Francisco and San Jose) and a centre in the south (around Los Angeles and San Diego). The North Atlantic cluster is centred around New York City and Boston. Four medium-sized clusters are detected around Seattle, Chicago, Detroit and Cleveland. Minneapolis, Buffalo, Dallas and Houston are minor clusters of innovation.

Figure 9.2 presents the spatial patterns of US university R&D expenditures for 1982. A simple comparison of the maps of innovations and university research highlights that university research activities follow a more even spatial distribution than innovations. Despite this relatively even location distribution, higher values of university research seem to concentrate around the areas where innovations are clustered. Table 9.2 reports the distribution of university research and US counties by university research ranges. University research follows a strong concentration tendency: while the majority of continental counties (2794 of 3107) do not exhibit any signs of high-technology university research, the top ten counties carry out one-third of the total university R&D ($1600 million out of $4800 million).

A comparison of the maps of innovations and university R&D reveals that the largest university research clusters are clusters of innovation activities as well. The North Atlantic region shows a strong concentration of both university research and high-technology innovations. Parallel intensification of innovative and university research activities characterizes the San Francisco–San Jose and Los Angeles areas. Similarly, regions of innovation around Chicago, Detroit and Houston are significant concentrations of university research as well. Interestingly, the St Louis, Atlanta and Raleigh–Durham university concentrations are not followed by innovation and research clusters.

The comparison of high-technology innovation and university research clusters indicates that innovative activities tend to concentrate in areas where academic research agglomerates, suggesting that university research may play an important

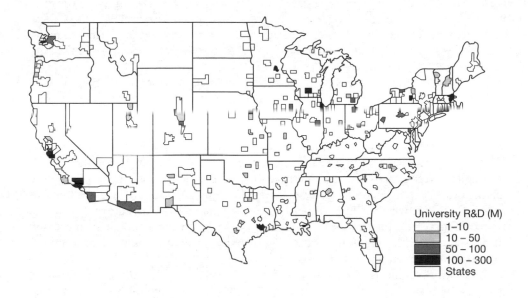

Figure 9.2 Spatial distribution of university R&D

Table 9.2 Distribution of university research expenditures and US counties by university research ranges (millions of 1982 US dollars)

University research ranges	University research	University research counties
0	0	2794
1–10	394	219
10–50	1670	67
50–100	1141	17
100–300	1592	10

Table 9.3 Concentration of academic research and innovation

University research ranges (millions of 1982 US dollars)	Average innovations per county	Percentage of innovating university counties
0	3	NA
0–10	9	42
10–50	14	67
50–100	20	82
100–300	97	100

role in the creation of new knowledge in high-technology industry. Table 9.3 provides further evidence of the common spatial concentration trends of academic research and commercial innovation. In this table, indicators of innovative activities were categorized by university research ranges: average number of innovations in innovating counties is sorted by university research expenditure ranges in the second column, while in the last column the percentage of counties that perform university research where at least one innovation was observed is categorized by university research expenditure ranges.

The second and third columns of the table demonstrate the similar spatial concentration tendencies of university research and commercial innovation. The column of average innovations per county reveals the trend that increased university research spending is associated with enlarged innovation productivity. Counties where university research activities are missing observe 3 innovations on average. This value increases with university research expenditures: even in counties where academic research activities are at a relatively modest level (i.e. in counties where academic research spending is less than $10 million), the average number of innovations is 9, which is three times larger than the number of innovations in the first category. The production of new knowledge is strongly linked to increased university research: the top range of university research counties produce 97 innovations on average.

Common concentration trends of academic research and commercial innovation gain further evidence in the last column of Table 9.3. This column shows that the probability of observing at least one innovation in a county increases with the size of university research activity. Forty-two per cent of the counties that perform academic research produce at least one innovation in the first research range. This proportion increases with university research expenditures. In the top range, every university county becomes innovative.

Relative importance of universities in local innovation systems

In the previous section, the spatial distribution of university research expenditures was related to the spatial pattern of commercial innovation in the United States. Common spatial distribution tendencies of the two sets of data suggest that knowledge transfers from local academic institutions may have an important effect on innovation activity. However, this observation was based on an investigation that considered potential local university knowledge transfer effects in separation from the complex environment of locally available external knowledge sources. These external effects are integral elements of the local innovation system of any particular high-technology region.

In addition to knowledge transferred from local academic institutions, the following external sources of innovation are considered in the relevant literature: knowledge transfers from local industrial R&D laboratories; technological information communicated within the network of related high-technology companies; and knowledge concerning commercialization and marketing assured by the presence of business services (for a review, see Feldman 1994a).

While most of the research carried out in universities has as its aim the accumulation of basic scientific knowledge, research in industrial laboratories, except in a few high-technology corporations, aims at the application of technical knowledge in product development. The tendency of industrial R&D to concentrate spatially has been widely recognized (e.g. Malecki 1980a, b, 1986; Varga 1998). Concentration of industrial research facilities in a high-technology region provides a rich source of the latest technological knowledge. This knowledge 'spills over' via the local network of industrial R&D scientists and engineers (Saxenian 1994; Almeida and Kogut 1995).

In many cases, new products are based on existing knowledge that is conveyed through local networks of production firms. Thus besides industrial and academic knowledge transfers, the local network of high technology firms is a significant source of externally available new technological information. As elements of this network, local competitor, supplier and end-user companies can be important sources of further innovations (for reviews, see Dosi 1988 and Feldman 1994a). In addition to knowledge created by R&D and knowledge communicated among industrial firms, the presence of business services provides important marketing, legal and financial information in the commercialization stage of a new technological idea (Feldman 1994a).

The complex effect of externally available local knowledge sources on innovation has been investigated in the literature in state-level US studies by Feldman (1994a), Feldman and Florida (1994) and Anselin, Varga and Acs (1997a), and in MSA-level investigations by Anselin, Varga and Acs (1997a, b). Both state- and MSA-level results strongly support the hypothesis of a significant local academic impact on innovative activities, even after controlling for the effects of other knowledge sources including industrial research spillovers, network of firms, and business services.

The impact of external knowledge sources on the creation of new knowledge is measured by the respective innovation elasticities in the above studies. The elasticity of innovation with respect to a given external knowledge source is expressed as the percentage change in innovation as a result of a 1 per cent change in a given innovation input. (More precisely: elasticity of innovation with respect to a given input = % change in innovation / % change in the given input.) At the level of US metropolitan areas, the effect of knowledge transfers from universities is a major external source of innovations: a 1 per cent change in local academic research expenditures results in about a 0.1 per cent change in innovations (Anselin, Varga and Acs 1997a). If, for example, the high-technology industry in a metropolitan area introduces 100 innovations and university research expenditures are currently $100 million, in order to raise innovations to 101, university research expenditures need to be increased to $110 million. (This example is valid, of course, if the only change affecting innovation in the MSA is the increase in academic research expenditures.)

The effect of university knowledge transfers on innovation is notable even after comparing it to the impacts of the other locally available external knowledge resources. The elasticity measuring the effect of the local network of high-technology companies seems to be the strongest, 0.65. A 1 per cent change in business services accounts for a 0.33 per cent change in innovations and the impact of industrial research spillovers is measured by an elasticity of 0.28 (Anselin, Varga and Acs 1997a).

University knowledge transfers follow a definite distance decay pattern. The

intensity of local university–industry connections (no matter whether they are facilitated through the local network of university and industry scientists, via formal
university–industry business relationships, or as a result of the application of university
physical facilities by private companies) shows a remarkable sensitivity to distance. The
effect of university research on the innovative activity of firms located in the metropolitan area, measured by the respective innovation elasticities, is 0.1 if the university
research is carried out within the boundaries of the MSA, 0.03 if the university is
situated within a 50-mile (80 km) range around the MSA border, and eventually
disappears if the distance is further increased (Anselin, Varga and Acs 1997a).

University knowledge transfers and the relative maturity of local innovation systems

In the previous section, evidence was given that technology transfers from universities are significant sources of innovations in the United States. However, several
observations support the hypothesis that the intensity of the effect of local academic
knowledge transfers on innovation is not stable over space and depends on the
development level of regional innovation systems. For instance, Feldman (1994b)
points out that even though Johns Hopkins University is the largest recipient of
federal research funds, technology transfer from the university has not become a
significant source of local economic growth. She argues that a missing 'critical mass'
of high-technology enterprises, together with the lack of producer services and
venture capital, is the main reason for the insufficient local academic spillover effect.
Perhaps similar factors justify the limited regional economic impact of the large
concentration of academic knowledge capital in Ithaca, New York. Despite the fact
that Cornell University and Stanford University disposed of comparable amounts of
R&D funds in science and engineering in 1982 ($110 million and $130 million,
respectively), high-technology industry in Ithaca produced only 2 innovations while
San Jose in California was responsible for 374 new high-technology products.

The above cases suggest that the amount of technological information transmitted
from the available pool of knowledge at local academic institutions depends on the
development level of the local innovation system. Thus, the larger the geographical
concentration of high-technology production, the more intensive the flow of information through the personal networks of university and industry professionals (for
example, concentration of production increases local demand for faculty consulting
services and raises the probability that graduates get jobs in the proximity of
universities). Similarly, the more advanced the local business services sector (e.g.
financial, legal, marketing services), the more intense the transfer of knowledge from
academic institutions through faculty spin-off companies or technology licensing.

The effect of agglomeration on the intensity of local academic knowledge transfers is demonstrated in Table 9.4. Local university technology transfers are
measured by the elasticity of innovations with respect to university research and
calculated by following the methodology developed by Varga (1998). On the basis of
the intensity of local university technology transfers, US metropolitan areas are
classified into four categories. Average innovation elasticities with respect to university research are presented in the second column. Average employment in
high-technology industry and in business services measure the development level of

Table 9.4 Innovations and the development level of local innovation systems

Tier	Elasticity of innovations with respect to university research	High-technology employment	Employment in business services	Population (thousands)
I	0.104	162,000	4,300	3,000
II	0.061	37,000	1,000	1,000
III	0.029	12,000	300	400
IV	0.022	3,000	130	200

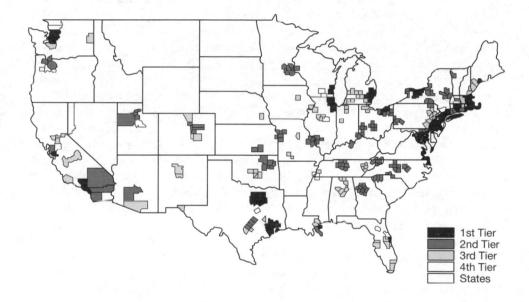

Figure 9.3 Regions by university technology transfer ranges

local innovation systems in the third and fourth columns, respectively, while in the last column population provides an indication of the average size of metropolitan areas belonging to each tier.

The second column of the table lists the values of average innovation elasticities by MSA categories. Although a 1 per cent change in university research results in a 0.1 per cent change in innovations in a typical first-tier MSA, this value is practically zero in the fourth tier. (Given that the average number of innovations in this tier of cities is only two, we can interpret the average elasticity value, −0.022, as an indicator of a missing university effect on local innovations.) The spatial distribution of the four tiers of high-technology MSAs is presented in Figure 9.3. Cities that absorb the university effect most efficiently are large agglomerations of the United States. The first five cities with the highest innovation elasticities are Los Angeles, Chicago, San Jose, Boston and Detroit.

There is an apparent positive relationship between the intensity of local university technology transfers and the development level of regional innovation systems: the average elasticity of innovation with respect to university research is the most intense in metropolitan areas where the highest levels of average high-technology and business services employment are observed. For the rest of the tiers, decreasing employment levels are associated with declining innovation elasticities.

Figure 9.4 demonstrates the dramatic differences in the 'productivity' of the same university research expenditure among the four typical MSA categories. The horizontal axis represents university research expenditures, while the vertical axis depicts expected innovations by research spending sizes and by MSA tiers (see Varga 1998 for the methodology of calculating expected innovations). The four curves in the figure stand for different innovation outcomes resulting from the same level of university research spending. It is clear from the figure that innovation productivity depends heavily on the development level of local innovation systems. While university research spending of $0.5 million can be expected to yield 63 innovations in an average top MSA, this number is 11 in the second tier, and 5 and 2 in the third and fourth tiers, respectively. The effect of increasing university research expenditures is even more striking. The curve of an average first-tier MSA increases sharply from 63 expected innovations to 115. In the second tier, the growth path is relatively modest: it ranges from 11 to 16. Academic impact on local innovations is basically non-existent in the third and fourth tiers. The return on the $324 million additional university research spending is zero: the number of expected innovations is the same for both the highest and the lowest possible university research expenditure levels. Examination of Figure 9.4 suggests that first-tier MSAs utilize university research expenditures with the highest productivity. There is an indication that increased university research funding makes basically no difference for the rest of the cities.

On the basis of the figure, the 'critical mass' of agglomeration required for significant effects of university knowledge transfers on regional innovation can be characterized as follows. In order to get university research expenditures to work for the regional economy, a typical (i.e. an 'average') city needs to have a size of about 3 million, and employment in high-technology production facilities and business service firms numbering around 160,000 and 4000, respectively. Note that the criteria presented here provide only crude estimates of the 'threshold location'. Cities can be (and are) successful in absorbing university research even if their actual combination of local characteristics does not match exactly the 'ideal' attributes. The point is that actual MSAs should not be 'too far' from the typical location in order to expect meaningful positive university research impacts on their economies.

Summary and conclusion

It is well known that knowledge transfers from universities have accounted for much of the economic growth in certain high-technology regions. Silicon Valley, Route 128 and the Cambridge Phenomenon are the most frequently cited success stories in this respect. Although sufficient information has been accumulated on the positive economic effects of university knowledge transfers in these regions, our understanding regarding the replicability of academic institution-generated local

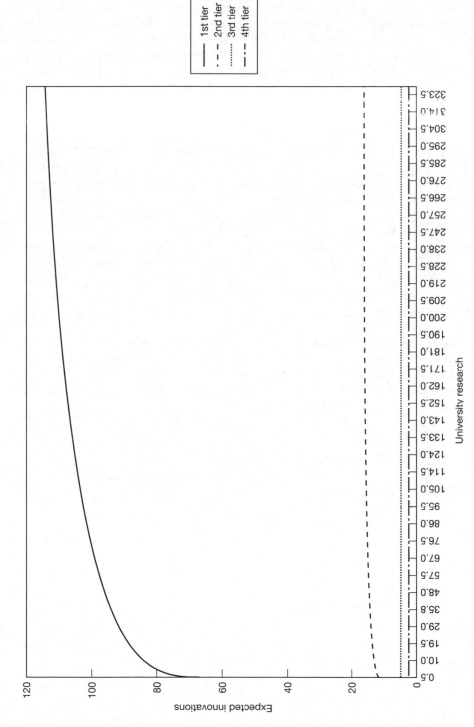

Figure 9.4 Expected innovations

economic development is still limited. It was the central issue in this chapter to search for the extent to which any of the US regional innovation systems can rely upon the positive effects of knowledge transfers from local academic institutions.

Applying US county and metropolitan area data, the chapter suggests that universities can be important actors in local innovation systems. It is found that university research and commercial innovation follow similar tendencies of spatial distribution, suggesting a positive relationship between academic research and local innovative activity. Another major finding of this chapter is that even if we compare the magnitude of the effect of university knowledge transfers on innovations to the impact of other locally available external knowledge sources on local innovative activities (i.e. private research laboratories, local networks of high-technology companies, and business services), the academic effect turns out to be still remarkable. It is demonstrated in this chapter that the effect of universities on the creation of new technological knowledge exhibits a strong dependence on the development level of the local innovation system. This finding has important regional economic development policy consequences. The efforts of several US states to advance local universities in order to develop their high-technology economic base have been widely recognized in the relevant literature (e.g. Vaugham and Pollard 1986; Schmandt and Wilson 1987; Fosler 1988; Osborne 1990). The positive relationship between the maturity of local innovation systems and the impact of academic research on local innovations suggests that strengthening universities in order to advance local economies can be a good option in relatively well-developed areas. However, there is strong evidence that MSAs that are far below the 'critical mass' cannot expect meaningful academic impact on their economies when considered in isolation. Instead, this suggests that in these regions a more comprehensive approach is needed, including a complex regional economic development plan that not only targets local academic institutions, but considers other elements of the local innovation system as well, such as high-technology employment and business services.

CHAPTER TEN

Towards a Conceptualization of Super-regional Systems of Innovation

Rebecca Morales

The issues

In the past decade, multi-state (super)regional trade pacts have become major actors in organizing the international economy, complementing a lead previously established by transnational private enterprises. The pacts clarify terms of trade and harmonize production processes in order to favour existing or anticipated regional flows and strengthen regional markets. Until now, their primary focus has been on market and production sharing. But in recent years, as firms have broadened their transnational activities to include R&D and the integration of product development across countries, the role of super-regional organizations with respect to knowledge-intensive activities has come under question.

At the national and state levels, governments have begun adopting policies that explicitly develop national or regional systems of innovation to support private-sector activities. However, the multi-state regional pacts have not kept pace. The super-regional pacts have been designed to stimulate trade and investment, not necessarily encourage innovation *per se*. As the influence of super-regional pacts continues to grow, spurred by the integration of regional markets, the need to define an explicit innovation policy is likely to increase. In anticipation of such, the purpose of this chapter is to examine the concept of a super-regional system of innovation and, further, to assess its implication for the North American region. Because the North American region combines nations of vastly different capability, the thrust is one of identifying the issues within a context of unbalanced multi-state regional growth.

Multi-state regionalization

Until recently, multi-state regional systems not only were non-existent or moribund, but were not anticipated to become a major international force. As late as 1989, renowned international trade economist Jeffrey Schott predicted that a 'U.S.–Mexico FTA [free trade area] or Mexican adherence to the Canada–U.S. FTA is not feasible in the short or medium term. A NAFTA [North American Free Trade Agreement will therefore remain an ideal, not a real policy option, for the next decade or more' (Schott 1989: 44). Nonetheless, NAFTA was signed in 1993 and implemented in 1994. What occurred somewhat unexpectedly worldwide was the rapid emergence of regional trade arrangements beginning in the 1980s and accelerating throughout the 1990s.

The movement towards regionalism took off when the European Community (now European Union) initiated a process of systematic economic integration through the Single European Act of 1986 and the Maastricht Treaty. Since then a number of regional institutions have emerged (de la Torre and Kelly 1992; Haggard 1996). Among the most notable are NAFTA, signed in 1993; the South American Southern Cone Common Market (MERCOSUR), signed in 1992; and the announcement by the Association of South East Asian Nations (ASEAN) in 1992 of its intent to create a free trade area. Throughout this period, a number of smaller regional associations have also coalesced, including the Central American Common Market, the Greater China Economic Zone (Hong Kong, Macau, Guangdong and Fujian provinces, and Taiwan), and the Australia–New Zealand Closer Economic Trade Agreement. In some cases the impetus to regionalism has been more organic than formal. For example, Asia has seen the rise of several 'growth triangles' consisting of Singapore, Bataan Island in Indonesia, and Johor Province, and among the border areas of Thailand, Laos and Cambodia (Yamazawa 1996). The movement towards regionalization has been so extensive that by the mid-1990s every country in the Western Hemisphere was a member of a regional agreement with the exception of Cuba, the Dominican Republic, Haiti, Panama and Surinam, a situation that could ultimately be addressed if NAFTA's proposed successor, the Western Hemisphere Free Trade Area (WHFTA), takes definition. Despite the remarkable growth of regional associations worldwide, whole parts of the globe nonetheless remain excluded from the trend, including the majority of Africa, the Middle East, South Asia and the ex-Soviet countries (Yamamoto 1996).

What has been the motivation behind the creation of these super-regions, and why were they so unexpected? In part the answer lies in the successes of the Bretton Woods institutions created during the 1940s, which encouraged lower tariffs in order to stimulate international trade. Fifty years later, the extent of trade overwhelmed the capacity of these institutions to respond. The heightened competition also undermined the ability of firms and governments to predict market demand with some certainty. In an effort to restore a semblance of market stability, many countries adopted non-tariff restrictions on imports as they looked for ways to strengthen regional markets. By the early 1990s approximately 40 per cent of world trade was thought to be managed, and the number of regional arrangements grew. Regional blocs expanded the market for goods and services while minimizing the risks and uncertainty that came with internationalization. The objective of regionalization, however, was to complement, not replace, the process of internationalization. As explained by political scientist Robert Gilpin,

> The two developments [i.e. economic globalization and economic regionalization] are in fact complementary and are responsive to each other. They reflect a world in which states want the *absolute* benefits of a global economy at the same time that they are seeking to increase their own *relative* gains through economic protectionism, the formation of regional arrangements, and managed trade. (Gilpin 1992: 28–9)

Following the post-Cold War breakdown of US hegemony in the international political economy, regional realignments became expressions of competitive power that replaced an order previously secured through military strength. In this new world order the major competitors consist of a triad of competing regions that have achieved economic parity – Europe, North America and Japan – augmented by a group of less affluent secondary regions (Golden 1996). Within these broad continental delineations, the nature of regional organization has been remarkably distinct. Linked by the Single European Act, unification of Western Europe redefines the institutional structure of its member nations. The legislation creates a European customs union, or unified internal market circumscribed by a common tariff on imports. The European Union harmonizes standards, establishes competition and regional policies through macro economic policy coordination and Community-wide institutions, and actively promotes redistribution among the members.

By contrast, the East Asian region has been driven by the actions of firms rather than of governments. As such, this area represents a type of 'natural' region which has grown and deepened in response to the trade and investment patterns of Japanese firms. Development of the region has occurred rapidly. In 1982 Japanese trade within the South-East Asian region was only $6.1 billion, but by 1989 it had reached $126.4 billion (Gilpin 1992: 25). Throughout this period Japanese firms became integrally linked with a vast network of East Asian firms and markets that formed the foundation to the region.

Providing yet another model is the North American Free Trade Agreement (NAFTA). NAFTA discriminates against non-members, stipulates rules regarding sector-specific investments, liberalizes financial markets, and specifies side agreements on labour and the environment, but it does not create a customs union. International trade economist and former director of economics at the US Trade Commission Peter Morici summarizes NAFTA accordingly:

> The agreement may be viewed as having four interwoven elements. First, it is a traditional free trade agreement. It eliminates tariffs and virtually all quantitative restrictions, and it seeks to end other unnecessary impediments to commerce through rules for government procurement, the activities of state-owned enterprises, product standards and testing, regulation of foreign investment, and the certification of business service providers.
>
> Second, it imposes on Mexico detailed timetables to phase out its remaining interventionist trade and industrial policies, such as those in the automobile, computer, secondary petrochemical, and pharmaceutical industries. Parallel timetables govern the opening of Canadian and American markets.
>
> Third, NAFTA mandates the modernization of Mexico's legal framework to ensure the security of property and the enforcement of contracts, and *commits Mexico to establish a modern antitrust regime and strong intellectual property protection*. NAFTA provides for international arbitration to ensure that Mexico's judicial system delivers fair treatment for United States and Canadian investors. [Emphasis added]
>
> Fourth, NAFTA requires follow-on consultations and negotiations across a broad range of issues. The agreement establishes separate committees and working groups to address procurement, subsidies, product standards, environmental regulation, and other nontariff issues.
>
> Overall, NAFTA addresses the central challenges inherent in achieving free trade between advanced industrialized countries and a developing country undergoing radical institutional change. (Morici 1996: 62)

These differences in regional design are consistent with and reflect the distinct philosophies towards growth and development underlying each area. For example, the European approach assumes that production and market sharing are optimized when partners share similar income and output capability. Consequently, the method of integration combines redistributive policies with programmes directed at increasing the competitiveness of lagging regions by upgrading their scientific and technological base. The North American approach, on the other hand, assumes that trade and investment among partners with dissimilar advantages is not only desirable but perhaps even necessary to maintain a 'virtuous cycle' where consumption stimulates investment and production in a positively reinforcing manner. Consequently, NAFTA is market-led and largely devoid of developmental programmes (with one exception being the North American Development Bank, a still new institution aimed at providing retraining and other assistance to companies and workers harmed by free trade). NAFTA does not stipulate policies directed towards upgrading the research and technological capability of North America as an integrated whole. By contrast, South-East Asian countries have become increasingly interlinked and have grown on the basis of 'market guidance' determined by national rather than regional policies (Wade 1990). Here, countries have typically identified national development goals bolstered by explicit science, technology or innovation policies. In contrast to the European approach of encouraging redistribution among member nations, redistribution occurs within nations (as reflected in their relative income parity) and is the result of educational and industrial policies (World Bank 1993). Within these three very distinct regions, firms have restructured in ways that are consistent with the demands of the knowledge economy.

Industrial reorganization and firm-level regionalization

Since the mid-1970s firms have undergone an extensive process of industrial restructuring. As markets became more demanding, inputs such as time, information and access to technology, or more specifically 'knowledge', became critical factors of production. Firms sought to broaden their markets and cost structures across countries while seeking a stable climate for trade and investment. The restructuring consisted of a combination of downsizing, outsourcing, technological and skills upgrading, and the creation of teams internal and external to firms for undertaking creative problem-solving. The result was a 'flattening' of large firms, and an emergence of industrial clusters or networks of firms engaged in production. Economist Masahiko Aoki traces this trend in Japan to the post-oil shock period, which triggered a process of 'quasi-disintegration'. He writes, 'larger firms started to hive off various activities in the form of subsidiaries in order to trim the number of their employees as much as possible', leading to a new set of contracting relations with 'more overlapping: [where] subcontractors have multiple relations with many prime manufacturers and vice versa. There is also increasingly more sharing of knowledge' (Aoki 1987: 282, 284). In other countries, notably in Europe, a similar process resulted in intense interactions among small and medium-sized firms that led to a related type of clustered system of production.

Among firms facing extremely congested or quickly changing markets, the sharing of knowledge has become extremely important. These firms redefined their product market objectives from an emphasis on price competitiveness and maximizing economies of scale to time competitiveness based on maximizing economies of scope or information aimed at bringing products to market rapidly, a process that is knowledge dependent (Stalk and Hout 1990; Meyer 1993; Cooper 1994). The emphasis on time over price, or what economist Kim Clark calls the new industrial competition, is the result of several factors:

> Three driving forces have introduced what I call the new industrial competition. These forces are (1) the emergence of intense international competitors, (2) the creation of fragmented markets, and (3) diverse yet transforming technological change. These three forces have created a new imperative for competition. (Clark 1989b: 2)

In an effort to correctly target their markets and gain a first-mover advantage, firms began to compress their product development cycle through use of concurrent or simultaneous engineering (Putnam 1985). This compression required the redeployment of workers into strategic project teams that replaced the rigid structures associated with functionally segregated, vertically defined organizations. It also necessitated greater integration of external suppliers and process equipment manufacturers into the product development cycle, especially those involved in the fabrication of production tools, prototype construction and major parts manufacture (K. B. Clark 1989b). The result was a certain amount of agglomeration of productive activities. As observed by Masahiko Aoki, 'This model implies that research and development are best carried out in geographical proximity – or at least with intimate communications links – to the sites of production and sales so close contracts can be maintained' (Aoki 1990: 30). The combined effect has been a regionalization of design and manufacture. Such regionalization is well documented at the substate level. However, it has also occurred at the multi-state level, especially in concert with the rise of multi-state regionalization. When undertaken by large transnational firms, the interlinked process of design, development and manufacture was transferred to the multi-state regions in which they operated (Morales 1994a, b). Thus, within these multi-state regions, innovation as well as the capacity to be innovative was transmitted by large firms to the major providers through the supplier chain.

Developing countries therefore depended upon foreign firms to set the standard for export competitiveness. The introduction of innovation through such means as incorporation into the product development process had a more transforming and lasting effect than through either government-promoted technology transfer programmes or investments in basic R&D because of the interdependent relationship among firms. Furthermore, when domestic firms were integrated into the product development process transnationally with larger firms, the capacity for innovation spilled over into the developing country regions. But initiating such innovative activity is often inhibited by a collective action problem. Investments in labour, technology and management required by any one firm intending to integrate developing country companies into the product development process carries both a high risk and a high cost. In developed countries, firms are equipped to share the risks and costs of collective action with other firms and institutions, but in developing countries, firms and institutions may not be sufficiently prepared to do the same (Golden 1996). Furthermore, in advanced industrialized nations, such cooperation among firms rarely inhibits competition because of the large field of competitors. However, in developing countries with emerging markets, knowing how to initiate cooperative behaviour while avoiding collusion and rent seeking among firms and governmental agencies remains an important issue. Governments have to be cata-lytic and market-responsive, a role that is often at odds with the process of liberalization these countries are presently undertaking. Neo-liberal policies often result in weak governments unable to 'organize' the market (Wade 1990), putting transnational corporations in the lead for transforming local capability. Cases of transnational knowledge sharing across developed and developing countries occur when firms operationalize multi-state regional design and production strategies. Within the North American auto industry, such regional integration has been the expressed policy of Honda, Nissan and Chrysler (Morales 1994a). Mexican supplier firms have since upgraded through participation in the product development pro-cess. The result has been a diffusion and sharing of knowledge, and an increased ability of Mexican suppliers to be innovative.

Knowledge as a factor of production

Despite the recent trend in industrial organization towards clustering among firms competing on the basis of time (i.e. the ability to bring products to market rapidly), which has led to both substate and multi-state regionalization, a large number of firms have continued to compete on the basis of cost, especially if they are operating in a high-volume segment of a market or in a mature industry. As these cost-competitive firms scan the globe for least-cost inputs, the result has been a diffused pattern of international development. Consequently, two opposing market strat-egies have emerged, as reflected in the form of industrial organization (i.e. hori-zontal versus vertical) and locational preferences (regional versus global) of firms, although it is still common to find the distinctions blurred.

The importance of time as a determinant of competitiveness is so important that it has even changed the way technological innovation is understood in the literature (Nelson 1993). Initially, technological innovation was defined as the acquisition of hardware and intermediate goods. Later, as new leading sectors termed 'high technology' emerged where production technologies were driven by knowledge-intensive processes of manufacture and design, the focus shifted towards industrial capability. More recently, with the rising importance of time and the creation of interdependent production systems, innovation is now understood to emanate from the interactions of public and private institutions linked in scientific and techno-logical activities. Because the interaction between private and public sectors defines competitiveness, it has become integral to the systematic design of innovation policies.

In contrast to science and technology policy, which are static concepts, innovation policy requires the establishment of an environment in which firms and institutions can interrelate in the creation of knowledge. Accordingly, economist Colin Bradford wrote the following for the Organisation for Economic Co-operation and Devel-opment:

> This [most recent] line of thought departs dramatically from the idea of the firm as a locus of internal decisions based on prices in the factor and goods markets. The net result of these new developments, theories and concepts is a focus on the inter-relationships among firms and between firms and other institutions. Strategic thinking and behaviour become critical. The whole notion of technological development broadens to include organizational and process innovations affecting the whole

network of firms involved in the particular production process, instead of being conceived of as technical and scientific inventions which then must be applied and internalized by individual firms. The emphasis of public policy shifts from science and technology policy, *per se* to a broader process of support for organizational and process innovations among complementary firms and institutions. This places more weight on diffusion of innovation and engagement of actors in complementary activities than the past science-based idea of technological change and high-technology industrialization. (Bradford 1994: 48)

Such interrelationships define what is known as the learning economy in reference to an economy that is capable of responding to constant shifts in the regional and global markets. Strategic problem-solving is undertaken by a number of agents towards the creation of knowledge. Such capability takes expression through the system of innovation. The United Nations Economic Commission for Latin America and the Caribbean uses the following definition for a system of innovation:

The term 'system of innovation' means all the agents, institutions, and behavioural norms of a society which determine the speed with which technological know-how is imported, generated, adopted and disseminated to all goods and service sectors. (United Nations Economic Commission for Latin America and the Caribbean 1996: 73)

The 'system' is the way firms, educational institutions, the public financial system and public-sector technology centres interrelate in the development of innovative capability (Nelson 1993; Dahlman 1994). Because it is dependent on having a coherent institutional framework, such a system has yet to be articulated at the super-regional level. The closest example of such is found in Europe, although here its focus is on science and technology policy, rather than innovation *per se*.

European super-regional research and technology policy

The European model of super-regional integration treats the upgrading of techno-logical capability among member nations as central to the process of development. As noted by Tom Higgins of University College Dublin,

A continuing major concern of the European Commission is how to minimize economic disparities among member nations and regions within the Community. To the extent that regional economic development depends increasingly upon innovation, entre-preneurship, and new business formation, disparities in the distribution of technological resources within the Community are of even greater concern. Since the natural tendency of technological resources is to flow to regions already blessed with a relative abundance of such resources, public policies are required to redress these imbalances. (Higgins 1993)

Accordingly, the European Commission has allocated substantial Community struc-tural funds towards reducing the technological deficit of weaker regions. These regions include Ireland, Northern Ireland, Portugal, Greece, Spain and southern Italy. From 1989 to 1993, ECU 1.3 billion was specifically targeted to Ireland, Portugal and Greece for research and technology development. Such targeted assistance to lagging regions is intentionally spatial in emphasis. Within these locations, the funds have gone to 'training programs, productivity drives, trans-border technology-transfer, science parks, regional development programs, centers of excellence, Research Center of Crete, the Standardization Institute of Greece, and the Confederation of Greek Industry' (Higgins 1993: 5). Notably absent have been firm-led strategies. Higgins refers to the European thrust as one in which development is 'predicated on technology push and which is supply driven, [as opposed] to one which is based on market opportunity and which is industry driven' (Higgins 1993: 10). The problem is that according to both theory and practice, it is now widely accepted that industry pull approaches to development are far more successful than technology push. Despite this significant limitation, the European case provides a clear instance in which super-regional institutions have been able to specify and implement science and technology policy transnationally.

Innovation and developing country issues

The rise of multi-state regionalization forces disparate countries with unequal learning capacities to interact through trade, investment and production. As argued by Europeans, countries need the capacity to upgrade technologically or they will face the prospect of falling further behind. The question of how to stimulate development among member nations – in contrast to economic growth of the region as a whole – has generated significant debate lately, especially in the wake of major efforts by a number of advanced industrializing countries in Latin America, Europe and Asia to accelerate their integration into the world economy through adoption of neo-liberal economic policies. For the most part, and often encouraged by multi-lateral institutions, neo-liberal macro-economic policies have combined trade promotion and tariff reduction with currency devaluation, privatization, financial and industrial deregulation, labour market reform and a reduction of social pro-grammes. However, in many instances the results have been disappointing. Growth has been slow and domestic income has been markedly skewed, owing to dramatic rises in poverty and inequality. Recent analysis suggests that the poor performance of traditional neo-liberal policies has been the result of an overemphasis on macro-economic policies and an underemphasis on micro-economics, including science, technology and innovation policy. Economist Fernando Fajnzylber explains the problem of an over-reliance on macro-economics accordingly:

> The main source of inspiration for economic policies – macroeconomics – is, in fact, based on the assumption that sectoral disaggregation serves no purpose in achieving the analytical goals pursued. These goals involve the definition of short-term macro-economic equilibria among variables which result from adding up the effect produced in the different sectors by the various agents participating in economic activity. Macroeconomics is concerned with defining to what extent it will be possible to achieve equilibria among product, consumption, and investment, and to balance public accounts and short-term external accounts. (Fajnzylber 1990: 40)

Economist Paolo Guerrieri extends the analysis further:

> In orthodox free trade thinking, change in industrial structure is seen as the automatic by-product of shifts in a country's comparative advantage, which is ensured, in open economies, by a correct price structure. In fact, trade barriers are considered primary constraints on growth because they prohibit the setting of market-clearing prices. Liberalization orthodoxy therefore involves adapting individual countries to inter-national norms and price structures ...
> [Yet] as the new trade theory and related developments elsewhere in economics have shown, in the presence of economies of scale, technological spillovers and externalities, a country's competitive advantage is much less a function of its national factor

endowments and natural comparative advantage, and much more a function of the complex trade, industrial and technological strategies followed by firms and nations.

. . . the key role in the innovation process is played by the firms themselves, which are the main actors in absorbing and incorporating technological advances.

. . . an export-oriented growth strategy could provide substantial benefits to a developing economy, especially because it exposes domestic firms to strong competition and forces them to invest, innovate and compete. This is not, however, a simple argument for free trade orthodoxy. When combined with premature import liberalization, the same strategy can generate very different outcomes by eliminating modern 'infant' companies and industries, and irreversibly penalizing a country's long-term technological and growth capacity. (Guerrieri 1994: 148–9)

The problem with a neo-liberal approach to economic opening is that it fails to address sectoral, or, more appropriately, industrial, deficiencies. Should such deficiencies be present, which is generally the case in industrializing countries, then efforts must be made to overcome them. This situation is particularly problematic under current conditions of accelerating rates of technological change. Because knowledge as a factor of production results in increasing rather than decreasing returns to scale, countries with even some capacity achieve significant gains. Countries able to harness the growing stock of knowledge have been able to pull ahead, while those lacking such capacity are falling further behind. Since the introduction of new production technologies has vastly reduced the cost of developing and delivering a product to market, cheap labour has become an insufficient condition for industrializing countries to remain competitive.

Because knowledge is a 'created' advantage, countries are now having to take a more proactive stance towards knowledge acquisition than before. In an admonition to Latin America, economist Hans Singer warned, 'Latin Americans who hope to follow the path of the prosperous East Asian NICs should remember that Korea, Taiwan, et al. achieved their stunning successes in export-oriented industrial development with significant government intervention and the strategic use of trade protection, not through deregulated "free markets" or complete trade liberalization' (Singer 1995: 137). Singer, among a growing number of other development economists, argues that continued integration of the Americas will only worsen economic disparities unless the lagging countries upgrade their innovative capacity.

In the light of the growing technology gap, a number of development economists are calling for the adoption of micro-economic along with macro-economic policies as countries continue on the path of liberalization. When Latin America experienced alarming rates of growing poverty and income inequality following the initial introduction of neo-liberal policies, the United Nations Economic Commission for Latin America concluded that 'excessive reliance on the "automatic" effectiveness of macro-economic price signals and reform has led to a tendency to underestimate the weakness of institutions, the failures of markets, and the importance of externalities' (United Nations Economic Commission for Latin America and the Caribbean 1996: 13). The combination of micro- and macro-economic policies suggested by the commission include the following:

- encouraging macro-economic stability and investments in tradable goods;
- increasing savings and productivity;

Table 10.1 Demographic characteristics: United States, Canada and Mexico, 1995

	United States	Canada	Mexico
Population (thousands)	263,090	29,606	88,402
GDP (billion US$ (current))	7,254	565	1,580
GDP per capita (US$ (current))	27,572	18,598[a]	3,991[a]

Source: OECD (1997) *Industrial Competitiveness: Benchmarking Business Environments in the Global Economy*, Paris: OECD, 18, 23, 31
Note:
[a] 1994 figures

- promoting innovation through inter-firm cooperation and relationships between firms and centres of learning and finance;
- developing skilled human resources;
- strengthening technology transfer to small and medium-sized businesses, especially through business associations; and
- establishing a legal framework and institutions needed to promote competitiveness. (United States Economic Commission for Latin America and the Caribbean 1996)

This combination of policies effectively redefines the nature of industrial governance within a country from a traditional neo-liberal approach which attempts to diminish the role of the public sector to one where the public sector is crucial and catalytic in the adoption of knowledge-enhancing practices and policies. In many industrializing countries which have recently liberalized, the prospect of engaging in such proactive policies remains largely unrealized. In any case, the focus of institutional change continues to be at the national, not the super-regional, level. The question remains whether it is possible to address these concerns at the super-regional level, especially as the process of regional integration accelerates. Here, examination of the North American case provides some insight into the problems at hand.

The North American region

Since adoption of NAFTA, a lingering issue of rectifying the disparate learning capacities of Canada, the United States and Mexico remains. There are several measures for understanding the uneven status of these countries. One is in their differences in GDP per capita (see Table 10.1). The United States is clearly among the world's wealthiest nations, while Canada has 67 per cent of the purchasing power of the United States and Mexico has only 14 per cent. A low per capita income significantly diminishes the ability of Mexicans, and to a lesser extent Canadians, to purchase high-value-added products. The uneven nature of the three economies is also apparent in the expenditures on R&D. The United States has a high government expenditure on R&D, in contrast to Canada and Mexico, where expenditure is significantly smaller (Table 10.2). But even more striking is the level of R&D performance by enterprises in the United States relative to that of Canada and

Table 10.2 Structure of the R&D system: United States, Canada and Mexico, 1994 (funding and performance of gross expenditure on R&D, in million US$)

	United States	Canada	Mexico
Government			
R&D expenditure[a]	65,578.00	3,550.30	1,613.00
R&D performance[b]	17,677.00	1,500.40	985.90
to enterprises	22,300.00	431.50	0.70
to higher education	21,011.00	1,620.00	626.40
to private non-profit	5,000.00	41.70	0
Enterprises			
R&D expenditure	99,652.00	3,544.00	182.70
R&D performance	199,700.00	4,557.40	157.20
to higher education	1,452.00	244.70	27.80
to private non-profit	800.00	23.00	0
to government	0	29.30	0
Higher education			
R&D expenditure	645.80	166.30	133.90
R&D performance	25,600.00	2,209.80	816.30
to enterprises	0	0	0.10
Private non-profit			
R&D expenditure	3,091.40	210.00	15.40
R&D performance	6,000.00	108.50	n.a.
to higher education	1,591.40	163.10	14.80
From abroad			
R&D expenditure	0	839.20	14.40
to government	0	4.00	0
to enterprises	0	813.10	0.90
to higher education	0	15.80	13.50
to private non-profit	0	6.30	0

Source: OECD (1997) *Industrial Competitiveness: Benchmarking Business Environments in the Global Economy*, Paris: OECD, 45, 55, 77.
Notes:
[a] R&D expenditure: all R&D funded by the sector performed in this and other sectors
[b] R&D performance: R&D performed in this sector

Mexico. Canada has only 2 per cent of the capability of the United States, while Mexico has only 0.08 per cent (Table 10.2). Seen as a whole, the US government, but most particularly US firms, engage in a much higher level of R&D than either Canada or Mexico. Furthermore, the institutional structures of the countries are not comparable. The United States has a well-developed private non-profit sector engaged in R&D, which is far less apparent in Canada and nearly negligible in Mexico (Table 10.2). By contrast, the United States receives no R&D inputs from abroad, as opposed to Canada, for which these represent a significant contribution to enterprises, and Mexico, which again has a significantly lower level of assistance across the board. Patterns of R&D expenditure and performance in higher education among the countries display a similar distribution, with the United States showing far more capability than either Canada or Mexico (Table 10.2). The data in

Table 10.2 illustrate the extent to which the R&D generated in the United States overwhelms that of Canada and Mexico.

The volumes of expenditures and output measure the extent to which the United States far outpaces its North American trading partners. That in itself sets up a momentum which propels the United States faster along its technological trajectory. But the United States is also actively changing the rules by which competition – and as such, cooperation – are defined through antitrust legislation. Over the years, antitrust legislation has been interpreted alternatively narrowly as well as leniently with respect to joint ventures among firms depending on the nature of domestic and international competition. At present a commonly held view in the United States is that domestic firms are at a disadvantage relative to foreign competitors in their ability to collaborate in the market. To rectify the situation, the National Cooperative Research Act (NCRA) 1984 was passed to permit pre-competitive R&D collaborations. Since passage of the act, there has been an exponential growth of such collaborations. Nine years after its passage, 300 research joint ventures were registered, in contrast to the estimated only 21 formed between 1976 and 1979 (Warner and Rugman 1994). Since implementation of the NCRA, calls for expansion of its coverage to include joint production ventures and joint marketing ventures have led to passage of the National Cooperative Production Amendments (NCPA) of 1993 and the National Cooperative Research and Production Act (NCRPA) of 1993.

These pieces of legislation relax the interpretation of antitrust to favour US firms, rather than NAFTA firms *per se*. Consequently, Canadian economists Mark Warner and Alan Rugman (1994), among others, argue that the legislation is discriminatory and inconsistent with the provisions of NAFTA. And while NAFTA attempts to make Mexican institutions more market responsive and to 'establish a modern antitrust regime and strong intellectual property protection' (see the passage by Morici quoted earlier), it does nothing to encourage cooperation among transnational R&D-intensive firms and institutions. Unless innovation policy is designed into NAFTA, or any other region for that matter, the nation that will benefit the most by protecting its lead will do so to the detriment of the region as a whole.

Towards the conceptualization of a super-regional system of innovation

What would be required to establish a coherent super-regional system of innovation? In contrast to national systems of innovation, super-regional systems involve trade relations among groups of countries. Whereas at the national level the primary focus is on industrial innovation as carried out by firms, followed by supporting institutions such as universities, government agencies and policies (Nelson 1993), at the super-regional level all the institutions and policies affecting trade and competition must be brought into play. Consequently, several considerations gain currency at the multi-state regional level.

First, it is important to recognize that translational innovation integrates nations with different learning capacities. These differences must be rectified or else the bloc faces the prospect of setting in motion even greater and growing disparities. Second, and learning from Europe, it is equally important to design an innovation policy that is demand driven, or these countries risk creating regional aid policies at the expense of public- and private-sector collaborations. Third, and drawing from NAFTA, it is important that trade arrangements not disadvantage partners because of preferential knowledge-enhancing mechanisms that on the surface do not appear to be trade related.

These issues are similar to those identified by Hans Singer when he asked whether a genuine partnership is possible among developed and developing countries in the Americas (Singer 1995). Here, he argued that a series of strategies would have to be undertaken simultaneously. First would be the strengthening of trade-creating effects, including a freer movement of labour. Second would be improving the trade efficiency of all countries by assisting the weaker developing countries. Third would be promoting partnerships between governments and businesses. And fourth would be modifying structural adjustment policies within countries to allow for regional cooperation.

A well-developed system of super-regional innovation would be derived from a combination of the policies identified by Singer with those previously outlined by the UN Economic Commission for Latin American directed at integrating micro- and macro-economic policies within countries. The latter list of conditions combines micro- and macro-economic concerns across countries.

Thus, an equitable and efficient approach for encouraging innovation at the super-regional level would combine elements of both the European and the North American systems. And while the European case illustrates how super-regional technology policies can be implemented, the North American case shows why it is necessary to go beyond technology policies towards development of a concerted innovation policy. As argued by a number of development economists, a coherent system of innovation requires institutional parity. Anything less could yield perverse results, especially as developing countries emerge as integral if not critical actors in the creation of super-regional trade arrangements.

PART IV

Regional Innovation Management

CHAPTER ELEVEN

Sources of Innovative Environments: A Technological Evolution Perspective

James M. Utterback and Allan N. Afuah

Introduction

Why do some regions or nations have a competitive advantage in some industries? A nation or region's local environment of factor conditions, demand conditions, related industries, and firm strategy, structure and rivalry can be a source of competitive advantage (Thomas 1989; Porter 1990). This immediately raises a simple but important question: if some environments are better sources of competitive advantage than others, how do such environments come about? In other words, what are the origins and evolution of environments that are conducive to competitive firms? Just as important is why and when such a competitive advantage can be lost. The answers to these questions are critical to firms' strategy and public policy formulation, and have been the subject of considerable research (Thomas 1989; Porter 1990). Porter (1990), for example, suggests that the environment often starts with an advantage in one of three determinants – factors of production, related and supporting industries, and demand conditions – and sets a process in motion in which other determinants assume greater roles, signalling the beginnings of a winning environment. Over time, the determinants reinforce each other, culminating in an environment that is the source of competitive advantage. For example, Sweden's speciality in the steel industry grew initially out of deposits of iron ore of low phosphorus content in Sweden (Porter 1990).

This chapter explores both questions by focusing on the evolution of the technologies that underlie a firm's low cost and product differentiation. The thesis of the chapter is that the local environment that is the source of national or regional competitive advantage is the result of the process of technological evolution driven by some initial and prevailing conditions. The type of environment that emerges is a function of how these initial conditions, chance events and the reaction (by firms and regional policy-makers) to firms' performance influence the processes of uncertainty resolution, capabilities building and survivor selection that are characteristic of technological evolution. Building on the Utterback and Abernathy dynamic model of innovation (Utterback and Abernathy 1975; Abernathy and Utterback 1978; Abernathy 1978; Utterback 1994), we develop a framework that can be used to explore how competitive environments evolve and the consequences for a firm's competitive advantage. We also argue that a region can lose its competitive advantage when a dominant design emerges during the evolution of the technology or when a technological discontinuity makes obsolete the localized technological capabilities not only of the manufacturer, but also of existing suppliers, customers and related industries.

The chapter is organized as follows. In the next section we lay the foundation for the framework that follows by drawing on the Utterback–Abernathy dynamic model of innovation to explore the processes that take place during the evolution of localized technological change and the impact of this evolution on firms' local environment. We then develop a framework for exploring how conditions at the beginning of, or during the evolution of, a technology can determine the nature of the local environment. In the section after that, we explore how the emergence of a dominant design or the arrival of a technological discontinuity can end a regional advantage. Finally, we use the case of the US semiconductor industry to illustrate our arguments.

Background

Technological evolution and a firm's local environment

The technological and market knowledge that underpins innovation is often tacit and idiosyncratic, and therefore learned by doing, using and interacting with customers, suppliers and related industries (Antonelli 1995: 2; Bell and Pavitt 1993; Rosenberg 1982; Nelson and Winter 1982). At the onset of an innovation it may not be clear to producers exactly what type of knowledge, components or related technologies they need, what customers want, and the markets that the product will address (K. B. Clark 1985). Utterback and Abernathy (1975) formalized the process of experimentation, error, correction, learning and interaction with the local environment of competitors, suppliers and customers that takes place during the life cycle of a technology. The coevolution of product, competition, suppliers and customers, which we now briefly explore, is summarized in Figure 11.1 and Table 11.1.

Uncertainty resolution, capabilities building and survival selection

According to Utterback and Abernathy (1975), there is a lot of product and market uncertainty early in the life of a technology. As the technology is in a state of flux, firms have no clear idea where to place their R&D bets. Custom designs are common, with the new product's technology often being crude, expensive and unreliable – but able to fill a function in a way that is desirable in some niche market. These designs are in some ways merely experiments in the marketplace (K. B. Clark 1985). The case of the personal computer (PC) illustrates some of these points. The first makers of PCs, like Altair or MITS, did not know just what the attributes of the personal computer should be and were not quite sure about the market they were going to address. Some of those first PCs were nothing more than a box with a microprocessor in it that was sold largely to hobbyists (Langlois 1992). As producers learn more about how to meet customer needs through producer–customer inter-action and product experimentation, some standardization of components, market needs and product design features takes place. Eventually a dominant design

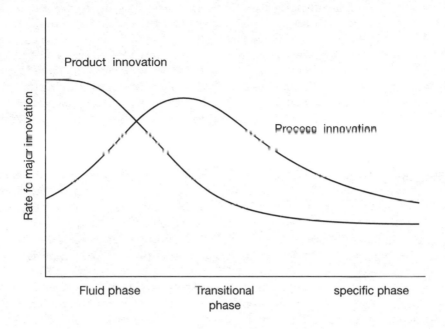

Figure 11.1 Coevolution of product, competition, suppliers and customers

Table 11.1 Key elements of the dynamic process of innovation

Product	From high variety, to dominant design, to incremental innovation on standardized products
Process	Manufacturing progresses from heavy reliance on skilled labour and general-purpose equipment to specialized equipment tended by low-skilled labour
Organization	From entrepreneurial *organic* firm to hierarchical *mechanistic* firm with defined tasks and procedures and few rewards for radical innovation
Market	From fragmented and unstable with diverse products and rapid feedback to commodity-like with largely undifferentiated products
Competition	From many small firms with unique products to an oligopoly of firms with similar products

Source: Utterback (1994)

emerges, signalling a substantial reduction in uncertainty, experimentation and major design changes. A dominant design is one whose major components and underlying core concepts do not vary substantially from one product model to the other, and the design commands a high percentage of the market share (Utterback and Suarez 1993; Utterback and Abernathy 1975; Henderson and Clark 1990; Anderson and Tushman 1990). Emphasis changes from major product innovation to process innovation, and incremental product innovations. As firms gain more experience in the dominant design, products become more highly defined, with differences between competitors' products often fewer than similarities. In the case of the personal computer, the dominant design emerged shortly after 1981 when IBM introduced its version. This quickly became the dominant design, as the firms that entered the market tended to use the IBM design. Following the emergence, many firms did not have to rethink what type of microprocessor architecture or operating system to use in their PC designs. Emphasis has since been largely in incremental product innovations and some process innovations.

Competition, industry structure and rivalry

Utterback and Abernathy (1975) and Utterback (1994) suggest that competition in an industry is a reflection of the changes in products and processes stemming from technological evolution. Thus, early in the life of the technology, when product and market requirements are still ambiguous, there is expected to be rapid entry of firms with very few or no failures. The basis of competition is on product features. Following the emergence of a dominant design, those firms that were not 'winners' of the dominant design are likely to exit. There are very few or no entries with designs that deviate substantially from the dominant design. In the personal computer example, there were very few or no entries that used a different design from the IBM one after it had emerged as the standard. Competitive emphasis shifts in favour of those firms with greater skill in process innovation and process integration, and with more highly developed internal technical and engineering skills focused on the dominant design. Many firms are unable to compete effectively and fail. Others may possess special capabilities and thus merge successfully with the ultimately dominant firms, whereas weaker firms may merge and still fail. Eventually the market reaches a point of stability in which there are only a few firms producing standardized or slightly differentiated products, and stable sales and market shares. The basis for competition becomes primarily low cost. Mueller and Tilton (1969) present similar arguments. Empirical evidence also supports this pattern (Gort and Klepper 1982; Klepper and Graddy 1990; Klepper and Simons 1993; Utterback and Suarez 1993; Utterback 1994).

Suppliers and customers

Early in the evolution of the technology, when product innovation dominates, input materials are largely off-the-shelf and manufacturing equipment mostly general purpose. The labour used in manufacturing is largely very skilled. This allows for process flexibility since process changes may be frequent. Following the emergence of the dominant design, the rate of product innovations decreases and emphasis shifts to process innovation. Materials become more specialized and equipment more specialized and expensive. The labour used becomes largely unskilled. Turning to the PC example again, early versions of PCs by the likes of MITS, Apple and Altair were assembled in garages or warehouses using different microprocessors and standard off-the-shelf microchips. Following the emergence of the dominant design, the Intel microprocessor became the microprocessor to be used in PCs.

Early in the life of the technology, customers may not know which of their needs the product can satisfy (K. B. Clark 1985). They may not even know whether they have such needs. Brand names may not count for much at this point, since producers are probably still unknown quantities. As time goes on, manufacturers and customers learn more about customer needs and expectations. Back in the late 1970s, most of today's PC users did not know that they needed one, let alone know what attributes it should have. But through interaction with computer makers, customers now know what some of their needs are.

The pattern described above repeats itself when a new technology with the potential to render the old one non-competitive is introduced, resulting in a technological discontinuity that starts the cycle all over again (Utterback and Kim 1986; Utterback 1994; Tushman and Anderson 1986, Tushman and Rosenkopf 1992). The technological discontinuity that ushers in a new cycle may render the existing localized technological knowledge and skills of a firm useless (Tushman and Anderson 1986). It can also have more far-reaching consequences: it can render the technological knowledge of existing suppliers, customers and related industries useless (Afuah and Bahram 1995).

The dynamics of local environments: a model

With the groundwork in place, we now turn to the first question: what determines the environment that gives a region a competitive advantage? In this subsection, we argue that this environment is a function of the impact of three factors – initial and prevailing conditions, the type of innovation, and the reaction by firms and policy-makers to the resulting firm and regional performance – on three important characteristics of technological evolution: uncertainty resolution, capabilities building and survivor selection. The elements of our model are shown in Figure 11.2. We will explore, first, how the type of innovation influences the uncertainty that must be resolved. We then explore how conditions such as a guaranteed market for outputs, very demanding customers, well-articulated product quality levels, the presence of a dominant firm, firm strategy and policies that force weak appropriability of technology or make venture capital easily available, determine what kind of environment emerges. (This list of initial conditions is not intended to be exhaustive but rather to serve as examples of those factors that help resolve uncertainty, build capabilities and select surviving firms during technological evolution.) These conditions do so in the way they help resolve technological and market uncertainty, select survivors, and build firm and related industry capabilities through the trial, error, correction and experimentation processes that take place during the evolution of localized technological innovation.

Types of innovation and associated uncertainties

An innovator faces both technological and market uncertainties (Freeman 1982: 149). Technological uncertainty is the additional information on the components, relationships among them, methods and techniques that go into making the new product or service work according to some specification. It is 'how to make a new product and how to make it work' (Geroski 1995: 92). At a discontinuity, this may include the additional information needed to choose between a new technology and an old one, or between competing new technologies. Market uncertainty is the additional information on who the customers are, what their needs and expectations

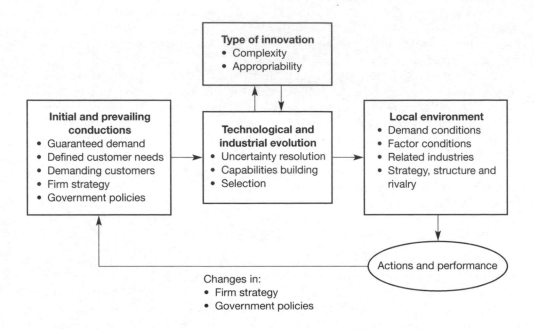

Figure 11.2 Determinants of local environments

are, how to get them to buy the product, and how to get it to them. It is 'how to sell the new product and make it a commercial success' (*ibid.*).

These uncertainties are a function of both the phase of the innovation life cycle and the complexity of the innovation (Tushman and Rosenkopf 1992; Utterback 1994). They are particularly rife early in the life of an innovation, and the more complex the innovation, the more the uncertainty. Complexity, in turn, is a function of: (a) the innovation's dimensions of merit – its attributes, as perceived by its local environment; (b) the number of interfaces between the innovation and peripheral innovations, and how interrelated they are (W. B. Arthur 1990), and whether the product exhibits network externalities[1] or not; and (c) the number of organizations in the innovation's local environment that are impacted by it, and the extent to which each organization must learn in order to play its role in the innovation. On this complexity scale, for example, simple non-assembled products such as paper or glass have the least complexity since their primary attributes are unit cost; they have limited interface with other products, and their primary focus is on customers. Open systems such as computer networks, radio, or telephone networks are the most complex. Computers, for example, have several dimensions of merit: type of operating system, amount of memory, disk capacity, upgradability, speed, power consumption, weight, user friendliness, the ability to run old software, and network characteristics. Interfacing with other computers, networks, and other software and hardware is important. A computer innovation can have an impact on customers, independent software vendors, hardware suppliers and communications network providers.

The more complexity, the more influential non-technical factors – e.g. complementary assets and organizations in the local environment – arc likely to be in determining the course of an innovation's evolution (Tushman and Rosenkopf 1992) and the less likely it is that the selection process reflects economic efficiency. That is, the best technology is more likely to win in simple products like glass than it is in computers. In any case, the extent to which uncertainties are resolved and the nature of the emergent local environment are a function of certain initial conditions.

Role of initial and prevailing conditions in shaping local environment

Dominant player's strategies

A dominant firm can greatly influence the timing and path of the evolution of a technology and the resulting local environment. This is particularly true for innovations which require complementary assets to be successful. IBM and the PC serve as a good example. When the company introduced its PC in 1981, the machine very quickly emerged as the dominant design, although it was not the most technically superior. There are several reasons for this not so efficient an economic outcome. First, IBM's entry reduced a major uncertainty in the minds of the PC's local environment. PC makers, suppliers of chips, independent software vendors and corporate customers had not taken the PC seriously, especially as a corporate business tool, until IBM 'legitimized' it when it entered the market. Second, customers care about what the size of the network they join now will be tomorrow (Katz and Shapiro 1985). This suggests that a firm's ability or reputation in building networks may be instrumental in customers' choice of the technology they adopt. IBM had such a reputation in computers, and many customers were quick to adopt its PC architecture, making it the dominant design. Emerging with this dominant design were chip suppliers like Intel and software makers like Microsoft whose products were compatible with IBM's. Their products were not necessarily technologically superior to competitors'. All three industries in the United States are very strong and often attributed to the PC's interrelatedness with chips and software.

Once the dominant design emerges, a dominant firm can also exert great influence on its local environment through its bargaining power. It can insist on having second sources for the components that it buys from suppliers, thereby reducing the appropriability of suppliers' innovations.

Guaranteed demand

A guaranteed market for products, with well-articulated customer needs, reduces market uncertainty. Such a reduction has several ramifications for an innovation. In the first place, firms that would have been prevented from entry by market uncertainty are now more likely to enter. Once in the market, they can concentrate on resolving technological uncertainties and translating customer needs into the appropriate product design. The more firms that enter, the higher the rate of competition and product innovation. Once IBM 'legitimized' the business market for PCs, entrants could concentrate on producing PCs for such a market. Defined customer needs also help in the choice of a technology from competing technologies. For example, the US government's demand in the 1950s and 1960s for reliable and lightweight electronic systems with low power consumption clearly pointed to the use of semiconductors over vacuum tubes (Utterback and Murray 1977).

In the second place, guaranteed demand for manufacturers' products means that they are, in turn, more likely to assure suppliers (of components and equipment) of demand for their own products. Moreover, a reduction in product uncertainty may also mean a reduction in market uncertainty for suppliers. That is, more firms will enter related industries, accelerating the rate of innovation for components, equipment and complementary products, and increasing the chances of having more competent surviving firms in related industries. Borrus (1988), Wilson, Ashton and Egan (1980) and Utterback and Murray (1977) suggest that US government guarantees to buy the output from US semiconductor start-up firms had an influence on the rapid pace of innovation and the types of competitors, suppliers and customers that emerged.

Very demanding customers – quality and quantity

A customer can be demanding in two ways: in the level of attributes of the products it expects (form, fit, function and reliability), and the quantity of parts that are needed. To satisfy the two types of demand requires a different kind of capability. For some products, meeting very high product attribute levels implies more product innovation than process. In the early part of the innovation cycle, such demand is likely to increase competition and result in an industry with surviving firms that are more competent at product innovation. The level of product attributes demanded can also influence the type of dominant design that emerges. In workstations, for example, processor speed is critical. Thus, reduced instruction set computer (RISC) technology has been able to replace the older CISC (complex instruction set computer) technology. In personal computers, where processor speed is not as important, however, CISC has continued to dominate.

Instead of emphasizing product attributes, demanding customers may want large volumes delivered on time at low cost. Such demands would force the manufacturer to emphasize process innovation, paying more attention to relations with suppliers of both materials and equipment, who are often the source or catalyst of process innovations. Over many product cycles, surviving manufacturers are likely to be more competent at process innovation than at product innovations. Learning-by-doing suggests that suppliers of materials and manufacturing equipment are likely to emerge stronger in such low-cost environments than in environments where emphasis is on product innovation.

Policies: weaker technological appropriability and availability of venture capital

If venture capital is readily available for innovations with low intellectual property protection, there is likely to be more entry. This allows entrepreneurs and technical gurus to move around more easily, often starting new firms. In either case, since technological knowledge is best transferred by moving people (Allen 1984; Roberts 1979), the rate of innovation, learning and quality of surviving firms is likely to increase.

Weak appropriability and availability of venture capital funds also have an impact on suppliers and related industries in two ways. First, some of the same funds are going to be available to suppliers of materials and equipment as well as to suppliers of complementary products from related industries. For example, some of the venture capital funds made available to PC makers would also be available to makers of PC components as well as to software developers. Second, the competitive pressures put on producers may be passed on to suppliers as they coevolve, resulting in surviving suppliers who are more competent.

Firm strategy

A firm's strategy can have an impact on the evolution of its local environment. Take Sun Microsystems, a maker of computer workstations whose strategy has been, since its founding in 1982, to maintain open standards. That is, in designing its workstations it has used standard components and technologies that are available to anyone. When RISC technology came along, Sun designed its own version of the technology and promptly licensed it to any chip or workstation maker who wanted it, instead of maintaining a proprietary hold on it, as had the likes of DEC. This had two consequences. First, many chip makers opted to manufacture the chip, which meant more opportunities to learn about the complicated microprocessor and to supply Sun with chips. Second, many workstation makers also opted to clone Sun's workstations, helping forge a large coalition for the competition for a standard in RISC workstation technology. This coalition assured customers of a large network and installed base of workstations, giving Sun an advantage (Garud and Kumaraswamy 1993; Khazam and Mowery 1994). So far, Sun's RISC technology has maintained the highest market share of the competing technologies.

The strategies pursued by Intel, Texas Instruments and Micron Technologies have also been credited with engineering the resurgence of the US semiconductor industry (Afuah 1996).

Combined effect of conditions

So far, for expository reasons we have considered each of these conditions alone. However, their combined effect may be more effective in shaping the local environment than each alone. For example, if intellectual property protection is weak, allowing employees to move around easily without any legal repercussions, venture capital is easily available, customers emphasize product features rather than large quantities, and the industry has short product life cycles, there is likely to emerge an environment in which product innovation thrives. Related industries such as product design tools and services are likely to thrive too. If, on the other hand, customers demand large quantities that must be delivered on time and without defects, and the industry is characterized by long product life cycles, survivors in such an environment are likely to excel at process innovation. Related process innovation industries such as suppliers of equipment and materials are also likely to thrive.

Chance events

Chance events and dynamic returns to scale play a significant role in explaining the outcome of competition between different technologies and the resulting competitive environment (David 1985; B. Arthur 1989). They can influence the local environment directly or indirectly via initial conditions. For example, one reason IBM obtained an operating system from Microsoft for its personal computer was because when it went to Microsoft, it just so happened that Microsoft knew of an operating system that it could buy, turn around and sell to IBM.

Feedback effects: reaction to firm performance

Upon realizing the significance of their local environment on their performance, firms and nations are likely to take some measures to influence it. They can, for example, alter the prevailing conditions by changing their strategies and policies (Figure 11.2). For example, in 1984 US legislation was changed to allow R&D collaboration between US firms following arguments that US firms were at a disadvantage when competing with Japanese firms, whose government encouraged such collaboration. Shortly thereafter, Sematech was formed by US firms with the help of the US government to develop more manufacturing technologies for US semiconductor makers, their customers and suppliers of equipment (Integrated Circuit Engineering 1995). Intel decided to exit the DRAM (dynamic random access memory) and SRAM (static random access memory) business to concentrate on microprocessors, where it now thrives (Burgelman 1994). These examples suggest that the local environment is not static but dynamic as firms and nations, in response to their performances, also influence the environment by changing strategies or altering some of the initial conditions.

Losing the advantage

Now we turn to the second question: why do regions lose their environmental competitive advantage? We argue that a region can lose its advantage during the evolution of the technology when a dominant design emerges, or at the arrival of a technological discontinuity when the discontinuity renders obsolete the localized technological capabilities not only of manufacturers but also of suppliers, customers and related industries.

Dominant design and advantage

As an innovation evolves, the local environment that is conducive to superior performance also varies. Drawing on the Utterback–Abernathy model, we use Porter's (1990) 'diamond' to summarize the elements of desirable environments before and after the emergence of a dominant design as shown in Table 11.2. Prior to the arrival of a dominant design, emphasis is on product innovation. This favours an environment with a large pool of skilled labour and whose research institutions emphasize product R&D. Demand conditions that emphasize product features and

Table 11.2 A firm's local environment as a source of advantage: before and after the emergence of a dominant design

Before the emergence of a dominant design	After the emergence of a dominant design
Factor conditions	
• Universities and other R&D institutions that emphasize product R&D	• Industry research that emphasizes manufacturing/process R&D
• Large pool of skilled labour	• Pool of low-cost labour
• Easy movement of employees	
• Availability of venture capital	
Demand conditions	
• Demand that emphasizes product features	• Demand that emphasizes low cost and high quality
• Presence of many lead users	• Large number of followers
Related and supplier industries	
• Presence of design tools and services	• Presence of suppliers of specialized materials and equipment for process innovations
• Broad scope of complementary products	
Firm strategy, structure and rivalry	
• Easy to start new firms	• Difficult to start new firms
• Inexpensive access to technological knowledge	• Mechanistic organizations
• Availability of venture capital	
• Organic organizations	

the presence of a significant number of lead users can also be valuable. Such lead users play a significant role in the experimentation to resolve market uncertainties (von Hippel 1986). The presence of industries that provide design tools such as computer-aided design (CAD) software as well as a broad scope of complementary products can also nurture product innovation. Finally, access to technological knowledge, availability of venture capital funds, and free movement of employees between firms allow new firms to exploit new product ideas from incumbents or universities.

Following the emergence of a dominant design, emphasis shifts to process innovation and incremental product innovation. Such innovations tend to thrive where universities and other R&D institutions emphasize manufacturing R&D and where there is a large pool of low-cost labour. Demand conditions that emphasize low cost and large number of customers who tend to be followers also favour the post-dominant design era. The presence of suppliers of special materials and equipment needed for the increased emphasis on process innovation can also be valuable. If the region is such that it is difficult to start new firms, incumbents will tend to dominate, and, given their tendency not to initiate new major product innovation, one can expect product innovation to be less frequent.

Thus an environment that is conducive to pre-dominant design firm performance may not be for post-dominant design, and a region whose local environment is conducive to product innovation may lose that advantage following the emergence of a dominant design.

Discontinuities and local environment

The emergence of a dominant design is not the only way a region can lose its competitive advantage. If the technological discontinuity that ushers in a new cycle makes obsolete not only the capabilities of manufacturers, but also those of its suppliers, customers and related industries, then a region that previously had an environmental competitive advantage may lose it. Why? Well, a primary reason why a firm can derive an advantage from its local environment is the relationships that it can forge with suppliers, customers and related industries that its competitors outside the region cannot (Porter 1990). If the competencies that allowed these parties to participate in the relationship are made obsolete by a technological discontinuity, the relationships themselves may not be worth as much. Take Japanese automobile makers and their suppliers. It has been estimated that an important part of their advantage in product development and manufacturing comes from their relationships with suppliers (K. B. Clark 1989a; Clark and Fujimoto 1991; Helper 1987). The electric car is a technological discontinuity and destroys the competencies of both automobile makers and their suppliers. This is because the components for the internal combustion automobile (engine, transmission, fuel injection and drive train), their underlying concepts and the linkages between them are radically different from those for the electric car (with the components electric motor, battery and electric motor control). In adopting the electric car, auto makers would have two choices: stay with the old manufacturers or switch to other suppliers. Staying with the old suppliers means using inferior components since the suppliers' existing localized technological knowledge of internal combustion engine automobiles has been rendered obsolete by the electric car. Switching suppliers means having to build relationships from scratch and incurring switching costs. Similar arguments can be made for the case when customer localized knowledge (from learning-by-using) or that of firms in related industries has been rendered obsolete. Thus if a discontinuity makes obsolete localized technological knowledge of members of the local environment – the core to the relationships that formed the basis for a region's advantage – the region is likely to encounter difficulties in sustaining its advantage.

The case of the US semiconductor industry

The United States led the world in semiconductor market share until the 1980s, when it lost that leadership position. In what follows, we argue that a strong US computer industry and US government policies that initially guaranteed demand for some products, forced firms to license out technology, stipulated high product quality (form, fit, function and reliability) and sponsored semiconductor R&D

resulted in a local environment that was conducive to product innovation and not the process innovation that is a critical success factor following a dominant design. Thus, while US firms have invented all the major semiconductor products in the market today and have been the first to commercialize them, their level of competitiveness has, with a few exceptions, dropped considerably once a dominant design has emerged and emphasis shifted from product to process innovation. We explore the cases of DRAMs (dynamic random access memories), EPROMs (electrically erasable read-only memories) and microprocessors.

The emergence of an entrepreneurial environment

The semiconductor industry was born with the invention of the transistor at AT&T's Bell Laboratories in 1948. One year later, the US Department of Justice initiated an antitrust case against AT&T which was settled in 1956 with a consent decree ordering AT&T to license all its existing patents to US domestic firms free of charge and future patents at reasonable rates (Tilton 1971; Borrus 1988). This lowered what might have otherwise been a high entry barrier for new entrants. In the years that followed, the US government also sponsored research at its own laboratories and at universities, further increasing the pool of technological knowledge on semiconductors available to US firms (Utterback and Murray 1977). With readily available technological knowledge, entrepreneurs, especially former employees of Bell Laboratories, took advantage of the free patents and left to start their own companies. These entrepreneurs usually went on to develop new products using new product ideas or technological knowledge from their former employers or other incumbents. In fact, intellectual property protection in the semiconductor industry was so low that one firm, MOSAID, actually specialized in opening up new products, painstakingly detailing how they were constructed, and selling the information to any firm that wanted to reverse-engineer the product. What is more, the US Defense Department had a practice, later followed by IBM and other computer companies, of requiring suppliers of semiconductors to have second sources. That is, firms were forced by their customers to license their technologies to competitors and therefore lose monopoly rents.

Uncertainty about the type of product to invent using semiconductor technology was greatly reduced by two factors. The first was the presence of an established and thriving computer industry in the United States which needed faster, cheaper and more reliable semiconductor components to replace components from less attractive technologies. For example, up to the 1970s computer memory used ferrite core devices, invented by Jay Forrester of MIT. These were magnetized iron ringlets strung with wire, and as such were bulky and consumed a lot of power, and so constituted a target for semiconductor replacement. Semiconductor companies knew that computer makers needed faster, cheaper and smaller semiconductor memories.

The second was the fact that the US military often bought most of the output from US firms and, in general, insisted on very high miniaturization, performance and reliability standards (Utterback and Murray 1977). This demand emphasized features and reliability and not large volumes. A guaranteed market encouraged many

Table 11.3 Popular semiconductor products and their inventors

Product	Inventor	First introduced	1994 sales (US$ million)[a]	US share (%)	Japan	Europe (%)	Rest of the world (%)
SRAM	Intel (USA)	1969	4,110	25	62	3	10
DRAM	Intel (USA)	1971	23,050	15	54	3	28
Microprocessor	Intel (USA)	1972	24,080	66	29	3	2
EPROM	Intel (USA)	1971	1,410	29	34	23	14
EEPROM	Xicor. Seeq (USA)	198?	500	51	12	24	13
Gate arrays	LSI (USA)	1980	5,200	38	38	15	9
ROMs	IBM? (USA)		2,075	15	72	2	11
Flash memory	USA	1990	860				

[a] Source for 1994 sales estimates: Integrated Circuit Engineering of Scottsdale, Arizona (Integrated Circuit Engineering 1995)

new entrants. Venture capitalists also financed more start-ups, given that there was already a buyer for output of the start-ups (Wilson, Ashton and Egan 1980).

Thus low intellectual property protection, free movement of employees and readily available venture capital led to a rather fragmented industry in which firms were started around some product or technology. Later in the product's life cycle, some of the employees, possibly founders, would defect to start another firm based on another product. With a flourishing computer industry that needed new products, many semiconductor firms had a good idea what products to produce.

The flourishing American computer industry and established research universities also played another role in shaping the product-oriented environment in the United States: that of supplier of the software tools that are critical to the design of semiconductor chips. The proximity of the supplier of such tools can be important, given the tacit nature of early concepts.

Although the features of the products demanded by the military had very high standards, the volumes required were very small. Large users of semiconductors like IBM and AT&T produced most of their own chips and sold none to anyone else. They were so-called captive manufacturers. Thus the incentive for semiconductor manufacturers was to develop new products with superior attributes and to deliver large volumes.

Product innovation

The entrepreneurial product innovation environment allowed US firms to invent most of the products whose sales have grown to a huge semiconductor market, worth $91 billion in 1994. The most popular of these products are shown in Table 11.3 together with their innovators. In this section we use DRAMs (dynamic random access memories), EPROMs (electrically erasable read-only memories) and microprocessors to show how the environment that evolved from the initial conditions, created largely by the US government and a thriving computer industry, was conducive more to invention and first commercialization, but once a dominant design emerged and emphasis shifted to process innovation, it no longer constituted a source of competitive advantage.

DRAMs (dynamic random access memories)

The DRAM is the gut of the computer and other logic systems; it is used as the main memory where programs are normally stored during execution. When PC manufacturers describe a system as having 16 megabytes of memory, they are usually referring to the amount of DRAM in the machine. In some computer products, such as workstations, the DRAM actually costs more than the microprocessor, the brain of the computer. Over \$23 billion worth of DRAMs were sold in 1994 alone (Integrated Circuit Engineering 1995).

Each bit of information in the DRAM is stored in the form of electrical charge in a capacitor. Since this charge can decay quickly, every millionth of a second or so, the capacitors have to be recharged (or 'refreshed', in the parlance of the industry). It is the fact that the product has to be refreshed every so often that gives it the description 'dynamic'. When Intel introduced the first DRAM in 1970, the device had three transistors per bit of information and was labelled a three-transistor cell device. The chip contained only 1024 bits of information, whereas today's DRAM chips can carry 256 million bits. That first DRAM also required two power sources, one to refresh the memory and the other to supply the power for moving the data. In the years that followed the invention, many firms entered the DRAM market and made many valuable product innovations. First, Intel developed a one-transistor cell. This was an extremely important innovation since the smaller the number of transistors required to store a bit of information, the more such bits chip makers could park on a given piece of silicon real estate. The next two innovations were made by Mostek, a start-up in Carrollton, Texas. In the first, it reduced the number of power sources needed for the DRAM to one, greatly simplifying the demands put on DRAM customers. In the second, it found a way to solve an important problem. To read or store information in a RAM, the computer must send it an address signal through the pins that normally stick out of the RAM. The way the address pins of the first DRAMs were designed was such that the number of pins grew very rapidly as the bit density of the chip increased. Mostek introduced an innovation called multiplexed addressing that allowed the DRAM to have considerably fewer address pins as the density increased. Both the one power supply innovation and multiplexed addressing were introduced with later versions of the 16K DRAM, and in going to the 64K DRAM, the dominant designed had emerged. Since then, there have been certain critical features that DRAM designers have not had to rethink each time they are introducing new DRAMs models, from that 64K chip to today's 24M. These features include a one-transistor cell, some kind of refresh mechanism to recharge the capacitor of the cell, one voltage source and multiplexed addressing.

The emergence of the dominant design shifted emphasis to process innovation. Thus the 64K required, among other things, design for manufacturability and better use of equipment from suppliers. Process innovations required closer working relations with suppliers of such equipment as automatic testers and photolithography machines. As newer generations of DRAMs were introduced – 256K, 1M, 4M – US firms dropped out. Inventor and pioneer Intel exited the market in 1984

(Burgelman 1994). Others followed, including Mostek, the firm that had been responsible for so much of the dominant design. At one point only two US firms remained in the industry. One of them was Micron Technology, a start-up by entrepreneurs from Mostek.

EPROMs (electrically programmable read-only memories)

The main disadvantage of DRAMs is that, unlike the ferrite core memory they replaced, they are volatile. That is, when power is switched off, they lose whatever data they were carrying. Thus an interesting question to chip makers in the 1960s was how to develop a random-access semiconductor memory that would preserve its data even when power was cut off. Intel's research for this novel device paid off when Dov Frolich-Benchkowsky invented the EPROM in 1971 with the development of the FAMOS (floating-gate avalanche injection metal oxide semiconductor) cell. Each bit of the memory device would be represented by the presence or absence of electrical charge on a gate buried in the oxide of a transistor. Like the early DRAMs, it needed two power sources: one large enough to 'force' the charge to the floating gate, and the other to supply the rest of the chip.

Shortly after Intel's introduction of the EPROM, other firms reverse-engineered the product and introduced similar parts. The dominant design emerged with the introduction of the 16K version, which needed only one power source. Again, following the dominant design, emphasis shifted from product innovation to process innovation, with relationships with suppliers of equipment now becoming critical. Even Intel, the innovator of EPROMs, de-emphasized them in 1991 to concentrate on microprocessors (Burgelman 1994).

Microprocessors

Intel invented the microprocessor in 1972, and shortly after that, other firms, including Motorola, TI and Zilog, entered the market. In the late 1970s and early 1980s Motorola's microprocessor was the processor of choice for high-performance applications such as computer workstations. In 1981, however, when IBM wanted a microprocessor for its PC, it chose Intel's architecture. As the popularity of the IBM PC increased, so did that of Intel's microprocessor. In the mid-1980s it emerged as the dominant design for PC microprocessors.

Following the emergence of the Intel architecture as the dominant design, foreign competitors did not take over the microprocessor market for two reasons. In the first place, the microprocessor's microcode is protectable under intellectual property laws and Intel has been able to legally protect its microprocessor copyrights. It has also pursued a so-called *run* strategy in which it introduces newer generations of microprocessors frequently, sometimes before sales of an existing generation have peaked (Afuah 1998). In the second place, all the software that users of IBM PCs have accumulated over the years cannot run on other architectures without very costly modifications. For this reason, the switching costs for customers can be high. Consequently, Intel and the United States have been able to maintain a leadership position in microprocessors despite the emergence of a dominant design and what would have been a shift from major product innovations favouring environments that are conducive to process innovations.

Summary of cases

With the exception of microprocessors, these cases show a very similar pattern. A US firm invents a product and is the first to commercialize it. Other firms enter and make valuable contributions, and a dominant design quickly emerges. Emphasis shifts from product innovations to process innovations, where relations with suppliers of lithography, test and other chip manufacturing equipment, and materials are critical. US firms quickly lose their lead. The microprocessor is the exception because of the nature of the installed base of computers that use the Intel architecture, the need for compatibility and, above all, Intel's strategies in protecting its entrepreneurial rents.

Summary and conclusions

Our goal was to explore the sources and dynamics of innovative environments, from a technological evolution perspective. We argued that such environments are the result of the process of technological evolution, driven by some conditions (initial and prevailing). The type of environment that emerges in an industry is a function of how these initial conditions and chance events influence the processes of uncertainty resolution, capabilities building and survivor selection that are characteristic of technological evolution. Given that success at each phase of the evolution requires a different set of capabilities and local environment, an environment that is conducive to a firm's competitive advantage early in the life of a technology may not be conducive in the later stages of the evolution. Firms' strategies and government policies, arising as a result of national and firm performance in the particular industry, also play a significant role in shaping the type of competitive environment that emerges.

We then used case studies from the US semiconductor industry to show that the presence of a strong US computer industry and US government policies shaped a local competitive environment that has been conducive to the introduction and first commercialization of products but not ideal for the large-volume manufacturing and process engineering that are critical success factors in the latter parts of the industrial innovation cycle. In particular, we suggested that the computer industry helped reduce product uncertainty and provide valuable software tools. We also argued that the US government policy of guaranteeing US firms a market for some of their output, encouraging weak technological appropriability and movement of personnel, and its high standards for miniaturization, performance and reliability all contributed to more industry competition and surviving firms that were very competent at product innovation but not process innovation. These firms went on to invent the DRAM, SRAM, EPROM, EEPROM (electronically erasable programmable read-only memory), the microprocessor, ASICs, the calculator chip and many others – products that today are at the heart of the semiconductor industry. However, because their local environments were not very suited to process innovations, each of the US inventors – with the exception of Intel and microprocessors – had to concede its initial leadership position to a Japanese firm following the emergence of a dominant design.

Note

1. A technology is said to exhibit network externalities if it becomes the more valuable to the users, the more people who use it (Katz and Shapiro 1985).

CHAPTER TWELVE

Network Models for Technology-Based Growth

Edward J. Malecki

Introduction

Among the simple models and easy solutions that have fallen to the findings of recent research is the linear model of technological change familiar to all who study technology. The linear model is a stereotypical deterministic model that simply represents the sequence from basic and applied research to product and process development to marketing of a commercial product. What it lacks most, in comparison to contemporary knowledge, is any notion of a *network*. As this chapter will show, network thinking opens up a wide variety of sources of ideas, which ultimately permit people and organizations – notably, but not only, firms – to better understand and (to some extent) to control their environment. Examples are drawn primarily from Japan, but these are illustrative rather than exclusive. Network models have become central to research on regional growth, and they have become central to understanding institutions and national systems of innovation.

The replacement of the linear model by a non-linear feedback model (Kline and Rosenberg 1986; Myers and Rosenbloom 1996) reflects a great deal of recent learning about the nature of technology and about the processes of learning that take place within and between firms and other organizations (Figure 12.1). The idea of a *learning corporation* acknowledges these relationships and, rather than merely exploiting them, works to facilitate the interactions on which people thrive and corporations profit. However, the responses of Japanese firms to continuous learning environments seem to be distinct from those of firms elsewhere.

National differences emerge regarding broad corporate strategies for new technologies. Japanese firms, for example, routinely enlarge their technology base and product range through an expansion of technological applications. What explains the routine nature of technological adaptation by Japanese firms? We first address this question, focusing on the systemic view of technology and innovation in Japan and the diverse sources of knowledge used, and then turn to other models from Europe that centre on networks as a mechanism for learning within firms and regions.

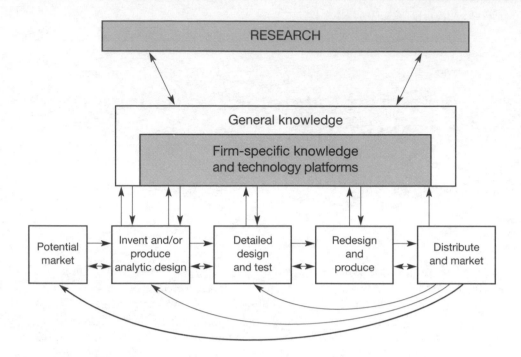

Figure 12.1 Feedback and interactions in the innovation process
Source: Malecki (1997: 53)

Managing innovation as a system

The most distinct and fundamental aspect of Japanese thinking is the perception of technology as a *system* that links various sources of knowledge. The firm functions not simply as a decision-making organization, but as an *information system* (Aoki 1994). This information system operates both within the firm and across a 'family' of related firms in an enterprise group, or *keiretsu*, in which cross-ownership is the norm, but that network is managed in a very different manner from that in US firms (Westney 1994). Complex cross-industry links, made possible within the family structure, make it difficult even for the Japanese to understand how their existing networks function (*ibid.*: 172). Corporate structure is less important than in non-Japanese firms, and corporate culture accomplishes what organizational form or structure attempts to do in firms from other countries (Song and Parry 1993).

The loosely structured Japanese organization, compared to hierarchical forms, is able to evolve and adapt and change, because continual information permits learning to be ongoing throughout the organization. Horizontal coordination, rather than hierarchical coordination, is based on sharing knowledge and information. Horizontal integration within the firm enables firms such as Nissan and NEC to master new technologies and to upgrade their capabilities in a dynamic manner. Long-term, persistent learning has permitted Japanese firms, for example, to learn new technologies and build competence in them more effectively than their competitors elsewhere. The horizontal 'family' structure has two other advantages: it

Table 12.1 Largest foreign sources of R&D investment in the United States, 1993

Country	Expenditures ($ billions)	R&D employees	Number of companies	Number of R&D facilities	Average number of R&D employees per company
Switzerland	2.524	14,700	16	45	919
Germany	2.321	19,200	32	95	600
United Kingdom	2.295	20,000	61	109	328
Japan	1.701	11,800	107	219	111
France	1.204	9,200	22	32	425

Source: Science (1995) Fertile US soil. 270 (December 1), 1445

provides 'internal' customers to test the market for new products, and it provides a 'place' for the interaction that is crucial to the innovation process (Imai 1994). In this way, affiliated companies add greatly to the technological capabilities of a firm.

The web of linkages, external as well as internal to the firm, provides an information redundancy that allows Japanese firms to take advantage of a large number of sources of tacit and explicit knowledge (Nonaka and Takeuchi 1995). These overlapping sources are especially effective in the process of innovation, where a large number of potential ideas is reduced by filtering them through the varied expertise and knowledge of team members. The use of a large number of information sources is evident from comparative data on R&D in the United States by foreign-owned firms. Japanese firms have adopted 'listening post' and 'global scanning' strategies: a large number of firms have R&D facilities in the United States, but their laboratories, in terms of the average number of R&D employees per firm, are the smallest of those in the major investor countries (Table 12.1). Japanese R&D spending continues to be located primarily in Japan.

In effect, the firm's network and system facilitate integration of technologies within managerial functions (Bowonder and Miyake 1993). Table 12.2 illustrates the various mechanisms for functional integration, which together provide several distinct advantages. For example, these integrative mechanisms allow Japanese firms to lower transaction costs, achieve fusion of different technologies, reduce the cycle time between design and commercialization, achieve rapid introduction of new products, and develop multidimensional competencies (*ibid.*: 154). These capabilities, in turn, permit Japanese firms to be competitive despite sometimes lower levels of R&D intensity.

An example of the systemic perspective is found in the Japanese concept of high technology. It includes both R&D intensity and a system orientation, and comprises a bundle or package of technologies rather than individual technologies. Isolated and independent technologies are excluded, even if R&D intensive. The focus is on those technologies that form the basis of entirely new economic infrastructures, such as microelectronics, biotechnology and new materials. The Japanese definition, then, is oriented towards core technologies associated with potential long-wave upswings. This perspective retains the importance of technological flows among sectors.

This systemic perspective has strengthened Japanese policy as well, thereby

Table 12.2 Mechanisms used by Japanese firms for functional integration in innovation

Mechanism	Characteristics
Organizational intelligence	Technical, commercial and financial intelligence obtained through a variety of channels. This is processed and disseminated to various departments
Technology fusion	Fusing diverse technologies to obtain new, more innovative technologies
Concurrent engineering	Overlapping the phases of development to facilitate information exchange, performance feedback and technological improvements
Horizontal information flow structures	Job rotation, teams for new product development and technology assimilation, large trading houses
Corporate networking	Quick exchange of data, information, designs, and other knowledge
Technology forecasting	An integrated, long-term vision of technologies, competencies and markets
Organizational learning	In-house, on-the-job training, new product subsidiaries, learning by doing, learning by using, learning by selling

Source: Modified from Bowonder and Miyake (1993: 148; table 1)

providing an institutional infrastructure that supports the efforts of companies. In contrast to mission-oriented policies, diffusion-oriented policies provide a broad capacity for adjusting to technological change throughout the industrial structure. The United States, the United Kingdom and France are regarded as having followed mission-oriented policies and political and industrial structures that have inhibited the sharing of technologies within and among firms (Nelson 1993). Japan, along with Germany, Sweden and Switzerland, on the other hand, has been diffusion-oriented, having developed institutional and industrial arrangements that encourage the transfer of know-how between activities. The Japanese market-pull emphasis on process innovation and manufacturing stands in sharp contrast to the stress on a technology-push model which has dominated most industries in the United States (Papadakis 1995).

Systemic thinking

The Japanese system facilitates hybrid technologies and technology fusion in a systemic manner that seems more difficult for non-Japanese firms to achieve. Three examples serve to illustrate this. The first is the *tree* model used to represent companies and technologies. NEC portrays itself as a tree, with technology as the roots, and several branches: communications, electronic devices, home electronics, computers and new opportunities (Branscomb and Kodama 1993: 27; Uenohara 1991). In the case of Sharp Corporation the tree model is more detailed, with roots in specific technologies such as digital recording, optical technologies and signal conversion, and 'branches' representing products such as electronic organs, satellite receivers, multi-channel recording and tapeless microcassettes (Tatsuno 1990: 83). A variation on the tree model is the 'bamboo innovation model' used by Sumitomo; bamboo begins as a single sprout, and other clumps of bamboo develop from the common roots over time to form clusters of related technologies (Branscomb and Kodama 1993: 26; Kodama 1995: 47–8).

The organic metaphor of a tree or bamboo plant embodies the connections between technologies and the relationship among various products and sectors. Linkages among technologies permit systemic products, such as robots, to be perfected by combining mechanics, electronics, sensors, new materials and software. Even the recent analogy of the 'living corporation' (de Geus 1997) fails to embody the organic nature of the interlinked systems of technologies found in these metaphors common in Japan.

A second example of Japanese systemic thinking is a *global*, rather than limited, search for new ideas and information (Tatsuno 1990: 76–80). The global 'knowledge spiral' utilizes a search of internal and external sources of tacit and explicit knowledge, permitting frequent feedback for improvements of existing products as well as development of new products (Nonaka and Takeuchi 1995: 70–3). Linkages and flows in intra- and inter-organizational networks, rather than science or the market, become the source of innovation. Networks transcend the boundaries between technologies, between departments within a firm, between firms and between sectors. Japanese firms rely on external sources of technology to a greater degree than European and North American firms.

The third example is the long-range *vision* and 'day after tomorrow' R&D. The development of generic technologies (the 'roots' of the trees) is carried out in central or corporate R&D laboratories for use in manufacturing divisions. In effect, the 'day after tomorrow' R&D provides long-range capabilities for the firm (Uenohara 1991). Long-range planning is common in large Japanese firms, and these plans help to form the basis of 'visions of the future' coordinated by the Ministry of International Trade and Industry (MITI) (Tatsuno 1990). Early 'visions' helped the shift from capital-intensive heavy industries (steel, shipbuilding, automobiles) and resource-dependent industries to knowledge-intensive machining and assembly industries, including general machinery, electronic and electrical equipment, transport equipment and precision instruments. The vision for the 1980s bluntly 'called for developing an industrial structure with high technology as its core', referred to as a 'creative, knowledge-intensive industrial structure' (Uekusa 1988: 97). The MITI vision for the 1990s emphasizes quality-of-life priorities and less strategic sectors, such as resorts, interior decorating and fashion. The latest 'vision' focuses on clean industrial technologies and aims to establish Japan as a leader in environmental technology.

The high-tech vision has largely succeeded in aerospace, where cooperative interaction among competing firms has allowed horizontal transfer of technology. The fact that the subcontractors are parts of large corporations and *keiretsu*, including Mitsubishi, Fuji and Kawasaki, has provided opportunities for vertical transfer within these organizations. The aircraft industry too has been portrayed in Japan by the tree metaphor – rooted in basic technologies, with 'fruits' in new and enhanced products for several sectors, including cars, shipbuilding, energy and housing – which represents 'how the Japanese understand linkages across industries and the consequent strategic value of aerospace in particular' (Samuels 1994: 245).

Sources of knowledge

Three sources of knowledge enable Japanese firms to master innovation: (a) workers and the knowledge they accumulate, (b) integration of technology within the firm, and (c) networks of other firms, especially the small firms with which subcontracting relationships are common.

Personnel as sources of knowledge

The Japanese innovation management system considers workers and their information networks to be critical to the success of the firm. Internal labour markets and widespread rotation of R&D workers integrate the knowledge of workers in production, marketing and R&D (Westney 1994). Job rotation ensures that engineers in particular have a holistic understanding of the technological, market and manufacturing requirements of a product. Horizontal information flow is maintained through tight links between central research and R&D labs in subsidiaries in other countries, reinforced by frequent job transfers. Perhaps most unusual is the direct transfer of research staff to the factory floor to follow a new product to production. The tacit knowledge learned by engineers in previous generations of technology can be carried on to new product development, reducing the learning time required. A Sony research director says that 'the transfer of researchers is like breathing: both necessary and natural' (Harryson 1997: 295). The practice remains far less common in non-Japanese firms.

Informal links with sources of knowledge are also prominent in Japan. Close ties are maintained between Japanese university professors and their former students, who may be working for a number of competing firms. Professors are sought out as contacts for their networks of colleagues and former students more than for their technical knowledge, which often is greater inside the major companies.

Inter-firm networks and flexible production

Within manufacturing, new forms of production organization are replacing the task fragmentation, functional specialization, mechanization and assembly-line principles of Fordism with a social organization of production based on work teams, job rotation, learning by doing, flexible production and integrated production complexes (Boyer 1995; Kenney and Florida 1993). Networks within the firms, whether called teams, quality circles or something else, are among the most frequent aspects of the 'Japanization' of industry. Teams are the central mechanism for achieving the functional integration of tasks, in response to continuous innovation, which is the heart of the Japanese model of work organization (Kenney and Florida 1993: 37).

Whether called flexible production, advanced manufacturing technology, computer-integrated manufacturing (CIM) or demand-flow technology, the ultimate goal is the combining of design, manufacture and coordination into an integrated whole. Shorter production runs and variety (economies of scope) are among the characteristics of this system, but manufacturing competitiveness goes beyond automation and robotics. Flexibility demands more than pieces of new equipment; it is a philosophy for improvement, and is organizational rather than technical in nature. The organizational changes necessary to implement such a system affect a firm both in its relations with other firms and in its internal organization of work and production processes. The new forms of production organization place severe demands on workers and on management – demands that are more easily met by Japanese practices. More skilled workers are needed and more training is required. A 'team approach' is a natural part of CIM implementation. Teams make communication better and faster, help to decentralize decision-making, and increase job rotation. In all of these areas, and most of all in their integration, Japanese firms are more advanced than those elsewhere (Sandoval 1994).

An additional consideration is significant: the corporate group or *keiretsu*. While there are several types of business groups, including those centred around banks and around trading companies, *keiretsu* is the term used commonly outside Japan to designate such corporate families. The corporate family structure permits and facilitates very efficient technology transfer across industrial sectors based on high knowledge content, including tacit knowledge, by providing a 'place' for interaction to occur smoothly (Imai 1994: 122; Samuels 1994). Internal job transfers and other forms of learning create skills that are enterprise specific or group specific (Patchell and Hayter 1995).

Networks with other firms

Japanese firms have led the way in demonstrating the competitiveness provided by cooperation with other firms. A network of firms reduces risk and uncertainty by providing a wide array of information – 'redundant, overlapping' knowledge (Nonaka 1990). A network may be formed between competitors, between manufacturers and suppliers, within channels of distribution, with spin-off enterprises and within corporate groups. Network strategies are pursued differently by different types of firms, and illustrate that a degree of control is still possible.

Perhaps as a result of their preference for network structures, Japanese companies also 'are the world's most aggressive participants in global alliances' (Okimoto and Nishi 1994: 204). Japanese firms, for example, prefer joint ventures in which they are dominant, taking advantage of the technology or market presence of smaller firms (Tyebjee 1988). The development of strategic alliances and international collaborative ventures is common among firms in most industries, including steel, motor vehicles, robotics, biotechnology, computers and new materials, and Japanese firms are well linked in most of these, with competitors both within and outside Japan.

Japanese firms also reduce uncertainty and maximize the intensity of their local networks through their location decisions. All global corporations tend to cluster R&D activities in noted high-tech centres within foreign countries, but Japanese firms seem to present an extreme case. Three-quarters of the R&D facilities of Japanese electronics firms in the United States are in California alone, and Japanese automotive firms have over 80 per cent of their R&D facilities in just two states, California and Michigan (Serapio 1993). By locating within the geography of the networks in these two industries, Japanese firms reduce uncertainty and maximize potential information.

Flexible production also depends on the ability of suppliers to deliver a tightly controlled stream of inputs tailored to the needs of production on both a short-term and a long-term basis. This in turn requires different relationships between a firm and its suppliers, epitomized in Japanese vertical de-integration and innovative supplier relationships. The distinction between Japanese supplier networks and those common in other firms is the rather strict hierarchical structure, in which a core firm utilizes a small number of large subcontractors which, in turn, are supplied by a larger set of sub-subcontractors, which are also served by an even larger lower tier of suppliers. The pyramidal structure of inter-firm links means that a Japanese firm has fewer direct suppliers than the typical European or North American firm. For example, General Motors and Volkswagen traditionally have had ten times the number of direct suppliers found in the networks of Nissan and Mazda (Howells and Wood 1993).

An added benefit of such arrangements is that, with bigger orders, a firm can demand faster service from suppliers. Close relationships with subcontractors form another 'important channel of information interchange on market and technology matters between large and small firms' (Fruin 1992: 287). The practice of developing a small number of *strategic suppliers* is slowly spreading throughout business in the United States. A small number of suppliers whose collaboration and technical skills are high are able to work with a company and solve design and production problems (Quinn and Hilmer 1994).

Small subcontractors are the essence of the *keiretsu* system. The loosely structured horizontal *keiretsu* provides a quasi-internal source of technical knowledge as well as material supplies. In this structure the hierarchical pyramid is replaced by a cobweb structure, in which cooperating small and medium-size firms interact (Groenewegen 1993; van Kooij 1991). *Keiretsu* result in few traditional measurable benefits, such as profitability, but they provide other advantages that may be more important, such as preferential financing, information exchange, fluid joint venture arrangements, and trademarks. The interaction-intensive ties permit close communication with, and job rotation in, the other firms in the group, thereby broadening the experience and knowledge of engineers and managers in subcontracting firms. Perhaps most importantly, these close relationships enable a high degree of trust to form (Ito 1994; Sako 1992).

Subcontracting relationships and trust

Subcontracting in the supply chain is a form of vertical collaboration, in contrast to horizontal collaboration, which occurs between partners at the same level in the production process. As in strategic alliances, these forms of collaboration provide several sets of benefits: increased scale and scope of activities; shared costs and risks; and improved ability to deal with complexity. Close, relational subcontracting, common in Japan, also contrasts with traditional, arm's-length relationships, and stresses one of the most 'non-economic' of variables: *trust* (Sako 1992).

The legalistic nature of relations common among Western firms (arm's-length contractual relations) contrasts sharply with the relational or obligational contractual relations found among Japanese firms, and may thwart the development of cooperative relationships. Obligational relations represent both an economic relationship, and the social relation between trading partners based on mutual trust. Because of this strong foundation, transactions can take place without prior agreement or specification of all the terms and conditions of trade.

Trust operates as a mechanism that facilitates communication and cooperation between firms. Trust relationships can result in a supplier exceeding contractual requirements, whether by early delivery, higher quality, or some other means of assuring goodwill (Sako 1992). Through the economic and social relationships in the network, diverse information becomes inexpensive to obtain.

The Japanese system of innovation

Strong intra-firm and inter-firm linkages are characteristic of the Japanese system of innovation (Odagiri and Goto 1993. 107). Japanese policies 'have converged on a national commitment to indigenise technology, to diffuse it throughout the economy, and to nurture firms that could benefit' (Samuels 1994: 55). One application of this commitment is seen in military technology. Japan identified earlier than US or European governments the concept of *dual use*: the recognition that technological advances interact between the military sphere and the civilian economy. The Japanese phrase to describe it, *spin-on*, involves the transfer of products and processes 'off the shelf' from civilian to military applications (Samuels 1994: 26). It now is seen as critical in the United States and Europe, but implementation has been difficult.

The policy component of a national system of innovation has a large impact on the competitiveness of firms (see Edquist 1997; Nelson 1993 and this volume, Chapter 2). Of all developed nations, Japan is thought to have perhaps the most conscious, focused and articulated technology policy, one whose roots date back to the nineteenth century. 'Administrative guidance', the management of competition and nurturing of technological development are seen in an elaborate system of 'protocols' and conventions – sometimes tacit, at other times explicit – to induce domestic firms, even as they compete, to negotiate constantly with their competitors and with bureaucrats, especially within MITI (Samuels 1994).

Despite a reputation for administrative guidance and informal cooperation, fierce competition, not cooperation, is the central force in Japan's economy (Callon 1995: 207). The success of several Japanese export industries was not based on MITI (or any other) policy. Products in which Japanese products dominate world markets include cameras, motorcycles, pianos, zippers, colour televisions, clocks, electric wire, machine tools, textile machinery, agricultural machinery, robots, compact disc players, facsimile (fax) machines, lasers and VCRs.

MITI's role may have declined, but Japanese institutions – Japan's national innovation system – remain robust. The interdependence of bureaucracy, firms and financial institutions provides information as well as financial capital, and reinforces the *keiretsu* and *keiretsu*-like linkages among firms (Bowonder, Miyake and Linstone 1994b; Fruin 1992). Evans (1995) suggests that Japan has the best-developed *embedded autonomy* in its government bureaucracies, strengthened by the relatively high regard in which the public service is held in Japan.

Bowonder, Miyake and Linstone (1994a) suggest several elements – some governmental, some industrial – as instrumental in Japan's growth:

- the status of manufacturing facilities in firms;
- availability of human skills;

- systems of information support;
- organizational and management systems;
- planning systems (government–firm linkages);
- technology diffusion systems (firm–market–government linkages);
- financial investment systems; and
- internationalization (international production and marketing networks).

In general, Japanese firms benefit from retaining strong links to the technology infrastructure in Japan. Japanese firms, for example, remain tied to their 'home base'; research takes places almost exclusively in Japan and is heavily dependent on both Japanese citations and Japanese collaborators (Hicks *et al.* 1994).

Weaknesses in Japan

Not everything works perfectly in the Japanese system of innovation. The failings of Japanese science and research – in contrast to engineering and product development – are widely recognized. Shortcomings have also appeared in high-technology regional development and in transplanting work practices abroad.

High technology

The universities are especially weak, certainly in comparison to corporate R&D labs (Odagiri and Goto 1993). In response to this situation, many Japanese firms have established research relationships with, and entire research institutes in, universities in the United States (Tatsuno 1990: 259–60). In addition, the Japanese government recently allocated a massive increase in basic research, in an attempt to raise the country's stature in pure science and inventiveness. Likewise, the 'mutual insurance system' of the *keiretsu* and other risk-sharing systems have produced an economy accustomed to 'competition without losers'. Risk-takers, including entrepreneurs, are scarce in such a system (Tezuka 1997).

Another failure is the lack of success of the Technopolis, a plan to reduce regional disparities and to transform all of Japan into a high-tech archipelago by building a network of regional high-tech cities (Tatsuno 1986). Tsukuba is the only success story of this policy, but even there too little 'frontier' R&D and little non-government R&D takes place. Although Tsukuba is modelled on Silicon Valley, Japanese culture has been slow to spawn commercial spin-off firms (Castells and Hall 1994). It is too early to know whether several environmental science institutes deriving from the New Earth 21 'Vision' in environmental technology in the new Kansai Science City near Osaka will have the same experience.

The technopolises have been unable to reduce the overpowering allure and advantages of Tokyo for R&D and other key corporate activities. As occurred in the implementation of growth centre policies in virtually all countries, intense competition among candidate regions diluted the potential to compete with the Tokyo region's dominance. The allure of the Tokyo agglomeration continues, if only because of the concentration in Tokyo of residential amenities, top universities and

existing corporate facilities. Indeed, the success of any technopolis is highly dependent on its proximity to Tokyo (Sternberg 1995).

Globalization and the challenge of 'flexible rigidity'

While the Japanese system is extremely flexible in adapting to new knowledge over
time, it retains a rigidity with regard to spatial adaptation. Japanese firms have been
'reluctant multinationals' because their production system is so difficult to relocate
to other countries and cultures (Hill and Lee 1994). Only part of the reluctance is the
costly capital-intensive nature of production to which firms have become accustomed in Japan (Fujita and Hill 1995). Foreign investment, like other strategic
actions, requires time for learning and for network formation. Investment by
Japanese firms in North America has taken place in two 'waves' that affect the
prevalence of 'new' forms of work organization. Older Japanese plants, dating from
the mid-1970s, did not attempt to incorporate teams or other Japanese work
practices, but instead tended to retain US work practices. These early overseas
operations also were strongly dependent on inputs imported from Japan. Beginning
in the mid-1980s, Japanese firms began to mesh their operations into networks more
similar to those in Japan, relying to a greater degree on local suppliers, many of them
Japanese firms themselves (Edgington 1993).

Although Japanese firms, more than others, coordinate by centralization, stagnant
conditions in Japan and a high yen have forced Japanese firms to decentralize
operations more in order to take advantage of both capabilities and lower costs in
other countries, creating a 'middle-up-down' management structure, rather than
purely top-down or bottom-up. Japanese structures are Triad-based, and multiple
independent 'international' headquarters in Europe, North America and South-
East Asia are intended to respond to specific local market needs (Hood, Young and
Lal 1994). Hybrid policies are developed explicitly in order to balance and interrelate central and local conditions. High levels of personnel interchange and travel
are still common in this system, with the benefit that they enhance the tacit
knowledge of a large number of people about diverse market conditions (Nonaka
and Takeuchi 1995).

Japanese work practices in North American 'transplants' vary considerably. In
particular, later investments have more effectively blended Japanese and American
work practices and management systems. Japanese analysts portray their locations
outside Japan as 'hybrid factories' in comparison to those at home. In a sense these
'hybrid' factories and other units are the logical outcome of the tension within any
transnational firm that comes from the tension between the need for integration
logic pursued by the parent corporation and the localization desired by subsidiaries
(Abo 1994).

It has proven difficult to transplant Japanese work organization to plants in
countries that represent major markets for Japanese producers. Resistance from
labour unions and cultural differences have led to significant differences in the work
practices used in North America and elsewhere. These differences include the hiring
of women workers and the presence of company slogans – both common in Nissan
and Toyota plants in the United States but not in the United Kingdom (Emmott
1993: 72–3). In part because the work environment cannot be duplicated exactly,

Table 12.3 Average assembly times for a car or truck by North American auto makers, 1995

Firm	Average assembly time (labour hours per vehicle)
Nissan	27.4
Toyota	29.4
Honda	31
Ford	37.9
Chrysler	43
General Motors	46

Source: Adapted from Suris (1996)

productivity levels remain lower in Japanese 'hybrid' plants abroad than in Japan (*ibid.*: 153–60). Another example of the difficulty of transfer of work environments is the General Motors joint venture with Toyota in the United States. While GM has learned a great deal from Toyota about work teams, learning bureaucracies and cooperative cultures, these have not spread within the firm sufficiently to affect overall efficiency (Table 12.3). The 'firm as community' may be the most difficult of Japanese work organization practices to transfer to other cultures and institutional settings (Dore 1987).

The just-in-time (JIT) or *kanban* system of inventory management, developed by Toyota during the 1950s, represents, along with new forms of production organization and lean production methods, what has been called Toyotism, the model of networked production, to succeed Fordism (Fujita and Hill 1995). The central goal of JIT is to eliminate waste in all areas: production, materials, labour, time, energy and money. Instead of a producer of cars maintaining inventories of all the many hundreds of parts needed for the vehicles to be produced, parts suppliers are required to deliver these several times per week – or per day. This system also demands that suppliers provide a higher level of quality: fewer defective parts per order with a goal of zero defects. In short, parts producers must operate at a higher frequency (shipping more often) and in smaller volumes than is the case under traditional (or Fordist) production organization. When put in place outside Japan, however, hybrid forms of JIT also are common (Hudson 1994).

Inter-firm networks: lessons from Europe

More from Europe than from Japan has emerged a recognition of a *network* model, which affects both large and small firms (Antonelli 1988; Cooke and Morgan 1993). The network form is neither a market nor a hierarchy, being distinct from both the hierarchical integrated firm and the arm's-length relationship of market transactions. As forms of governance – a term which refers to the rules and procedures that govern the behaviour of coordinating transactions – networks are very different. Markets are a coordination mechanism that offers choice, flexibility and opportunity, but markets do not require trust, and agreements are enforced by legal sanctions. In networks, on the other hand, relationships and transactions are able to change as the circumstances dictate. Problems and conflicts can arise, because the participants remain in one way or another competitors. In short, networks are a flexible

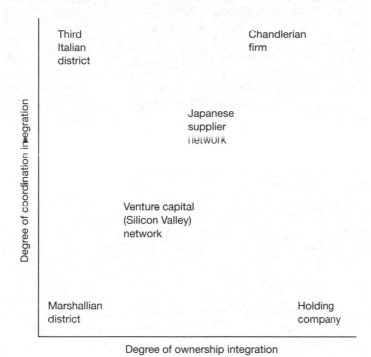

Figure 12.2 Organizational control versus network coordination
Source: Based on Robertson and Langlois (1995: 548)

intermediate response ('make together') to the ever-present 'make or buy' decision (Camagni and Rabellotti 1992). Small firms, in particular, unable to maintain an R&D effort and 'a systematic technology watch', use networks as 'antennas' and 'filters' of information (Estimé, Drilhon and Julien 1993: 56).

The simple market–hierarchy dichotomy, however, also masks some important differences which were hinted at above concerning Japanese networks. The prototypical hierarchical 'Chandlerian' firm includes high degrees of both ownership integration and coordination integration. Several network forms contain varying degrees of integration of ownership and coordination. The Japanese network, with its combination of cross-ownership and inter-firm cooperation, is a truly intermediate case. Venture capital networks common in California's Silicon Valley have less ownership control, but more than is found in either Marshallian districts or industrial districts of the type found in Italy (Robertson and Langlois 1995) (Figure 12.2).

Regional systems of innovation

In Europe it is regional and local innovation systems, rather than national or corporate systems, that stand out. The regional system links global knowledge of generic technologies to specific applications produced by local firms (Arcangeli 1993). Industrial districts in Denmark, Germany and Italy have all provided models for other places. In a local system, institutions provide training, information and R&D that support innovation. In Baden-Württemberg, for example, small firms do not have to bear the burden of flexible production; 'many of the costs ... are shared by or embedded in a deep network of organizations and practices in the political economy' of the region (Herrigel 1993: 17). The institutional structures are sufficiently widespread and redundant that Baden-Württemberg is a model of a networked region (Cooke and Morgan 1994a). Increasing globalization and necessity for the skill-intensive R&D of flexible production have caused a serious need for collaboration so that the regional system of innovation does not break down (*ibid.*). Despite the allure of the industrial district phenomenon, the accumulation of knowledge, and the institutions to support that accumulation, are country-specific, so universal answers are not possible (Belussi 1996).

Webs of local linkages and subcontracting are the basis of the agglomeration advantages of such industrial districts.[1] Information flow among firms, cooperation, and sharing of new equipment are commonplace. Such interlinked production systems are far more common in Europe than in North America. In the United States, only Silicon Valley appears to have the characteristics of districts elsewhere; Saxenian (this volume, Chapter 8) stresses the region's uniqueness. As a model of regional innovation based on networks, Silicon Valley is perhaps unique, largely because of difficult-to-pinpoint cultural factors. These traits include tolerance of failure, risk-seeking, reinvestment in the community, enthusiasm for change and rapid response to technological change, and collaboration. The cultural attributes, in turn, result in easy entry of new firms and a variety of firms in size and specialization.

Other research findings point to the unique character of Silicon Valley as an environment for entrepreneurship. For example, Silicon Valley provides a large number of entrepreneurial role models and examples. This environment comprises a unique 'ecosystem' within which firms form and re-form through continual entrepreneurship. Networks of interpersonal relationships support both entrepreneurship and links among enterprises, large and small alike (Bahrami and Evans 1995).

Other areas in the United States have had difficulty creating the institutional structures found in Silicon Valley and in Europe. Institutional cooperation and support for firms is found to some degree in Austin, Texas, where cooperative institutional arrangements, especially among governments, firms, universities and other groups, support entrepreneurship (Smilor, Gibson and Kozmetsky 1989). By contrast, A. J. Scott (1996) has shown the shortcomings of the weak institutional environment for sectors in southern California. Few areas are willing to take the time to develop local industries, especially those based on small firms, for which a degree of 'chaos' exists (Smilor and Feeser 1991).

For many authors the current best practice for a region is to be, or become, what some authors call a 'learning region' or innovative milieu (Florida, this volume, Chapter 14). The learning region incorporates two distinct processes that must operate in such a region: *interaction* and *learning* (Maillat 1995). In an innovative milieu, two sets of effects operate simultaneously: proximity effects, such as reductions in costs because of quicker circulation of information, face-to-face contacts and lower costs of collecting information; and socialization effects, related to collective learning, cooperation and socialization of risks. These two processes are collective rather than explicitly cooperative and thus spread beyond any single bilateral inter-firm linkage. As with innovative, learning-based firms, the technological vitality of learning regions revolves around cultural norms that are not easily created or transplanted. It takes decades for a regional technological infrastructure to develop, a fact that regional and local governments, like national governments, may find difficult to accept (Castells and Hall 1994).

Generally, the importance of learning, of external sources of knowledge, and of incremental innovation (in contrast to formal R&D and radical innovations) has become the mainstream of understanding technical change (Freeman 1994). Non-R&D activities may account for more than half of corporate effort on innovation in products and services. However, 'unlearning' or 'forgetting' what has accumulated in the past is as important a process as learning itself, especially in a time of rapid change.

Lessons of systemic thinking

Systemic thinking is spreading into the policy arena as well. Competitiveness originates at the firm level, but it requires a 'systemic competitiveness' based on interaction between government, enterprises, and other actors in order to craft a supportive environment specific to each place. *Systemic competitiveness* refers to the interaction of the components of the national economy, including the financial, production, innovation and governance systems. As a framework for thinking about policy and the role of government, the systemic paradigm is 'consistent with a redefined state capable of supporting initiative, innovation and investment in the private sector by providing a strategic framework for investment decisions, channels for interaction between the public and private sectors, and supportive polices for economic growth' (Bradford 1994: 58).

Regional and local policies for industrial modernization

At the state and local level too, towards which policy initiatives have largely devolved, the need for a systemic approach is gaining recognition. In the context of industrial modernization, which affects small firms in particular, Shapira, Roessner and Barke (1995: 69) observe:

> Industrial modernization is a complex problem, involving technology, information, management, training and financing, and raising questions of structures, private and public–private relationships, attitudes, policies and practices. It is a problem with multiple dimensions. Addressing the problem at the 'micro' level of the firm and its managers is critical; but the problem also involves 'macro' economic, technological and social policies, as well as 'meso' issues of business relationships and practices, institutional linkages and inter-firm networks, and public–private cooperation.

Regional technology transfer has become a common policy objective, following the example of Japan's excellent Kohsetsushi centres (Shapira 1996). Technology transfer is not guaranteed to work, even if it is ostensibly part of a regional innovation policy, unless it is targeted towards small and medium-sized firms.

National differences in technology transfer programmes reflect large-scale differences in national system of innovation and mission or diffusion orientation. Even policies aimed at small firms may fail unless they become a routine element of the culture, seeking out small-firm clients (rather than waiting for active firms to seek out information) and providing long-term financing to ensure continuity.

Hyperarchies: neither market nor hierarchy nor network

Hierarchical models are threatened even more by the *hyperarchy* of the World Wide Web. Without a hierarchical structure, the Web allows the possibility of random access and symmetry of information (Evans and Wurster 1997). The Internet transcends any single organization, and similar free-wheeling intranets are unlikely to be an appropriate structure for a firm, even a transnational corporation (TNC) that is attempting to combine global and local strengths. The goal of *globalization* represents achieving this balance between being global, with the scale advantages associated with size and global scope, and being local within each regional or national market and network of resources. For many firms, information flow from the centre to the corporate units elsewhere is easier to achieve than information flow from various units to the centre and to other units (Cerny 1996; Gustavsson, Melin and Macdonald 1994). Rather than control and dependence, a firm must create a 'shared concern' for change among its subsidiaries. In other words, a hierarchy has control advantages balanced against the fact that its standardization is not in tune with local needs, whereas a heterarchy, comprising many different kinds of centres, has the principal disadvantage of being more local than meshed into the global enterprise (Hedlund 1986). Because of the challenges to globalize, it is difficult to construct and maintain a perfect network firm that balances control, learning and evolutionary change.

In R&D and sales/marketing, firms such as Hewlett-Packard are able to benefit from new-product development in several locations, including Japan, Singapore and the United Kingdom (Leonard-Barton 1995). R&D is becoming more mobile geographically, more similar to the pattern found in production and sales operations. Multiple linkages, representing cross-functional communication, take place between headquarters and subsidiaries in firms such as Matsushita Electric and Philips. Managing innovation and R&D in large firms is among the most difficult aspects of a TNC, and R&D remains the least globalized of all corporate activities. The world's largest firms, which are also the largest holders of US patents, have not dispersed R&D as much as they have centralized it within their home countries.

'Listening posts' or surveillance units to follow competitors and to keep track of technological changes in various settings have grown rapidly, as have international strategic alliances, but global firms continue to rely most on their domestic base. The corporate form is that of a 'polyp' firm, 'using its tentacles to acquire from each country its excellence in research rather than to decentralise its brain' (Archibugi and Michie 1995: 135). The objective of accumulating technical knowledge from many sources is the principal reason for firms to undertake internationalized R&D. Listening posts and intelligence scanning are productive, however, only if the best practices and other new ideas identified are communicated among other corporate units.

The role of institutions

From the successes of East Asia it has become clear that the key process in industrialization is 'the constant and uncertain process of learning', to be superseded by innovating (Lall 1994: 648). The uncertain, evolutionary, disequilibrium process of learning requires 'a complex network of economic and social relations' and 'institutional diversity' rather than rigidity (Chang and Kozul-Wright 1994: 884). Despite a trend towards less government in North America and Europe, it seems that policies are needed to address weaknesses in entrepreneurial learning.

Perhaps more important than formal structures and institutions are the conventions that support learning and movement along a technological trajectory – creating and sustaining a *technical culture* within an economy (Storper 1995; Sweeney 1991). This culture is needed to keep pace with innovations and international technical knowledge (Lynn, Reddy and Aram 1996). Inter-firm linkages facilitate collective learning and represent an indicator of development far more advanced than employment alone. Local linkages support other firms, with impacts on local economic development, seen most vividly in innovative milieux and industrial districts.

National competitiveness and technological capabilities are represented, first, by skilled technical workers and, second, by the general educational level of the labour force. Skill acquisition is one of the central areas where policies either enhance or inhibit the development of a learning economy. Public effort must complement private-sector efforts to develop human resources. Different labour models are found not only in Japanese firms or those trying to emulate them. They are also central to corporate efforts to improve product and service quality and to organizational responses to new technologies and competition. The Japanese system, and its counterparts in Germany and Sweden, has advantages in the context of flexibility and its demands for labour skills (Boyer 1995).

In the Swedish, German and Japanese models, extensive intra-firm, or enterprise-based, training has been the norm, albeit with variations. All three models, while different, have contributed to a strong structural competitiveness in their economies (Boyer 1995). The German system of lengthy apprenticeships is looked to by many as a model for producing highly skilled workers. In the United States, by contrast, firms underinvest in training because these investments can relatively be lost as workers take their expensive training to other firms in return for higher personal compensation. The Anglo-American system is considered to be the 'low road' approach that relies on a dual labour market, with serious weaknesses compared with other systems (Doeringer 1994).

Towards knowledge-based systems

If firms are 'learning organizations' then they must be able to learn – to gain knowledge – from many sources (Leonard-Barton 1995). The simplest form of learning is 'learning by doing', suggested over thirty years ago by Arrow as a form of technology acquisition outside of formal R&D. The list of types of learning has expanded greatly over the years as it has gained greater prominence among experts on technological change (Table 12.4). In order to obtain tacit knowledge – embodied in people, rather than in written form or in objects – firms generally pursue a number

Table 12.4 Types of technological learning

Learning by doing
Learning by using
Learning by operating
Learning by changing
Learning by training
Learning by hiring
Learning by searching
Learning by trying
Learning by interacting
Learning by selling
Learning from inter-industry spillovers
Learning to borrow
Learning by failing

Source: Adapted from Malecki (1997: table 2.3)

of strategies in addition to training, such as hiring, R&D and interpersonal networking (Nonaka and Takeuchi 1995). Japanese firms have provided models for these forms of knowledge acquisition. Regions, in turn, also must become 'learning regions' in order to keep their regional economies agile and innovative.

In this chapter I have tried to show that the Japanese and European models have a great deal of relevance for each other, for America, and for other places. They have been adopted and adapted to some extent, but there is room for more of this. The network models from Europe and Asia have brought a new awareness of the importance of learning, of trust, of institutions and civic society. These and other ideas will need to be absorbed by both firms and regions as we cross into the twenty-first century.

Notes

1. Industrial districts also have been identified in Japan; see Friedman (1988).

CHAPTER THIRTEEN

Venture Capital's Role in Regional Innovation Systems: Historical Perspective and Recent Evidence

Donald F. Smith, Jr, and Richard Florida

Introduction

Venture capital plays a critical role in technological innovation and economic development. California's Silicon Valley and Massachusetts' Route 128 area clearly owe much of their vibrant, rapidly growing economies and their development as high-technology centres to the infusion of significant amounts of venture capital. The successful revitalization of these regions stands in sharp contrast to the stagnation and decline of the older, more traditionally oriented manufacturing regions. Venture capital has played a catalytic role in the formation of new technologies, and indeed entirely new industries. The revolutionary innovations and inventions of numerous venture capital-backed start-ups like Fairchild, Intel, DEC, Apple Computer, Cray Computer, Sun Microsystems, Genentech, and countless others have set in motion tremendous gales of industrial restructuring and economic renewal. Many of these companies would never have got off the ground at all, or attained commercial success so quickly, without the financial backing and managerial expertise of venture capitalists. Three-quarters of all venture investments go to high-technology companies.

Venture capitalists invest in new, unproven enterprises, exchanging their investment capital for an equity or ownership stake in the companies they finance. Venture capitalists are active investors, providing a wide range of assistance that encompasses business, managerial, financial and legal issues. Thomas Doerflinger and Jack Rivkin, prominent Wall Street analysts, characterize venture investing as '"smart money" – money that is imbued with the entrepreneurial savvy, business contacts, executive talent and patience of financiers with long experience in helping small companies succeed' (Doerflinger and Rivkin 1987: 16). And Venture Economics, the leading authority on the venture capital industry, describes venture capitalists as investors who seek 'to add value through long term involvement with continuing business developments' (*Venture Capital Journal*, March 1987, p. 10).

The past ten years have witnessed an explosion in the number of venture capital investments. The total venture capital pool increased by over 800 per cent between 1980 and 1995, from $4.5 billion to $37 billion, with most of the increase occurring between 1980 and 1987, when the venture capital pool surged from $4.5 billion to $29

Table 13.1 Venture capital industry estimated funding and disbursements, 1986–95 ($ millions)

Year	Total pool	Disbursements to portfolio companies
1986	14,693	3,219
1987	17,799	3,971
1988	20,216	3,849
1989	23,153	3,379
1990	24,138	2,301
1991	24,757	1,359
1992	25,867	2,542
1993	28,924	3,071
1994	32,670	2,741
1995	37,154	3,859

billion. Table 13.1 shows that venture capital investments also increased over these years – from $2.7 billion in 1985 to $3.9 billion in 1995 (all in current dollars).

Venture capital resources and investments are geographically concentrated. A few areas – California's Silicon Valley, Boston's Route 128 area, New York City and Chicago – account for the majority of venture capital resources. Venture capital investments are even more concentrated than this: California's Silicon Valley and Boston's Route 128 are by far the largest attractors of venture capital.

Venture capitalists seldom invest alone. Instead, they participate in co-investment syndicates that consist of two or more venture investors. Co-investment provides access to a much wider range of investment possibilities, and enables venture capitalists to spread risk by investing in a larger number of deals.

Given these facts, it is not surprising that the public sector has become enamoured with venture capital as a mechanism for generating technology-based economic development. Indeed, government now views venture capital investment as an essential ingredient of economic change. Over the past fifteen years, a number of states and localities have committed public funds to finance public venture capital programmes. While Connecticut and Massachusetts were the only states with venture capital programmes prior to 1980, the number increased to 28 by 1988 (Malecki 1987: 50; Lyne 1987: 582). Much of this policy is premised on the notion that regional gaps exist in the distribution of venture capital, and that by alleviating such gaps, states and localities can stimulate technology and entrepreneurship. Still, it remains to be seen precisely what role venture capital plays in stimulating new business formation, job creation and economic development outside the primary regions of investment. And it is unclear that simply closing capital gaps will generate technology-oriented economic development along the lines of a Silicon Valley.

The venture capital industry

The venture capital industry has experienced tremendous growth over the past three decades. In 1969 the size of the venture capital pool was $2.4 billion. Today, it exceeds $37 billion. The number of venture capital firms also increased dramatically over the past two decades. There are over 600 professional venture capital firms in the United States with over 1100 offices. These firms employ thousands of professionals. These venture capital companies invested in approximately 1200 companies in 1995 alone.

There are a variety of types of venture capital firms: private limited partnerships, venture capital subsidiaries of industrial corporations, venture capital subsidiaries of financial institutions, federally assisted small business investment companies (SBICs) and wealthy individuals known as angel investors. Private limited partnerships are currently the dominant type of venture capital firm, making up nearly 84 per cent of venture capital resources and having the greatest number of offices.

The origins of venture capital

Venture capital, as an institutional form of investment, is a relatively new phenomenon. Prior to World War II the functions of today's venture capitalists were performed by wealthy individuals and families on an *ad hoc*, informal basis. The economist Joseph Schumpeter used the term 'entrepreneurial financiers' to refer to these early venture capitalists. More organized types of risk finance or venture capital emerged to finance the US railroad system and steel industry. This was especially important since traditional financial institutions were unwilling and/or unable to absorb the risk of investing in new industries during the late nineteenth century.

The post-war years

Venture capital emerged in its modern institutional form in the years following World War II. Wealthy individuals such as J. H. Whitney, Laurance Rockefeller and others established private risk capital investment firms which, in the words of Rockefeller, sought to promote 'pioneering projects that with proper backing will encourage sound scientific and economic progress in new fields – fields that hold the promise of tremendous future development' (Morris 1953: 169). The Rockefeller family made numerous risk investments in the immediate post-war era.

American Research and Development (ARD) was the first professional venture capital firm to raise funds from the sale of shares to private investors. ARD was founded in Boston in 1946 by Ralph E. Flanders, president of the Federal Reserve Bank of Boston, Merrill Griswold, head of Massachusetts Investors Trust, and Karl T. Compton, president of the Massachusetts Institute of Technology. These men then chose Georges Doriot, a former general and Harvard Business School professor, to serve as president of the company, which sought to provide not only risk capital to technology-oriented businesses, but also 'encouragement and advice ... [through the] powerful team of financial experts, skilled business managers, and leading scientists' assembled by the founders of ARD (Bylinsky 1967: 132). Under Doriot's leadership, ARD invested in such phenomenally successful firms as Digital Equipment Corporation and Teradyne, Inc. Surely Doriot is the father of venture investing. The *Venture Capital Journal* (1980: 13) said of Doriot that 'His original concepts have remained. Long term development with active management assistance and support was the keystone of his investment philosophy.'

The Small Business Investment Act

A major impetus behind the rise of the modern venture capital industry was the Small Business Investment Act of 1958. The early 1950s witnessed increased concern over the financing of small businesses among business officials and public policy-makers. Organizations like the Committee for Economic Development began to develop a variety of alternatives for public vehicles to provide entrepreneurial risk capital. In 1954 the Small Business Administration (SBA) was created, partly as a result of these efforts, to direct federal resources to aid small business development. The subsequent Small Business Investment Act of 1958 made federal long-term loans available for the formation of SBICs. These companies in turn would invest in small, independent businesses via equity financing, debt issuance or some combination of both. Many of the earliest venture capital funds began as either independent or bank-affiliated SBICs.

Recent growth of the venture capital pool

The development of what we now refer to as the venture capital industry has occurred mainly over the past three decades. A number of reasons have been offered to explain this dramatic growth in the venture capital pool. First, since the mid-1960s traditional manufacturing industries have been beset by falling profits, making venture investments a more attractive investment option. Second, the high returns offered by new technology-intensive industries like semiconductors, computers and biotechnology have tended to 'pull' investments towards these new fields. Third, there was 'escalating' stock market activity in the 1980s and 1990s, which made it easier to take new companies into the new issues market. And fourth, a series of changes in US public policy – most notably reductions in the rate of taxation on capital gains and the liberalization of restrictions of public pension investments under ERISA statutes – helped to channel additional capital into the venture capital pool. A model developed by William Bygrave and Jeffrey Timmons (1985) shows strong positive correlations between the volume of new public offerings, the liberalization of declining capital gains taxes, and the increase in the total venture capital pool.

Changes in the venture capital pool have closely followed changes in the tax rate on capital gains. The steady increase in the tax rate on capital gains from 25 per cent in 1969 to 49 per cent in 1976 was followed by a decline in the venture capital pool (measured in constant dollars) from $6.1 billion in 1969 to $4.3 billion in 1977. The lowering of the capital gains tax rate to 35 per cent in late 1978, and then again to 28 per cent in 1979 and 20 per cent in 1981, has been followed by a dramatic increase in the venture capital pool.

Structure of the venture capital industry

There are a variety of types of venture capital funds: private limited partnerships, corporate financial-related venture capital funds, corporate industrial venture capital funds, SBICs and 'angels'. The following sections examine each of these in detail. Table 13.2 shows the percentage of resources controlled by each of the different types of venture capital companies.

Table 13.2 Venture capital resources by type of firm, 1995

	Capital ($ billions)	Firms
Independent private/public	31.00	513
Corporate financial	5.77	83
Corporate industrial	0.38	14
Total	37.15	610

Venture capital limited partnerships

One of the most striking features of the venture capital industry over the past two decades is the dramatic growth in limited partnerships as the primary vehicle for venture capital investment. In 1977 limited partnerships accounted for 44 per cent of all venture capital companies and controlled 35 per cent of the total venture capital pool. By 1995 limited partnerships represented 83 per cent of all venture capital firms and 84 per cent of venture capital resources.

The emergence of limited partnerships as the dominant form of venture investing was the result of a lengthy period of experimentation and evolution. Basically, the limited partnership eclipsed other models because it provided an effective way to mobilize large amounts of funds from outside investors and enabled venture capitalists to realize significant financial gains. Today, partnerships are often piggy-backed one on top of another, giving rise to the phenomenon of 'megafunds' with value in excess of $500 million. While early partnerships were run by one or two venture capitalists and a skeleton staff, modern partnerships may have five to ten general partners, a dozen associates and a sizeable support staff. To effectively manage their assets, modern partnerships have adopted increasingly formal organizational schemes.

Private limited partnerships are composed of both general and limited partners. General partners are the professional venture capitalists who secure capital commitments for a fund and make and manage its investments, while limited partners are the financial investors in the fund. On average, limited partnerships have a fixed life span of seven to ten years. The first few years are ones of active investment, while the remaining period is used to build companies to the point of public stock offerings, mergers or other forms of exit. Because of their limited life expectancies, partnerships seek to build companies rapidly in order to realize large capital gains, the proceeds of which are then invested into new venture funds or kept accordingly.

Corporate venture capital funds

There are two primary types of corporate venture funds: financial and industrial. The first group of corporate venture capital funds are affiliated to banks and other financial institutions. In 1995 there were approximately 83 venture capital subsidiaries of financial institutions which controlled nearly $6 billion in resources (*Venture Capital Journal*, April 1988, p. 10). Examples of bank-related venture capital funds include Citicorp and First National Bank of Chicago. Those affiliated to investment banks and brokerage firms include Merrill Lynch; Drexel, Burnham,

Lambert (Lambda); Smith Barney (First Century Partnership); and Donaldson, Lufkin & Jenrette (Sprout Group). Many traditional financial institutions, such as commercial and investment banks and brokerage firms, helped establish the venture capital industry when they founded SBICs, in order to take advantage of the new investment opportunities provided by the federal subsidiaries.

Bank-related funds often operate on different incentives as compared with limited partnerships. Since they have access to significant blocks of capital, venture capital concerns tied to large commercial banks do not face competitive pressures to generate funds from external sources. In addition, sponsoring banks often encourage venture capital affiliates to commit capital which will generate rates of return in excess of that of the sponsor, but which may fall short of the rate of return achieved by pre-eminent venture partnerships.[1]

As of 1995 there were fourteen venture capital funds operating as subsidiaries of industrial corporations. These venture funds controlled approximately $0.5 billion in venture capital, or approximately 1 per cent of total venture capital resources. The objectives of corporate venturing are many. They range from pursuit of an attractive return on investment, to growth and diversification, to securing a 'window on technology', to enhancement of entrepreneurial spirit within the corporation, to acquisition or development of a strategic partnership with a successful small company.[2]

The relative importance of all corporate venture capital firms has decreased in recent years. Corporate firms, both financial and industrial, controlled 41 per cent of venture capital resources in 1977. However, by 1995 corporate venture capital firms controlled only 17 per cent of the total.

Small business investment companies (SBICs)

SBICs were created under the enabling legislation contained in the federal Small Business Act. They are privately organized and managed investment firms, licensed by the Small Business Administration. These investment companies have access to long-term federal loans in return for their agreement to invest solely in small businesses. Today there 271 active SBICs, controlling over $3.5 billion in private capital, along with $1.1 billion in government leverage.

SBICs have access to federal leveraging funds under provisions of the 1958 Small Business Investment Act. SBICs provide a range of financing alternatives. These include traditional venture capital funds, combined debt and equity, and long-term loans. Between 1958 and 1968 SBICs were the primary financial resource for small business development. Today, even though there are a relatively large number of SBICs, they comprise only a little over 10 per cent of the venture capital resource base. SBICs are generally smaller than other types of venture capital funds.

SBICs have been an important source of equity for smaller, moderate-growth firms, such as those located in the service, manufacturing, and transportation and communication sectors.[3] SBICs' contribution to the total venture capital industry pool of capital declined from 24 per cent in 1977 to 8 per cent in 1987, but has rebounded somewhat with changes to the programme made in 1992 to contribute nearly 12 per cent today.

'Angels' and other types of venturing

The discussion in this chapter has centred on the activities of formal, professional venture capital firms. Informal investors known as 'angels' provide an additional source of venture capital. Angels generally invest smaller amounts of capital in ventures with higher risks or lower rewards than traditional venture capital firms. Though the amount of individual angel investment is usually quite small, their aggregate contribution to the venture capital industry can be significant. In fact, it has been estimated that angels may account for one-half to two thirds of all venture capital investment (*New England Business* 1986). William Wetzel, a professor at the University of New Hampshire, has focused his research on the role of angel investments in the New England economy. Wetzel estimates that there are approximately 15,000 angel investments in New England. His research has shown that angel investment patterns are more localized than professional venture capital firms. Angels are more likely to invest in a relatively restricted geographic region than professional venture capital firms. Wetzel believes that angels play an important role in localized economic development.

What do venture capitalists do?

Venture capitalists are involved in a variety of tasks that are vital to technological innovation and economic development. They play an active role in the development of start-up companies by lending substantial managerial, legal, marketing and financial assistance to fledgling firms. This chapter explores the various functions they perform, tracing the nature of their involvement from the inception of a new business concept until a viable business is formed.

Venture capital and the stages of business development

Venture capitalists play a role at a number of different stages of a business's development. As Figure 13.1 shows, they invest primarily in the start-up and early stages of business development. Their role is to help new companies get off the ground, nurturing their firms' development until they are ready to enter the public offering market or become merger candidates. Venture capitalists typically target only a minor amount of their funding at the earliest stages of business development (i.e. the seed stage) and tend to increase their commitments over time.

A number of analysts, such as William Abernathy and James Utterback (1978), view the process of business development in terms of a life cycle or 'S-curve'. A firm proceeds through three stages: emergence (initiation and rapid growth), consolidation (increasing economies of scale and steady expansion) and maturity (oligopoly and decline). Figure 13.1 shows that venture capital is most important during the emergence stage, which begins with a major breakthrough or innovation. This phase is marked by experimentation with new technology, uncertainty regarding future progress, wide-open markets, low entry barriers and diseconomies of scale. During this stage, venture capitalists evaluate the technological potentials, financial requirements and organizational capabilities of new businesses and the products upon which they are based (Bean, Schiffel and Mogee 1975). These firms are also assisted in their recruitment of management, location of production facilities,

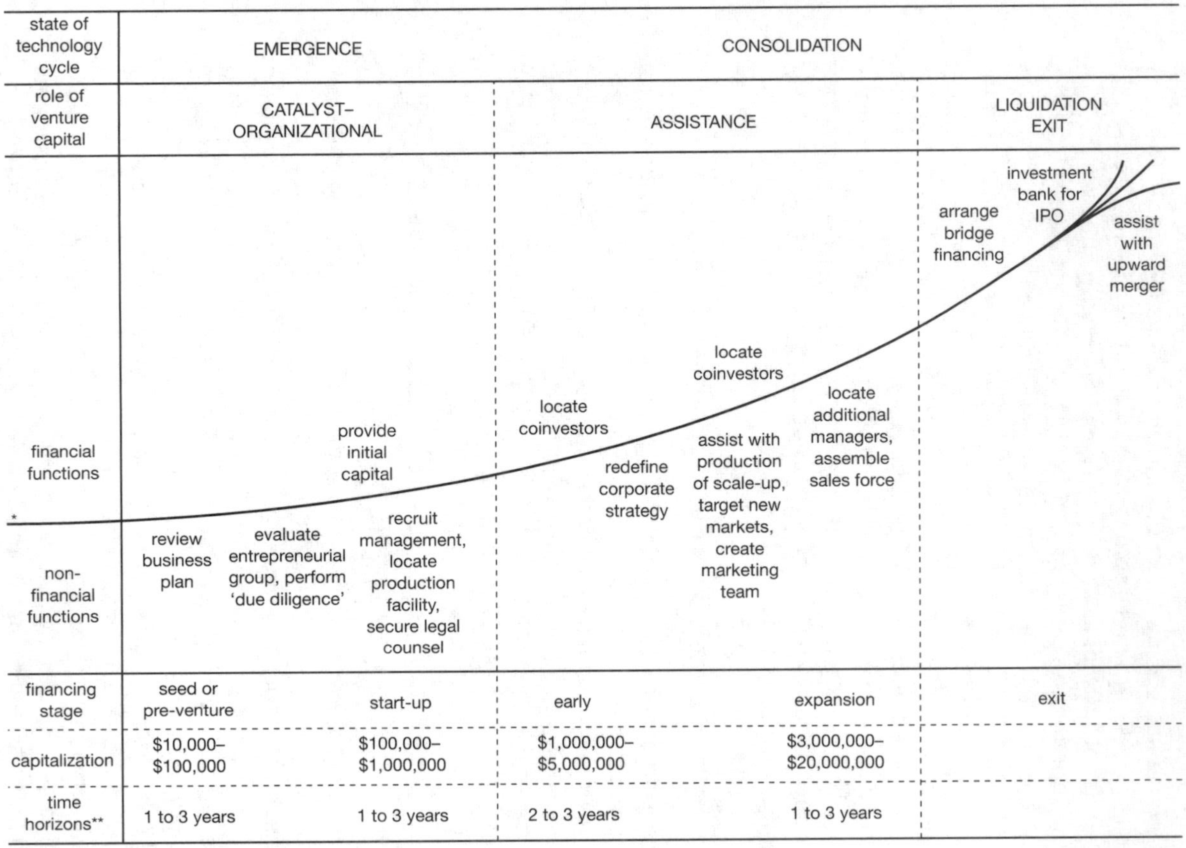

	seed or pre-venture	start-up	early	expansion	exit
state of technology cycle	EMERGENCE	EMERGENCE	CONSOLIDATION	CONSOLIDATION	LIQUIDATION EXIT
role of venture capital	CATALYST–ORGANIZATIONAL	CATALYST–ORGANIZATIONAL	ASSISTANCE	ASSISTANCE	LIQUIDATION EXIT
financial functions		provide initial capital	locate coinvestors	locate coinvestors	arrange bridge financing; investment bank for IPO; assist with upward merger
non-financial functions	review business plan; evaluate entrepreneurial group, perform 'due diligence'	recruit management, locate production facility, secure legal counsel	redefine corporate strategy; assist with production of scale-up, target new markets, create marketing team	locate additional managers, assemble sales force	
financing stage	seed or pre-venture	start-up	early	expansion	exit
capitalization	$10,000–$100,000	$100,000–$1,000,000	$1,000,000–$5,000,000	$3,000,000–$20,000,000	
time horizons **	1 to 3 years	1 to 3 years	2 to 3 years	1 to 3 years	

* growth curve of a new technology intensive business

** average of 7 years

Figure 13.1 Venture capital in the technology cycle

securing of legal counsel, and other services crucial to a young firm's survival and growth. As the business evolves, venture capitalists arrange additional rounds of financing, attract co-investors, redefine corporate strategy, assist with production scale-up, target new markets, create a skilled marketing department, and work to maintain an effective management team. In these ways venture capitalists add real value to new firms that transcends the provision of mere financial resources.

Narrowing the field: identifying investment opportunities

Venture capitalists select their investments from literally hundreds and, for some venture capital funds, thousands of business proposals each year. Only a fraction of these receive serious evaluation, and an even smaller percentage actually result in funding. For example, during 1987 the 100 most active venture capital firms received on average roughly 1000 proposals each, with the actual number of proposals ranging from a minimum of 10 to a maximum of 6500. Of these proposals, less than 4 per cent received funding. When 'follow-on' investments are excluded, this figure falls to only 2 per cent (Judak *et al.* 1988).

Venture capitalists rely heavily on personal contacts in their search for and initial screening of quality venture opportunities. These referrals are a critical factor in venture capitalists' investment decisions. Survey research indicates that nearly two-thirds of all proposals are referrals from other venture capitalists, personal acquaintances, banks or investment brokers. Executives of successful portfolio companies are particularly important to this referral process. Their industry experience and contacts afford them preferential access to high-potential entrepreneurial groups and business proposals, which they, in turn, refer to venture capitalists. Law firms specializing in venture capital are also important; they provide a steady stream of referrals, match entrepreneurs to potential investors, and are involved in negotiations that are critical to forging new business alliances. Law firms that specialize in new venture activity are retained by both venture capitalists and high-technology start-ups. For example, one of the top West Coast venture law firms, Wilson, Sonsini, Goodrich & Rosati, has a client list that includes venture capital firms such as Mayfield Fund, Hambrect & Quist and Sequoia Capital, as well as high-tech companies like ROLM Corporation and Apple Computer (*Venture Capital Journal*, January 1987, pp. 48–54).

A high-technology orientation

Venture capitalists invest primarily in high-technology enterprises. This is illustrated in Table 13.3, which shows the industry orientation of venture capital investments in 1994 and 1995. During this period technology-intensive companies, in industries such as computers, software, telecommunications, etc., received between 66 and 75 per cent of all venture capital investment. Computer software has consistently received the greatest portion of venture capital financing, claiming, for example, one-quarter of the total venture capital disbursed in 1995. In addition, the venture capitalists interviewed indicated a near-unanimous preference for technology-intensive investments. Non-high technology companies (i.e. consumer-related

Table 13.3 Venture capital investments by industry

Industry	No. of companies
Biotechnology	98
Computer hardware systems	50
Energy-related	5
Industrial automation	9
Industrial products and machinery	37
Medical/health care-related	156
Other electronics	66
Software and services	250
Telephone and data communications	130
Commercial communications	37
Consumer-related	103
Other products and services	134
Total	1,075

products, services, and commercial communications) represent a minority of investments, accounting for less than 25 per cent of the total disbursements in 1995.

The start-up phase

Once the business plan is accepted, capital is infused into the new enterprise. In return, venture capitalists receive a significant ownership stake in the new company, ranging from 10 per cent to 90 per cent, though 51 per cent is common. By opting for equity investment over traditional debt financing, venture capitalists and their portfolio companies eliminate the problem of scheduled repayment. Loans that are made to new businesses generally carry high interest rates and short terms. Repayment can be an onerous burden for young companies which require substantial inflows of capital during early growth stages and, therefore, cannot afford sizeable outflows to cover interest and principal payments. In addition, the loan officers employed by banks frequently do not understand the technical dimensions of high-technology business formation (US Small Business Administration 1986). In contrast, equity investment allows young companies to reinvest all earnings in the company and provides an asset base which can be used to attract outside capital and enhance a company's credibility with vendors, suppliers and traditional financial institutions.

Just as important as the funding provided by venture capitalists is the significant management assistance they render to small, technology-intensive businesses. Generally, they attempt to foster the growth of new companies with advice rather than becoming actively involved in the time-consuming daily management of the company (although if a venture capitalist believes that a venture is headed for disaster under the original founders, that venture capitalist will step in and assume control over a firm's operation). Along with their equity in the corporation, venture capitalists commonly gain active representation on the corporate board of directors. Donald Valentine has termed venture capitalists' 'managerial' contribution 'intelligence equity', which he defines as 'experience the companies don't have, contacts they don't have, perspectives they don't have' (Valentine 1985: 46–7). Venture capitalists' substantial experience and extensive contacts help new companies secure legal counsel, patent attorneys, accounting services, outside technical experts, public relations consultants and a wide variety of ancillary business services, as well as locate office or production facilities.

The provision of financing from a reputable venture firm in established technology regions, like Silicon Valley or Route 128, can function as a 'seal of approval' for new companies which need to establish working relationships with suppliers, financial institutions and related businesses. Venture capitalists may also organize strategic partnerships between portfolio companies and larger corporations through technology exchanges, original equipment manufacturer, other customer agreements, and minority equity investments.

Perhaps the most crucial contribution to a new firm's development by a venture capitalist is its recruitment of managers for business start-ups. To assist with such efforts, most venture firms have executive search firms on retainer. A survey of 77 important venture capital firms indicated that the venture capital community views management recruitment as the single most important form of assistance provided to young companies (Case 1986). Indeed, the Mayfield Fund has recently added a 'recruiting partner' who specializes in filling management positions at portfolio companies (T. Davis, General Partner in the Mayfield Fund, interview with authors, December 1986). Venture capitalists often lure top-level personnel from secure academic or corporate posts by offering them equity stakes in fledgling businesses and the concomitant possibility of realizing large capital gains in return for their expertise.

Building a business

The role of venture capitalists changes as new businesses and technologies proceed through the business development cycle (Figure 13.1). Over time, technological and entrepreneurial skills diminish in importance relative to managerial and marketing capabilities, and the young company establishes a more formal organizational structure. At this stage the role of the venture capitalist shifts from active intervention to one of advice and assistance. The venture capitalist's expertise in particular industries and prior experience with business expansion provides a reservoir of knowledge which can be critical for the survival of a growing company. 'Real value is added in a venture activity', according to Arthur D. Little, 'not on the front or buy end and not on the back or sell end, but through working with people in the company in the middle' (Christie 1985: 93). At times, some venture capital funds may also encourage collective problem-solving by managers of portfolio companies, creating an intensive information exchange among entrepreneurs which eliminates or diminishes the severity of many problems associated with new business development.

The relationship between venture capitalists and the companies they finance is not always devoid of conflict. Although venture capitalists and entrepreneurs typically work together to build new companies, the reasons why they do so are often quite different. Of primary importance to venture capitalists are the profits or capital gains made on investments. While entrepreneurs are also interested in financial gain, they are also likely to be driven by some combination of profit, long-term economic security, sense of mission, and attachment to their enterprise. These differences may underscore more obvious disagreements, which can at times lead to bitter confrontations over corporate policy. In such cases, venture capitalists can use their control of board positions or leverage over further rounds of financing to coerce management to make changes or to remove the founder or entrepreneurial group. If disagreements are serious enough, they will endeavour to replace managers. In some instances, the venture capitalists may assume direct operating positions themselves, though our interviews lead us to conclude that they will do so only in the most dire situations.

Investment syndicates and co-investing

Venture capital-financed start-up investments increasingly occur with the involvement of multiple venture capital firms. Our interviews with venture capitalists suggest that the most highly regarded investments are 'self-organizing' – that is, two or more venture capital firms will simultaneously evaluate a potential investment and mutually agree to invest and form a syndicate (W. Burgin, General Partner of Bessemer Venture Partners, interview with authors, June 1987).

Investment syndication, or 'co-investing', links venture capital firms together in local, regional and national networks. According to the Congressional Joint Economic Committee, approximately 90 per cent of all venture capital investments involve syndicates. This process enables venture capitalists to pool expertise, diversify their portfolios, and share information and risk. Co-investment is also a mechanism by which venture capital firms ensure themselves of a steady stream of quality investment opportunities, exchanging a portion of a current deal flow for consideration in future investments.

Venture capital firms use investment syndicates to secure additional rounds of financing for new companies. The original lead investor may arrange two or three investment syndications involving as many as fifteen other investors. Lead investors typically use personal networks to secure co-investors, trading opportunities to participate in each other's investments. While investment syndications are primarily accomplished to provide capital, venture capitalists typically seek co-investors with complementary skills and supplementary contacts.

Bringing companies to market and other forms of exit

Venture capitalists' participation in new businesses culminates when they 'exit' from their investments. This is typically accomplished through a public stock offering or upward merger that transforms investments into liquid capital. Between 1978 and 1984, nearly 300 venture-backed companies were brought into the market for initial public offerings (IPOs) (Soussou 1985). From 1985 to 1990 there were 343 venture-backed IPOs, and in the superheated IPO market of the 1990s there were 783 venture-backed IPOs from 1991 to 1995. The push to go public is embedded in the very structure of the venture capital industry. The more quickly investment portfolios are liquidated (at high multiples of the original investment) and the limited partners receive their return, the sooner the venture capitalist can launch another fund.

There is a significant economic rationale for this. Venture capitalists usually receive a management fee of approximately 2–3 per cent of paid-in capital per year. Since this management fee covers only salaries and business expenses, the pay-off for the professional venture capitalist comes after returning an agreed-upon percentage to the limited partners, at which point an override share of approximately 20 per cent of further profit is retained by the general partner.

The large potential return provided by equity financing enables venture capitalists to assume substantial investment risks, since one enormously successful investment can more than offset a series of break even investments or outright losses. An unpublished study by the consulting firm Horsley, Keough & Associates of the performance of ten leading venture capital funds indicates that of 525 separate investments made during the period 1972–83, just 56 'winners' (or 10.7 per cent) generated more than half ($450 million) of the total value held in portfolio ($823 million), while roughly half (266) either broke even or lost money.

The intervention of venture capitalists in the early life of a firm has proved essential to the success of new technology-oriented companies. Venture capitalists provide managerial, marketing, legal, financial and other types of experience that most likely would be unavailable through conventional sources of funding. In doing so, they function as catalysts in the evolution of new technologies, new businesses, and even entirely new industries. The next section elaborates on these themes, providing a conceptual basis from which to understand venture capital's role in technological innovation.

Venture capital and technological innovation

Venture capitalists play a critical role in the process of technological innovation by helping to organize embryonic technology. They sit at the centre of multifaceted networks of financial institutions, large corporations, universities and entrepreneurs, and in doing so forge important linkages between large and small institutions. Venture capital serves in large measure to formalize the roles historically played by the entrepreneur and independent financier, and lend structure to the innovation process and attendant 'gales of creative destruction' that are so vital to the wave-like expansions of capitalist societies (Schumpeter 1934).

Entrepreneurial versus corporate innovation: the Schumpeterian tradition

The rise of venture capital has dramatically transformed the way that innovation takes place. Economists working in the tradition of Joseph Schumpeter have traditionally made a distinction between entrepreneurial and corporate forms of innovation. Under entrepreneurial innovation, individual entrepreneurs or entrepreneurial groups drive the innovation process. These actors either utilize ideas drawn from science or employ technical know-how to launch new products and forge new product markets. The technological and organizational changes brought about by these innovations generate strong bandwagon effects which lead to the creation of new industries, the revitalization of some older ones, and the disappearance of still others.

Under corporate innovation, large corporations organize R&D within specialized research laboratories, thereby internalizing innovation. These corporations use internal R&D to remain at the forefront of new technology and to generate successive waves of innovation. According to Christopher Freeman and his colleagues at the Science Policy Research Unit, this creates 'a strong positive feedback loop from successful innovation to increased R&D activity, setting up a virtually self-reinforcing circle' (Freeman, Clark and Soete 1982). The internalization of innovation within large corporations makes technological change a less sporadic, more continuous process.

Venture capitalists as technological gatekeepers

In organizing many of the elements necessary for technological innovation, venture capitalists function to a large extent as 'technological gatekeepers' – setting the direction of technological change. The idea of 'natural' or 'technological' trajectories suggests that the given path of technological development both channels and constrains future technological progress. The organizational and institutional context of society acts as an additional constraint on technological change. Since innovation and technological change take place largely within these relatively fixed constraints, only critical technological or organizational breakthroughs can disrupt existing socio-technical pathways and open up new technological frontiers.

Venture capitalists are a crucial part of the context within which such breakthroughs occur. Owing to the intensive flows of information at their disposal, venture capitalists are well positioned to spot the opportunities that arise as critical barriers are breached. It is at these junctures that they perform a 'gatekeeping' function, by intervening to help create new companies and actualize important breakthroughs. At the same time, they are able to capture the 'economic rents' that come from being first across such boundaries. Although only a small subset of all venture investments ultimately pay off, the most important choices or 'technological bets' made by venture capitalists in fields such as semiconductors, personal computers and biotechnology have disrupted existing socio-technical trajectories and opened up whole new frontiers for technological progress, setting the stage for clusters of imitative activity and swarms of improvements and innovations.

This does not imply that large corporations are unimportant in placing technology bets. The historic role played by Bell Laboratories in pioneering a series of important innovations in the United States is exemplary. However, recent years have seen large corporations recede from directly innovative activity, although they certainly help to establish the technological base from which innovative activity can originate. This is in part the result of venture capital-based innovation, which has generated increased incentives for employees to leave large corporations.

In short, venture capital-financed innovation is more than just a mid-point between entrepreneurial and corporate models of innovation. By organizing and capitalizing on the complementary strengths of a variety of organizations, venture capital-driven investment presents a new, integrative model of innovation. In addition, venture capital-financed innovation plays an important technological gatekeeping function, moving the US economy across new technological frontiers and setting in motion the 'gales of creative destruction' which establish the context for economic restructuring.

An example of venture capital-financed innovation: the semiconductor industry

The operation of this new model of venture capital-financed innovation can be illustrated through the example of the semiconductor industry, but was also crucial for both the personal computer and the biotechnology industries.

The linkage between large corporations and venture backed companies is clearly evident in the semiconductor industry. The basic technology used in semiconductors was developed at Bell Laboratories during the 1950s by William Shockley, Gordon Teal and their collaborators. In 1951 Teal left Bell Labs to join Texas Instruments, and in 1954 Shockley left to launch his own firm. The establishment of Fairchild Semiconductor in 1957 by Eugene Kleiner, Robert Noyce and six other of Shockley's former employees catalysed the nascent semiconductor industry. Fairchild was one of the first important venture capital-backed start-ups. Its financing was arranged by Arthur Rock, who was then an investment banker with a prominent New York City firm.[4] Fairchild laid crucial groundwork for the genesis of the Silicon Valley innovation complex, becoming an important 'incubator organization' for both entrepreneurial spin-offs and venture capitalists. Fairchild alumnus Jerry Sanders launched Advanced Micro Devices in 1967. That same year Robert Noyce, Andy Grove and Gordon Moore left Fairchild to found Intel, with backing from Rock. Rock also provided venture capital for Intersil, Inc., which was started by Jean Hoerni, another of Fairchild's original founders (Wilson 1985: 38).

In the early 1980s another group of top Fairchild executives, led by then president Wilfred Corrigan, left Fairchild to launch LSI Logic, a leading producer of custom semiconductors. According to recent estimates, more than 80 semiconductor start-ups can trace their origin to Fairchild. Moreover, Fairchild alumni have also gone on to form prominent venture capital partnerships. Eugene Kleiner, one of Fairchild's founding eight, is a key principal in Kleiner Perkins, while Donald Valentine runs the Sequoia Partnership.

Venture capital and innovation

The emergence of a formalized venture capital industry has transformed the nature of innovation. Venture capital-financed innovation overcomes a variety of barriers that obstruct technological progress, including the risk aversion of established financial markets, the organizational inertia of large corporations, and the multifaceted technological, organizational and financial requirements of new business development. Generally speaking, venture capital-financed innovation accelerates the processes of technological innovation by combining resources and personnel drawn from a variety of organizations. In addition, venture capital-financed innovation occupies a particular niche in the technology cycle. It is of special importance during the early and chaotic stages of a technological thrust, when the nature of nascent technology, its applications and market potentials are in flux.

Venture capitalists are agents of innovation, performing a technological gate-keeping function. They are not omniscient with regard to technological change but

Table 13.4 Venture capital resources by geographic region

Region	1995		1994	
	Capital ($ billions)	Percentage of total	Capital ($ billions)	Percentage of total
Northeast	16,673.7	44.9	15,101.0	46.2
West Coast	10,921.7	29.4	9,046.8	27.7
Midwest	4,174.6	11.2	3,401.4	10.4
Mid-Atlantic	2,330.1	6.3	2,289.8	7.0
Southeast	1,079.4	2.9	900.4	2.8
Southwest	1,079.4	2.9	1,016.4	3.1
Rocky Mountains	471.9	1.3	484.7	1.5
Northwest	423.2	1.1	429.2	1.3
Total	37,154.01	100	32,669.7	100

draw their power from the wide-ranging contacts and networks at their disposal. As focal points of social structures of innovation, they organize the myriad transactions and reduce the uncertainty associated with new business formation. In doing so, they catalyse the dynamic complementarities which exist between large corporations, universities, small companies and a variety of related organizations.

Where is venture capital?

Venture capital is tightly concentrated in a few distinct pockets across the United States. Our research shows that venture capital funds are formed in areas with high concentrations of high-technology business, financial resources, or both.

   This section provides a detailed look at the geography of venture capital activity – the places where venture capital is concentrated. The major conclusion is that venture capital is highly concentrated at the regional, state and metropolitan levels. Table 13.4 illustrates the degree of industry concentration at the level of regions, and Table 13.5 lists the leading states. The Northeast and Pacific regions together account for 75 per cent of all venture capital resources. Furthermore, just three states – California, New York and Massachusetts – control 64 per cent of the national venture capital pool. Within these states, just three metropolitan areas (San Francisco, New York City and Boston) are home to approximately 50 per cent of the nation's venture capital resources. The tight clusters or complexes of venture capital are readily apparent here, particularly in San Francisco/Silicon Valley and Los Angeles in the West, Chicago in the Midwest, and New York and Boston in the Northeast.

Regional concentration of the venture capital industry

Venture capital is concentrated in two broad regions of the country, the Northeast and Pacific. Over the past decade the proportion of venture capital resources controlled by these two regions has remained fairly constant. In 1987 the Northeast and Pacific regions accounted for nearly three-quarters of all venture capital

Table 13.5 Venture capital resources by leading states

Region	1995		1994	
	Capital ($ millions)	Percentage of total	Capital ($ millions)	Percentage of total
1 California	10.92	29	9.04	28
2 New York	7.88	21	7.38	23
3 Massachusetts	5.22	14	4.27	13
4 Connecticut	2.24	6	2.20	7
5 Illinois	2.10	6	1.07	0
6 Maryland	1.42	4	1.46	5
7 New Jersey	1.26	3	1.13	4
8 Texas	0.94	3	0.91	3
9 Minnesota	0.73	2	0.56	2
10 Pennsylvania	0.63	2	0.63	2

Table 13.6 Concentration of venture capital offices within states

State	Total no. of offices	No. in leading city
California	277	160 in San Francisco/Silicon Valley
New York	174	140 in New York City
Massachusetts	105	67 in Boston
Illinois	63	44 in Chicago
Georgia	23	21 in Atlanta

resources, and roughly two-thirds of all venture capital offices. During the past decade or so, there has been a shift in venture capital resources from the East to the West Coast, as Silicon Valley has increased its dominance as the premier high-technology and venture capital region of the United States.

Concentration of venture capital in the states

The venture capital industry is extremely concentrated at the state level as well. Table 13.5 shows the top ten states in terms of venture capital resources. California is the leading state for venture capital resources with $10.92 billion in 1995, or 29 per cent of the total venture capital pool. It is followed by New York with $7.88 billion, or 21 per cent of the venture industry's resources. Massachusetts is third with $5.22 billion, or 14 per cent. Together, these states control almost two-thirds of the $37 billion US venture capital pool.

Concentration of venture capital within states

The venture capital industry is further concentrated within states at the metropolitan level, as evidenced in Table 13.6. For example, nearly 60 per cent of the venture capital offices in California are located in the San Francisco Bay/Silicon Valley area, with most of the remaining offices in the Los Angeles/San Diego area. In fact, the

San Francisco/Silicon Valley area contains more venture capital offices than any other state except New York – over 16 per cent of the national total. More than 80 per cent of New York's venture capital offices are concentrated in the New York City area, while Chicago is home to some 70 per cent of Illinois' venture capital offices. Boston and its suburbs account for over two-thirds of Massachusetts' venture capital industry.

Where does venture capital go?

Venture capital investments are even more highly concentrated than venture capital resources – primarily flowing to a few limited areas. Although a logical assumption might be that venture capital investments tend to concentrate in areas that possess venture capital resources, our findings indicate that this is only partly true. Venture capital mainly flows to the nation's premier high-technology centres, most notably California's Silicon Valley and Route 128 around Boston. In contrast, venture capital centres like Chicago and New York City receive a relatively minor share of venture investments.

The major findings of our work can be summarized as three major points. First, venture capital investments are highly concentrated by region. Just two regions – the Northeast and the Pacific – account for a clear majority of the venture capital invested each year. Second, at the state level, just two states – California and Massachusetts – accounted for over 50 per cent of all venture capital invested in 1995. And third, venture capital investments are highly concentrated within most states. According to our data, the San Francisco–Silicon Valley area accounts for over 50 per cent of all venture capital investments made in California, and over 20 per cent of all venture capital investments made nationwide; the Route 128 area around Boston received about 95 per cent of the venture capital investments in Massachusetts. Moreover, this pattern is also observable in states that are not leading centres of venture capital. A prime example of this is Georgia; almost all of the venture capital investments in that state are concentrated in the Atlanta area.

Together, these three findings lead us to conclude that venture capital investments flow to areas with *established concentrations of high-technology businesses*. Many researchers have explored the following 'chicken or the egg' question: does venture capital attract or create high-technology industry or does high technology attract the venture capital dollars? While both are doubtless partially true, our research supports the latter interpretation. An area is much more likely to be a recipient of venture capital if it is home to high-technology firms.

Concentration of venture capital investments

The geographic distribution of venture capital investments is highly uneven and tightly clustered. As Table 13.7 shows, California attracted the lion's share of the investment dollars, with $1.8 billion or nearly 50 per cent of the national total in 1995. Massachusetts was second – receiving approximately $337 million, or 9 per cent of the total venture capital invested, while Texas, Virginia, New Jersey, North Carolina, Pennsylvania, Minnesota and Michigan each attracted between $107 and

Table 13.7 Disbursements for top ten state recipients (ranked by capital disbursed in 1995)

Rank	State	Dollars invested ($ millions)	Percentage change, 1994–5
1	California	1,820	65
2	Massachusetts	337	(2)
3	Texas	136	(40)
4	Virginia	119	98
5	New Jersey	116	4
6	North Carolina	110	588
7	Pennsylvania	110	02
8	Minnesota	107	78
9	Michigan	107	3,467
10	Washington	97	62

$119 million. Although in recent years California and Massachusetts have commanded the majority of the venture capital industry's disbursements, this pattern of investment did not always hold. In the period prior to the industry's boom of the late 1970s, the *combined* share of investments for these two states was only 35 per cent.

Venture capital is also highly concentrated within states. Silicon Valley receives more than two-thirds of all venture capital investments made in California, with investments tightly clustered in the cities of Sunnyvale, Santa Clara and San Jose. These cities received 30 per cent of the California total, and 12 per cent of total investments. Of the states, only Massachusetts received more venture capital investments than this three-city area.

A similar level of concentration is noticeable in the Route 128 area. The eighteen cities and towns along the Route 128 corridor received almost 75 per cent of that state's investments. And just three communities – Newton, Waltham and Woburn – received 62 per cent of the Route 128 investments – almost 3 per cent of the *national* total of venture capital investments.

Interestingly, this pattern is also true of states that control only minor amounts of venture capital. Atlanta, Georgia, which was the leading recipient of venture capital in the South, has been evolving a high-technology industrial base in recent years. A similar trend was especially evident in Colorado, where the distribution of venture financings went primarily to high-technology firms located along Interstate 25, a corridor that is becoming a well-known centre for technology-intensive defence industries.

Venture capital and regional innovation

Clearly, venture capital is a vital component of US regional innovation and economic development; without exception, thriving innovation and technology-driven regional economies are home to above-average shares of venture capital investment. Through their role as technological gatekeeper, venture capitalists not only support the development of new technologies, but also shape their evolution. Abundant venture capital provides strong incentives for researchers to look for commercial application for their work. In addition, venture capitalists help provide the infra-structure and expertise that can help these commercial ventures to grow and succeed.

Some have argued that the unique presence of venture capital in the United States has led to a national innovation system that favours 'breakthrough' innovations which can be capitalized into venture-backed companies. Many point to Silicon Valley and the Route 128 corridor as prime examples of the powerful effects caused by the combination of world-class research universities and abundant venture capital. The story is simple, they say: Silicon Valley and Route 128 are the premier regional innovation centres in the United States, and they are also among the leading centres of venture capital resources and are the pre-eminent recipients of venture capital funding. Regional venture capital and regional innovation seem to go together.

There is a cautionary tale to be told. New York City and Chicago are among the top five regions for venture capital resources, and yet they receive precious little venture capital investment, and are not thought of as high-technology regions. Obviously, venture capital resources alone are insufficient to generate regional innovation. In fact, pooling their financial resources in venture capital causes the investment dollars of New York and Chicago to be exported to innovative industrial concerns in other regions. Venture capital, while playing an important role in regional innovation systems, is not a panacea for policy-makers seeking to re-create the Silicon Valley effect in their locale.

Numerous European and Asian technology and economic development officials have visited the premier US innovation regions in an effort to learn about the role of venture capital in their development. And many have attempted to stimulate indigenous venture capital in their home country in an effort to develop their own innovation systems. However, tax climates that do not favour capital gains, and the absence of a historical culture of private ownership and accumulation, have ham-pered the development and effectiveness of home-grown venture capital industries in most countries outside the United States. The United Kingdom is the most successful example of efforts to build a venture industry.

Venture capital outside the United States

While the United States remains the dominant venture capital market, other countries have experienced rapid growth in venture activity. Most notable is the growth of the venture capital industry in the United Kingdom and throughout Europe. As recently as 1984, the sum total of European venture activity was trivial in comparison to US activity. Since then, through a combination of public policy actions, regulatory changes and increased attention to the success of US venture capitalists, the pool of European venture capital has grown dramatically. In 1988 the European Venture Capital Association identified resources of just over ECU $9 billion. Today that total stands at ECU $23.1 billion. In the United Kingdom, which accounts for roughly half of European venture activity, today's venture pool is more than seventeen times larger than it was in 1984. Clearly, Europe and the United Kingdom have taken quickly to the venture capital model, and are growing rapidly.

By some calculations, Europe as a whole will invest more in new venture capital investments during 1999 than the United States.

Policy implications

Venture capital's role in innovation translates into important implications for regional innovation and economic development policy. The past fifteen years have seen a surge in state and local activity designed to overcome gaps in the availability of venture capital and to promote economic development. Only four states were financing new enterprises prior to 1900, today more than half are actively providing some type of venture assistance. Total capitalization of these efforts currently exceeds $1 billion.

Recent state programmes to enhance venture capital

State and local governments are actively experimenting with a variety of mechanisms for providing or stimulating venture capital. These efforts are predicated on the twofold belief that venture capital stimulates regional innovative activity and that there exist regional venture capital gaps that limit the development of regions outside of venture capital centres. Evidence on these programmes is decidedly mixed. Many states have scrapped their programmes as ineffective, while other states are adding new venture initiatives.

A number of states use public money to underwrite privately managed venture capital partnerships. Public entities generally function as passive limited partners in these arrangements, placing few stipulations on the type or location of investments. The New York Business Venture Partnership is a $40 million limited partnership backed by two public pension funds and managed by Rothschild Ventures. The Michigan Investment Fund counts the State of Michigan, public pension funds and the University of Michigan endowment among its limited partners. It is managed by Doan Associates, a Michigan-based venture firm, and invests on a national basis. The Primus fund in Cleveland, Ohio, is a $30 million limited partnership backed in part by public capital. Although its charter originally limited investments to Ohio and the Midwest, Primus currently invests across the country.

Many states – including Ohio, Pennsylvania, Michigan, New York, Utah, Oregon and Washington – allow public pension funds to commit a small percentage of assets to venture capital, according to the Small Business Association in 1985. Pension funds have generally invested in established partnerships without regard for location. But, as the examples above indicate, some states have employed this mechanism to create local venture partnerships. A number of others, most notably Ohio and Michigan, have experimented with direct investment in new enterprises, according to the Ohio Department of Development in 1985.

Tax incentives have also been used to stimulate private venturing. The Montana Capital Companies Act offers a 25 per cent state tax credit for the formation of private venture funds. Louisiana and Minnesota offer similar tax credits. Finally, a number of jurisdictions have established venture capital conferences, seminars or networks that link entrepreneurs to private sources of venture capital. Notable among these efforts is the Venture Capital Network of New Hampshire, which employs a computerized matching process to link prospective entrepreneurs to informal investors or so-called 'angels'. According to Wetzel, such efforts stimulate economic development by reducing the information costs involved on both the entrepreneurial and the investment sides of the venturing process.

What can we expect from these efforts?

Government risk capital programmes must face the fact that finance is only a small part of the activities of a venture capitalist. The success of new ventures is highly contingent upon the support services supplied by venture capitalists. It is questionable whether the public sector can or should attempt to compete with private venture capitalists to recruit individuals with the skills necessary to provide such services. There may also be barriers prohibiting representatives of public funds from accessing private venture capital networks.

A different set of problems crop up when public funds are managed by private venture capitalists. This may turn out to be a catch-22 situation. Placing tight restrictions on the investment activities of public venture capital pools is problematic because it narrows potential investment opportunities, constrains deal flow and is likely to negatively influence the fund's rate of return. When no such strings are attached, however, investments will flow to areas where the most attractive investments and highest rates of return are available, resulting in interregional transfers of capital and further depletion of local resources. It will be difficult for many states to balance successfully the goals of high rates of return and local venture investment to spur economic development.

The single most important implication for economic development policy is that, despite the very important contribution venture capital has made to the making of high-technology regions (i.e. Silicon Valley and Route 128), we should not expect public venture capital to be a cure-all for an area's economic woes. Public provision of venture or risk capital is likely to be effective only in a very limited number of areas.

The reason for this is simple. Venture capital is just one of a host of necessary inputs to technology-intensive economic development. As the cases of New York and Chicago illustrate, the presence of abundant venture capital does not necessarily translate into high-technology development. The consensus view in the literature on high technology and regional development is that only a very limited set of areas possess the attributes needed to generate and sustain a high level of high-technology entrepreneurship and development. Increasing the volume of venture capital in areas that lack such conditions is likely to have little effect on their technological capabilities and can have perverse effects if this capital simply flows to established centres of high technology. It is quite possible that current models of public equity finance will confer disproportionate benefits on already advantaged regions, enabling them to consolidate their hold on high-technology development.

In fact, public provision of venture capital may be most appropriate in areas that are just developing the 'social structures of innovation' needed for high-technology growth. Since venture capital is just one of many important inputs into the technology development process, public intervention in venture capital will be most successful in areas that already have a supply of the other inputs, but do not have sufficient venture capital. In these few cases (and only in these cases), relief of the venture capital constraint is likely to have a significant impact.

A key aspect in determining the efficacy of public provision of venture capital is whether or not so-called regional 'capital gaps' exist in the venture capital industry. Our research indicates that venture capitalists are quite proficient in locating the high-technology firms that offer such good investment opportunities. In other words, while 'capital gaps' may in fact exist, this is a function of an area's underlying technology base – not an absence of financial capital. Simply put: capital gaps exist because there are few good deals to attract venture capital in the first place.

Given this reality, the rapid expansion of public venture capital programmes may end up generating yet another round of inter-locality competition, pitting jurisdiction against jurisdiction in the scramble for high-technology businesses and jobs. The costs of such duplicative activity may well exceed potential benefits. Despite the rhetoric of indigenous job generation that surrounds them, entrepreneurial programmes are confronted by the same 'zero-sum' consequences evidenced by more traditional economic development strategies.

While venture capital is an important element of high-technology complexes, it is not a panacea for the problems of declining states or localities. In the light of our findings, public policy-makers would do well to avoid 'quick-fix' remedies like venture capital programmes, and get back to the business of building integrated strategies to bolster the underlying economic and technological capacities of states and regions.

Notes

This chapter significantly draws its historical background on the venture capital industry from research completed by the authors with Martin Kenney (Florida, Kenney and Smith 1990).

1. This point was reinforced in our discussions with John Dougery, a former Citicorp employee who is now a member of the limited partnership Dougery, Jones & Wilder, and with David Wegman, who is currently with Citicorp Ventures in Palo Alto, California.

2. For further detail on venture capital subsidiaries of large industrial corporations, see Charles River Associates (1976), Mears (1981) and *Venture Capital Journal*, November 1985, pp. 6–13.

3. A thorough discussion of the early history of the SBIC programme is provided by Noone and Rubel (1970).

4. For a history of Fairchild Semiconductor, see Braun and MacDonald (1982). On venture capital's role, see Wilson (1985: 33–4).

PART V

The City and the World

CHAPTER FOURTEEN

The Learning Region

Richard Florida

Introduction

A new age of capitalism is sweeping the globe. In Silicon Valley a global centre for new technology has emerged, where entrepreneurs and technologists from around the world backed by global venture capital invent the new technologies of software, personalized information and biotechnology that will shape our future. In the financial centres of Tokyo, New York and London, computerized financial markets provide instantaneous capital and credit to companies and entrepreneurs across the vast reaches of the world. In the film studios of Los Angeles, computer technicians work alongside actors and film directors to produce the software that will run on new generations of home electronics products produced by television and semiconductor companies in Japan and throughout Asia. Computer scientists and software engineers in Silicon Valley and Seattle work with computer game-makers in Kyoto, Osaka and Tokyo to turn out dazzling new generations of high-technology computer games. In Italy, highly computerized factories produce designer fashion goods tailored to the needs of consumers in Milan, Paris, New York and Tokyo almost instantaneously. Teams of automotive designers in Los Angeles, Tokyo and Milan create designs for new generations of cars, while workers in Kyushu work to the rhythm of classical music in the world's most advanced automotive assembly factories to produce these cars for consumers across the globe. Throughout Japan, a new generation of knowledge workers operate the controls of mammoth automated factory complexes to produce the most basic of industrial products: steel. A new industrial revolution sweeps through Taiwan, Singapore, Korea, Malaysia, Thailand, Indonesia, and extends its reach to formerly undeveloped nations such as Mexico and China. And regions once written off, like the former Rust Belt of the United States, are being revived through international investment and the creative destruction of traditional industries.

Despite continued predictions of the 'end of geography', regions are becoming more important modes of economic and technological organization in this new age of global, knowledge-intensive capitalism. Although there have been numerous excellent studies of the dynamics of individual regions, the role of regions in the new age of knowledge-based global capitalism remains rather poorly understood. And, while several outstanding studies have chronicled the rise of knowledge-based capitalism, outlined the contours of the learning organization, and described the knowledge-creating company, virtually no one has developed a comparable theory of what such changes portend for regions and regional organization.

This chapter suggests that regions are a key element of the new age of global, knowledge-based capitalism. Its central argument is that regions are themselves becoming focal points for knowledge creation and learning in the new age of capitalism, as they take on the characteristics of *learning regions*. Learning regions, as their name implies, function as collectors and repositories of knowledge and ideas, and provide an underlying environment or infrastructure which facilitates the flow of knowledge, ideas and learning. Learning regions are increasingly important sources of innovation and economic growth, and are vehicles for globalization. In elaborating this thesis, the following sections provide brief descriptions of the new era of knowledge-based capitalism and its global scope, before we turn to our discussion of the dynamics of learning regions.

The knowledge revolution

Capitalism, as writers as diverse as Peter Drucker and Ikujiro Nonaka point out, is entering a new age of knowledge creation and continuous learning. This new system of knowledge-intensive capitalism is based on a synthesis of intellectual and physical labour – a melding of *innovation* and *production*, or what I have elsewhere termed innovation-mediated production. In fact, the main source of value and economic growth in knowledge-intensive capitalism is the human mind. Knowledge-intensive capitalism represents a major advance over previous systems of Taylorist scientific management or the assembly-line system of Henry Ford, where the principal source of value and productivity growth was physical labour. The shift to knowledge-based capitalism represents an epochal transition in the nature of advanced economies and societies. Ever since the transition from feudalism to capitalism, the basic source of productivity, value and economic growth has been physical labour and manual skill. In the knowledge-intensive organization, intelligence and intellectual labour replace physical labour as the fundamental source of value and profit.

The new age of capitalism makes use of the entirety of human intellectual and creative capabilities. Both R&D scientists and workers on the factory floor are the sources of ideas and continuous innovation. Workers on the factory floor use their deep and intimate knowledge of machines and production processes to devise new, more efficient production processes. This new system of economic organization harnesses the knowledge and intelligence of the team – the group social mind – a sharp break with the conception of individual knowledge embodied in the lone inventor or great scientist. Teams of R&D scientists, engineers and factory workers become collective agents of innovation. The lines between the factory and the laboratory blur.

The factory is itself becoming more like a laboratory – a place where new ideas and concepts are generated, tested and implemented. Like a laboratory, the knowledge-intensive factory is an increasingly clean, technologically advanced and information-rich environment. In an increasing number of factories, workers perform their tasks in clean room environments, alongside robots and machines which conduct the physical aspects of the work. In some knowledge-intensive factories, laboratory-like spaces are available for workers, which may include sophisticated laboratory-like equipment: computerized measuring equipment, advanced monitoring devices, and test equipment. Workers use these laboratory-like spaces together with R&D scientists and engineers to analyse, fine-tune and improve products and production processes.

The global shift

This new age of capitalism is taking the form of an increasingly integrated economic system, with globe-straddling networks of transnational corporations and high levels of foreign direct investment between and among nations. Such investment is a vehicle for diffusing advanced technologies and state-of-the-art management practices, and is a powerful contributor to the global flow of knowledge. Indeed, international investment has surpassed global trade as the defining feature of the new global economy. A United Nations report shows that today transnational corporations operate some 170,000 factories and branches throughout the globe. In 1992 this worldwide network of foreign affiliates generated $5.5 trillion in sales, exceeding world exports of $4 trillion, one-third of which took the form of intra-firm trade.

Globalization is increasingly taking place through *transplant* companies and in some instances through integrated complexes of transplant factories and surrounding supplier and product development activities. The best examples of such complexes include Toyota and Honda's massive production complexes in the United States. In fact, Japanese automotive production in North America takes the form of an integrated transplant complex comprising seven major automotive assembly complexes and more than 400 suppliers located in and around the traditional industrial heartland region of the United States.

Transplant investment is the source of important productivity improvement and economic growth. According to a recent study by the McKinsey Global Institute (1993), transplants increase productivity by accelerating the adoption and diffusion of best-practice organization and management, and placing pressure on domestic industries to adopt those best practices. The McKinsey study notes that:

> Transplants from leading-edge producers: (1) directly contribute to higher levels of domestic productivity, (2) prove that leading-edge productivity can be achieved with local inputs, (3) put competitive pressure on other domestic producers, and (4) transfer knowledge of best-practices to other domestic producers through natural movement of personnel. Moreover, foreign direct investment has provoked less political opposition than trade because it creates jobs instead of destroying them. Thus, it is likely to grow faster in years to come. (p. 2)

A recent OECD study provides additional empirical evidence of the link between foreign direct investment, productivity improvement and economic growth. Comparing investment and productivity patterns in fifteen advanced industrial nations, the OECD study found that foreign-owned companies are typically more efficient than domestic firms both in absolute levels and in rates of productivity growth. The study found that these productivity gains resulted from more advanced technology than domestic industries, or from adding capacity. By contrast, productivity increases at locally owned companies more often resulted from downsizing and lay-offs. The study also found that international investment has been a key source of employment growth across the advanced industrial nations. In ten of fifteen countries studied, foreign-owned companies created new employment more rapidly than did their domestically owned counterparts, sometimes expanding their operations while domestic firms were contracting. In three others they eliminated jobs, but they did so more slowly than domestically owned enterprises. The study found that the largest employment declines occurred in Japan and Germany, where soaring costs during the 1980s caused international investors to cut a significant number of jobs. Furthermore, the OECD study points to a link between investment and trade, as foreign subsidiaries tended to export and import more than domestic firms, with most of the imports taking the form of intra-firm trade.

Foreign direct investment has played a key role in the economic revival of the United States. For example, productivity grew more rapidly in foreign-owned transplant manufacturing companies in the United States than for the manufacturing sector as a whole during the 1980s. The real output of transplant manufacturers rose nearly four times as fast as that of manufacturing establishments taken as a whole between 1980 and 1987. Transplant companies generated productivity increases and value-added which outdistanced US-owned companies. From 1987 to 1990, for example, the rate of increase in plant and equipment expenditures for transplant industrial enterprises (e.g. non-bank, non-agricultural business) was five times greater than that for US-owned business. As of 1989, value-added per employee was substantially higher in transplants than for US-owned manufacturers. And transplant companies have played an important role in the economic resurgence of the US industrial Midwest – a region which produced more than $350 billion in manufacturing output, making it the third largest manufacturing economy in the world.

Technology and innovative activity are also undergoing considerable globalization. For most of the Cold War, the United States was the world's overwhelming generator of research and technology. However, by the early 1990s the combined R&D expenditures of the European Community and Japan exceeded those of the United States, and their R&D efforts were much more focused on commercial technology. Furthermore, the share of patents taken by non-US inventors has increased dramatically, with non-US inventors accounting for nearly half of all US patents in 1992.

As the pace of innovation has accelerated and the global sources of technology have grown, corporations have expanded their global innovative activities and cross-border alliances. A global survey of companies in the United States, Europe and Japan found that corporations are substantially increasing their reliance on external sources of research and technology for both basic research and product development. Furthermore, a growing number of corporations are establishing R&D facilities abroad. US companies conducted roughly 12 per cent of their total R&D activities abroad in 1991, the most recent year for which reliable data are available. Japanese companies have established a global network of more than 200 research, development and design facilities.

The past decade has seen the progressive globalization of the US technology base, as the United States has become the hub in the global science and technology system. Since 1980, foreign companies have invested tens of billions of dollars in roughly 400 research, development and design centres in the United States. The annual R&D outlays of these facilities have risen from $4.5 billion in 1982 to $10.7 billion in 1992, and the share of total industrial R&D they comprise has grown from 9 per cent to nearly 17 per cent over the same period, roughly one out of every six dollars of industrial R&D spending in the United States. R&D spending by foreign companies is highly concentrated in sectors where foreign industries are highly competitive: European companies in chemicals and pharmaceuticals, and Japanese and German companies in automotive-related technologies and electronics. The globalization of innovation is required to tap into the sources of knowledge and ideas, and scientific and technical talent, which are embedded in cutting-edge regional innovation complexes such as Silicon Valley in the United States, Tokyo or Osaka in Japan, Stuttgart in Germany, and many others.

Towards the learning region

The shift to knowledge-intensive capitalism goes beyond the particular business and management strategies of individual firms. It involves the development of new inputs and a broader infrastructure at the regional level on which individual firms and production complexes of firms can draw. The nature of this economic transformation makes regions key economic units in the global economy. In essence, globalism and regionalism are part of the same process of economic transformation. In an important and provocative essay in *Foreign Affairs*, Kenichi Ohmae (1993) suggests that regions, or what he calls *region-states*, are coming to replace the nation-state as the centrepiece of economic activity.

> The nation state has become an unnatural, even dysfunctional unit for organizing human activity and managing economic endeavor in a borderless world. It represents no genuine, shared community of economic interests; it defines no meaningful flows of economic activity. On the global economic map the lines that now matter are those defining what may be called region states. Region states are natural economic zones. They may or may not fall within the geographic limits of a particular nation – whether they do is an accident of history. Sometimes these distinct economic units are formed by parts of states. At other times, they may be formed by economic patterns that overlap existing national boundaries, such as those between San Diego and Tiajuana. In today's borderless world, these are natural economic zones and what matters is that each possesses, in one or another combination, the key ingredients for successful participation in the global economy. (p. 79)

Region-states, Ohmae points out, are fundamentally tied to the global economy through mechanisms such as trade, export, and both inward and outward foreign investment. The most competitive region-states not only are home to domestic or indigenous companies, but are attractive to the best companies from around the world. Region-states can be distinguished by the level and extent of their insertion in the international economy and by their willingness to participate in global trade:

> The primary linkages of region states tend to be with the global economy, and not with host nations. Region states make such effective points of entry into the global economy because the very characteristics that define them are shaped by the demands of that economy. Region states tend to have between five million and 20 million people. A region state must be small enough for its citizens to share certain economic and consumer interests but of adequate size to justify the infrastructure – communications and transportation links and quality professional services – necessary to participate economically on a global scale. It must, for example, have at least one international airport and, more than likely, one good harbor with international-class freight-handling facilities. A region state must also be large enough to provide an attractive market for the broad development of leading consumer products. In other words, region states are

not defined by their economies of scale in production (which, after all, can be leveraged from a base of any size through exports to the rest of the world) but rather by having reached efficient economies of scale in their consumption, infrastructure and professional services. (*ibid.*)

For most of the twentieth century, successful regional as well as national economies grew by extracting natural resources such as coal and iron ore, making materials such as steel and chemicals, and manufacturing durable goods such as automobiles, appliances and industrial machinery. The wealth of regions and of nations in turn stemmed from their abilities to leverage so-called natural comparative advantages that allowed them to be mass producers of commodities, competing largely on the basis of relatively low production costs. However, the new age of capitalism has shifted the nexus of competition to ideas. In this new economic environment, regions build economic advantage through their ability to mobilize and to harness knowledge and ideas. In fact, regionally based complexes of innovation and production are increasingly the preferred vehicle used to harness knowledge and intelligence across the globe.

The new age of capitalism requires a new kind of region. In effect, regions are increasingly defined by the same criteria and elements which comprise a knowledge-intensive firm: continuous improvement, new ideas, knowledge creation and organizational learning. Regions must adopt the principles of knowledge creation and continuous learning; they must in effect become learning regions. Learning regions provide a series of related infrastructures which can facilitate the flow of knowledge, ideas and learning.

Regions possess a basic set of ingredients that constitute a production system (see Table 14.1). They all have a *manufacturing infrastructure* – a network of firms that produce goods and services. Mass-production organization was defined by a high degree of vertical integration and internalization of capabilities. External supplies tended to involve ancillary or non-essential elements, were generally purchased largely on price, and stored in huge inventories in the plant. Knowledge-intensive economic organization is characterized by a much higher degree of reliance on outside suppliers and the development of co-dependent complexes of end-users and suppliers. In heavy industries, such as automobile manufacturing, large assembly facilities play the role of hub, surrounding themselves with a spoke network of customers and suppliers in order to harness innovative capabilities of the complex, enhance quality and continuously reduce costs.

Regions have a *human infrastructure* – a labour market from which firms draw knowledge workers. Mass-production industrial organization was characterized by a schism between physical and intellectual labour – a large mass of relatively unskilled workers who could perform physical tasks but had little formal involvement in managerial, technical or intellectual activities, and a relatively small group of managers and executives responsible for planning and technological development. The human infrastructure system of mass production – the system of state schools, vocational training, and college and university professional programmes in business and engineering – evolved over time to meet the needs of this mass production system, turning out a large mass of 'cogs in the machine' and a smaller technocratic elite of engineers and managers. The human infrastructure required for a learning region is quite different. As its name implies, a learning region requires a human

Table 14.1 From mass production to learning regions

Basis of competitiveness	Mass-production region	Learning region
	Comparative advantage based on: • Natural resources • Physical labour	Sustainable advantage based on: • Knowledge creation • Continuous improvement
Production system	Mass production • Physical labour as source of value • Separation of innovation and production	Knowledge-based production • Continuous creation • Knowledge as source of value • Synthesis of innovation and production
Manufacturing infrastructure	Arm's-length supplier relations	Firm networks and supplier systems as sources of innovation
Human infrastructure	• Low-skill, low-cost labour • Taylorist workforce • Taylorist education and training	• Knowledge workers • Continuous improvement of human resources • Continuous education and training
Physical and communication infrastructure	Domestically oriented physical infrastructure	• Globally oriented physical and communication infrastructure • Electronic data exchange
Industrial governance system	• Adversarial relationships • Command and control regulatory framework	• Mutually dependent relationships • Network organization • Flexible regulatory framework

infrastructure of knowledge workers who can apply their intelligence in production. The education and training system must be a learning system that can facilitate lifelong learning and provide the high levels of group orientation and teaming required for knowledge-intensive economic organization.

Regions possess a *physical and communications infrastructure* upon which organizations deliver their goods and services and communicate with one another. The physical infrastructure of mass production facilitated the flow of raw materials to factory complexes and the movement of goods and services to largely domestic markets. Knowledge-intensive firms are global players. Thus the physical infrastructure of the new economy must develop links to and facilitate the movement of people, information, goods and services on a global basis. Furthermore, knowledge-intensive organization draws a great portion of its power from the rapid and constant sharing of information and, increasingly, electronic exchange of key data between customers, end-users and their suppliers. For example, seat suppliers for Toyota receive a computer broadcast of what seats to build as Toyota cars start down the assembly line. A learning region requires a physical and communications infra-structure which facilitates the movement of goods, people and information on a just-in-time basis.

To ensure growth of existing firms and the birth of new ones, regions have a capital allocation system and financial market which channel credit and capital to firms. Existing financial systems create impediments to the adoption of new management practices. For example, interviews with executives and surveys of knowledge-intensive firms in the United States indicate that banks and financial institutions often require inventory to be held as collateral, creating a sizeable barrier to the just-in-time inventory and supply practices which define knowledge-intensive economic organization. The capital allocation system of a learning region must create incent-ives for knowledge-based economic organization; for example, by collateralizing knowledge assets rather than physical assets.

Regions also establish mechanisms for *industrial governance*: formal rules, regula-tions and standards, and informal patterns of behaviour between and among firms, and between firms and government organizations. Mass-production regions were characterized by top-down relationships, vertical hierarchy, high degrees of func-tional or task specialization, and command-and-control modes of regulation. Learning regions must develop governance structures which reflect and mimic those of knowledge-intensive firms; that is, co-dependent relations, network organization, decentralized decision-making, flexibility, and a focus on customer needs and requirements.

Learning regions provide the crucial inputs required for knowledge-intensive economic organization to flourish: a manufacturing infrastructure of interconnected vendors and suppliers; a human infrastructure that can produce knowledge workers, that facilitates the development of a team orientation, and that is organized around lifelong learning; a physical and communications infrastructure which facilitates and supports constant sharing of information, electronic exchange of data and informa-tion, just-in-time delivery of goods and services, and integration into the global economy; and capital allocation and industrial governance systems attuned to the needs of knowledge-intensive organizations.

Building the future

For most of the past two decades, experts predicted a shift from manufacturing to a post-industrial service economy, or from basic industries to high technology. In the wake of the predictions, efforts were undertaken to invest in new critical technolo-gies and industries. But the change under way is not one of old sectors giving way to new, but a more fundamental change in the way goods are produced and the economy itself is organized – from mass production to a knowledge-based economy. The implications of the epochal economic transformation are indeed sweeping.

For firms and organizations, the challenge will be to shift towards the principles of knowledge-based organization, and to adopt new organizational and management systems which harness knowledge and intelligence at all points of the organization from the R&D laboratory to the factory floor. Maintaining a balance between cutting-edge innovation and high-quality and efficient production will be a critical issue. To do so, organizations will increasingly adopt best-practice techniques throughout the world, creating new and more powerful forms of knowledge-intensive organizations. Such organizational mechanisms are likely to blend the ability of 'Silicon Valley'-style high-technology companies to spur individual genius and creativity, with strategies and techniques for continuous improvement and the collective mobilization of knowledge. Knowledge-intensive firms and organizations will be called on to build integrated and dense global webs of innovation and production. And these firms will increasingly be forced to build and maintain new regional infrastructures which can support knowledge-based production systems.

The new age of capitalism holds even greater challenges for regions. The very fabric of regional organization will change, as regions gradually adopt the principles of knowledge creation and learning. Learning regions will be called on to supply the requisite human, manufacturing and technological infrastructures needed to support knowledge-intensive forms of innovation and production. Rather than ushering in the 'end of geography', globalization is likely to occur increasingly through complex systems of regional interdependence and integration. And as the nation-state is squeezed between the poles of accelerating globalization and rising regional economic organization, regions will become focal points for economic, technological, political and social organization.

At a broader level, there is likely to be a shift from strategies and policies which emphasize national competitiveness to ones which revolve around the concept of sustainable advantage at the regional as well as national scale. *Sustainable advantage* means that organizations, regions and nations shift their focus from short-run economic performance to re-creating, maintaining and sustaining the conditions required to be world-class performers through continuous improvement of technology, continuous development of human resources, the use of clean production technology, elimination of waste, and a commitment to continuous environmental improvement. Indeed, the concept of sustainable advantage has the potential to become the central organizing principle for economic and political governance at the international, national and regional scales. In this sense, there is some possibility that over time it may come to replace the increasingly dysfunctional Fordist model of nationally based political-economic regulation.

The industrial and innovation systems of the twenty-first century will be remarkably different from those which have operated for most of the twentieth. Knowledge and human intelligence will replace physical labour as the main source of value. Technological change will accelerate at a pace heretofore unknown: innovation will be perpetual and continuous. Knowledge-intensive organizations based on networks and teams will replace vertical bureaucracy, the cornerstone of the twentieth century. The intersection of relentless globalization and the emergence of learning regions are likely to erode the power and authority of the nation-state – the paragon of nineteenth- and twentieth-century political economy. Whole new institutions for international trade, investment, environment and security will doubtless be created. While the new century holds out great hope, it will require tremendous energy and effort to set in motion the necessary changes, and an unparalleled collective effort to bring them about.

CHAPTER FIFTEEN

Cities, Information and 'Smart Holes'

Zoltan J. Acs and John de la Mothe

The preceding chapters of this volume have collectively made the strong point that in order to understand the complex processes that are popularly, if somewhat glibly, referred to as 'globalization' or 'global change', we must not allow ourselves to be uncritically seduced by ungrounded notions of 'virtual' or 'cyber' economics. Instead we must pay close attention to the dynamics of exchange as they actually take place on the ground, in what Karl Polanyi referred to as 'real' economies. To be sure, some influential commentators, such as Kenichi Ohmae (1995) and Jean Marie Guéhenno (1995), have argued persuasively that the politico-economic functions of the nation-state are being greatly diminished by new information technologies. But this, so boldly put, is to overstate.

To be sure, global changes in the nature of economic activity are provoking a re-examination of cornerstone factors of production, investment and trade. But because of our growing understanding of constructed endowments such as knowledge, the literature dealing with the economics of innovation and growth has allowed us to move beyond the neo-Ricardian notion of land-locked 'comparative advantage' and beyond Porter's variation of market-locked 'competitive advantage' to the point where we can now speak of 'constructed advantages' which are conditioned by bounded rationalities, technological and organizational complexities, and badly behaved dynamics. It allows us to move towards endogenous views of growth in which skills, learning, creativity, entrepreneurship, quality and other knowledge-based intangibles are key. And it allows us to begin to analyse the knowledge-laden content of foreign direct investment (FDI), international technology flows, and so on. Witness the emergence of Singapore, a tiny state geographically but one which attracts a disproportionate world share of FDI and technology-intensive multinational enterprises (MNEs).

As this book has shown in some detail, these broad observations mean that, far from calling for 'the end of geography' or 'the end of the state', locations, regions and complex organizational interactions (between government, business and local community-based organizations) instead matter decisively in a competitive globalizing economy. Moreover, this volume has articulated a series of mechanisms and processes that helps to explain the conditions or pre-conditions of knowledge-based economic success. It has outlined that regional systems of innovation feature a number of architectures for inter-firm relationships, including a requirement for network economics, the presence of web systems, cooperation and trust, as well as a heightened importance of supplier chains.

In terms of knowledge infrastructures, the regional presence of research universities, the capacity to capture the benefits of external sources of knowledge, local spillovers from R&D, and a tendency to focus on new product development are all key. Firms, in such regional clusters, tend to focus on the development of cultures which can promote or foster continuous innovation, and these firms tend to be organically organized – capable of bottom-up decision-taking or subsidiarity.

The financial servicing of regional systems of innovation tends to be informal, adaptive or custom-fit (featuring venture capital, for example), in contrast to the more formal and highly structured arrangements of national financial systems which try to operate to broad global markets through scale and scope (witness, for example, the 1998 mega-merger mania that swept the banking and insurance sectors). Notice, too, the unique importance of community partnerships of all kinds (especially between public and private interests), entrepreneurship (particularly in the realm of start-ups), and the presence of local champions. Together these observations go a long way to explaining the factors of success of regional innovation systems within the context of a globalizing economy.

However, although we have made such progress in understanding, a cluster of questions deserve further attention. For example, why do information and knowledge alight in one place rather than another? At what point or under what conditions is sufficient information accumulated in one place for it to become a 'smart region'? At what point does a smart region become the gravitational fulcrum of an economy?

Such questions are in some ways fundamental, and are of direct interest to policy-makers (who wonder how they can help 'grow' the next Silicon Valley) as well as to economic researchers. Consequently, in considering such research horizons, it is appropriate to wonder how best to approach such questions. Here we might fruitfully follow the lead of James Kenneth Galbraith, who, writing in *The American Prospect*, has noted certain complementarities between economics and cosmology in the work of Keynes and Einstein. In this vein, images or analogies drawn from cosmology might usefully lead to new conceptualizations, new research and new insights into the dynamic between regional innovation, knowledge and global change.

Take this preliminary notion further. We study the origins of the universe as part of the study of the universe as a whole, in much the same way that authors in this book have asked questions about location, innovation and growth as part of a larger project to understand the economy. Cosmology and astrophysics have brought us to consider many different types of celestial objects and many different ways of observing them. All this observational knowledge and all these techniques must be brought to bear on cosmological problems in order that we can understand the most fundamental questions about the universe. Similarly, observational knowledge about regional innovation and globalization raises queries about information, knowledge, learning agglomerations and the attributes of successful (and less successful) locations, almost as if they shared certain attributes with light, particles, gravity, and so on where the questions concern the mechanisms behind how stars form, where they form, under what conditions they emit light, and so on.

Let's follow this lead. If, in cosmology, we ask questions such as 'Is the universe expanding or contracting?' and 'How big is it?', then in the study of regional innovation, knowledge and global change we can ask the economic corollary questions, like 'When the principal economic resource becomes intangible (capital, knowledge, learning, ideas, R&D), then where will value accrue?', 'What attracts information and knowledge?' and 'How far out can the economic spillovers be felt?' This book has approached answers on these important topics. But if we are going to theorize with effect on such core queries, then perhaps it would be fruitful to discard, temporarily, traditional frameworks which prize or privilege the marketplace, prices, cost theories and rational actors in favour of mental maps that focus on spillovers, the mechanisms of scale and scope, and organization.

One starting point through which to begin this closing exploration is to consider the loose parallels between studying processes of globalization, the nature of expanding markets, and the direction of economic change and questions regarding the origins and destiny of our universe. For example, in Armagh, Ireland, in the mid-seventeenth century, Bishop Ussher declared that the physical universe was created at 9 a.m. on Sunday 23 October in the year 4004 BC. Nowadays we are less certain of the details of our origins in time or space. But still, well into the 1960s many cosmologists held that while we did not (or could not) know with precision the date or nature of our beginnings, they could, with confidence, subscribe to a static theory of the universe (Bondi 1960). This view is now under considerable attack, in much the same way that static equilibrium theories of economic growth and change are under review and revision, leading us to economic models of spontaneous order, surprise generating mechanisms and badly behaved dynamics (Nelson and Winter 1982; Mankiew 1997).

A next step can be found in the observation that many of the deepest questions of cosmology, as in economics, can be very simply stated. Take the question 'Why is the sky dark at night?' or, put differently, 'Why is the light in the night sky where it is?' This seems analogous to the economic questions regarding why information, knowledge and exchange activities develop and remain in some locations rather than in others. Analysis of such simple observations has led to profound conclusions about the physical universe. For example, we certainly know that the night sky is basically dark, with light from the stars and planets scattered about against a dark background.

This immediately tells us what we know through observation, namely that there is no even distribution of bright matter in the night sky, just as there is no even distribution of economically prosperous activity across a nation. After all, growth is lumpy and accrues in certain locations rather than in others. What is this process? As this book has discussed in detail, successful regions are able to act as magnets for jobs, capital, skills, competition, ideas, foreign direct investment, and other intangible assets around which institutions form.

But when considering the dark sky, a bit of thought shows that if there was a uniform distribution of stars in space (or if there was a uniform distribution of 'smart regions' driven by knowledge-based innovation and value-added activities), then it would not be dark anywhere in the sky, for if we looked in any direction our eyes would alight upon a star. The fact that this argument does not work and that the sky *is* dark is called Olber's paradox, named after Heinrich Olber, who formulated this problem in 1826.

One solution to Olber's paradox lies, in part, in the existence of the red shift of light – meaning that objects are moving away from us – and thus in the expansion of the universe. This concept can be clearly stated. Imagine a raisin cake that is about to go into the oven. The raisins are spaced a certain distance away from each other. Then, as the cake rises, the raisins spread apart from each other. If we were able to sit on one of the raisins, we would see our neighbouring raisins move away from us at a certain speed. It is important to realize that raisins further away from us would be moving away faster: not only would the distance from us to the neighbouring raisins have increased, but also the additional distance beyond the neighbours to the furthest raisin would have increased.

Thus, in no matter what direction we looked the raisins would be receding from us, with the velocity of recession being proportional to the distance – a relationship established in Hubble's constant. Of course, this does not mean that the answer to the paradox is just that visible light from distant galaxies is red-shifted out of the visible, for at the same time ultraviolet (invisible) light is being red-shifted out of the ultraviolet into the visible. (New economic players come into the picture.) The point is that each quantum of light undergoes a real diminution of energy as it is red-shifted. Thus we do not see the level of brightness emitted at the surface of a faraway star or galaxy because the energy that was emitted has been diminished by this red-shift effect before it reached us. (The energy is local.)

Olber's paradox suggests interesting questions which have derivative logics for the economic study of regional innovation. These will be drawn out further below. But first, it is worthwhile sketching two other sets of cosmological observations which are portentous for our continuing examination of these issues. These, in particular, deal with star formation and black holes.

The processes and mechanisms of star formation are of related economic interest from the perspective of both scholars and local or regional economic development officers. Understanding the mechanisms through which value can be built and attracted is not moot. Stars form out of interstellar gas and dust in galaxies. (This discussion draws on Jastrow (1967) and Avrett (1976).) Economic parallels might be information and ideas. The process of star formation begins with a region of gas and dust of slightly higher density than its surroundings.

If the density is high enough, the gas and the dust begin to contract under the force of gravity. (Here, the corollaries might be the availability of capital and people – not just as consumers but as a social structure through which culture and trust are developed and shared.) As the gas and dust contract, energy is released and it turns out (from a basic theorem) that half of that energy heats the matter. As they are heated, they begin to give out an appreciable amount of radiation. (Ideas are born.) Also, as the temperature rises, the peak of the emitted radiation moves through the infrared spectrum to shorter and shorter infrared wavelengths.

The evolutionary track of this proto-star can be sketched easily, as evidenced by the Hertzsprung–Russell diagram, which plots star temperature along the x-axis and brightness or 'luminosity' in absolute magnitude along the y-axis. In such a way, the full array of star types – from white dwarfs and main-sequence stars (like our sun) to red giants, blue dwarfs and super giants – can be placed. Again, the economic parallel might be with cities or regions: Silicon Valley might be a neutron star, New York City a red giant, Mexico City a super giant of the future, Amsterdam a main-sequence star, and so on. At first, the proto-star brightens, and tracks upward and to the left on the Hertzsprung–Russell diagram.

While this occurs, the centre part of the proto-star continues to contract and the temperature rises. The higher temperature results in a higher pressure, and this acts as a force moving in the outward direction. Eventually a point of stability is reached, where this outward force balances the inward force of gravity for the central region. By this time the gas has vaporized and the dust is opaque, so that the energy emitted from the central core does not escape directly. The outer layers continue to contract. Since the surface area is decreasing, the luminosity decreases and the Hertzsprung–Russell track of the proto-star begins to move downward. Clearly, less massive stars contract in a much more leisurely fashion than more massive ones.

While a fuller discussion of stellar evolution is not needed here, one further relevant key observation on this can be made. As the balancing act of outward and inward forces mediating the nuclear fusion that fuels stars continues, and they swing through their cycles of scale and scope, many stars find their most powerful expression as neutron stars. As fusion continually burns the outer shell of a star, it burns first through the lightest elements such as helium. In the star's most mature phase, these lighter elements are no longer available and the star burns heavier elements, like iron. As iron fills the inner core of a massive star, the temperatures rise to such a level that the iron nuclei begin to break apart into smaller units. The pressure is no longer high enough to counteract gravity and the outer layers collapse. The result is a neutron star, which may only be 20 kilometres in diameter but which contains one or more solar mass! (A Silicon Valley is formed.)

It seems clear from empirical observation that neutron stars and their related pulsars have a maximum mass. The value of this maximum is theoretically calculated to be about 2 solar masses. As the mass continues to contract, radiation is continuously and increasingly red-shifted. Eventually, when the mass has been compressed to a certain size, radiation from the star can no longer escape into space. The star has in effect 'withdrawn' from our observable universe, in that we can no longer receive radiation from it. It has become a black hole. Black holes attract matter, and matter accelerates towards them, in much the same way that information, skills and capital are attracted by smart regions. Spillover effects can be felt directly only within a parameter of roughly 50 miles (80 km) (Anselin, Varga and Acs 1997a).

Outside that region, export economics can be felt but not participated in. Yet the light (cultural and economic influence) can be seen, just as the influence of Paris or New York, London or Hollywood, is felt widely. Some of the light – or economic information and knowledge – will be pulled directly into the black hole, but some will orbit around it and will orbit at a very high velocity, developing a variety of new services, entrepreneurial activities and supplier lines.

In the foregoing brief discussion of Olber's paradox, star formation and black holes, there are indeed many intricate questions that could be posed. But the point of invoking these cosmological analogies is not to pursue these intricacies, or even to suggest direct mechanical parallels. Rather, it is to try to reframe some observations in the hope of permitting some fresh postulations for future work. Surely the dynamic role of information and regional innovation – or 'smart holes' – in the larger, knowledge-intensive environment deserves such attention.

References

Abernathy, W. J. (1978) *The Productivity Dilemma: Roadblock to Innovation in the Automobile Industry*. Baltimore: Johns Hopkins University Press.

Abernathy, W. J. and Utterback, J. M. (1978) Patterns of innovation in technology. *Technology Review*, **80** (7), 40–7.

Abo, T. (ed.) (1994) *Hybrid Factory: The Japanese Production System in the United States*. New York: Oxford University Press.

Acs, Z. J. (1990) High technology networks in Maryland: a case study. *Science and Public Policy*, **17** (5), 315–25.

Acs, Z. J. (1995) Does research create jobs? In J. de la Mothe and G. Paquet (eds), *Technology, Trade and the New Economy*. Ottawa: PRIME, pp. 77–87.

Acs, Z. J. (1996) U.S. clusters of innovation. In J. de la Mothe and G. Paquet (eds), *Evolutionary Economics and the New International Political Economy*. London: Pinter, pp. 183–219.

Acs, Z. and Audretsch, D. (1988) Innovation in large and small firms: an empirical analysis. *American Economic Review*, **78**, 678–90.

Acs, Z. J. and Audretsch, D. B. (1990) *Innovation and Small Firms*. Cambridge, MA: MIT Press.

Acs, Z. and Audretsch, D. (1993a) Analyzing innovation output indicators: the US experience. In A. Kleinknecht and D. Bain (eds), *New Concepts in Innovation Output Measurement*. New York: St Martin's Press.

Acs, Z. J., and Audretsch, D. B. (1993b) Innovation and technological change: the new learning. In G. Libecap (ed.), *Advances in the Study of Entrepreneurship*. Greenwich, CT: JAI Press, pp. 143–76.

Acs, Z., Audretsch, D. and Feldman, M. (1991) Real effects of academic research: comment. *American Economic Review*, **81**, 363–7.

Acs, Z. J., Audretsch, D. B. and Feldman, M. P. (1992) Real effects of academic research. *American Economic Review*, **82** (1), 363–7.

Acs, Z. J., Audretsch, D. B. and Feldman, M. P. (1994a) R&D spillovers and innovative activity. *Managerial and Decision Economics*, **15**, 131–8.

Acs, Z. J., Audretsch, D. B. and Feldman, M. P. (1994b) R&D spillovers and recipient firm size. *Review of Economics and Statistics*, **76**, 336–40.

Acs, Z. J., de la Mothe, J. and Paquet, G. (1996) Local systems of innovation. In P. Howitt (ed.), *Implications of Knowledge-Based Growth for Micro-economic Policies*. Calgary: University of Calgary Press, pp 339–58.

Acs, Z., FitzRoy, F. and Smith, I. (1999) High technology employment wages, and university R&D spillovers: evidence from U.S. cities. *Economics of Innovation and New Technology*, **8**, 57–78.

Acs, Z. J. and Morck, R. (1999) *Small and Medium Sized Enterprises in the Global Economy*. Ann Arbor: University of Michigan Press.

Afuah, A. N. (1996) Strategic choice, capabilities, or environmental determinism: explaining the resurgence of the US semiconductor industry. Working Paper, University of Michigan Business School.

Afuah, A. N. (1998) *Innovation Management: Strategies, Implementation, and Profits*. New York: Oxford University Press.

Afuah, A. N. and Bahram, N. (1995) The hypercube of innovation. *Research Policy*, **24**, 51–76.

Allen, T. (1984) *Managing the Flow of Technology*. Cambridge, MA: MIT Press.

Almeida, P. and Kogut, B. (1995) The geographic localization of ideas and the mobility of patent holders. Paper presented at the Conference on Small and Medium-Sized Enterprises and the Global Economy, organized by CIBER, University of Maryland, 20 October.

Amin, A. and Thrift, N. (1995) Globalization, institutional 'thickness' and the local economy. In P. Healey, S. Camerson, S. Davoudi, S. Graham and A. Madani-Pour (eds), *Managing Cities: The New Urban Context*. Chichester: Wiley, pp. 91–108.

Anderson, P. and Tushman, M. L. (1990) Technological discontinuities and dominant designs: a cyclical model of technological change. *Administrative Sciences Quarterly*, **35** (4), 604–33.

Andrew, C. *et al.* (1993) New local actors: high technology development and the recomposition of social action. In J. Jenson *et al.* (eds), *Production, Space, Identity*. Toronto: Canadian Scholars' Press, pp. 327–46.

Anselin, L., Varga, A. and Acs, Z. (1997a) Entrepreneurship, geographic spillovers and university research: a spatial economic approach. Paper presented at CBR Workshop, Cambridge, March.

Anselin, L., Varga, A. and Acs, Z. J. (1997b) Local geographic spillovers between university research and high technology innovations. *Journal of Urban Economics*, **42**, 422–48.

Antonelli, C. (1988) The emergence of the network firm. In C. Antonelli (ed.), *New Information Technology and Industrial Change: The Italian Case*. Dordrecht: Kluwer, pp. 13–32.

Antonelli, C. (ed.) (1992) *The Economics of Information Networks*. Amsterdam: North-Holland.

Antonelli, C. (1995) *The Economics of Localized Technological Change and Industrial Dynamics*. Dordrecht: Kluwer Academic Publishers.

Aoki, M. (1987) The Japanese firm in transition. In K. Yamamura and Y. Yasuba (eds), *The Political Economy of Japan*, vol 1. Stanford: Stanford University Press.

Aoki, M. (1990) Frontiers in corporate globalization. *Japan Echo*, **17**, 26–32.

Aoki, M. (1994) The Japanese firm as a system of attributes: a survey and research agenda. In M. Aoki and R. Dore (eds), *The Japanese Firm: The Sources of Competitive Strength*. Oxford: Oxford University Press, pp. 11–40.

Arcangeli, F. (1993) Local and global features of the learning process. In M. Humbert (ed.), *The Impact of Globalization on Europe's Firms and Industries*. London: Pinter, pp. 34–41.

Archibugi, D. and Michie, J. (1995) The globalization of technology: a new taxonomy. *Cambridge Journal of Economics*, **19**, 121–40.

Archibugi, D. and Pianta, M. (1992) *The Technological Specialization of Advanced Countries*. London: Kluwer.

Arthur, B. (1989) Competing technologies, increasing returns and lock-in by historical events. *Economic Journal*, **99**, 116–31.

Arthur, B. (1990) Positive feedbacks in the economy. *Scientific American*, **262** (2), 92–9.

Arthur, W. B. (1990) 'Silicon Valley' locational clusters: when do increasing returns imply monopoly? *Mathematical Social Sciences*, **19**, 235–51.

Association of University Technology Managers (1995) *AUTM Licensing Survey. Fiscal Year 1991–Fiscal Year 1994.* AUTM.

Audretsch, D. B. (1995) *Innovation and Industry Evolution*. Cambridge, MA: MIT Press.

Audretsch, D. and Feldman, M. (1996) R&D spillovers and the geography of innovation and production. *American Economic Review*, **86**, 630–40.

Avictt, E. (ed.) (1976) *Frontiers in Astrophysics*. Cambridge, MA: Harvard University Press.

Backhaus, A. and Seidel, O. (1997) *Innovationen und Kooperationsbeziehungen von Industriebetrieben, Forschungseinrichtungen und unternehmensnahen Dienstleistern: Die Region Hannover–Braunschweig–Göttingen im interregionalen Vergleich Effekt* (Innovations and cooperative relationships between manufacturing firms, research institutions and business services: the region of Hanover–Brunswick–Göttingen in an international comparison). Hannoversche Geographische Arbeitsmaterialen 19. Hanover: Geographisches Institut Universität Hannover.

Bahrami, H. and Evans, S. (1995) Flexible re-cycling and high-technology entrepreneurship. *California Management Review*, **37** (3), 62–89.

Bania, N., Calkins, L. and Dalenberg, R. (1992) The effects of regional science and technology policy on the geographic distribution of industrial R&D laboratories. *Journal of Regional Science*, **32**, 209–28.

Beam, A. and Frons, M. (1995) How Tom Vanderslice is forcing Apollo Computer to grow up. *Business Week*, 25 March, pp. 96–8.

Bean, A., Schiffel, D. and Mogee, M. (1975) The venture capital market and technological innovation. *Research Policy*, **4**, 380–408.

Begg, I. and Mayes, D. (1993a) Cohesion, convergence and economic and monetary union. *Regional Studies*, **27**, 29–38.

Begg, I. and Mayes, D. (1993b) Regional restructuring: the case of decentralised industrial policy. Regional Science Association, Nottingham (mimeo).

Beise, M. and Spielkamp, A. (1996) *Technologietransfer von Hochschulen: Ein Insider–Outsider-Effekt* (Technology transfer of universities: an insider–outsider effect) Discussion Paper 96–10. Mannheim: Zentrum für Europäische Wirtschaftsforschung.

Bell, A. and Corliss, E. (1989). Apollo falls to the west. *Mass High Tech*, **1** (9), 24 April.

Bell, M. and Pavitt, K. (1993) Technological accumulation and industrial growth: contrasts between developed and developing countries. *Industrial and Corporate Change*, **2**, 157–210.

Belussi, F. (1996) Local systems, industrial districts and institutional networks: towards a new evolutionary paradigm of industrial economics? *European Planning Studies*, **4**, 5–26.

Benko, G. and Lipietz, A. (eds) (1992) *Les régions qui gagnent*. Paris: Presses Universitaires de France.

Bernstein, J. I. (1986) Issues in the determinants and returns to R&D capital in Canada, mimeo, February.

Best, M. (1990) *The New Competition*. Cambridge, MA: Harvard University Press.

Bianchi, P. and Bellini, N. (1991) Public policies for local networks of innovators. *Research Policy*, **20** (5), 487–97.

BMBF (ed.) (1996) *Bundesbericht Forschung 1996* (Federal research report 1996). Bonn: Bundesminister für Bildung, Wissenschaft, Forschung und Technologie.

BMBF (ed.) (1997) *Zur technologischen Leistungsfähigkeit Deutschlands* (Germany's technological performance). Bonn: Bundesminister für Bildung, Wissenschaft, Forschung und Technologie.

BMBF (ed.) (1998) *Faktenbericht 1998* (Federal research report 1998). Bonn: Bundesminister für Bildung, Wissenschaft, Forschung und Technologie.

Boddy, M. and Lovering, J. (1986) High technology in the Bristol sunbelt-region: the aerospace/defence nexus. *Regional Studies*, **20**, 217–31.

Bonaccorsi, A. and Piccaluga, A. (1994) A theoretical framework for the evaluation of university–industry relationships. *R&D Management*, **24** (3), 229–47.

Bondi, H. (1960) The steady state theory of the universe. In H. Bondi, W. B. Bonnor, R. A. Littleton and G. J. Whitrow, *Rival Theories of Cosmology*, London: Oxford University Press.

Borrus, M. (1988) *Competing for Control: America's Stake in Microelectronics*. Cambridge, MA: Ballinger.

Boschma, R. (1997) National innovation systems and technology policy in Western Europe: the experience of Great Britain, France, Germany and the Netherlands. Paper presented at Regional Science Association 37th European Congress, 26–29 August, Rome.

Boulding, K. E. (1970) *A Primer on Social Dynamics*. New York: Free Press.

Bowonder, B. and Miyake, T. (1993) Japanese innovations in advanced technologies: an analysis of functional integration. *International Journal of Technology Management*, **8**, 135–56.

Bowonder, B., Miyake, T. and Linstone, H. A. (1994a) The Japanese institutional mechanisms for industrial growth: a systems perspective – Part I. *Technological Forecasting and Social Change*, **47**, 229–54.

Bowonder, B., Miyake, T. and Linstone, H. A. (1994b) The Japanese institutional mechanisms for industrial growth: a systems perspective – Part II. *Technological Forecasting and Social Change*, **47**, 309–44.

Boyer, R. (1995) Training and employment in the new production models. *STI Review*, **15**, 105–31.

Braczyk, H.-J., Cooke, P. and Heidenreich, M. (eds) (1997) *Regional Innovation Systems: The Role of Governances in a Globalized Economy*. London: UCL Press.

Bradford, C. I., Jr (1994) The new paradigm of systemic competitiveness: why it matters, what it means and implications for policy. In C. I. Bradford, Jr (ed.), *The New Paradigm of Systemic Competitiveness: Toward More Integrated Policies in Latin America*. Paris: Organisation for Economic Co-operation and Development, pp. 41–65.

Branscomb, L. M. (1993) National laboratories: the search for new missions and structures. In L. M. Branscomb (ed.), *Empowering Technology: Implementing a U.S. Strategy*. Cambridge, MA: MIT Press.

Branscomb, L. M. and Kodama, F. (1993) Technology strategies of Japanese high-tech companies. In R. S. Cutler (ed.), *Technology Management in Japan*. Boulder: Westview Press, pp. 11–29.

Braun, E. and MacDonald, S. (1982) *Revolution in Miniature: The History and Impact of Semiconductor Electronics*, 2nd edn. New York: Cambridge University Press.

Breheny, M. and McQuaid, R. (eds) (1987) *The Development of High Technology Industries*. London: Croom Helm.

Brett, A., Gibson, D. and Smilor, R. (1991) *University Spin-Off Companies*. Savage, MD: Rowman & Littlefield.

Brezinski, H. and Fritsch, M. (1995) Transformation: the shocking German way. *Moct-Most* 5, 1–25.

Brodsky, N., Kaufman, H. and Tooker, J. (1980) *University/Industry Cooperation: A Preliminary Analysis of Existing Mechanisms and Their Relationship to the Innovation Processes*. New York: Center for Science and Technology Policy, Graduate School of Public Administration, New York University.

Brösse, U. (1996) *Industriepolitik* (Industrial policy). Munich: Oldenbourg.

Brzezinski, Z. (1997) *The Grand Chessboard: American Primacy and Its Geo-strategic Imperative.* New York: Basic Books.

Bulkeley, W. M. (1987) Culture shock: two computer firms with clashing styles fight for market niche. *Wall Street Journal,* 6 July, p. A1.

Burgelman, R. A. (1994) Fading memories: the process theory of strategic business exit in dynamic environments. *Administrative Sciences Quarterly,* **39**, 24–56.

Butchart, R. L. (1987) A new UK definition of the high technology industries. *Economic Trends* 400 (February), 82–8.

Bygrave, W. and Timmons, J. (1985) An empirical model of the flows of venture capital, In J. Hornady, E. B. Shils, J. A. Timmons and K. H. Vesper (eds), *Frontiers of Entrepreneurial Research.* Wellesley, MA: Center for Entrepreneurial Research, Babson College.

Bylinsky, G. (1967) General Doriot's dream factory. *Fortune,* August, p. 132.

Callon, S. (1995) *Divided Sun: MITI and the Breakdown of Japanese High-Tech Industrial Policy, 1975–1993.* Stanford: Stanford University Press.

Camagni, R. and Rabellotti, R. (1992) Technology and organization in the Italian textile–clothing industry. *Entrepreneurship and Regional Development,* **4**, 271–85.

Case, D. (1986) An overview of venture capital. Unpublished paper, Hambrecht & Quist, San Francisco.

Castells, M. (1989) *The Informational City: Information Technology, Economic Restructuring, and Urban-Regional Process.* Oxford: Blackwell.

Castells, M. and Hall, P. (1994) *Technopoles of the World.* London: Routledge.

Cerny, K. (1996) Making local knowledge global. *Harvard Business Review,* **74** (3), 22–38.

Chandler, A. D. (1977) *The Visible Hand: The Managerial Revolution in American Business.* Cambridge, MA: Belknap.

Chandler, A. (1990) *Scale and Scope: The Dynamics of Industrial Capitalism.* Cambridge, MA: Belknap.

Chang, H.-J. and Kozul-Wright, R. (1994) Organising development: comparing the national systems of entrepreneurship in Sweden and South Korea. *Journal of Development Studies,* **30**, 859–91.

Charles, D. and Howells, J. (1992) *Technology Transfer in Europe Public and Private Networks.* New York: St Martin's Press.

Charles River Associates (1976) *An Analysis of Capital Market Imperfection.* Cambridge, MA: Charles River Associates.

Chesnais, F. (1991) Technological competitiveness considered as a form of structural competitiveness. In J. Niosi (ed.), *Technology and National Competitiveness.* Montreal: McGill-Queen's University Press, pp. 142–76.

Christie, C. M. (1985) Venture capitalist as private detective. *New England Business,* 18 March.

Ciborra, C. U. (1992) Innovation, networks and organisational learning. In C. Antonelli (ed.), *The Economics of Information Networks.* Amsterdam: North-Holland, pp. 91–102.

Clark, K. B. (1985) The interaction of design hierarchies and market concepts in technological evolution. *Research Policy,* **14**, 235–51.

Clark, K. B. (1989a) Project scope and project performance: the effects of parts strategy and supplier involvement on product development. *Management Science,* **35** (10), 1247–63.

Clark, K. (1989b) High performance product development in the world auto industry. Harvard Business School Working Paper, 90–004.

Clark, K. B. and Fujimoto, T. (1991) *Product Development Performance: Strategy, Organization, and Management in the World Automobile Industry.* Boston: Harvard Business School Press.

Clark, N. (1985) *The Political Economy of Science and Technology.* Oxford: Blackwell.

Coleman, J. S. (1988) Social capital and the creation of human capital. *American Journal of Sociology*, **94**, Supplement, 95–120.

Comerford, R. (1992). How DEC developed Alpha. *IEEE Spectrum*, July, pp. 26–31.

Committee of Vice-Chancellors and Principals (1986) The future of the universities. CVCP, 29 Tavistock Square, London WC1H 9EZ, January.

Company Reporting (1994) *The 1994 UK R&D Scoreboard*. Edinburgh: Company Reporting.

Cooke, P., Boekholt, P. and Tödtling, F. (1999) *The Governance of Innovation in Europe: Regional Perspectives on Global Competitiveness*. London: Pinter.

Cooke, P. and Morgan, K. (1993) The network paradigm: new departures in corporate and regional development. *Environment and Planning D: Society and Space*, **11**, 543–64.

Cooke, P. and Morgan, K. (1994a) The creative milieu: a regional perspective on innovation. In M. Dodgson and R. Rothwell (eds), *The Handbook of Industrial Innovation*. Aldershot: Edward Elgar, pp. 25–32.

Cooke, P. and Morgan, K. (1994b) Growth regions under duress: renewal strategies in Baden-Wurtemberg and Emilia-Romagna. In A. Amin and N. Thrift (eds), *Globalization, Institutions and Regional Development in Europe*. Oxford: Oxford University Press, pp. 91–117.

Cooke, P. and Morgan, K. (1998) *The Associational Economy*. Oxford: Oxford University Press.

Cooper, R. (1994) *Cost Down: Lessons in Japanese Cost Management*. Cambridge, MA: Harvard Business School Press.

CorpTech (1993) *Technology Company Information: Regional Disks*. Woburn, MA: Corporate Technology Information Services.

Dahlman, C. (1994) New elements of international competitiveness: implications for developing economies. In C. I. Bradford, Jr (ed.), *The New Paradigm of Systemic Competitiveness: Toward More Integrated Policies in Latin America*. Paris: Organisation for Economic Co-operation and Development.

Dahmen, E. (1988) Development blocks in industrial economics. *Scandinavian Economic History Review*, **36**, 3–14.

Dalum, B. (1995) Local and global linkages: the radio communications cluster in northern Denmark. Department of Business Studies, University of Aalborg (mimeo).

David, P. A. (1985) Clio and the economics of QWERTY. *American Economic Review*, **75** (2), 332–6.

David, P. A. (1992) Information network economics. In C. Antonelli (ed.), *The Economics of Information Networks*. Amsterdam: North-Holland, pp. 103–5.

David, P. and Foray, D. (1994) Accessing and expanding the science and technology knowledge base. Paris: OECD Working Group on Innovation and Technology Policy.

David, P., Mowery, D. C. and Steinmeuller, W. E. (1994) University–industry research collaborations: managing missions in conflict. Paper presented at the CEPR/AAAS conference 'University Goals, Institutional Mechanisms, and the "Industrial Transferability" of Research', Stanford, CA, 18–20 March.

Davidow, W. H. and Malone, M. S. (1992) *The Virtual Corporation*. New York: Harper.

Davis, C. H. (1991a) *Local Initiatives to Promote Technological Innovation in Canada: Eight Case Studies*. Ottawa: Science Council of Canada.

Davis, C. (1991b) *Metropolitan Science Councils*. Ottawa: Science Council of Canada.

DeBresson, C. and Amesse, F. (1991) Networks of innovators: a review and introduction to the issue. *Research Policy*, **20** (5), 363–79.

DeBresson, C. and Walker, R. (eds) (1991) Special issue on networks of innovators. *Research Policy*, 20 (5).

de Castro, N., Hawkins, J., Stevens, L. and Constantino, I. (1996) *Regional Innovation Systems Profile of the Portuguese Centro Region*. TSER-REGIS Working Paper, Aveiro.

de Geus, A. (1997) *The Living Company*. Boston: Harvard Business School Press.

de la Mothe, J. (1992) The revision of international science indicators: the Frascati manual. *Technology in Society*, **14**, 401–6.

de la Mothe, J. and Paquet, G. (1994a) The dispersive revolution. *Optimum*, **25**(1), 42–8.

de la Mothe, J. and Paquet, G. (1994b) The technology–trade nexus: liberalization, warning blocs, or negotiated access? *Technology in Society*, **16** (1), 97–118.

de la Mothe, J. and Paquet, G. (1994c) The shock of the new: a techno-economic paradigm for small economies. In M. Stevenson (ed.), *The Entry into New Economic Communities: Swedish and Canadian Perspectives on the European Economic Community and North American Free Trade Accord*. Toronto: Swedish–Canadian Academic Foundation, pp. 13–27.

de la Mothe, J. and Paquet, G. (1994d) Circumstantial evidence: a note on science policy in Canada. *Science and Public Policy*, **21** (4), 261–8.

de la Mothe, J. and Paquet, G. (eds) (1996a) *Evolutionary Economics and the New International Political Economy*. London: Pinter.

de la Mothe, J. and Paquet, G. (eds) (1996b) *Corporate Governance and the New Competition: The Second PRIME Lectures*. Ottawa: PRIME.

de la Mothe, J. and Paquet, G. (1998) Finance and the technology–trade nexus. *Technology in Society*, **20** (5).

de la Torre, A. and Kelly, M. (1992) *Regional Trade Arrangements*. Washington, DC: International Monetary Fund.

Dodgson, M. (1996) Learning, trust and inter-firm technological linkages: some theoretical associations. In R. Coombs, A. Richards, P. P. Saviotti and V. Walsh (eds) *Technological Collaboration*. Cheltenham: Edward Elgar, pp. 54–75.

Doerflinger, T. M. and Rivkin, J. L. (1987) *Risk and Reward*. New York: Random House.

Doeringer, P. B. (1994) Can the US system of workplace training survive global competition? In S. Asefa and W.-C. Huang (eds), *Human Capital and Economic Development*. Kalamazoo, MI: W. E. Upjohn Institute for Employment Research, pp. 91–107.

Dore, R. (1987) *Taking Japan Seriously*. London: Athlone.

Dorfman, N. (1983) Route 128: the development of a regional high technology economy. *Research Policy*, **12**, 299–316.

Dorgan, M. (1997) Eye on Asia: is what's good for Silicon Valley good for America? *San Jose Mercury News*, 8 July.

Dosi, G. (1988) Sources, procedures and microeconomic effects of innovation. *Journal of Economic Literature*, **26**, 1120–71.

Dosi, G. and Nelson, R. R. (1994) An introduction to evolutionary theories in economics? *Journal of Evolutionary Economics*; **4** (3), 153–72.

Dosi, G., Freeman, C., Nelson, R., Silverberg, G. and Soete, L. (eds) (1988) *Technical Change and Economic Theory*. London: Pinter.

Drucker, P. (1993) *Post-capitalist Society*. New York: Harper Business.

Dunning, J. (1993) *Multinational Enterprises and the Global Economy*. London: Pinter.

Dunning, J. (1995) The role of foreign direct investment in a globalizing economy. *Banco Nationale del Lavoro Quarterly Review*, **193**, 125–44.

Dyer, J. (1993) The Japanese vertical keiretsu as a source of competitive advantage. Paper presented to the Vancouver Network Conference.

The Economist (1994) Welcome to Cascadia, 21 May, p. 52.

Edgington, D. W. (1993) The globalization of Japanese manufacturing corporations. *Growth and Change*, **24**, 87–106.

Edquist, C. (ed.) (1997) *Systems of Innovation: Technologies, Institutions and Organizations*. London: Pinter.

Electronic Business (1992) The Top 100 Exporters. *Electronic Business*, 16 March, pp. 4–42.

Emmott, B. (1993) *Japanophobia: The Myth of the Invincible Japanese*. New York: Times Books.

Ergas, H. (1987) Does technology policy matter? In B. R. Guile and H. Brooks (eds), *Technology and Global Industry: Companies and Nations in the World Economy*. Washington, DC: National Academy Press, pp. 191–245.

Estimé, M.-F., Drilhon, G. and Julien, P.-A. (1993) *Small and Medium-Sized Enterprises: Technology and Competitiveness*. Paris: Organisation for Economic Co-operation and Development.

Etzkowitz, H. (1989) Entrepreneurial science in the academy: a case of transformation of norms. *Social Problems*, **36** (1), 14–27.

Evans, P. B. (1995) *Embedded Autonomy: States and Industrial Transformation*. Princeton: Princeton University Press.

Evans, P. B. and Wurster, T. S. (1997) Strategy and the new economics of information. *Harvard Business Review*, **75** (5), 71–82.

Ewers, H. J. and Wettmann, R. W. (1980) Innovation-oriented regional policy. *Regional Studies*, **14**, 161–79.

Fajnzylber, F. (1990) *Unavoidable Industrial Restructuring in Latin America*. Durham, NC: Duke University Press.

Faulkner, W. and Senker, J. (1995) *Knowledge Frontiers: Public Sector Research and Industrial Innovation in Biotechnology, Engineering Ceramics, and Parallel Computing*. Oxford: Clarendon Press.

Feldman, M. (1994a) *The Geography of Innovation*. Boston: Kluver Academic.

Feldman, M. (1994b) The university and economic development: the case of Johns Hopkins University and Baltimore. *Economic Development Quarterly*, **8**, 67–76.

Feldman, M. and Florida, R. (1994) The geographic sources of innovation: technological infrastructure and product innovation in the United States. *Annals of the Association of American Geographers*, **84**, 210–29.

Feller, I. (1990) Universities as engines of R&D based economic growth: they think they can. *Research Policy*, **19**.

Ferguson, C. H. (1988) From the people who brought you voodoo economics. *Harvard Business Review*, **89**, 55–62.

Florida, R. (1995) Towards the learning region. *Futures*, **27**, 527–36.

Florida, R. and Kenney, M. (1990) Silicon Valley and Route 128 won't save us. *California Management Review*, **33** (1), 68–88.

Florida, R., Kenney, M. and Smith, D. (1990) *Venture Capital, Innovation and Economic Development*. Report to the Department of Commerce, Economic Development Administration, Washington, DC.

Foley, P. and Watts, D. (1996) Production site R&D in a mature region. *Tijdschrift voor Economische en Sociale Geografie*, **87** (2), 136–45.

Foray, D. and Freeman, C. (eds) (1993) *Technology and the Wealth of Nations*. London: Pinter.

Fosler, R. (ed.) (1988) *The New Economic Role of American States*. New York: Oxford University Press.

Fraunhofer-Institut für Systemtechnik und Innovationsforschung (ISI) (1997) *Technologische Position Deutschlands im internationalen Wettbewerb: Beitrag im Rahmen der gemeinsamen Berichterstattung 1996 zur technologischen Leistungsfähigkeit Deutschlands* (Technological position of Germany in international competition: contribution in the context of mutual reporting for 1996 on Germany's technological performance). Karlsruhe: ISI.

Freeman, C. (1982) *The Economics of Industrial Innovation*. Cambridge, MA: MIT Press.

Freeman, C. (1988) Japan: a new national system of innovation. In G. Dosi, C. Freeman, R. Nelson, G. Silverberg and L. Soete (eds), *Technical Change and Economic Theory*. London: Pinter.

Freeman, C. (1993) ???

Freeman, C. (1994) The economics of technical change. *Cambridge Journal of Economics*, **18**, 463–514.

Freeman, C. (1996) Why growth rates differ: the case of Latin America and Asia. In J. de la Mothe and G. Paquet (eds), *Evolutionary Economics and the New International Political Economy*. London: Pinter, pp. 160–79.

Freeman, C., Clark, J. and Soete, L. (1982) *Unemployment and Technical Innovation*. London: Pinter.

Friedman, D. (1988) *The Misunderstood Miracle: Industrial Development and Political Change in Japan*. Ithaca, NY: Cornell University Press.

Fruin, M. (1992) *The Japanese Enterprise System*. Oxford: Oxford University Press.

Fruin, M. (1993) The visible hand and invisible assets: network organization and supplier relations in the electronics industry in Japan. Paper presented to the Vancouver Network Conference.

Fujita, K. and Hill, R. C. (1995) Global Toyotaism and local development. *International Journal of Urban and Regional Research*, **19**, 7–22.

Garud, R. and Kumaraswamy, A. (1993) Changing competitive dynamics in network industries: an exploration of Sun Microsystems' open systems strategy. *Strategic Management Journal*, **14**, 351–69.

Gehrke, B. and Schasse, U. (1993) *Automobilbezogene Forschungskapazitäten un Universitäten, Fachhochschulen und außeruniversitären Forschungseinrichtungen in der Region Hannover–Hildesheim–Braunschweig (ohne betriebliche FuE)* (Car-related research capacities at universities, technical colleges and non-university research institutions in the Hanover–Hildesheim–Brunswick region). Hanover: Niedersächsisches Institut für Wirtschaftsforschung.

Gerlach, K. and Wagner, J. (1994) Regional differences in small firm entry in manufacturing industries: Lower Saxony 1979–1991. *Entrepreneurship and Regional Development*, **6**, 63–80.

Geroski, P. (1995) Markets for technology: knowledge, innovation and appropriability. In P. Stoneman (ed.), *Handbook of Economics of Innovation and Technological Change*. Oxford: Blackwell.

Gerschenkron, A. (1962) *Economic Development in Historical Perspectives*. Cambridge, MA: Harvard University Press.

Gibbons, M. (1995) *The New Production of Knowledge*. London: Sage.

Gilpin, R. (1989) *The Political Economy of International Relations*. Princeton: Princeton University Press.

Gilpin, R. (1992) The new world political and economic order. Paper presented at the Foro Nacional, International Conference on the New International Order, Rio de Janeiro, 13–14 April.

Golden, J. R. (1996) Economics and national strategy: convergence, global networks, and cooperative competition. In B. Roberts (ed.), *New Forces in the World Economy*. Cambridge, MA: MIT Press, pp. 102–36.

Gomes-Casseres, B. (1996) *The Alliance Revolution*. Cambridge, MA: Harvard University Press.

Gort, M. and Klepper, S. (1982) Time paths in the theory of product innovations. *Economic Journal*, **92**, 630–52.

Grabher, G. (ed.) (1993) *The Embedded Firm: On the Socio-economics of Industrial Networks*. London: Routledge.

Grandinetti, R. and Schenkel, M. (1996) The economic development of Friuli-Venezia Giulia. REGIS Working Paper, Cardiff.

Granovetter, M. (1985) Economic action and social structure: the problem of 'embedded-ness'. *American Journal of Sociology*, **91** (3), 481–510.

Greene, T. (1990) Can HP find the right direction for the '90s? *Electronic Business*, 22 January, pp. 26–9.

Griliches, Z. (1990) Patent statistics as economic indicators: a survey. *Journal of Economic Literature*, **28**, 1661–707.

Groenewegen, J. (1993) The Japanese group. In J. Groenewegen (ed.), *Dynamics of the Firm: Strategies of Pricing and Organisation*. Aldershot: Edward Elgar, pp. 96–113.

Grotz, R. and Braun, B. (1997) Spatial aspects of technology-oriented co-operation: examples from the German mechanical engineering industry. *Regional Studies*, **31**, 545–57.

Guéhenno, J.-M. (1995) *The End of the Nation State*. Minneapolis, University of Minnesota Press.

Guerrieri, P. (1994) International competitiveness, trade integration and technological inter-dependence. In C. I. Bradford, Jr (ed.), *The New Paradigm of Systemic Competitiveness: Toward More Integrated Policies in Latin America*. Paris: Organisation for Economic Co-operation and Development.

Gustavsson, P., Melin, L. and Macdonald, S. (1994) Learning to globalize. In P. Shrivastana, A. S. Huff and J. E. Dutton (eds), *Advances in Strategic Management*, vol. 10B: *Interorganizational Relations and International Strategies*. Greenwich, CT: JAI Press, pp. 255–88.

Haggard, S. (1996) The political economy of regionalisation in Asia and the Americas. In V. R. Whiting, Jr (ed.), *Regionalisation in the World Economy: NAFTA, the Americas and Asia Pacific*. New Delhi: Macmillan India.

Hall, P. and Markusen A. (1985) *Silicon Landscapes*. Boston: Allen & Unwin.

Handy, C. (1992) Balancing corporate power: a new federalist paper. *Harvard Business Review*, **70** (6), 59–72.

Handy, C. (1994) *The Age of Paradox*. Boston: Harvard Business School Press.

Harryson, S. J. (1997) How Canon and Sony drive product innovation through networking and application-focussed R&D. *Journal of Product Innovation Management*, **14**, 288–95.

Harvey, D. (1988) Urban places in the global village: reflections on the urban condition in the late 20th century. In L. Mazza (ed.), *World Cities and the Future of the Metropolis*. Milan: Electra.

Hedlund, G. (1986) The hypermodern MNC – a heterarchy? *Human Resource Management*, **25** (1), 9–35.

Helper, S. (1987) Supplier relations and technical change: theory and application to the US automobile industry. Unpublished doctoral dissertation, Harvard University.

Henderson, R. and Clark, K. B. (1990) Architectural innovation: the reconfiguration of existing product technologies and the failure of established firms. *Administrative Sciences Quarterly*, **35**, 9–30.

Herrigel, G. (1993) Large firms, small firms, and the governance of flexible specialization: the case of Baden-Württemberg and socialized risk. In B. Kogut (ed.), *Country Competitiveness: Technology and the Organizing of Work*. New York: Oxford University Press, pp. 15–35.

Hicks, D., Ishizuka, T., Keen, P. and Sweet, S. (1994) Japanese corporations, scientific research and globalization. *Research Policy*, **23**, 375–84.

Higgins, T. (1993) Promoting innovation and development in Europe's weaker regions: the achievements and lessons of recent investment programmes for research and technology development. Paper presented at the International Workshop of Regional Science and Technology Policy Research titled 'Regional of Science and Technology Resources in the Context of Globalization', 13–16 June, Tokyo.

Hill, R. C. and Lee, J. (1994) Japanese multinationals and East Asian development: the case of the automobile industry. In L. Sklair (ed.), *Capitalism and Development*. London: Routledge, pp. 289–313.

Hilpert, U. (ed.) (1991) *Regional Innovation and Decentralisation: High Tech Industry and Government Policy*. London: Routledge, ch. 1.

Hilpert, U. and Ruffieux, B. (1991) Innovation, politics and regional development: technology parks and regional participation in high tech in France and West Germany. In U. Hilpert (ed.), *Regional Innovation and Decentralisation: High Tech Industry and Government Policy*. London: Routledge, pp. 61–88.

Hirst, P. and Thompson, P. (1996) *The Globalization Question*. Cambridge: Polity.

Hoffmann, S. (1995) Review of *The European Sisyphus: Essays on Europe 1964–1994*. *Foreign Affairs*, **74** (4), 143.

Hollingsworth, R. (1993) Variation among nations in the logic of manufacturing sectors and international competitiveness. In D. Foray and C. Freeman (eds), *Technology and the Wealth of Nations*, London: Pinter, pp. 301–21.

Hood, N., Young, S. and Lal, D. (1994) Strategic evolution within Japanese manufacturing plants in Europe: UK evidence. *International Business Review*, **3**, 97–122.

Howells, J. and Wood, M. (1993) *The Globalization of Production and Technology*. London: Pinter.

Hudson, R. (1994) New production concepts, new production geographies? Reflections on changes in the automobile industry. *Transactions of the Institute of British Geographers*, NS **19**, 331–45.

Imai, K. (1989) Evolution of Japan's corporate and industrial networks. In B. Carlsson (ed.), *Industrial Dynamics*. Boston: Kluwer.

Imai, K. (1994) Enterprise groups. In K. Imai and R. Komiya (eds), *Business Enterprise in Japan*. Cambridge, MA: MIT Press, pp. 117–40.

Integrated Circuit Engineering (1995) *Status 1995: A Report on the Integrated Circuit Industry*. Scottsdale, AZ: ICE.

Inter-American Development Bank (IDB) and Economic Commission for Latin America and the Caribbean (ECLAC) (eds) (1995) *Trade Liberalization in the Western Hemisphere*. Washington, DC.

Isaksen, A. (1997) Regional clusters and competitiveness: the Norwegian case. *European Planning Studies*, **5**, 65–76.

Isserman, A. (1994) State economic development policy and practice in the United States: a survey article. *International Regional Science Review*, **16**, 49–100.

Ito, M. (1994) Interfirm relations and long-term continuous trading. In K. Imai and R. Komiya (eds), *Business Enterprise in Japan*. Cambridge, MA: MIT Press, pp. 105–15.

Jaffe, A. B. (1989) 'Real effects of academic research. *American Economic Review*, **79**, 957–70.

Jastrow, R. (1967) *Red Giants and White Dwarfs*. New York: Harper & Row.

Johnson, L. (1984) *The High-Technology Connection: Academic/Industrial Cooperation for Economic Growth*. ASHE-Eric Higher Education Research Report, no. 6. Washington, DC: Clearinghouse on Higher Education, George Washington University.

Jordan, S. (1995) Industrial change, labour mobility and regional economic development: the case of high technology industry in Oxfordshire. Dissertation, Honours School of Geography, Oxford University.

Judak, J. *et al.* (1988) *Venture*, June, pp. 36–42.

Katz, M. L. and Shapiro, C. (1985) Network externalities, competition and compatibility. *American Economic Review*, **75** (3), 424–40.

Keck, O. (1993) The national system for technical innovation in Germany. In R. R. Nelson (ed.), *National Innovation Systems: A Comparative Study*. New York: Oxford University Press, pp. 115–57.

Keeble, D. B., Moore, F., Wilkinson, C. and Smith, H. L. (1996) *Territorial Development and Innovative Milieu*. ESRC Centre for Business Research, Cambridge University.

Kelly, K. (1994) *Out of Control*. Reading, MA: Addison-Wesley.

Kelly, K., Weber, J., Friend, J., Atchison, S., DeGeorge, G. and Holstein, W. (1992) Hot spots: America's new growth regions are blossoming despite the slump. *Business Week*, **19** (October), 80–8.

Kenney, M. and Florida, R. (1993) *Beyond Mass Production: The Japanese System and Its Transfer to the U.S.* New York: Oxford University Press.

Khazam, J. and Mowery, D. (1994) Commercialization of RISC: strategies for the creating of dominant designs. *Research Policy*, **23**, 89–102.

Kindleberger, C. and Audretsch, D. B. (1983) *The Multinational Corporation in the 1980s*. Cambridge, MA: MIT Press.

Kirchoff, B. and McAuliffe, R. (1988) Economic redevelopment of mature industrial areas. Report prepared for Technical Assistance and Research Division, Economic Development Administration, US Department of Commerce.

Kirzner, I. M. (1997) Entrepreneurial discovery and the competitive market process: an Austrian approach. *Journal of Economics Literature*, **35** (1), 60–85.

Klepper, S. and Graddy, E. (1990) The evolution of new industries and the determinants of market structures. *RAND Journal of Economics*, **2**, 27–42.

Klepper, S. and Simons, K. L. (1993) Technological change and industry shakeouts. Unpublished manuscript, Department of Social and Decision Sciences, Carnegie-Mellon University.

Kline, S. J. and Rosenberg, N. (1986) An overview of innovation. In R. Landau and N. Rosenberg (eds) *The Positive Sum Strategy*. Washington, DC: National Academy Press, pp. 275–305.

Kodama, F. (1995) *Emerging Patterns of Innovation*. Boston: Harvard Business School Press.

Koestler, A. (1970) *The Ghost in the Machine*. London: Pan.

Krugman, P. (1991) *Geography and Trade*. Cambridge, MA: MIT Press.

Krugman, P. (1995) *Development, Geography and Economic Theory*. London: MIT Press.

Kumon, S. (1992) Japan as a network society. In S. Kumon and H. Rosovsky (eds), *The Political Economy of Japan*, vol. 3. Stanford: Stanford University Press, pp. 109–41.

Lall, S. (1994) The East Asian miracle: does the bell toll for industrial strategy? *World Development*, **22**, 645–54.

Langlois, R. N. (1992) External economies and economic progress: the case of the microcomputer industry. *Business History Review*, **66**, 1–50.

Lawson, C., Moore, B., Keeble, D., Lawton Smith, H. and Wilkinson, F. (1997) Inter-firm links between regionally clustered high-technology SME firms. ESRC Centre for Business Research, Cambridge, May.

Lawton Smith, H. (1990) The location and development of advanced technology industry in Oxfordshire in the context of the research environment. Unpublished DPhil thesis, University of Oxford.

Lawton Smith, H. (1991) Industry and academic links: the case of Oxford University. *Environment and Planning C*, **20** (4), 405–16.

Lawton Smith, H. (1993) Externalisation of research and development in Europe. *European Planning Studies*, **1** (4), 465–82.

Lawton Smith, H. (1995) The contribution of national laboratories to the European scientific labour market. *Industry and Higher Education*, **31** (1), 41–54.

Lecoq, B. (1989) *Réseau et système productif régional*. Dossiers de l'IRER, 23.

Leonard-Barton, D. (1995) *Wellsprings of Knowledge*. Boston: Harvard Business School Press

Levine, J. B. (1988) Sun Microsystems turns on the afterburners. *Business Week*, 18 July, pp. 114–18.

Licht, G. (1997) Technology diffusion networks in Germany. In Organisation for Economic Co-operation and Development (ed.) *Diffusing Technology to Industry: Government Policies and Programmes*. Paris: OECD, pp. 85–97.

Lindholm, A. (1997) Entrepreneurial spin-off enterprises in Goteborg, Sweden. Paper presented to the European Network Meeting on 'Networks, Collective Learning and RTD in Regionally-Clustered, High-Technology SMEs', Munich, March.

Lipietz, A. (1992) The local and the global: regional individuality or inter-regionalism? *Transactions of the Institute of British Geographers*, **18** (1), 8–18.

Lipnack, J. and Stamps, J. (1994) *The Age of the Network*. Essex Junction, VT: Omneo.

List, F. (1841) *Das nationale System der politischen Oekonomie*. Basel: Kyklos-Verlag.

Luger, M. I. and Goldstein, H. A. (1991) Universities, the Urban Milieu, and Technology Development. Paper presented at 1991 ACSP-AESOP Conference, Oxford.

Lundvall, B.-Ä. (1988) Innovation as an interactive process: from user–producer interaction to the national system of innovation. In G. Dosi, C. Freeman, R. Nelson, G. Silverberg and L. Soete (eds), *Technical Change and Economic Theory*. London: Pinter, pp. 349–69.

Lundvall, B.-Ä. (ed.) (1992) *National Systems of Innovation: Towards a Theory of Innovation and Interactive Learning*. London: Pinter.

Lundvall, B.-Ä. (1997) The globalizing learning economy: implications for technology policy at the regional, national and European level, EU-TSER Framework Programme (mimeo).

Luttwak, E. N. (1993) *The Endangered American Dream*. New York: Simon & Schuster.

Lyne, J. (1987) Numerous state, provincial incentives pave the road for high-tech facility locations. *Site Selection Handbook*, **32**, 582.

Lynn, L. H., Reddy, N. M. and Aram, J. D. (1996) Linking technology and institutions: the innovation community framework. *Research Policy*, **15**, 91–106.

Lynn, W. and Long, F. (1982) University–industrial collaboration in research. *Technology in Society*, **4**, 199–212.

McKinsey Global Institute (1993) *Manufacturing Productivity*. Washington, DC: McKinsey Global Institute.

McWilliams, G. (1992) Crunch time at DEC. *Business Week*, 4 May, pp. 30–3.

Maddox, J. and Gee, H. (1994) 'Mexico's bid to join the world'. *Nature*, 28 April, pp. 789–804.

Maillat, D. (1992) Milieux et dynamique territoriale de l'innovation. *Canadian Journal of Regional Science*, **15** (2).

Maillat, D. (1995) Territorial dynamic, innovative milieus and regional policy. *Entrepreneurship and Regional Development*, **7**, 157–65.

Malecki, E. (1980a) Corporate organizations of R&D and the location of technological activities. *Regional Studies*, **14**, 219–34.

Malecki, E. (1980b) Dimensions of R&D location in the United States. *Research Policy*, **9**, 2–22.

Malecki, E. (1986) Research and development and the geography of high-technology complexes. In J. Rees (ed.), *Technology, Regions and Policy*. Boston: Rowman & Littlefield, pp. 51–74.

Malecki, E. J. (1987) Hope or hyperbole? High tech and economic development. *Technology Review*, 90 (7), 50.

Malecki, E. (1991) *Technology and Economic Development: The Dynamics of Local, Regional and National Change*. Harlow: Longman.

Malecki, E. (1994) Entrepreneurship in regional and local development. *International Regional Science Review*, **16** (1/2), 119–53.

Malecki, E. J. (1997) *Technology and Economic Development: The Dynamics of Local, Regional and National Competitiveness*, 2nd edition. London: Addison Wesley Longman.

Malecki, E. and Tödtling, F. (1995) The new flexible economy: shaping regional and local institutions for global competition. In C. S. Bertuglia, M. M. Fischer and G. Preto (eds), *Technological Change, Economic Development and Space*. Berlin and New York: Springer-Verlag, pp. 276–94.

Malmberg, A. (1996) Industrial geography: agglomeration and local milieu. *Progress in Human Geography*, **20** (3), 392–403.

Malmberg, A. and Maskell, P. (1997) Towards an explanation of regional specialization and industry agglomeration. *European Planning Studies*, **5**, 1–15.

Mankiew, G. (1997) *Macro-economics*. New York: John Wiley.

Marshall, A. (1920) *Industry and Trade*. London: Macmillan.

Markusen, A. (1996) Sticky places in slippery space: a typology of industrial districts. *Economic Geography*, **72**, 293–313.

Maskell, P. and Malmberg, A. (1995) Localised learning and industrial competitiveness. Paper presented at the Regional Studies Association Conference on 'Regional Futures', Göteborg, 6–9 May 1995.

Massey, D. (1984) *Spatial Divisions of Labour*. London: Macmillan.

Massey, D. (1994) *Spatial Divisions of Labour: Social Structures and the Geography of Production*, 2nd edition. Basingstoke: Macmillan.

Mears, W. (1981) Corporate venture capital: can it be successful? Master's thesis, Sloan School of Management, Massachusetts Institute of Technology, Cambridge, MA.

Meyer, C. (1993) *Fast Cycle Time: How to Align Purpose, Strategy, and Structure for Speed*. New York: Free Press.

Mihell, D. (1996) *Biotechnology Sector in Oxfordshire*. Oxford: Oxford Innovation Ltd, September.

Mitchell, J. (1989) HP sets the tone for business in the valley. *San Jose Mercury News*, 9 January

Morales, R. (1994a) Product development and production networks: evidence from the U.S.–Mexican automobile industry. *Journal of Industry Studies*.

Morales, R. (1994b) *Flexible Production: Restructuring of the International Automobile Industry*. Oxford: Polity Press.

Morck, R. and Yeung, B. (1997) Why investors sometimes value size and diversification: the internalization theory of synergy. Mitsui Life Financial Research Center Working Paper 97–9, School of Business Administration, University of Michigan.

Morici, P. (1996) An architecture for free trade in the Americas. *Current History*, February, pp. 59–64.

Morris, J. A. (1953) *Those Rockefeller Brothers*. New York: Harper.

Mowery, D. and Nelson, R. (eds) (forthcoming) *The Sources of Industrial Leadership*. New York: Cambridge University Press, forthcoming.

Mueller, D. and Tilton, J. (1969) Research and development as barriers to entry. *Canadian Journal of Economics*, **2**, 570–9.

Myers, M. B. and Rosenbloom, R. S. (1996) Rethinking the role of industrial research. In R. S. Rosenbloom and W. J. Spencer (eds), *Engines of Innovation*. Boston: Harvard Business School Press, pp. 209–28.

Naisbitt, J. (1994) *Global Paradox*. New York: William Morrow.

Nash, J. and Hayes, M. (1993) Key DEC project moving to Palo Alto. *Business Journal (San Jose and Silicon Valley)*, **1**, 17.

National Governors Association (1983) *State Initiatives in Technological Innovation: Preliminary Report of Survey Findings*. Washington, DC: National Governors Association.

National Science Board (1982) *University–Industry Research Relationships: Myths, Realities, and Potentials. Fourteenth Annual Report of the National Science Board*. Washington, DC: Office of Technology Assessment.

National Science Board (1996) *Science and Engineering Indicators*. Washington, DC: NSB.

National Science Foundation (1982) *Academic Science and Engineering: R&D Expenditures, Fiscal Year 1982*. Data obtained from *CASPAR* data files.

Nee, E. (1991) Back to basics at Hewlett-Packard. *Upside*, June/July, pp. 38–78.

Nelson, R. (1988) *Institutions Supporting Technological Change in the United States*. In G. Dosi, C. Freeman, R. Nelson, G. Silverberg and L. Soete (eds), *Technical Change and Economic Theory*. London: Pinter, pp. 312–29.

Nelson, R. (ed.) (1993) *National Innovation Systems: A Comparative Analysis*. New York: Oxford University Press.

Nelson, R. and Rosenberg, N. (1993) Technical innovation and national systems. In R. Nelson (ed.), *National Innovation Systems: A Comparative Analysis*. New York: Oxford University Press, pp. 3–22.

Nelson, R. R. and Winter, S. G. (1977) In search of a useful theory of innovation. *Research Policy*, **6** (1), 36–76.

Nelson, R. and Winter, S. (1982) *An Evolutionary Theory of Economic Change*. Cambridge, MA: Belknap Press.

New England Business (1986) Angels give wing to entrepreneurs. 1 December, p. 31.

Niosi, J., Saviotti, P., Bellon, B. and Crow, M. (1993) National systems of innovation: in search of a workable concept. *Technology in Society*, **15** (2), 207–27.

Nishiguchi, T. (1989) Strategic dualism: an alternative in industrial societies. PhD dissertation, Nuffield College, Oxford University.

Nohria, N. and Eccles, R. (1992a) Face-to-face: making network organizations work. In N. Nohria and R. Eccles (eds), *Networks and Organizations: Structure, Form, and Action*. Boston, MA: Harvard Business School Press.

Nohria, N. and Eccles, R. (eds) (1992b) *Networks and Organizations: Structure, Form, and Action*. Boston, MA: Harvard Business School Press.

Nonaka, I. (1990) Redundant, overlapping organizations: a Japanese approach to managing the innovation process. *California Management Review*, **32** (3), 27–38.

Nonaka, I. and Takeuchi, H. (1995) *The Knowledge-Creating Company*. New York: Oxford University Press.

Noone, C. and Rubel, S. (1970) *SBIC's Pioneers in Organized Venture Capital*. Chicago: Capital.

Nye, J. (1996) Hard power. *Foreign Affairs*, July–August, pp. 114–17.

Odagiri, H. and Goto, A. (1993) The Japanese system of innovation: past, present, and future. In R. R. Nelson (ed.), *National Innovation Systems: A Comparative Analysis*. New York: Oxford University Press, pp. 76–114.

OECD (1993) *Localized Production of Technology for Global Markets*. DSTI/EAS/STP/ NESTI 1993 4. Paris: OECD.

OECD (1994a) *National Systems for Financing Innovation*. Paris: OECD.

OECD (1994b) *National Systems of Innovation: General Conceptual Framework*. DSTI/STP/ TIP 94 4. Paris: OECD.

OECD and EUROSTAT (1997) *Oslo Manual: Proposed Guidelines for Collecting and Interpreting Technological Innovation Data*. Paris: OECD.

Ohmae, K. (1993) The rise of the region state. *Foreign Affairs*, **72** (Spring), 78–87.

Ohmae, K. (1995) *The End of the Nation State*. New York: Free Press.

Okimoto, D. I. and Nishi, Y. (1994) R&D organization in Japanese and American semi-conductor firms. In M. Aoki and R. Dore (eds), *The Japanese Firm: The Sources of Competitive Strength*. Oxford: Oxford University Press, pp. 178–208.

Osborne, D. (1990) *Laboratories of Democracy*. Boston, MA: Harvard Business School Press.

Osborne, D. and Gaebler, T. (1992) *Reinventing Government*. New York: Addison-Wesley.

O'Toole, J. and Bennis, W. (1992) Our federalist future. *California Management Review*, **34** (4), 73–90.

Oxfordshire County Council (1997) *Economic Development Strategy for Oxfordshire 1997/8*. Oxford: County Hall.

Papadakis, M. (1995) The delicate task of linking industrial R&D to national competitiveness. *Technovation*, **15**, 569–83.

Paquet, G. (1989) A social learning framework for a wicked problem: the case of energy. *Energy Studies Review*, **1** (1), 55–69.

Paquet, G. (1990) The internationalization of domestic firms and governments: anamorphosis of a palaver. *Science and Public Policy*, **17** (5), 327–32.

Paquet, G. (1992) The strategic state. In J. Chrétien (ed.), *Finding Common Ground*. Hull, Quebec: Voyageur Publishing, pp. 85–101.

Paquet, G. (1994) Reinventing governance. *Opinion Canada*, **2** (2), 1–5.

Paquet, G. and Roy, J. (1995) Prosperity through networks: the bottom-up strategy that might have been. In S. Phillips (ed.), *How Ottawa Spends 1995–96*. Ottawa: Carleton University Press, pp. 137–58.

Parker, D. and Zilberman, D. (1993) University technology transfers: impacts on local and US economies. *Contemporary Policy Issues*, **11**, 87–99.

Patchell, J. and Hayter, R. (1995) Skill formation and Japanese production systems. *Tijdschrift voor Economische en Sociale Geografie*, **86**, 339–56.

Patel, P. and Pavitt, K. (1994) National innovation systems: why they are important, and how they might be measured and compared. *Economics of Innovation and New Technology*, **3**, 77–95.

Pavitt, K. (1984) Sectoral patterns of technical change: towards a taxonomy and a theory. *Research Policy*, **13**, 343–73.

Peck, J. (1994) Regulating labour: the social regulation and reproduction of local labour markets. In A. Amin and N. Thrift (eds), *Globalization, Institutions and Regional Development in Europe*. Oxford: Oxford University Press.

Perroux, F. (1960) *Économie et société*. Paris: Presses Universitaires de France.

Piore, M. J. (1992) Fragments of a cognitive theory of technological change and organizational structure. In N. Nohria and R. G. Eccles (eds), *Networks and Organizations*. Boston: Harvard Business School, pp. 430–44.

Piore, M. and Sabel, C. (1984) *The Second Industrial Divide: Possibilities for Prosperity*. New York: Basic Books.

Polanyi, K. (1957) The economy as instituted process. In K. Polanyi, C. M. Arensberg and H. W. Pearson (eds), *Trade and Markets in the Early Empires*. New York: Free Press, pp. 243–70.

Polanyi, K. (1968) The economy as instituted process. In K. Polanyi, *Primitive, Archaic and Modern Economies*. New York: Anchor Books, pp. 139–74.

Polanyi, M. (1958) *Personal Knowledge*. Chicago: University of Chicago Press.

Porter, M. E. (1980) *Competitive Strategy: Techniques for Analysing Industries and Competitors*. New York: Free Press.

Porter, M. (1990) *The Competitive Advantage of Nations*. New York: Free Press.

Porter, P. (1993) Executive interview: HP's Gary Eichorn tackles enterprise computing. *Mass High Tech*, **3**.

Powell, W. (1987) Neither market nor hierarchy: network forms of organization. In B. Staw (ed.), *Research in Organizational Behavior*. Greenwich, CT: JAI Press.

Putnam, A. O. (1985) A redesign for engineering. *Harvard Business Review*, May–June, pp. 139–40.

Putnam, R. D. (1993) *Making Democracy Work*. Princeton: Princeton University Press.

Quinn, J. B. and Hilmer, F. G. (1994). Strategic outsourcing. *Sloan Management Review*, **35** (4), 43–55.

Reich, R. (1992) *The Work of Nations*. New York: Knopf.

Resnick, M. (1994) Changing the centralized mind. *Technology Review*, **97** (5), 32–40.

Rheingold, H. (1993) *The Virtual Community*. Reading, MA: Addison-Wesley.

Rifkin, G. and Harrar, G. (1990) *The Ultimate Entrepreneur: The Story of Ken Olsen and Digital Equipment Corporation*. Rocklin, CA: Prima Publishing.

Rivlin, A. M. (1992) *Reviving the American Dream*. Washington, DC: Brookings Institution.

Roberts, E. B. (1979) Stimulating technological innovation: organizational approaches. *Research Management*, **6**.

Roberts, P. (1981) Commercial innovations from university faculty. *Research Policy*, **10**, 108–26.

Robertson, P. L. and Langlois, R. N. (1995) Innovation, networks, and vertical integration. *Research Policy*, **24**, 543–62.

Rogers, E. (1986) The role of the research university in the spin-off of high-technology companies. *Technovation*, **4**, 169–81.

Rogers, E. and Larsen, J. (1984) *Silicon Valley Fever*. New York: Basic Books.

Rosenberg, N. (1982) *Inside the Black Box: Technology and Economics*. Cambridge: Cambridge University Press.

Ruigrok, W. and Van Tulder, R. (1995) *The Logic of International Restructuring*. London: Routledge.

Sabel, C. (1988) Flexible specialization and the reemergence of regional economies. In P. Hirst and J. Zeitlin (eds), *Reversing Industrial Decline? Industrial Structure and Policy in Britain and Her Competitors*. Oxford: Berg.

Sabel, C. F. *et al.* (1987) Regional Prosperities Compared: Massachusetts and Baden-Wurtemberg in the 1980s. WZB Discussion Paper IIM/LMP 878, Berlin.

Sako, M. (1992) *Prices, Quality, and Trust: Inter-firm Relations in Britain and Japan*. Cambridge: Cambridge University Press.

Samuels, R. J. (1994) *'Rich Nation, Strong Army': National Security and the Technological Transformation of Japan*. Ithaca, NY: Cornell University Press.

Sandoval, V. (1994) *Computer Integrated Manufacturing (CIM) in Japan*. Amsterdam: Elsevier.

Save British Science (1994) Public investment in research and development. Oxford: SBS.

Saxenian, A. (1983) The genesis of Silicon Valley. *Built Environment*, **9**, 7–17.

Saxenian, A. (1985) Silicon Valley and Route 128: regional prototypes or historic exceptions? In M. Castells (ed.), *High Technology, Space, and Society*. Beverly Hills: Sage, pp. 91–105.

Saxenian, A. (1991) The origins and dynamics of production networks in Silicon Valley. *Research Policy*, **20**, 423–37.

Saxenian, A. (1994) *Regional Advantage: Culture and Competition in Silicon Valley and Route 128*. Cambridge, MA: Harvard University Press.

Saxenian, A. (1997) Transnational entrepreneurs and regional industrialization. Paper presented to Conference on Social Structure and Social Change, Institute of European and American Studies, Academia Sinica, Taiwan.

Schein, E. (1985) *Organizational Culture and Leadership*. San Francisco: Jossey-Bass.

Schmandt, J. and Wilson, R. (1987) *Promoting High-Technology Industry: Initiatives and Policies for State Governments*. Boulder: Westview Press.

Schott, J. (ed.) (1989) *Free Trade Areas and U.S. Trade Policy*. Washington, DC: Institute for International Economics.

Schumpeter, J. (1934) *The Theory of Economic Development*. Cambridge, MA: Harvard University Press.

Science (1995) Fertile US soil. 270 (December 1), 1445.

Science Council of Canada (1984) *Canadian Industrial Development: Some Policy Directions*. Ottawa: SCC.

Science Council of Canada (1990) *Grassroots Initiatives, Global Success: Report of the 1989 National Technology Policy Roundtable*. Ottawa: Science Council of Canada.

Scott, A. (1998a) *Metropolis: From the Division of Labor to Urban Form*. Berkeley: University of California Press.

Scott, A. (1988b) *New Industrial Spaces: Flexible Production Organization and Regional Development in North America and Western Europe*. London: Pion.

Scott, A. (1996) Regional motors of the global economy. *Futures*, **28**, 391–411.

Scott, A. J. (1996) Economic decline and regeneration in a regional manufacturing complex: southern California's household furniture industry. *Entrepreneurship and Regional Development*, **8**, 75–98.

Secretaria de Comercio y Fomento Industrial (SECOFI) (1996) *Program of Industrial Policy and International Trade*. Mexico, DF: SECOFI.

Segal Quince Wicksteed (1988) *Universities, Enterprise and Local Economic Development: An Exploration of Links*. London: HMSO.

Serapio, M. G. (1993) Macro–micro analyses of Japanese direct R&D investments in the U.S. automotive and electronics industries. *Management International Review*, **33**, 209–25.

Shapira, P. (1996) Modernizing small manufacturers in the United States and Japan: public technological infrastructures and strategies. In M. Teubal, D. Foray, M. Justman and E. Zuscovitch (eds), *Technological Infrastructure Policy (TIP): An International Perspective*. Dordrecht: Kluwer Academic, pp. 285–334.

Shapira, P., Roessner, J. D. and Barke, R. (1995) New public infrastructures for small firm industrial modernization in the USA. *Entrepreneurship and Regional Development*, **7**, 63–84.

Sheff, D. (1989) A new ball game for Sun's Scott McNealy. *Upside*, November–December, pp. 46–54.

Sherwood-Call, C. (1992) Changing geographic patterns of electronic components activity. *Economic Review* (Federal Reserve Board of San Francisco), **2**, 25–35.

Singer, H. W. (1995) Is a genuine partnership possible in a Western Hemisphere free trade area? In Inter-American Development Bank and Economic Commission for Latin America and the Caribbean (eds), *Trade Liberalization in the Western Hemisphere*. Washington, DC.

Smilor, R. W. and Feeser, H. R. (1991) Chaos and the entrepreneurial process: patterns and policy implications for technology entrepreneurship. *Journal of Business Venturing*, **6**, 160–70.

Smilor, R. W., Gibson, D. V. and Kozmetsky, G. (1989) Creating the technopolis: high-technology development in Austin, Texas. *Journal of Business Venturing*, **4**, 49–67.

Solow, R. (1994) Perspectives on growth theory. *Journal of Economic Perspectives*, **8** (1), 45–54.

Song, X. M. and Parry, M. E. (1993) How the Japanese manage the R&D–marketing interface. *Research-Technology Management*, **36** (4), 32–8.

Soussou, H. (1985) Note on the venture capital industry – update. No. 0-286-060. Cambridge, MA: Harvard Business School.

Stalk, G., Jr, and Hout, T. M. (1993) *Competing against Time: How Time-Based Competition Is Reshaping Global Markets*. New York: Free Press.

Standard & Poor's (1992) Compustat PC+ database.

Staudt, E. (1987/88) Technologie- und Regionalpolitik der Länder: Vom Leistungs- zum Subventionswettbewerb (Technology and regional policy of the states: from performance to subsidy competition). *List Forum*, **14**, 93–110.

Steed, G. and De Genova, D. (1983) Ottawa's technology-oriented complex. *Canadian Geographer*, **27** (3), 263–77.

Sternberg, R. (1992) Technology transfer from universities: needs of small and medium-sized enterprises and standards for transfer agencies – the example of Hanover. In E. Frackmann and P. Maassen (eds), *Towards Excellence in European Higher Education in the 90s*. Proceedings of the 11th European AIR Forum in Trier. Utrecht: Lemma, pp. 151–65.

Sternberg, R. (1995) Supporting peripheral economies or industrial policy in favour of industrial growth? An empirically based analysis of goal achievement of the Japanese 'Technopolis' program. *Environment and Planning C: Government and Policy*, **13**, 425–39.

Sternberg, R. (1996a) Government R&D expenditure and space: empirical evidence from five advanced industrial economies. *Research Policy*, **25**, 741–58.

Sternberg, R. (1996b) Regional institutional and policy frameworks and the recent evolution of RTD-intensive enterprises in the Munich region. Paper presented at the Networks, Collective Learning and RTD in Regionally Clustered High Tech Small and Medium Enterprises Project Meeting, Nice, 27–28 September.

Sternberg, R. (1998) *Technologiepolitik und High-Tech Regionen: Ein internationaler Vergleich* (Technology policies and high-tech regions: an international comparison), 2nd edition. Münster and Hamburg: Lit (Wirtschaftsgeographie, 7).

Sternberg, R. and Tamásy, C. (1999) Munich as Germany's no. 1 high technology region: empirical evidence, theoretical explanations and the role of small firm/large firm relationships. *Regional Studies*, **33** (4), 367–78.

Sternberg, R., Behrendt, H., Seeger, H. and Tamásy, C. (1996; 2nd edn 1997) *Bilanz eines Booms: Wirkungsanalyse von Technologie- und Gründerzentren in Deutschland* (Outcome of a boom: evaluation of innovation centres and science parks in Germany). Dortmund: Dortmunder Vertrieb für Bau- und Planungsliteratur.

Stoffaes, C. (1987) *Fins de mondes*. Paris: Éditions Odile Jacob.

Stopford, J. (1996) The globalization of business. In J. de la Mothe and G. Paquet (eds) *Evolutionary Economics and the New International Political Economy*. New York: Pinter, pp. 118–38.

Storper, M. (1989). The transition to flexible specialization in the U.S. film industry: external economies, the division of labor, and the crossing of industrial divides. *Cambridge Journal of Economics*, **13**, 273–305.

Storper, M. (1992) The limits of globalization: technology districts and international trade. *Economic Geography*, **68** (1), 60–93.

Storper, M. (1993) Regional worlds of production: learning and innovation in the technology districts of France, Italy and the USA. *Regional Studies*, **27** (5), 433–55.

Storper, M. (1995) Territorial development in the global learning economy: the challenge to developing countries. *Review of International Political Economy*, **2**, 394–424.

Storper, M. and Scott, A. (1995) The wealth of regions: market forces and policy imperatives in local and global context. *Futures*, **27**, 505–26.

Suris, O. (1996) Chrysler leads big three in efficiency of car factories, but all trail Japanese. *Wall Street Journal*, 30 May pp. A2, A4.

Sweeney, G. P. (1991) Technical culture and the local dimension of entrepreneurial vitality. *Entrepreneurship and Regional Development*, **3**, 363–78.

Tannenwald, R. (1987) Rating Massachusetts' tax competitiveness. *New England Economic Review*, November–December, pp. 33–45.

Tassey, G. (1992) *Technology Infrastructure and Competitive Position*. Norwell: Kluwer.

Tatsuno, S. (1986) *The Technopolis Strategy*. New York: Prentice-Hall.

Tatsuno, S. M. (1990) *Created in Japan: From Imitators to World-Class Competitors*. New York: Harper Business.

Teece, D. J. (1992) Foreign investment and technological development in Silicon Valley. *California Management Review*, Winter, pp. 88–106.

Teich, A. (1982). Research centers and non-faculty researchers: a new academic role. In D. Phillips and B. Shen (eds), *Research in the Age of the Steady-State University*. Boulder: Westview Press, pp. 91–108.

Tezuka, H. (1997) Success as the source of failure? Competition and cooperation in the Japanese economy. *Sloan Management Review*, **38** (2), 83–93.

Thomas, L. G. (1989) Spare the rod and spoil the industry: vigorous competition and vigorous regulation promote global competitive advantage: a ten nation study of government industrial policies and corporate pharmaceutical advantage. Working Paper, Columbia Business School.

Thurow, L. (1992) *Head to Head*. New York: Morrow.

Thurow, L. (1996) *The Future of Capitalism*. New York: William Morrow.

Tilton, J. E. (1971) *International Diffusion of Technology: The Case of Semiconductors*. Washington, DC: Brookings Institution.

Tödtling, F. (1994) the uneven landscape of innovation poles: local embeddedness and global networks. In A. Amin and N. Thrift (eds), *Globalization, Institutions and Regional Development in Europe*. Oxford: Oxford University Press, pp. 68–90.

Tödtling, F. and Sedlacek, S. (1997) Regional economic transformation and the innovation system of Styria. *European Planning Studies*, **5**, 43–64.

Tuller, D. (1988) HP plans to buy 10% stake in Octel. *San Francisco Chronicle*, 12 August.

Tushman, M. L. and Anderson, P. (1986) Technological discontinuities and organizational environments. *Administrative Science Quarterly*, **31**, 439–65.

Tushman, M. L. and Rosenkopf, L. (1992) Organizational determinants of technological change: towards a sociology of technological evolution. *Research in Organizational Behaviour*, **14**, 311–47.

Tyebjee, T. T. (1988) A typology of joint ventures: Japanese strategies in the United States. *California Management Review*, **31** (1), 75–86.

Tylecote, A. (1996) Managerial objectives and technological collaboration: the role of national variations: In R. Coombs, A. Richards, P. P. Saviotti and V. Walsh (eds), *Technological Collaboration*. Cheltenham: Edward Elgar, pp. 34–53.

Uekusa, M. (1988) The oil crisis and after. In R. Komiya, M. Okuno and K. Suzumura (eds), *Industrial Policy of Japan*. Tokyo: Academic Press, pp. 89–117.

Uenohara, M. (1991) A management view of Japanese corporate R&D. *Research-Technology Management*, **34** (6), 17–23.

United Nations Economic Commission for Latin America and the Caribbean (1996) *Strengthening Development: The Interplay of Macro- and Microeconomics*. Santiago, Chile: ECLAC.

US Small Business Administration (1986) *The State of Small Business. A Report to the President*. Washington, DC: US Government Printing Office.

Utterback, J.M. (1994) *Mastering the Dynamics of Innovation*. Cambridge, MA: Harvard Business School Press.

Utterback, J. M. and Abernathy, W. (1975) A dynamic model of process and product innovation. *Omega*, **33**, 639–56.

Utterback, J. M. and Kim, L. (1986) Invasion of a stable business by radical innovation. In P. R. Kleindorfer (ed.), *The Management of Productivity and Technology in Manufacturing*. New York: Plenum Press.

Utterback, J. M. and Murray, A. (1977) Influence of defence procurement and sponsorship of research and development of civilian electronics industry. Working Paper, MIT.

Utterback, J. M. and Suarez, F. F. (1993) Innovation, competition, and industry structure. *Research Policy*, **22**, 1–21.

Valentine, D. (1985) Peaks and valleys. *INC*, May, pp. 46–7.

van Kooij, E. (1991) Japanese subcontracting at a crossroads. *Small Business Economics*, **3**, 145–54.

Varga, A. (1998) *University Research and Regional Innovation*. Boston: Kluwer Academic Publishers.

Varga, A. and Stough, R. (1997) Innovation in the high technology industry: an assessment of the local factors enhancing the innovative potential of US high technology regions. Research Paper, Regional Research Institute, West Virginia University, Morgantown, WV.

Vaugham, R. and Pollard, R. (1986) State and federal policies for high-technology development. In J. Rees (ed.), *Technology, Regions and Policy*. Boston: Rowman & Littlefield, pp. 268–81.

Venture Capital Journal (1980) The evolution of an industry: venture capital redefined for the 1980s, January, p. 13.

Vernon, R. (1960) *Metropolis 1985*. Cambridge, MA: Harvard University Press.

Vickery, G. (with C. Casadio) (1996) The globalization of trade and investment. In J. de la Mothe and G. Paquet (eds), *Evolutionary Economics and the New International Political Economy*. London: Pinter, pp. 83–117.

Voelzkow, H. (1990) *Mehr Technik in die Region: Neue Ansätze zur regionalen Technikförderung in Nordrhein-Westfalen* (Putting more technology into the region: new approaches to regional technology policies in North Rhine-Westphalia). Wiesbaden.

von Hippel, E. (1986) Lead users: a source of novel product concepts. *Management Science*, **32** (7), 791–805.

Voyer, R. and Roy, J. (1996) European high-technology clusters. In J. de la Mothe and G. Paquet (eds), *Evolutionary Economics and the New International Political Economy*. London: Pinter, pp. 220–37.

Voyer, R. and Ryan, P. (1994) *The New Innovators*. Toronto: Lorimer.

Wade, R. (1990) *Governing the Market: Economic Theory and the Role of Government in East Asian Industrialization*. Princeton: Princeton University Press.

Warner, M. A. A. and Rugman, A. M. (1994) Competitiveness: an emerging strategy of discrimination in U.S. antitrust and R&D policy? *Law and Policy in International Business*, **25** (3), 945–82.

Webber, A. M. (1993) What's so new about the new economy? *Harvard Business Review*, **71** (1), 24–42.

Weiss, J. and Delbecq, A. (1987) High technology cultures and management: Silicon Valley and Route 128. *Group and Organization Studies*, **12** (1), 39–54.

Westney, D. E. (1994) The evolution of Japan's industrial research and development. In M.

Aoki and R. Dore (eds), *The Japanese Firm: The Sources of Competitive Strength*. Oxford: Oxford University Press, pp. 154–77.

Whiting, C. (1987) For flexible, quality manufacturing don't do it yourself. *Electronic Business*, 15 March, pp. 46–7.

Whiting, V. R., Jr (ed.) (1996) *Regionalisation in the World Economy: NAFTA, the Americas and Asia Pacific*. New Delhi: Macmillan India.

Wicksteed, S. (1985) *The Cambridge Phenomenon: The Growth of High Technology Industry in a University Town*. London: Segal Quince Wicksteed.

Williamson, O. E. (1970) *Corporate Control and Business Behavior*. Englewood Cliffs, NJ: Prentice-Hall.

Willis, T., Kingham, D. and Stafford, J. (1996) Oxfordshire's motor sport industry: building on local strengths. Report commissioned by Heart of England Training and Enterprise Council, Oxford Innovation, February.

Wilson, J. (1985) *The New Venturers*. Reading, MA: Addison-Wesley.

Wilson, R. W., Ashton, P. K. and Egan, T. P. (1980) *Innovation, Competition and Government Policy in the Semiconductor Industry*. Lexington, MA: Lexington Books.

Womack, J. and Jones, D. (1996) *Lean Thinking*. New York: Simon & Schuster.

World Bank (1993) *The East Asian Miracle: Economic Growth and Public Policy*, New York: Oxford University Press.

Wriston, W. B. (1992) *The Twilight of Sovereignty*. New York: Scribner's.

Yamamoto, Y. (1996) Regionalization in contemporary international relations. In V. R. Whiting, Jr (ed.), *Regionalisation in the World Economy: NAFTA, the Americas and Asia Pacific*. New Delhi: Macmillan India.

Yamazawa, I. (1996). Economic integration in the Asia Pacific region: a Japanese view. In V. R. Whiting, Jr (ed.), *Regionalisation in the World Economy: NAFTA, the Americas and Asia Pacific*. New Delhi: Macmillan India.

Yoder, S. (1991) A 1990 reorganization at Hewlett-Packard already is paying off. *Wall Street Journal*, 22 July, p. A1.

Index